War Termination

The Proceedings of the
War Termination Conference
United States Military Academy West Point

Colonel Matthew Moten
General Editor

Combat Studies Institute Press
US Army Combined Arms Center
Fort Leavenworth, Kansas

War Termination

The Proceedings of the
War Termination Conference
United States Military Academy West Point
21 June 2010

Colonel Matthew Moten
General Editor

Combat Studies Institute Press
US Army Combined Arms Center
Fort Leavenworth, Kansas 66027

Published by Books Express Publishing
Copyright © Books Express, 2011
ISBN 978-1-780390-17-8

Books Express publications are available from all good retail
and online booksellers. For publishing proposals and direct
ordering please contact us at: info@books-express.com

Foreword

Conference Proceedings – War Termination Conference

West Point, New York, June 2010

Anyone who has ever studied the history of American diplomacy, especially military diplomacy, knows that you might start in a war with certain things on your mind as a purpose of what you are doing, but in the end you found yourself fighting for entirely different things than you had ever thought of before. In other words, war has a momentum of its own and it carries you away from all thoughtful intentions when you get into it.

– George Kennan, Oct 2002

This conference investigates war termination, one of the most important issues facing military and political leaders as they use or contemplate the use of use of military force in the pursuit of national aims. Prompted by the Unified Quest Training and Leader Development theme and discussions about the use of history in training and leader development, the US Army Training and Doctrine Command and the United States Military Academy partnered on this war termination project and invited renowned military historians to provide their views on the subject. The study began with several seminars following Unified Quest in May of 2009. Each contributor provided a brief essay and presented their views on the topic at a War Termination Conference at West Point in June of 2010. These scholars represented a broad range of the American experience from the Revolutionary War to the first Gulf War. The assembled essays and interviews reflect the thoughts of these historians about America's wars, their concluding battles or final campaigns, and ultimately how they ended. While they provide no answers and no formula for successful war termination, they do provide thoughtful reflections from years of study and they suggest important implications for civilian and military decisionmakers today.

Among the discoveries of this project is that war termination is a curiously neglected topic. Little has been written about the subject that is of practical use in educating military leaders. This project represents an important first step to raise awareness and enrich the Army's leader development as well as education and training. This volume is intended to support instructors and students in academic courses, seminars, and individual study focused on the topic of war termination in the hope of answering these important questions: What is the American experience? How has America ended its wars? What can we learn from that experience?

Colonel Matthew Moten
Professor and Deputy Head
Department of History
United States Military Academy
West Point, New York

Table of Contents

Introductory Remarks

Colonel Matthew Moten

I am a bit of a stranger to a lot of you. I sometimes work here. My name is Matt Moten. I am the once and future deputy head of the department, affectionately known around here as the knot head. I have been on sabbatical for the last year, putting this project together. I want to introduce our keynote speaker for this conference on war termination. Often, when one brings a general officer in, it's simply to throw holy water on things, but in this case we are bringing in the person who is the driving force behind this war termination project. I have gotten to know him fairly well over the last year as we have worked on it. I won't say very much about General Dempsey other than that I know that he reads widely and thinks deeply. So, without further ado, the Commanding General of the United States Army Training and Doctrine Command, General Martin Dempsey.

General Martin E. Dempsey, Commanding General, US Army Training and Doctrine Command (TRADOC)

I am extraordinarily excited about this project, for reasons that I think I'll try to make clear. That's why I'm here by the way, to tell you why we're doing this. I wouldn't call myself the driving factor in this at all actually, but I'll explain why and who I think are the driving forces.

When I took command of Training and Doctrine Command, there was a bit of a convergence of things coming my way that I didn't fully understand at the time. I think I understand them better and I'll tell you what those are and show you where this effort fits. But as I was sitting at my desk in the — and I'm in the same desk, in the same office, in the same space that General DePuy was in and Donn Starry was in. No pressure there, but one day with Mike Starry in the office, we discussed an e-mail to me from General Donn Starry commenting on a Training Strategy I had sent him. In his response he talked about the value of history in leader education and development and he mentioned *America's First Battles* which I had on my bookcase. You may recall that book from the 1980s. I remember, as really a senior company grade officer at the time, that that had a catalytic effect on me becoming interested in readiness. Now that's kind of a tactical issue, but it occurred to me, or I began to wonder, what book or project or think piece or essay could have that kind of catalytic effect on our intellect. What could get us to think and argue about what we're about in this 21st century, and particularly after nine years of war.

So I asked, "what am I going to do about this?" And from that kind of modest thought, this project was born, because what we discussed later, and with Matt Moten and others, was we've got plenty of stuff that tells us how to get into a fight, and what are the principles that underpin the beginning of a conflict. We don't have much in the way of deep thinking about what happens when you get into a fight and how do you extricate yourself from it. I don't know if this was the right title by the way, War Termination. It might be. I'm going to leave that up to you all to help me understand. I've read some of the essays and one might stand here and say, what ever happened to good old fashioned victory? It's a good question actually.

So here are the things that are coming upon me, that I want to use this project to help me knit together. One of them is the work that Brigadier General H.R. McMaster is doing on the Army Capstone Concept. The Army Capstone Concept is important, because what we've done is taken a look at the raison d'être for a land force, notably the Army in this case. We began to ask ourselves some questions about that, and among the themes that have come out — some of you are aware of the work — is the idea of full spectrum operations. As you know, we've embraced stability operations as somewhat of a co-equal — well, as a co-equal to offense and defense — and decided that it's really a matter of weight of effort and where you are in the life of a campaign.

So, Army Capstone Concept, full spectrum operations, offense, defense, stability, and importantly, that as an Army, as a land force, you develop the situation through action, that you have to be in contact with the environment in order to understand it, that you can't understand from a distance. You can see things from a distance, you can interpret things from a distance, but you can't gain the kind of understanding you need, to understand the population, the terrain, your adversary, and so an important theme of this Army Capstone Concept is developing the situation through action, in contact. That's not kinetic. It doesn't take you immediately to kinetics, but it takes you toward kinetics, and we have to understand them to imply them proportionately and so forth. So that's the big ideas in the Army Capstone Concept.

There's a subordinate document to that called the Army Operating Concept. How's it going to fight? What does full spectrum operations really mean? That work is being done right now. In fact, there's a draft on the street. But importantly in that work, what H.R. and a wide variety of people who have collaborated have helped us begin to see, is that instead of arguing about whether we're going to be optimized for COIN or major combat, because when you optimize for COIN or major combat, you're giving the vote to the enemy. The enemy then in some way, will decide the way you optimize yourself. And furthermore, as we have learned and will continue to learn, and in fact we'll learn in this conference here, when you enter a conflict in a given set of circumstances, in a given environment, the only certainty is that your presence will change it and therefore the enemy will change, you'll change, the political dynamic will change. It's just a constant effort to understand change that goes on, and I think we'll see here.

One of the themes of this conference is that we rarely finish conflicts for the purposes we think we fully understand as we enter them. That's an important thing, and where that takes you as an Army, is that we've got to be able to do two broad mission sets. We've got to be able to do wide area security. Wide area security is the condition in which you would perform peacekeeping, you would perform counterinsurgency operations, humanitarian relief, mass atrocity response, a variety of things; but when you're responsible for producing stability and security in a wide area, you tend to decentralize things. So you hear all this discussion these days about empowering the edge, and we are, as you know, decentralizing. That takes a certain kind of leader development.

And then on the other side of it, you've got this requirement for combined arms maneuver, not necessarily synonymous — in fact, not synonymous with major combat, but the notion that you have to maneuver forces, probably large formations of forces, for offensive and defensive missions, and in that environment, you typically centralize resources for any number of reasons. But you can see where that takes us as an Army. We can't afford to optimize, because there is combined arms maneuver in wide area security and there's wide area security in combined arms maneuver, but the point is, it's a different way of thinking about what our Army has to do, and should allow us to see the capability gaps and in some cases the redundancies. That's the important point.

The third thing that is coming my way is the Army Leader Development Strategy, and the fact that I and others get a lot of feedback from folks inside and outside the Army, that say we're not developing our leaders for the environment in which we find ourselves and the future environment in which we anticipate. And in particular, we're not developing leaders who are capable of providing military advice at the strategic level, and we're not developing leaders who understand how to run the institution of the Army. In other words, we're doing a pretty good job of producing leaders who are enormously skilled and talented at the tactical level, but we're not developing leaders capable of operating at the strategic level. This is the feedback. And in fact, if I reflect back on my own career, not only are we not developing them with educational experiences, we're also finding it very difficult to find time to take them out of the tactical fight and put them in an experience that could be broadening, whether it's the joint staff or combatant command position, whether it's to one of the nongovernmental organizations or with our interagency partners. The estimate is that on the current path, 45 percent of the colonels that appeared before the Brigadier General Board, in the next two years will not be joint qualified. And as you know, you're just not getting over into that next rank unless you're joint qualified. So we're about at the point where half of the colonels that reach the point in their career where they'll be considered for general officer, will not have the joint credential and therefore will not be competitive until we get him that joint credential. That's a function of the pace of current events and, in particular, the individual augmentations. But the larger issue here is that when we do have to them to educate, we really haven't changed anything about our leader development models in a very long time. One of the things that I hope comes out of this conference is some emerging insights into how we might begin to take on that task of developing strategic leaders. Where do you begin that process?

The other thing in the Army Leader Development Strategy is that we've introduced, as part of our planning process, the concept of design. Some of you are familiar with it. How did we get to this thing called design? A couple of ways. And by the way, what is design? It's a commander's or a leader's cognitive tool, to help them seek to understand the problem before they decide to solve it. Now, that's a very simple description. It's a significantly more complicated idea, but it really resonates with me, and I'll just give you one personal vignette to tell you why.

I commanded the 1st Armored Division in 2003/2004, in Baghdad. As you know, the Division's mission in the beginning of OIF, was to go from Kuwait to Baghdad, movement to contact, hasty attack. A very understandable problem. METT-T, mission, enemy, terrain, troops available, and time. I knew how to figure that out; it was me against them and I knew who "them" were, and I knew where the ground was, I knew where I was, and could make this kind of mathematical — I could lay down this geometric formation and move it to Baghdad. Having arrived in Baghdad, the mission of the Division was changed to establish a safe and secure environment. In a city of 7 million, with huge sectarian issues, separated both physically and psychologically by a river. So, this old, at that time 55-year-old or so, Irish-Catholic from Bayonne, New Jersey, was perplexed. And you know, in our manuals, we say that the commander's responsibility is to visualize, understand, decide, direct, and assess. We've got all kinds of tools for decide, direct and assess. We've got almost no tools, cognitive tools, to help senior leaders understand, and so design is our effort to help leaders understand; to actually seek complexity before they seek simplicity. It's our instinct, of course, to go for simplicity, and then to hand it to your staff and say give me a plan that will fix that problem.

So design is also part of this effort and you'll see how it fits together, because I think someone — it might have been H.R. McMaster or it could have been [Major General] Joe Martz. One of them said to me, "If you want a new idea, go find an old book." So this issue of design encourages the kind of deeper, richer, more nuanced understanding. It encourages the military leader to look more broadly than just at the military instrument. We've begun to use it with combatant command staffs, with significant success. So that was two things in the Leader Development Strategy. This idea of you better figure out a way to develop strategists, or at least military officers who know how to give advice to senior civilian leaders when they ask for it, and secondly, this idea of understanding complex problems or seeking to understand them before you try to solve them.

And then the last thing was pretty recent, we had a conference right here at West Point on talent management, or the management of the Army's talents, for the good of both the individual and the institution. But what came out of that conference in unexpected ways — and by the way, I hope we have some unexpected insights, because those are the ones that really seem to be the most important. Out of that conference came the notion that — we're talking about leader development, we're talking about managing the Army's talent. Who is talking about the Army as a profession? But Dr. Don Snider, who as you know is an adjunct professor here in the Social Sciences Department, at one point he raised his hand and pointed out to us that we were talking about managing talent and talking about leader development as though they existed in isolation from this thing we call a profession. And he said, "You know, General, you're not a profession just because you say you are. Your client has to consider you to be a professional." Our clients, of course, are the people of the United States.

We are considered a profession today, undoubtedly. In fact, if you look at the polls, which I try not to, but if you were to look at the polls, you'd note that the military profession is very well respected and is considered a profession. But maybe what the point would be here is we had better not take that for granted. One of the things that defines a profession, among the five, six or seven total characteristics — and we're still tinkering around the edges of what it means to be a profession in a changing environment such as we face today — is the study of that profession's history. And so when you think about the requirement for military leaders to give solid strategic advice to civilian leaders and government, and when you think about the need to constantly reinforce to ourselves and others that we are a profession, then the kind of thinking at this level, the kind of thinking about conflict, not only the beginning of conflict but the end of conflict, not only how it starts but how it ends, is extraordinarily important. And that's not to say that we're going to talk ourselves into the conclusion that war is so unpredictable that we're never going to do it, it's just too hard, we're not going to do it. Of course we all know, you don't get to pick all the time. Sometimes wars pick you and sometimes you pick a war and then it changes and picks you, and I think we would admit, we're probably in a situation like that today.

So this effort here is a thread for me, it's a thread that runs through the Army. Capstone Concept, the Operating Concept, the Leader Development Strategy, and the work that we have just really begun, to look at ourselves as a profession. And as we look at ourselves as a profession in the context of all those things, this work will be, I think, extraordinarily important, because one of the things that I've seen in the essays, — and I've read about a third of the essays. One of the things I've seen, even behind the words, you can see senior leaders struggling with how to articulate that which they are doing, that which they need to do, and then to have the civilian leaders with whom they're interacting understand it. But, by the way, that's our job. That's not — it's not their fault, in my view; now you may come to a different conclusion. It's not a particular civilian leader's fault if they can't understand what we're trying to tell them. And I think this work has the potential to give us a bit of a — I won't call it a common vocabulary — a framework in which we can understand strategy. We're damn good at tactics. With this work, we can begin to understand strategy in a way that maybe we haven't really tried to understand it before.

But the point is that we categorize conflict at our great peril. I think this conference and the work that's coming out of it is critical. The pace at which you have worked was described to me as light speed for academia. I told Roger Spiller, I should probably get a drill sergeant hat to award to Matt Moten here at the end of the process.

But I do appreciate the depth. First of all, I appreciate those of you who have agreed to be part of it. The depth of the thought that I've seen. I really appreciate the pace at which you've produced it, because if we want to generate this examination of our profession, if we want to have part of that examination be the idea of strategic leadership, if we want to emphasize that we really need to understand our history, if we're going to be able to give good advice, good solid military advice to senior leaders, then I've got to keep these things moving apace. Capstone Concept is on the street, Operating Concept probably August, I think, Leader Development Strategy is out there. This work on the profession is, I've got a goal of having a White Paper out by the end of this calendar year, and that's about the same timeline as we hope this happens. And then the more introspective among us will see, I hope, that these things are threaded together in a way that should raise the bar on our intellectual energy, in a way that probably hasn't been attempted since the mid-'80s. But I think we need to do it, and I think the time is now.

Session 1
War Termination:
Theory and American Practice

by

Dr. Roger Spiller

The way we commonly see war and how it ends comes to us from the world of the soldier. This world is highly utilitarian and quite simple in its most basic form: if I kill enough of the enemy the rest will stop fighting and I can live. In this way, the soldier hopes to impose control over events that are fundamentally unpredictable and chaotic. The "chain of command" from which he and his comrades receive their orders does not only describe how this control is managed, the chain of command is also a chain of knowledge. It prescribes how military ideas are organized, too. In its ideal form, this chain of military thought is hierarchical and deductive, proceeding from the general to the specific. Strategy sets the terms and objectives for how campaigns are designed. Campaigns are in turn designed to meet those terms and objectives by means of engagements and battles, which are composed of smaller unit actions and minor tactical events.

This is a world where causes are meant to be translated into effects, in which decision is to lead as directly as possible to action. Successful actions are supposed to result in successful engagements whose sum will produce successful campaigns leading to the attainment of final victory. The ideal map to victory has one straight road on it. It is somewhat amazing that for some time the world's armies, great and small, have fought in consonance with this worldview, especially as it has often proved to have little relevance to real war.

This highly structured world is also suffused with a unique value system built on good and practical reasons. In earlier days, war was a blunt instrument, no more fit for surgery than an axe. Orchestrating the use of military power was difficult even in ideal conditions, and soldiers regarded with a jaundiced eye any scheme that required them to reserve or limit their strength. Even now, the principle of economy of force is sometimes seen as subtracting from an army's main effort. Soldiers have always preferred to be stronger than their enemy everywhere, so strong that the outcome of their war will be in no doubt. If one is very much stronger, so much the better; the enemy may be compelled to surrender without a fight. If the enemy stands, he may be defeated more quickly and thoroughly, thus sparing lives and treasure on all sides. For these reasons, a soldier is bound to regard any sort of limitation on his strength as playing with his life.

We in the outside world are not obliged to see war in this way. To do so would be like a physician who only sees an illness from the patient's point of view. The soldier's perspective might serve him well, but that is not to say it advances our knowledge of war equally well.

This essay addresses the conduct of war and how it ends, seen from the perspective of the American military experience. Although this essay's chief concern is how America's conflicts drew to a close, it is based on the premise that the actions of war and the conclusions they produce cannot be separated from one another or indeed from the influences of the world beyond the battlefield. To that end, this essay advances six general propositions about the history of American war termination and its implications for the conduct of modern limited war, propositions that may at first glance seem counterintuitive from the soldier's perspective.

First: Wars are defined not by their extremes but by their limitations. Concepts of total war or complete victory are abstractions whose function is to depict an ideal case against which real war can be understood and conducted.

Second: War's original aims and methods are constantly revised by the stresses and actions of war. The way in which a war ends, therefore, depends on the strategic and operational context that the war itself has created during its course.

Third: The public face of war is ever more cosmopolitan and so, therefore, is the conduct of war itself, which can no longer be quarantined from the influence of the world beyond, if it ever could.

Fourth: In every war, the aims of all sides, no matter how opposed at the beginning, gradually converge toward an agreement to stop fighting.

Fifth: This convergence of aims is not produced on the battlefield alone. It derives not only from military actions but also from influences well beyond the battlefield, only some of which may be within the reach of control by policymakers, strategists, and operational commanders.

Last: Within the confines of war itself, a war's terminal campaign exercises the greatest influence over the manner in which it ends and, therefore, is not always a war's last campaign. This means that the concept of a decisive campaign or victory is of less utility than orthodox military thought has traditionally assumed.

Contemporary American military doctrine refers to "war termination" as the conclusion of "operations on terms favorable to the United States." Defense strategists and operational planners are enjoined to keep the question of how a conflict might end uppermost in their minds as they go about their work. The doctrine makes clear that strategies and operational plans should be designed to achieve a certain "end state." Once the strategic course of action is decided on, the doctrine recognizes that plans may well be interrupted by "unforeseen events" that force a "reassessment" of the terms on which hostilities will be concluded.

That the subject of war termination is addressed at all is somewhat surprising. As a term of art, "war termination" is of fairly recent vintage, having made its appearance in legal studies during the First World War, but there was no serious work on the subject between the two world wars, and although there was official and scholarly interest in nuclear war termination during the Cold War, even that seems to have faded from view. Now, the term is not one frequently heard in war and staff colleges, and over the past 20 years professional military journals have carried only two essays on the subject.

For centuries, statesmen, soldiers, and scholars have made do with a much more elastic concept of how wars are terminated: victory. Yet, today you will search in vain for any definition of victory in American military doctrine. Exactly when the idea of victory disappeared from official doctrine is an open question but its absence invites the thought that at some time in the recent past, victory, a concept so long dominating military thought and practice, lost some of its official appeal. Since President Bush's declaration of victory in Iraq seven years ago aboard the USS Abraham Lincoln, political and military authorities have been reluctant to describe how and under what circumstances victory will be achieved in either of America's current wars beyond "staying the course until the job is done." Regardless of its status in public discourse or as a doctrinal term, however, victory has by no means gone out of fashion and there is no reason to think that the concept of war termination, with its vaguely clinical, antiseptic feel, is likely to supplant it anytime soon. Nevertheless, the idea that conflicts can be deliberately guided toward a practical, durable solution acceptable to all sides is especially relevant to our times. The history of war and the history of American war in particular, can contribute importantly to this relatively new way of understanding how modern war ends.

Despite any present reservations about victory, in earlier days the ideal of victory was very potent indeed. In its ideal form, victory was believed to settle all questions. Victory was unambiguous, a complete triumph by force of arms to which one's enemy could not reply. Once victory was achieved, the victor was at complete liberty to define the peace that followed. This was what General Norman Schwartzkopf had in mind when he recalled the end of the First Gulf War. "Our side had won," he wrote, "so we were in a position to dictate terms." His meeting with Iraqi commanders at Safwan that halted the fighting, he insisted, was in no way a transaction. "I'm here to tell them exactly what we expect them to do;" he told reporters.

Historically, if one were to ask a soldier what he or she expected to accomplish in a war, victory was the automatic reply. If one were to ask those who have been at war since World War II, the answer might be more equivocal. A veteran of the Korean War might say that victory in his war meant preventing the unification by force of the peninsula under the banner of North Korea. The veteran of Vietnam might say that if the United States had done the same, that is to defend the sovereignty of a friendly nation from aggression, this would have been enough. Those were in fact the aims of the United States in those wars as well as in the First Gulf War, although how they were defined varied considerably as the war evolved. In the end, they were strictly limited. Said differently, the kind of victory envisioned by our statesmen and soldiers fell considerably short of the ideal and some have argued, far too short of it.

Given America's history of war, especially the nation's two world wars, it is understandable that the outcome of our more limited wars would have aroused considerable official and popular disappointment. The first half of the 20th century saw wars that approached totality and the victories they produced seemed closer to the ideal than those of the nation's subsequent wars. These two great wars, if not examined too closely, are held up as examples of war properly done, their outcome commensurate with uncompromising aims and sacrifices paid, so complete that the defeated enemy had little say in what followed. The Second World War especially has been used as a benchmark against which all subsequent wars, including our present conflicts, have been measured. Yet, to paraphrase Clausewitz, when war is examined in reality, rather than in its imaginary form, the whole thing looks quite different.

However one may imagine war in the abstract, in reality, wars are defined by their limitations. Real wars are creatures of their unique place and time. The purposes for which they are fought, the manner in which they are fought, the ways in which they end, and their lasting results arise from their social, political, and material circumstances. Even in societies fully committed to general war, the translation of social and material resources into military power is far from comprehensive. During the Civil War, the Confederacy mobilized an astonishing 80 percent of its white males of military age but intentionally did not recruit its huge slave population. For social and political rather than purely military reasons, the Confederacy willingly paid a high cost that President Davis would try to rectify very late—too late—in the war. During World War II, the United States mobilized more extensively than any time before or since but reserved much of its potential strength for industrial mobilization, with the result that only one-sixth of its male population served in the armed forces. More than six million draftees were rejected for service on grounds that, according to one authority, would not have excused them in other armies. The United States' calculations of the number of men needed on the fighting lines were so fine [that] the Army came close to running out of infantrymen during the critical last year of the war.

The limits imposed on war by material resources are even more pronounced. The state of science, technology, and industry directly influences a war's geographic scope, its pace of operations, and the effectiveness with which these resources are employed from the strategic to the tactical level. Moreover, the mere existence of such resources is no guarantee their potential can be fully exploited. Decades passed, for instance, before modern armies adjusted to machine guns. In 1912, the Army still regarded them as a "weapon of emergency."

To these limitations, one must add those exacted by the actions of the enemy. Combat soldiers know well the cliché that the enemy always gets a vote. Yet the list of wars—including American wars—in which statesmen, strategists, and generals embarked on and directed wars with scant reference to the enemy is depressingly long. The common conceit is that if one is strong enough, if one's plans are well laid, if one's operations are well generalled, how the enemy responds is of little relevance. During the Vietnam War, President Lyndon Johnson and Secretary of Defense Robert McNamara occasionally took notice of the enemy and found their knowledge lacking. Their solution was to imagine what they would do if they were Ho Chi Minh. The historian Douglas Pike found in the writings of Aldous Huxley the perfect term for this conceit: "vincible ignorance" or "that which one does not know and realizes it but does not regard as necessary to know." Put differently, no enemy is going to tell me how to run my war.

In all too many cases, a state of war is assumed to create such an impenetrable wall of enmity that the adversaries have no relation to one another except when they meet in battle. Yet even the most vicious wars have been shot through with formal and informal agreements about how they shall be fought. All sides foreswore the use of chemical weapons in combat in World War II, not in the interests of humanity but because of the prospect of retaliation. With one exception, this common understanding held fast. For the briefest moment at the beginning of the European war, Great Britain and Germany imposed limits on the bombing of cities and "non-military" targets, although those limits were violated soon enough as the war escalated.

In the opening pages of "On War," Clausewitz famously described war as a duel but he wisely chose not to take this metaphor, with its connotation of sequential action, thrust and parry, too far. Instead, he wrote later on of war as "a continuous interaction of opposites." The practical result of this interaction can be seen as the original aims and methods of the adversaries are constantly revised by the stresses of war. Motives that seem unimpeachable at the outset and ambitions for what the war might accomplish rarely if ever survive intact. This reciprocal nature of war, in which the actions of one define the other, is perhaps the single most difficult feature of war to comprehend and act upon.

Sixty-one wars, many of them revolutions or civil wars, broke out in the two decades following the Second World War. The United States was involved at least indirectly in 18 of these. Despite the nation's overwhelming military strength, in both the Korean and Vietnam Wars the United States strictly controlled its power so as not to ignite a general war with its closest competitors, the Soviet Union and China, and they followed the same policy. The threat that these limited wars might escalate to ignite a nuclear war served as a powerful counterweight against the United States' aims in both Korea and Vietnam, not only in official circles but in public opinion as well. War could no longer be quarantined from the outside world, if it ever really could.

Most of America's wars have attracted public criticism and sometimes outright resistance. It is easily enough forgotten that the national unity of World War II was more the exception than the rule in American history, but since the first stirrings of the Cold War, each military action has been subjected increasingly to an ever more immediate public scrutiny and aided by advances in communications, that public scrutiny was not only national but global. Military actions have counted for more, not less, in the public world. Minor tactical actions that in World War II would not have warranted an entry in daily situation reports can attract national attention. Commanders in the field could no longer direct their operations as if they were masters of the universe. The public face of war became ever more cosmopolitan and so had the conduct of war itself. Especially since World War II, more than one American policymaker or general has been made to pay a price for what the public sees as a strategic or operational miscalculation, and events that seem to have little tactical or operational importance can have strategic consequences.

So it is all the more ironic that at the same time the idea should have arisen that war could be treated as if it took place in a laboratory, grown in a Petri dish under strictly controlled conditions. By the late 1950s and early 1960s, influential civilian strategists were arguing that military actions in and of themselves were almost incidental to the management of a given conflict. Conflict was seen as a bargaining process between national security elites in a closed environment, segregated from the larger world beyond executive briefing rooms. In this environment, military actions counted for less than the "signals" the elites sent one another, signals to which the other side would then respond. No part of war, or no important part, was believed beyond intellectual control. This approach is now associated with our strategy during the War in Vietnam but it was not so novel as the theorists supposed. It had already been attempted without the aid of theory in the Korean War, and one can find traces of it stretching throughout the nation's military history. While it is true that modern communications had compressed the loop between decision and action, it was more than ever true that the loop was not a closed one.

Wars do not begin by accident but deliberately and with purpose; that is how they are fought and that is how they end but that is not to say that all the parts of war can be controlled. If that were true, the way a war ends would correspond precisely to the aims that set it in motion. Yet the difference between the original aims of a war and the terms on which it actually ends is often considerable and it is only during the course of the war itself that the combatants' aims converge toward an agreement to stop fighting.

One might think that in a war where one side is overpoweringly stronger than its enemy, this process of convergence is somehow nullified but its traces can be found in every war, regardless of disparities in strength. In the American Revolution, the Americans were vastly outmatched by any military standard of the day and seemed to stand little chance against the most powerful empire in the world. That the Americans would successfully fight their way through eight years of warfare to the negotiating table seems the very definition of a miracle, until one calculates the enormous burdens of empire, not least the enmity of France and Spain that Great Britain carried throughout the war. Seen from this wider perspective, the Americans' victory at Yorktown was decisive only in a narrower sense, indeed so narrow that General Washington expected to resume campaigning and with good reason. The British had already lost an army at Saratoga and kept fighting nonetheless. They still had more men in the field than Washington did and still occupied New York City and Charleston, lodgments from which new offensives could be launched. The course of the war had educated Great Britain about how wrong its original calculations had been and far from being complete, the Americans' victory left unsettled questions that would not be resolved for generations. Their ambitions thus redefined by the course of the war, Great Britain's interests and those of its former colonies began to intersect in the aftermath of Yorktown even though the war officially continued for another two years.

In all of American history, no conflict seems less conducive to this process of convergence than the Second World War. Nazi Germany and Imperial Japan's ambitions were so vast as to seem to have no limits at all, encompassing as they did the domination between them of the entire Eurasian land mass. Almost at the outset, President Franklin Roosevelt committed the United States to the objective of unconditional surrender, an objective formally approved by the Allied powers at the Casablanca Conference in 1943. Exactly what Allied aims at that stage of the war meant for Germany was spelled out by Secretary of the Treasury Henry Morgenthau, who drafted a plan for postwar Germany that was agreed to by the President and British Prime Minister Winston Churchill at the Quebec Conference in late 1944. The plan called for Germany's permanent enfeeblement by reducing it to a state of agricultural peonage.

The plan also called for the summary field execution of leading Nazi officials as soon as they were taken prisoner. Although Churchill had reservations about the extent of economic punishment to be meted out against Germany, his views on how its leaders should be treated were more in keeping with Morgenthau's. In his history of the war, Churchill recounts an exchange with Russia's Joseph Stalin in which the Soviet leader suggested field executions for the entire German General Staff, some 50,000 officers in all. Although he joked Stalin's suggestion away, or thought he did, Churchill did not mention that he and General Dwight Eisenhower had discussed standing every General Staff officer above the rank of major up against the wall. Such ideas were reflections of a bitter war still being fought at white hot intensity all around the world, one whose end was still very far from view.

Morgenthau's plan seems to have been written with little thought that it might affect the operational conduct of the war but its implications were not lost on the enemy. Hitler's Minister of Propaganda, Joseph Goebbels, was quick to seize on the news as proof that the Allies intended to enslave the German people. American officials saw its operational implications too. Secretary of War Henry Stimson and Chief of Staff of the Army General George C. Marshall pointedly warned Morgenthau that German resistance all along the front was stiffening because of the news and OSS Chief William Donovan reported to the White House that the German people no longer fought to preserve the Nazi regime but Germany itself. One well placed American officer with entre to the White House told the President that the plan was worth 30 German divisions.

The Carthaginian peace envisioned by Morgenthau was muted by the strategic situation, not in 1944, but as it had developed by 1945. The fears of a German resurgence after the war that had driven policymakers toward extremes of retribution were subordinated to new concerns over how the Soviet Union would capitalize on its own victory. The deindustrialization and denazification programs imposed on Germany were pale reflections of Morgenthau's original recommendations. Nazi leaders were not stood against the wall after all and not very many of them were called to account for their crimes before the Allied tribunal at Nuremberg.

One might argue that the way the war in Europe ended makes a poor case for convergence. After all, Germany had little say in how the peace was imposed but just as the course of the war cannot be understood without reference to the larger world in which it occurs, convergence is not produced on the battlefield alone. The members of the Allied coalition pursued their own aims and fought their own wars, sometimes in harmony with their allies and sometimes not, and in the end it was skillful wartime diplomacy that guided them toward a strategic convergence. These purposes intersected to set a far less draconian course for the future of Germany than the goal of unconditional surrender as it was originally defined might have otherwise produced. Germany benefited from these accommodations to strategic reality in terms it might have sought itself, had it negotiated from a position of greater strength at the end.

If anything, the war in the Pacific seemed to hold out even less promise for a moderate termination. Depths of enmity not present in the war against Germany, fed by racial animosity that was intensified by Japan's surprise attack on Pearl Harbor and their conduct in the campaigns that followed, sustained the Americans to the very end of the war. Most Americans would not have minded if Japan had been erased from the face of the earth. Any sort of concession to this enemy was unthinkable. For their part, Japan's leaders could not conceive of surrender in any form. For some in Japan's highest councils, even the atomic attacks against Hiroshima and Nagasaki were insufficient to dissuade them from fighting on.

Yet President Roosevelt's views were not so absolute. At the same time Roosevelt was offhandedly discussing the mass castration of all German males after the war, a far more reserved vision for a defeated Japan was taking form. Although some of his advisors looked forward to imposing the severest form of peace possible on Japan, including the execution of the Emperor, other advisors convinced Roosevelt that the Emperor system should be preserved in the interests of postwar stability. Instead, the United States would preside over a purposeful rebuilding and reform of an undivided Japan.

The reason President Roosevelt and his successor President Harry Truman decided on this approach was because the war changed East Asia's strategic landscape as profoundly as it had Europe's. Roosevelt lost confidence in nationalist China's ability to survive, and although he pressed the Soviets to enter the war against Japan, he was concerned about the role they would play once they did. Gradually, he and Truman after him began to see Japan as the bulwark of American strategy in the Far East. Neither the horrendous final campaign for Okinawa nor the grim forecasts that the war could only be won when Allied ground forces invaded the Japanese home islands were enough to disrupt the convergence of American and Japanese interests. The use of atomic weapons only accelerated a process that had already been at play for nearly two years. In the end, the Emperor was not punished for his part in the war, and, as in Germany, a substantial number of civilian and military leaders escaped judgment. Japan was rapidly transformed into America's strategic mainstay in East Asia.

Although the problem of war termination is fundamentally a strategic one, it cannot be divorced from the conduct of the war itself. Soldiers will insist, and rightly so, that their sacrifices count for more than bargaining chips to be played by statesmen but the process of convergence toward the termination of a war, even in the extreme case of a huge general war, suggests that military campaigning should be thought of differently. Seen from the perspective of war termination, the role of individual campaigns in the actual shaping of the peace is today far less obvious than traditions of military thought and practice imply.

For the professional soldier and policymaker, no less than for the historian of war, one of the most important questions arising from this different perspective is whether the terminal campaign, the campaign that has the most influence on the termination of a war, is the same as the final campaign? In the nation's most recent history, the course of the War in Vietnam poses this question most vividly. Chronologically, North Vietnam's offensive of 1975 was the war's final campaign but seen from the present, it was the Tet Offensive in 1968 that exercised the greatest influence over how the war would end. Although North Vietnam's confederates in the South suffered heavy battlefield loses during Tet, its strategic effect was profound, forcing the retirement of President Johnson as well as the removal of his principal commander in the field and a sea change against the war in American and world opinion. From that campaign onward and despite attempts by America's commanders in the field to reverse these effects, the United States was on the strategic defensive. In that light, North Vietnam's final offensive was the consummation of its strategic success during Tet, and it is in the period between the two campaigns that the process of convergence can be seen most clearly. The immediate results of the Tet Offensive certainly gave North Vietnam's leaders little cause for celebration and the full scope of its strategic consequences played out only gradually over the next seven years. Yet the ultimate outcome challenged orthodox views on how campaigns affect the course of a war.

Professional soldiers are likely to recoil at the thought that a battlefield defeat might in some way contribute to their ultimate goal of victory. The survivors of Japan's victory at Pearl Harbor are not likely to take kindly to the suggestion that their defeat exercised a far greater influence over the outcome of the Pacific War than if they had successfully repelled the attack with little loss of life or damage to the Pacific Fleet. Yet the defeat at Pearl Harbor drove the United States to declare war sooner than it might have. The damage to its battleships forced the United States to depend more on carriers that would bear the burdens of its early naval war. For Americans on the home front as well as those who fought, the defeat served as a powerful incentive for retribution until the day the Enola Gay appeared over Hiroshima. In the longer view that statesmen and field commanders do not have the luxury of enjoying, campaigns won and lost take on a far different shape.

If military action still plays a crucial role in moving a war toward its termination, of what value is it to redefine the terms of victory that have sustained armies for centuries? The reason is that modern war, no less than any other, is a creature of its unique place and time. The terms by which war was understood in the past have been overturned by the view that modern war must be more precisely attuned to the limited objectives for which it is being fought—limited objectives that must be designed precisely as well.

The demands made on those who direct war today are therefore substantially different than those of the past. The use of military power in pursuit of national objectives in the age of modern war is more a question of its efficient employment than use of its full potential. That today the United States accepts these limitations at risk to its interests means that its enemies benefit from advantages they might not otherwise enjoy, including the deliberate protraction of conflict as well as the expansion of its scope beyond its immediate operational zones to regions that have no direct involvement in the war. Under these circumstances, the United States' immense military power is no guarantee that it can seize and sustain the strategic and operational initiative, and steering a war toward a desirable end is no small task even in the most favorable circumstances. The policymaker who decides for war must first understand that there will be mutually acceptable terms in the end, that these terms may bear little resemblance to those originally envisioned, and that in any case no one nation is the sole author of the peace. Thus every military action should be designed with a view to the contribution it might make along with that of the enemy to the nature of the peace that will inevitably follow and on no other basis.

General George C. Marshall once wrote that the art of war has no traffic with rules. No book of rules on the art of ending war is likely to grace the bookshelves of the Oval Office or the doctrinal libraries of the Pentagon. The propositions advanced in this essay derive from America's own military experience. Although these propositions may appear to be self evident, it is also true that every one of America's major conflicts have been fought in ignorance - or defiance - of one or more of them. It is for that reason that they are now offered as aides to both the policymaker and the soldier as they confront the challenge of ending America's wars in the future.

Bibliographic Note

Every study of war should begin with Carl von Clausewitz's "On War," edited and translated by Michael Howard and Peter Paret (Princeton: Princeton University Press, 1976), which, despite his preoccupation with battle, has much to say about how wars actually end. How military thinking evolved since Clausewitz is surveyed in Azar Gat's "A History of Military Thought from the Enlightenment to the Cold War," (Oxford: Oxford University Press, 2001), and in "The Makers of Modern Strategy from Machiavelli to the Nuclear Age," edited by Peter Paret (Princeton: Princeton University Press, 1986).

For the global context in which the American experience of war arose, Christian Archer, John R. Ferris, Holger Herwig, and Timothy H. E. Travers' "World History of Warfare," (Lincoln: University of Nebraska Press, 2002), is of considerable value. The long sweep of American military history is covered in Allan R. Millet and Peter Maslowski's "For the Common Defense: A Military History of the United States," revised and expanded edition (New York: The Free Press, 1994).

Military historians have had little to say about the subject of war termination. Geoffrey Blainey's "The Causes of War," (New York: The Free Press, 1973); and Fred Ikle's "Every War Must End," (New York: Columbia University Press, 1991) are notable exceptions.

Recommended Reading

A substantial body of scholarly literature in the social sciences has emerged since the end of the Vietnam War; these are surveyed in Berenice Carroll's "How Wars End: An Analysis of Some Current Hypotheses," *Journal of Conflict Resolution*, volume 392 (November, 1970): 14-29; and William T. R. Fox, editor, "How Wars End," *The Annals of the American Academy of Political and Social Science* (Philadelphia: The American Academy of Political and Social Science, 1970). The state of contemporary thought in the social sciences is on display in Dan Reiter's "How Wars End," (Princeton: Princeton University Press, 2009).

Session 1

Interview

Dr. Roger Spiller

Interviewer

As a term of art, the notion of war termination is a fairly recent one dating to legal studies during the First World War. Why was the phrase "war termination" really created then? Before that, how did they refer to the ends of wars?

Dr. Roger Spiller

My suspicion is that it was a part of the evolution of the laws of war, which had really made their appearance with the Lieber Code in the American Civil War.

The international community had taken an interest in the termination of war, how war is finished, not only how they were conducted but how they were finished. This led to a kind of minor school of literature and to international laws of war to insure that justice was done on all sides.

The ultimate hope, of course, was that war could be prevented all together. This coincided at the same time with the rise of the world peace movement, the most famous part of which being the great Hague conferences at the turn of the century, and ultimately, right after the conclusion of World War I, the establishment of the League of Nations, which, notably, the United States did not sign up for.

Interviewer

And the focus on war studies grew from there.

Dr. Roger Spiller

Especially after World War I, western governments were concerned about the use of poison gas and the use of airplanes to bomb civilian populations. Unfortunately, some nations were getting experience in advance doing that, notably the Italians in North Africa. So there was a great deal of concern, especially in the UK, which was vulnerable to air attack. It was, I think, Stanley Baldwin, the Prime Minister in the 1930s, who said the bomber will always get through. What they were getting through to was not war industries.

It was the civilian population itself, this idea that in order to win a great war, you had to break the will of the enemy people. So the people become a target. Whether there was a legitimate military target or not is another question. So by the turn of the century, some people were beginning to interest themselves in how, if we were so unfortunate as to have a war, that war might be limited both in duration and in the cost and destruction of the war. So there was a great interest in mitigating the effects of war in some way whether by means of law or by means of technology or simply common agreement that it was in no one's interest to engage in some forms of warfare.

Interviewer

Is it consistent with the rise of democracy in the 20th century that the popular voice becomes significant as a tool for beginning and ending wars?

Dr. Roger Spiller

I think there was a great public change of mind in the late 19th and early 20th century about what war was, about the nature of war, about how war should be conducted. Before World War I and maybe even before that, if you asked the educated man on the street in the western nations whether war was inevitable he would say yes. If you asked him whether war was a natural phenomenon like a thunderstorm that you couldn't predict and you had difficulty controlling or impossible to control, he would say yes. After World War I, the answer would have been "no" to both of those. So the public was increasingly interested in war in the 19th and certainly in the 20th century.

There are two great revolutions in warfare in the 19th century. One of them is always talked about, the technological or industrial revolution, but another one hasn't been addressed so systematically, and that's the Democratic Revolution.

With the emergence of the idea during the Napoleonic Wars that the entire nation would go to war, that to the degree possible you would mobilize every asset you had to protect vital interests of state and nation. It was the revolution that gave some substance to that idea of total mobilization.

It was a notion that came to be very popular in Europe, especially Germany, after World War I. In fact, it was General Ludendorff who coined the term "total war." By total war, he meant the complete mobilization, militarization of a society for the purposes of war. So you have these competing impulses. On the one hand, there are people such as the English barristers who are writing about international laws of war and how to terminate war equitably to sort of overcome the mistake of starting the war to begin with. On the other hand, you have this other impulse toward total war. Both schools were aiming in directions that were unattainable. I mean, they were ideals more than the realities. That's one of the things that I especially wanted to talk about in this essay.

Interviewer

As the will of the people seems to take hold in governance, it seems as though the great masses of the people are then equally brought into the experience of war-making.

Dr. Roger Spiller

That's right. For a limited war, you sort of go to war with what you have but for a national war, one that engages the national interest, the whole population is in some way involved. In World War II, which was the most completely mobilized this country has ever been, an enormous number of able-bodied men who in other countries would have been eligible for active military service were held back for purposes of industrial production. We could have drafted into service upwards of eight or nine million people.

Interviewer

But it is not only that the great masses of people are fighting the war. The masses must also be in support of the war.

Dr. Roger Spiller

That's true…The age of modern war really begins in 1945. You see the workings of public opinion and the policymaker's attentiveness to public opinion, intensifying.

That's a process which has continued to intensify, fed by nothing other than the revolution in communications that's occurred since the 1950s. There's just no precedent for that sort of thing. Now, almost every day includes an electronic referendum on the conduct of the war. We may not be very interested in it day to day; citizens may not be very interested in it but they know about it. It's hard for them not to be exposed to what is happening in Iraq or Afghanistan. Ten years ago, the average citizen would have had trouble locating them on a map. Now, they know where Baqubah is.

Interviewer

And it is a vivid picture, too.

Dr. Roger Spiller

It's a dramatic picture. It's fed by image. In news, you don't go looking for places where nothing happens…You don't go looking for images of normal traffic on the interstate. You go for the multi-car wrecks.

Interviewer

In that old expression, news is when "man bites dog" not when "dog bites man. "

Dr. Roger Spiller

Yes, something like that.

Interviewer

Nonetheless, another factor to this has to be that for most of the 20th century, we had conscription.

Dr. Roger Spiller

Yes.

Interviewer

…and since 1973, we had the volunteer army so that public opinion takes on a more diminished role.

Dr. Roger Spiller

Yet the heightened technical capacities of public media insure that the emotional impact on the general population is every bit as intense, maybe more so, than the mass wars of World War I and World War II.

I was involved in a project a few years ago, a film project. We were discussing how the ordinary citizen in America received war news. How was the ordinary citizen informed about the progress of American forces in the fighting theaters of war?

Well, they got letters. When it was really bad news, they got telegrams from the War Department. Then, once a week, MovieTone News and News of the World were playing at the local theater. These are wonderful to look at now for how little they informed the audience but in those days, that was the information...So if you compare the input of information about war to the public citizenry in let's say 1944 to the amount of information coming to the citizen now, today we are constantly getting a more vivid picture of war and it affects the audience. It affects their opinions. No matter how intellectual they are,

The policymaker who attempts to ignore that ignores it at his peril. The American policymaker, that is.

Interviewer

How influenced is something like the Powell Doctrine by that reality, do you think? The Powell Doctrine as being massive force used for very clearly stated aims, quick and out and therefore less likely to endure the kinds of hardships that are vivified by public image.

Dr. Roger Spiller

Yeah. Well, it's a very appealing idea. The Powell Doctrine of course is a product of the Vietnam War

But...sometimes you don't get to choose which wars you fight. The Army certainly doesn't get to vote and neither does the chief of staff nor the secretary of defense. That decision rests with one person only.

I think the Powell Doctrine made it all a bit too clinical. I was working in a joint command for a four star general, one of the so called CINCs at the time that the Powell Doctrine came out. We saw it in draft. I objected to it. We were supposed to write a response, and I wrote the response. I objected to it on those grounds. It was too restrictive a formula, and I felt that if the United States followed that formula, essentially it would entail a great deal more risk than otherwise.

There are times, such as in the Balkans, our intervention in the Balkans and Kosovo, where it's not overtly in America's interest to be there. Even at the time it was asked, "Well, where are the Europeans? If this is such a problem for the Balkans, where is the European community?" Well, they were there but it wasn't the same as when America intervened.

In that case, it turned out positively and probably prevented a conflagration and perhaps even genocide.

In Somalia, it turned out very badly. Very badly indeed. In both cases, we violated the Powell Doctrine. Not perversely, or out of ignorance I think but because it was decided the United States had a moral obligation to intervene in those places. I don't know how far I would go with moral intervention, the moral necessity of intervention.

You have to, in any case, even if you're a great power like the United States, be very selective about which fights you choose if you do indeed choose them.

...You take your chances, and I'm not sure that one formula like the Powell Doctrine is adequate for all the contingencies the United States faces.

Interviewer

It seems as though the Powell Doctrine is framed in part to do the best one can to avoid uncertainty.

Dr. Roger Spiller

Well, one of the underlying assumptions in the Powell Doctrine is that it's going to be quick and decisive. Use overwhelming force, get in as fast as you can, hit the enemy as hard as you can and get out soon. The only problem with expeditions like that is they tend to last a lot longer than we expect them to. The so-called phase four of the operation, that is to say post-hostilities phase always involves some degree of humanitarian rescue, perhaps reconstruction, perhaps political reformation.

That certainly was the case in Panama. There was plenty to do after the fighting stopped but it was the fighting itself that helped shape the peace that followed.

Interviewer

Well one of the themes of your essay and in general I think it seems somewhat of your work in general is that war is unpredictable. There are myriad agents of change in all directions. You cannot prepare, really, effectively, for what you are going to do, what war is going to do. Given that, what would the "Spiller Doctrine" be?

Dr. Roger Spiller

Intellectual preparation. If there's one deficiency, it's the deficiency of imagination.

And yet saying that war is unpredictable and fundamentally chaotic is not to be confused with the counsel for inaction…The great paradox is that even knowing all that, at some point you will have to act, you will act.

You might not like it. It might be under conditions that you never yourself would have chosen but you must act to sustain the interests of the nation. It goes with the territory. To paraphrase Mao, it's not a dinner party and it's not a seminar.

Interviewer

So, to you, imagination seems to be the key.

Dr. Roger Spiller

If at the beginning of our involvement in Vietnam we had understood the roots of the Vietnamese independence movement, if we had understood the historic connections, the historic relationship between China and Indochina, and how much animosity there was between the two; if we had understood the political landscape with any kind of acuity at all, inside both North Vietnam and South Vietnam, our courses of action would have been different. We wouldn't have been so blithely confident that we could shoot our way to peace.

Interviewer

You write something in your essay, and I have gone over it several times because I want to make sure I understand it. You said that Robert McNamara tried to imagine what he would do if he were Ho Chi Minh instead of imagining what Ho Chi Minh himself would do.

Dr. Roger Spiller

That's exactly right. In every disaster, there's always one guy who knows. When the investigations come out of the oil spill in the gulf, I'll bet you a dollar we find that there was one guy in BP who said; "Wait a minute, you don't want to do it this way. This oil head is not fitted for this kind of operation. There are all sorts of technical problems here."

He's probably going to be in middle management somewhere, or maybe a technical expert. He may look funny. He may dress funny. He may have bad habits; have a pugnacious personality, be disliked by his fellow employees but he's right. The management blows him off.

This is almost a hypothesis but if you go back to any disaster, military or industrial or otherwise, and dig deeply enough, you'll find one of these guys. The trick, I think, for the leader is to be sufficiently open of mind to recognize that guy and to take him seriously long enough to consider what he has to say.

Interviewer

There is a lesson in leadership built into what you just described.

Dr. Roger Spiller

I'll speak directly to the army. As you grow up as an officer, you gradually become committed to our corporate narrative…and it sets up boundaries to your thinking. You tend to be less flexible as you go along. Within the orbit, within your immediate orbit, you may be known as a free thinker but there's always a limit about how free you can be.

For good and practical reasons, armies must operate in unison if they can. I mean it's certainly a pre-democratic institution and a pre-industrial institution, even a pre-historic institution. It bears all the signatures of those origins. It is a unique subculture. It is very much a subculture. It has all the signatures of a subculture.

So it enforces certain patterns of thought along its members which are very difficult to break out. It is a practical problem. You don't want a commander who's running around willy-nilly, changing his mind every second…You always have to weigh the practicalities of changing your mind against the necessity of changing your mind. That's not an easy task. That takes some practicing and it takes some thinking about before the event occurs.

Interviewer

Here in the army you have men and women who are trained on a certain plane of conformity and then leap into positions of strategic importance and are asked to make decisions. According to the Spiller Doctrine, they should listen for the eccentric voice in the crowd and at least take it seriously.

Dr. Roger Spiller

Right. Sometimes it takes a great deal of courage. After Pearl Harbor, we could have just built more battleships. We lost two, a few were damaged. The strike was certainly intended to disable the battle fleet. We could have said, "Okay, we'll delay our entry into the Pacific War a little bit. It'll just take us a little while to build more battleships but we'll get there.

Indeed we could have…but against that was the cost of wasting time and trying to reverse Japanese advances against the Pacific which had grown just exponentially since the spring. So…the American government could have made a very wrong decision at that point. Instead, we took what carriers we had and they really carried the burden of the Pacific War.

Interviewer

There have been enormous technological advances in the last quarter century. Do you look at the future of wars in the 21st century as within the scope of the imagination of the leaders in charge right now?

Dr. Roger Spiller

I don't think we know. I don't think we can know until the event. We can make forecasts but we may be far wrong. That's the other vexing part about it. If it were all predictable, we would have fixed it a long time ago, wouldn't we have?

Interviewer

This is a great segue into going back more directly to the topic of war termination and the traditional notion of victory. Would you say that this word has become somewhat archaic?

Dr. Roger Spiller

I think it's limiting. I think it obscures the complexity of what we're doing. It may once have been possible to think that all wars ended in a great victory that you could paint on a mural. I don't. In closer examination, if you look at how wars actually finish and the nature of the peace that follows, you find that victory is not really an event. I mean, the end of war is not really an event like victory, I should say, and that its effects can reverberate for years.

As late as the 1840s, the United States was still dealing with questions that had arisen during the American Revolution. The treatment of the native peoples and the expansion to the west, what was then the old northwest but in the 1840s, we're still having disputes with Great Britain over boundaries. I mean there was a war cry there for awhile, not a serious one, nothing that took us to the brink of war with Great Britain but there was a diplomatic crisis of some magnitude. I mean that's more than half a century later.

How many years have we been in a semi-state of war in Korea after the armistice? That was in, what, 1953? Over half a century. If someone had come to President Truman just after the North Koreans invaded South Korea in the summer of 1950 and said, "Mr. President, we have to go to war to defend the sovereignty of South Korea, to prevent its being overtaken by the Communist North. The price for this is probably going to be about 60,000 casualties and 100,000 more wounded. Oh yes, by the way, we're going to have to occupy the southern part of the country for the next half century," what do you think his response would have been?

Interviewer

So in a sense, what you're also saying is wars can never really terminate or terminate a century later, that the end is not necessarily related to battlefield victories, to last campaigns.

Dr. Roger Spiller

No.

Interviewer

…or necessarily related to the original goals of war.

Dr. Roger Spiller

Those are always in a state of motion, always in a state of motion.

Interviewer

You mention in the essay that one thing that is rarely understood is the way that the enemy can change the conduct and the outcome of the war. Even the loser can change the conduct.

Dr. Roger Spiller

Losers are not without their resources. It's very interesting to look at the end of our involvement in Vietnam from that angle. Even though we had telegraphed our intentions to leave South Vietnam no matter what the cost…we nevertheless had certain advantages we could have played in the peace negotiations but the Nixon administration was hell bent on getting out as soon as possible for reasons of political discord at home as much as anything.

The American people were having their vote. The North Vietnamese played that advantage very well but we had advantages, too. We had enormous, overwhelming strength and we mostly cut back on that strength as fast as we could. I think we had other ways to orchestrate our departure from that war, essentially leave Southeast Asia in a much more equitable way than we did. It's still quite an emotional subject, the way in which we left that war. I think we may get over it in another couple of generations but not any time soon.

Interviewer

Well, you would agree that the way that we left has had an impact on the future wars.

Dr. Roger Spiller

It has an impact right now.

Interviewer

Explain that.

Dr. Roger Spiller

The shadow of Vietnam hangs over every one of our communications with Hamid Karzai and with the government of Afghanistan, with our attitude toward the enemy or the enemies in Afghanistan and Iraq; with our putative allies in Pakistan. Vietnam is right there behind the curtain. Even more than the first Gulf War.

Historical memory has a savage way about it. It's not symmetrical, and it's not uniform and it's not arranged chronologically. You sort of look back and you pick the things that impress you the most. Those are the things that tend to influence your behavior in the future. I mean, the best analogy is the old Munich and appeasement analogy. How long did Munich play in the political imagination?

Interviewer

Munich is still holding on.

Dr. Roger Spiller

Fewer people understand the analogy these days.

Interviewer

Right but you can call somebody a Chamberlain now. People will know what that means.

You say the great distance between executive decision and military action which generals and policymakers often pray for appears to strengthen rapidly during these years. Can you explain that in a little bit more depth? Why is it that generals pray for a great distance between executive decisions?

Dr. Roger Spiller

Because they have independence.

Interviewer

They want to own their own war?

Dr. Roger Spiller

Yes.

Interviewer

Particularly in American history, they fear the input of a naive civilian.

Dr. Roger Spiller

It's not just American history. Napoleon, when he was on campaign in Russia, in order to receive communication from Paris, I think the loop was about two weeks. He had the best communication system in continental Europe. Very fast. Probably faster than the Rothschild communication system, which was for the financial network. It was very advanced for its time. It still was two weeks between decision and action, essentially. What is it now? One email away. You know? The theater commander will walk around with a Blackberry in his hand and be having a running conversation with his president. That's pretty tight.

Interviewer

Do you think that the speed with which decisions may be made works negatively upon the conduct of the use of deadly force?

Dr. Roger Spiller

It does. In this instance, in this restrictive instance, I'd like a lot less efficiency, actually. I'd like a little lag time, because the stakes are so high not only for us but for the enemy population. It would be nice to have a little less efficiency in that regard but we're not going in that direction. It's not the way war is going. It's going the opposite direction.

Interviewer

Wars do not begin by accident but deliberately with purpose. That is how they are fought and that is how they end.

Dr. Roger Spiller

The notion that there is an accidental war, I don't know where that comes from. It's a very soothing idea but we do it to ourselves. It may be wrong but we start it on purpose.

We have something in mind. It may be a stupid idea. The cause may be pernicious, may be dreadful, but we start it in the hope that we can advance that cause of it. That's very deliberate. That's a choice. Even those who are attacked have a choice. They can submit.

They can do other things. The alternatives may not be acceptable to them, so they fight. They defend themselves. ...There is nothing mysterious about this. This is a very human act; a very human act.

Interviewer

Would you say that they end in the same way?

Dr. Roger Spiller

They do end deliberately but not as a consequence of deliberation by policymakers alone or strategists alone...You can more manage a war's termination than you can the totality of the war while it's going on. Some factors are beyond your reach to control or manipulate.

Interviewer

Yet with all the chaos associated with wars, we nonetheless associate what we would call our greatest presidents with specific wars and with their heroic conduct in those wars. Washington, Lincoln, Roosevelt.

Dr. Roger Spiller

It may be the greatest test a president could ever face. It may well be...

Interviewer

Yet you could argue that some presidents who worked to avoid war are less glorified by histories. Think of Eisenhower.

Dr. Roger Spiller

I think if one were to ask candidate Obama whether he would rather have taken office during the war or when it was at peace, I think he would choose peace. Were it within his power to affect, I think he would like to make the war disappear. I mean, the war is not going to disappear. So he has a limited range of options, a limited number of roads to go down. As usual in circumstances like this, some of the choices, most of the choices perhaps, are unpalatable. You have to choose between lesser evils.

Interviewer

Talk to me about Morgenthau's plan and the wish for wars to end with retribution.

Dr. Roger Spiller

Henry Morgenthau, Secretary of the Treasury to Franklin Delano Roosevelt. The author or the patron, if you like, of a plan put together in the Department of the Treasury. It really

Wasn't treasury's mission to think about the fate of post-war Germany but that's what it was aimed at. It was a Draconian plan that in general called for the permanent agricultural enfeeblement of occupied Germany. It was encouraged at least in part, by early talk in the Roosevelt Administration during World War II, from 1942-1943 about what to do with the Germans if we won.

Of course, those were days in which the outcome of this war was not certain. It was still very much a crapshoot but nevertheless, they were talking about it. Both Roosevelt and Prime Minister Winston Churchill entertained a very punitive peace for Germany.

…Morgenthau's plan was meant to translate the policy of unconditional surrender into a reality on the ground in Germany. First of all, de-Nazifying their population. Exactly how was not specified. De-industrializing was just completely reducing all the industry in Germany.

By those two principle methods, Roosevelt and Churchill were agreed that they wanted to create a post-war Germany that could not in a few years times work a resurgence of its military strength as it had after World War I. So in 1942-1943, western policy makers and Stalin are dealing with the problems of war termination that were born in World War I. Unconditional surrender is essentially a reverberation of World War I and Germany's eventual rearmament after World War I…

The scent of vengeance was in the air in 1943 or so. Morgenthau, who was just as seized with the idea of vengeance as anyone else or maybe more so, gave voice to these impulses with his plan and talked Roosevelt into approving a draft of the plan in the fall of 1944. Of course, it was a confidential or classified plan but it was soon enough leaked… and a summary of it was published, I think, in the Washington Post.

There was a tremendous outcry, mainly from editorial writers. The American public opinion wasn't so concerned. It didn't bother them all that much but opinion writers such as Walter Lippmann at the time came out square against it.

There was also a movement inside the Roosevelt Administration at the time to counter the pernicious effects of the Morgenthau Plan because it was believed that as soon as the plan became public, it encouraged stiffer resistance on the part of the Germans at the front.

In fact, the Office of Strategic Services reported from Bern that that's exactly what was happening inside Germany. One American Army officer who had access to the White House said that the Morgenthau Plan was worth 30 German divisions. His numbers, I think, were off but the point was made well enough even though the Roosevelt Administration eventually repudiated the substance of the Morgenthau Plan.

Interviewer

How interesting within that short period of time that such a transformation was made. I imagine that already there was a deeper understanding that the total surrender that had been demanded of Germany from World War I was one of the reasons why Germany rose to World War II.

Dr. Roger Spiller

Exactly, I think when President Truman succeeded President Roosevelt in May of 1945, that Truman instinctively understood that. I think by that time, of course Henry

Stimson had just enormous prestige within the government. He's dying by inches in front of everybody and he refuses to retire. If you read his diaries, you can see how he's kind of triangulating between his deteriorating personal health and the seriousness of the problems facing him. At the same time he's trying to moderate what Morgenthau has put in motion, he's trying to do the same thing with regard to Japan. That's a story with a completely different twist but again it all turns in the policy of unconditional surrender.

Interviewer

Talk about war termination as to the story of Japan, the introduction of the bomb at the end of the Second World War.

Dr. Roger Spiller

First of all, Roosevelt and even Truman were much less concerned with the post war fate of Japan than they were of Germany. They just spent more time with Germany than they did with the war against Japan. Inside the Department of State at the Assistant Secretary of State level, there was a fellow named Joseph Grew around whom there crystallized a movement of people who really knew something about Japanese life and culture, who had lived in Japan, who had studied and worked in Japan, who as far as they were able understood Japanese culture. They knew more about Japanese culture than anybody else in America probably, with a possible exception of a couple of scholars in universities.

The policy of unconditional surrender sort of collided with their knowledge of Japan and how it might be possible to construct a peace. It would have to be painstakingly constructed and if you did it the wrong way you would create even more disaster. So from about late 1942 onward, which is really quite early, Grew and some of his colleagues began to lobby very powerfully.

Public opinion polls at the time showed that enormous numbers wanted just the outright execution of the emperor. They wanted the dismantlement of Japan, the complete partitioning of Japan into little principalities that would never rise again as a unified state, essentially, the destruction of Japanese culture and life.

Interviewer

This was because Japan and not Germany actually struck the United States?

Dr. Roger Spiller

Yes, and also because of its conduct during the war which was judged by Americans as inhuman, bestial, barbaric, so on and so forth, which in point of fact was perfectly consonant with the history of Japanese military culture. What they were doing had a cultural basis. It was of relatively recent vintage and several new works on Japan have pointed out, and it was kind of an ersatz culture or pseudo-military culture that Japan went to war with but it was their culture and they had been working at it. The Japanese military certainly had been working at it very intensely since the ascent of Hirohito to the throne in the early 1920s. So they had plenty of time to prepare the public.

Interviewer

So, on one side a kind of bloodthirstiness and on the other a kind of thirst for revenge and unconditional surrender which concludes with the A-bomb.

Dr. Roger Spiller

The Bomb is part of the great sea change I think in public opinion that has occurred in the past two centuries but certainly in the 20th century. And that is that war cannot be allowed to run its course because the course it runs toward is the extension of a large part of the human race.

There is a large trend which should be recognized and which should play an important role in all our future considerations about war and peace.

At the beginning of the 20th century, 10 percent of all those who died in wars were civilians. At the end of the 20th century, 90 percent of all those who died in wars were civilians. So statistically speaking, at the end of the century it's much safer to be in uniform than out of it. At least there you're surrounded by your weapons. That's not a trend that I think is going to reverse.

Interviewer

As a final question I want to come back to the subject of about American and world history because we're the ones that declare the people to be sovereign. Here we are with the people sovereign and we are in a sense more vulnerable because of it with more power to the people as a mass.

Dr. Roger Spiller

It may well be that the future army doctrine will turn in the direction of saying that the population centric warfare is the way of the future. There's a powerful argument to be made for that. It means that our style of warfare will have to change if that's true in which the minimizing of casualties, not the taking of casualties, not the creating of casualties is the aim. How to express military power in nonviolent means? That might be the great challenge of the 21st century.

Session 1
From Cowpens to Yorktown:
The Final Campaign of the War for American Independence

by

Dr. Ira D. Gruber

On New Year's Day of 1781, the War for American Independence was in its sixth year with no end in sight. The war had begun in 1775 when the British government used force in Massachusetts to put down a rebellion that had been building in its North American colonies for more than a decade. Fighting soon spread from Massachusetts to other British colonies on the Atlantic seaboard from New Hampshire to South Carolina. By the summer of 1776, the colonists had raised a Continental army, declared their independence, created republican state governments, and come together in a loose confederation of states to wage war and conduct foreign affairs. When American forces captured a British army at Saratoga, New York, in fall of 1777, the new United States secured both treaties and an alliance with France, turning their war of independence into a world war. The British had to fight not just their former colonists but also France, Spain, and the Netherlands in a war that stretched from North America to the West Indies, the English Channel, the Mediterranean Sea, and the coasts of Africa and India. In North America, the British managed to carry on the war with smaller regular forces and had some success maintaining a base at New York City, capturing Savannah and Charleston, and by 1780 establishing posts from the interior of Georgia and South Carolina to the Chesapeake. Even after promising not to tax the colonists or to interfere in their internal affairs, the British had not been able to restore royal government anywhere beyond the reach of their armies nor had the Americans been able to exploit the opportunities that had come with a wider war such as to raise the forces needed to cooperate effectively with French squadrons that reached North America each year or to take advantage of the reduction and redeployment of the British fleet and army in the United States. Indeed, at New Year's Day in 1781, the war seemed far from over. No one could have predicted confidently that 1781 would have the final campaign of the War for American Independence.

The war had dragged on indecisively in America because each side had great difficulty in using force to achieve its war aims. The British had never been able to find a combination of force and persuasion to restore royal government beyond a few ports and outposts. The new United States had had nearly as much difficulty as the British in using force. Since 1776, Americans had fought for independence, a national domain, and republican government. Having rebelled against a remote and oppressive imperial administration, Americans were also determined to win their independence without creating a central government or a standing army that could coerce the states or deprive the people of their liberties. They hoped first to defeat the British with an army of short-term volunteers supported by militiamen and supplied by the states, but the campaign of 1776 at New York made it clear that such forces could not wage war successfully against the British regular army. Congress agreed to strengthen the Continental Army by enlisting men for at least three years and by adopting a code of military discipline that would help turn raw recruits into effective soldiers, measures that significantly improved the army by the spring of 1778. Even so, without the power to tax, Congress had to depend on loans from European nations and contributions from the American states to pay, feed, clothe, house, and arm its forces and those loans and contributions were rarely adequate. Continental soldiers who were hungry and unpaid went home or mutinied with increasing frequency after 1779, and American commanders were forced to limit their operations and to rely more than they wished on poorly trained and wasteful militia. They were never able to cooperate adequately with the French squadrons that came to North America each year from 1778 to 1780.

Although Congress and the Continental Army would continue to labor under severe constraints, Americans would find ways to make the campaign of 1781 unexpectedly decisive. In December of 1780, Nathanael Greene had reached Charlotte to take command of Continental forces in the southern states. Greene brought wide experience as well as exceptional energy, political skill, and imagination to the daunting tasks of rebuilding his own small army and checking an enemy that was shifting its forces from New York to the South and threatening, with the help of Loyalists, to restore royal government to Georgia and the Carolinas. Greene began with what seemed a hazardous decision. In late December of 1780, he divided his army in the face of a much superior enemy, placing those units under his immediate command about 70 miles to the northeast of the principal British camp at Winnsboro, South Carolina, with the remainder of his men under General Daniel Morgan about 70 miles to the northwest of Winnsboro. He did so not only to make it easier to feed his men and screen the North Carolina frontier but also to tempt the British to divide their forces and attack his. He hoped that he or Morgan would have an opportunity to fight a defensive battle with a portion of the enemy's army. In mid-January, Morgan got just such an opportunity, inflicting a crushing defeat on a British detachment at Cowpens in the northwest corner of South Carolina. At a cost of fewer than 75 killed and wounded, Morgan killed, wounded, and captured more than 800 of the enemy. He also had the good judgment to preserve his victory by retreating rapidly into North Carolina with his prisoners.

In the ensuing two and a half months, Greene was able to use the American victory at Cowpens to draw the British into a most destructive campaign. On learning that the British commander, Charles Lord Cornwallis, had burned his baggage and was pursuing Morgan's detachment into North Carolina, Greene joined forces with Morgan to check Cornwallis and look for another opportunity to fight a defensive battle. Because Cornwallis had more than 2,500 men with him, a force nearly three times larger than that which had attacked Morgan at Cowpens, Greene was unwilling to risk battle until he could get reinforcements from North Carolina and Virginia. He could do no more until late February than to retreat from one swollen river to another until he reached Virginia. When Cornwallis at last turned back from the Dan River, Greene followed him toward Hillsborough, still waiting for reinforcements and using detachments to harry the British so as to keep them from raising Loyalists and gathering provisions in North Carolina. By 11 March, Greene had the forces he needed to offer battle. Deploying his army as Morgan had at Cowpens with militia in front, Continentals to the rear, and cavalry on the wings, he awaited attack in an open wood near Guilford Court House. When that attack came on 15 March, his army fought well enough. If his militia fired and fled too quickly, his Continentals stood firm until one unit broke and endangered the rest of his line. Greene withdrew, covered by his cavalry and Continental infantry, but not before his men had killed and wounded 532 of the British while losing 257 of their own. Because the British held the field and because over 1,000 of the Americans had fled, Greene was slow to appreciate that his men had had the better of the fighting at Guilford Court House. By 22 March, he was following a retiring Cornwallis toward Wilmington. Greene did not have the men or supplies to attack. He did have the courage to make a most unusual decision, to leave Cornwallis at Wilmington and invade South Carolina. On 7 April, he marched for Camden.

Greene knew that invading South Carolina would risk losing North Carolina to the British but he thought the risk was worth taking. If Cornwallis followed him south, North Carolina would be secure. If he did not, Greene would have an opportunity to drive the British from the back country and reestablish patriot governments in South Carolina and Georgia. His strategy would prove remarkably successful, in part because Cornwallis went to the Chesapeake rather than to the Carolinas and in part because Greene made skillful use of his forces. Within three months of reaching Camden on 19 April, he had lured the British into another destructive battle and employed detachments of cavalry, partisans, and militia to evict the British and Loyalists from all of their fortified posts in the interior. The British were still able to camp and forage in the vicinity of Charleston and to send an occasional detachment into the interior but by the summer of 1781, Greene was pushing the British ever closer to Charleston and encouraging patriots to restore republican governments in the rest of South Carolina and Georgia. By then he was anticipating the arrival of a powerful French fleet and army which he thought might be used decisively in the Chesapeake, if not at New York or Charleston, and preparing his own army for more ambitious operations. In early September he attacked a British detachment of more than 2,000 men that was attempting to establish a camp at Eutaw Springs, about 25 miles northwest of Charleston. In four hours of intense inconclusive fighting, his troops killed or wounded more than a quarter of the enemy. On the next day, the British retired toward Charleston and Greene retired to the High Hills of Santee where his men could recuperate while he sought to contain the British in Charleston or, with French help, capture them there. Greene was to be disappointed in his hopes of getting the French to cooperate against Charleston, but he had already done more than anyone might have expected in the campaign of 1781: to clear the British from all of the lower South except three ports, to restore republican government to Georgia and South Carolina, to encourage a reconciliation with the Loyalists, and to assist American diplomats in preserving the territorial integrity of the United States whenever the war might end.

While Greene was campaigning in the Carolinas and Georgia, George Washington, Commanding General of the Continental Army, was adopting a strategy that would take full advantage of French aid, complement what Greene had done, and make the campaign of 1781 truly decisive. By 1781, Washington was a thoroughly sound and experienced commander, a man who could be trusted as much for his republican principles as for his ability to lead men and wage a prudent war against the British. Since the summer of 1780, he had repeatedly recommended that the French and Americans join forces to attack the British in New York City. The French, knowing the weaknesses of the Continental Army, consistently rejected such an attack. In the spring of 1781, when they learned that their government was sending a powerful squadron for a summer offensive in North America, the French began recommending a campaign against the British in the Chesapeake. Washington continued to press for an attack on New York City until in late July he conducted a reconnaissance of the British lines on Manhattan and received a letter from Nathanael Greene expressing a clear preference for trapping Cornwallis in the Chesapeake. Greene thought it would be far easier to capture Cornwallis than to take either New York City or Charleston. By 30 July, Washington was beginning to waver — to make plans for going to the Chesapeake if unable to attack New York. Within two weeks, he had agreed to join the French for a campaign in Virginia. It was then sure that a massive French fleet under Count de Grasse was en route from the West Indies to the Chesapeake. Washington lost no time in urging the French Commodore Barras at Rhode Island to join de Grasse and in ordering his and the French troops on the Hudson to start overland for Virginia. By 21 August, Washington's Army was marching south through New Jersey.

Within two months, the French and American allies would achieve a remarkable victory; a victory founded not just on British mistakes but also on their own courageous decisions, good timing, and luck. They were able to take advantage of Cornwallis having made the Chesapeake the seat of the war in 1781 and of a British admiral's failure to match de Grasse's redeployment from the West Indies to the Chesapeake in August of 1781. De Grasse had the courage to take the whole of his fleet, his 28 ships of the line, to Virginia and the good luck to reach the Chesapeake on 30 August, five days ahead of a British fleet. He also had the good judgment to use his fleet to disperse the British and bring Barras' eight ships from Rhode Island safely into the Chesapeake. De Grasse was fortunate that he had arrived before the British, that his fleet was superior to theirs, that Barras had not been intercepted en route from Rhode Island to Virginia, and that Cornwallis remained in the Chesapeake. De Grasse had made the most of his opportunities in sealing the Bay, trapping Cornwallis, and allowing Washington and his allied army to make the campaign decisive. Washington, who had been passing through Philadelphia when the French engaged the British off the Chesapeake, reached Williamsburg on 14 September. As soon as he knew that de Grasse and Barras were safe within the Chesapeake, he ordered his army to embark at the Head of Elk for a voyage down the Bay to besiege Cornwallis' posts on the York River. The ensuing siege of Yorktown, which began on 1 October, did not last long. The British defensive lines were tightly placed against the river and all too easily enfiladed. By 14 October, the allies had captured redoubts guarding the British eastern flank and opened batteries that commanded the rest of the British works as well as their communications across the York. On 19 October, Cornwallis surrendered his army of nearly 8,000 men together with more than 200 cannon and 7,300 muskets.

Although no one could then be sure, the campaign of 1781 would prove to be the final campaign of the War for American Independence. Fighting would go on sporadically in North America for another year and a half. British forces would continue to occupy New York City for more than two years. Negotiations to end the war would take even longer, but gradually the belligerents realized that the campaign of 1781 had been decisive. In the days following Cornwallis' surrender, Washington sought to both continue the allied offensive against British posts in the South and to prepare for an even more ambitious effort in 1782. Even before he sent news of the surrender to Europe, he tried to persuade de Grasse to join in evicting the British from Charleston or Wilmington so as to reduce thereby the amount of territory that the British held in the southern states and the amount they might try to claim in any peace negotiations. When de Grasse refused to join in an autumn offensive, Washington asked Congress and the states to raise the men, money, and supplies for an allied offensive in the spring of 1782. Fortunately for Washington, he would not need to mount another offensive. Cornwallis' surrender had an even greater impact in Europe than in America. In February of 1782, the British House of Commons voted to abandon the American war and in March, King George III accepted a ministry that would begin to negotiate the independence of the United States. By November, American representatives in Paris had agreed to preliminary terms that were most favorable to the new nation: independence, the withdrawal of all British forces, and a domain that included lands north of Florida and south of Canada from the Atlantic Ocean to the Mississippi River. These terms, which took effect with the signing of treaties between Britain and France and Britain and Spain in January of 1783, were part of the definitive Peace of Paris of 1783.

The campaign of 1781 in Virginia and the Carolinas, the final campaign of the War for American Independence, had served the United States remarkably well. It helped Americans win a war and make a peace that realized nearly all of their war aims, even those aims that made the war difficult to wage and that would not long seem to be in the nation's interest. Americans succeeded not just in gaining independence, the withdrawal of British forces along the Atlantic seaboard, and a generous national domain but a more generous domain than Spain and France might have wished. They also managed to win the war without creating a central government and standing army that threatened the independent republican governments of the States or the liberties of the people.

Recommended Reading

The place to begin understanding the campaign of 1781 is with John C. Fitzpatrick, ed., "The Writings of George Washington, 1745-1799" (Washington, 1931-1944), volumes 22-23, and Richard K. Showman et al, eds., "The Papers of General Nathanael Greene" (Chapel Hill, 1976-2005), volumes 7-9. For the campaign and the principal commanders see J. T. Flexner, "George Washington in the American Revolution (1775-1783)", (Boston, 1968), John D. Grainger, "The Battle of Yorktown, 1781" (Woodbridge, Suffolk, England, 2005), Theodore Thayer, "Nathanael Greene: Strategist of the American Revolution" (New York, 1960), and Franklin and Mary Wickwire, "Cornwallis The American Adventure" (Boston, 1970). For a broad view of the war see Stephen Conway, "The War of American Independence, 1775-1783" (London, 1995) and Piers Mackesy, "The War for America, 1775-1783" (Cambridge, Massachusetts, 1964). For specialized studies that enhance an understanding of the campaign of 1781: E. Wayne Carp, "To Starve the Army at Pleasure: Continental Army Administration and American Political Culture, 1775-1783" (Chapel Hill, 1984), Jonathan R. Dull, "The French Navy and American Independence . . . 1774-

1787" (Princeton, 1975), Richard H. Kohn, "Eagle and Sword: the Federalists and the Creation of the Military Establishment in America 1783-1802" (New York, 1975), James Kirby Martin and Mark Edward Lender, "A Respectable Army: The Military Origins of the Republic, 1763-1789" (Arlington Heights, Illinois, 1982), Richard B. Morris, "The Peacemakers: The Great Powers and American Independence" (New York, 1965), Charles Royster, "A Revolutionary People at War: The Continental Army and American Character, 1775-1783" (Chapel Hill, 1979), and Gordon S. Wood, "The Creation of the American Republic 1776-1787" (Chapel Hill, 1969).

Session 1
Interview
Dr. Ira Gruber

Interviewer

Your work focuses on the 1781 Southern Campaign of the American Revolutionary War, particularly Cowpens and Yorktown. When considering the outcome of American Wars, why do you think this campaign has such relevance?

Dr. Ira Gruber

Well, the United States had gone into the fighting with Britain. It was a war of rebellion and at the outset, the United States hoped simply to get a redress of grievances. That would have been the first stage. The British were not very interested in redressing grievances.

They thought they were an aggrieved party, that they were victims of a rebellious selfish people or at least of rebellious leaders who were misleading the population into resistance to British authority.

The fighting that took place over the next six or eight months gave the colonists no hope that they were going to get redress of grievances and so, they were by the summer of 1776, ready to declare their independence and when they declared their independence their ambitions and aims changed substantially.

It's one thing to be part of an empire and to get somebody to say he won't tax you, or except by your own representatives, or that he won't interfere in your domestic affairs but it's quite another thing to get somebody to say he would grant you independence and recognize you as an independent state among nations of the world. The United States fought from July of 1776 for independence, recognition of its republican governments, and its loose national confederation. It fought for a national domain and for sort of complementary war aims - to avoid creating a central government in the course of the war but maintain the fighting with a loose confederation; not to have a standing army that would be oppressive to the people; [and] not to have destructive taxation. They were fighting against those things.

Consequently they thought they could win their independence without developing their own tyrannical government, which would be quite an undertaking. Well, they did reasonably well for about a year with a voluntary spirit of getting people to join up, contribute funds, provide supplies, and they tried essentially to operate without what we would call a highly disciplined and trained national force. That really sort of evaporated. The hope of that evaporated in the summer and autumn of 1776 when they suffered a lot of reverses and were driven out of Long Island, Manhattan through Westchester County, New York and out of New Jersey.

By the end of 1776, they were just lucky to survive it all and only because Washington in desperation won the little victories at Christmas and New Year's, first at Trenton and then at Princeton. Little victories sort of kept the rebellion alive.

Congress had voted an army. Congress had voted a code of discipline for the army. They had tried to create a national force but they were never comfortable with it and they'd hope that General Washington would make really short work of the revolution.

He knew better in a sense. He had an inexperienced army. To make too short work of the war would have been to risk losing the army and losing the rebellion. So, from his aspirations to create an army [and] Congress giving in to using the army, the war went along without any kind of resolution. The British were able to occupy the middle colonies to try to cut off New England and when they lost an army everything had to change for everyone.

Interviewer

…at Saratoga.

Dr. Ira Gruber

…at Saratoga, exactly. General Howe, who commanded the British Forces in the middle colonies, was to have cooperated with General Burgoyne in advancing from Canada.

Howe was preoccupied with Pennsylvania. He didn't cooperate. Burgoyne discovered that he was at the end of his tether, 300 miles from his space in a sparsely populated wilderness without his supplies and he was eventually stopped, blockaded and forced to surrender in upstate New York. That changed the whole war for everybody. France ended the war.

Britain was then involved in a world war and the world war sort of took over from Britain. Of course they lost an army. They lost Burgoyne's army but much more important was the intervention of the French to be followed by the Spanish and then the Dutch joined in a League of Armed Neutrality, against the British and they had a big problem on their hands.

Interviewer

So the campaign, then, of 1781 was that the British attempt to decisively end the war?

Dr. Ira Gruber

Well, the British, under the circumstances I've just described, the British were at a great disadvantage in North America, so how to proceed? How to keep the American War going? With fewer troops, with worldwide commitments, with enemies everywhere, the French sent forces to America every year from 1778 to 1781. There's a paradoxical effect.

The British were under great duress and they had to turn to the population. They had to ask the Loyalists to help them and rely on the Royal Navy. So, we could understand that but from the American perspective, the intervention of the French seemed to promise victory and Washington was suddenly without the kind of support he'd had before.

He was all right in 1778 because that was the winter of Valley Forge and they had advanced training and the army was pretty good. It could fight the British as it did at Monmouth, New Jersey in June of 1778, effectively but thereafter, they didn't succeed in cooperating with the French as they had hoped and Washington's army just simply melted away because the American people relaxed their support for the war.

Interviewer

And so it is this that will finally get us to the campaign of 1781.

Dr. Ira Gruber

Yes. The American forces, through 1778, 1779, and 1780 had been on such a low level, a couple thousand; two, three thousand men at times, and nobody was supporting them.

Congress had to depend on loans or contributions from the states. It tried printing money. You can't print money indefinitely. Inflation ensued anyway. Without support, the US forces had to look for a way somehow to get some kind of decision in the war.

How could they work together with the French? Washington would propose things and the French took one look at him and his scrawny little army and they usually said they weren't interested in whatever, he would propose attacking New York City. The British after the war had shifted and it had become a world war, they held New York City and then they tried to shift their forces to the southern colonies which they did and they were surprised at how successful they were.

So they added force. They reinforced the south and they recovered Savannah and Georgia and they recovered Charleston and South Carolina and they took over the interiors of those states. They sent expeditionary forces to the Chesapeake and they held the Chesapeake.

So, at the beginning of 1781 the British had forces at New York City, in the Chesapeake, at Wilmington, Charleston, and Savannah, and in the interior of the Georgia and South Carolina. I mean they had forces scattered over maybe what? That would be probably five or six hundred miles of the Atlantic seaboard and the Americans were trying to sort of monitor them and match them, which brings us to those really decisive and really interesting operations.

Washington's 2,000 couldn't do anything until a French fleet showed up but Nathanael Greene tried to convert his 2,000, or fewer continentals, into an effective force. He did that by enlisting the support of militia, enlisting the support of partisans. Militia and partisans are not very good soldiers. They might be good at ambushing you but unless they can be fighting on the defense, unless they surprise you or fight down the defensive, they don't have the discipline to undertake some kind of planned and disciplined campaign.

What Greene did was to attract the British into attacking him repeatedly. He did that to the extent that from Cowpens he divided his forces, the British divided theirs and they attacked his forces at Cowpens in northwestern South Carolina in January of 1781 and they were badly beaten.

That was the beginning and then they had the good sense to retreat because they weren't good enough against the whole, at that moment, of the British Regular Forces in the south. Green and Daniel Morgan led Charles Earl Cornwallis, who was the British commander in the south, through North Carolina and into Virginia just getting out of the way and hoping to retreat far enough until they could gain additional forces, build up their forces, and try again.

It took them from January until March to do that, to accomplish that withdrawal, essentially a strategic withdrawal, and then an operational recovery and a kind of counter offensive into North Carolina. They succeeded in attracting Cornwallis into attacking them once again at Guilford Courthouse in March. He did and he was severely punished for his efforts. He held the field at the end and it took people a while to figure it out but he'd lost.

He had then to withdraw and he withdrew to Wilmington on the coast. Nathaneal

Greene followed him far enough. He couldn't attack him but he could follow him and monitor him. Then Greene did something very surprising to everybody. He left Cornwallis at Wilmington and invaded the interior of South Carolina, letting Cornwallis do whatever he pleased.

If Cornwallis didn't follow Greene, Greene would be free then to attack British garrisons in the interior and perhaps liberate South Carolina and Georgia. Cornwallis, in his tattered shape, went to Virginia of all things. So he liberated North Carolina and Greene, in the ensuing period from March or early April of 1781 until July, he recovered the whole of the interior of South Carolina, which is an amazing achievement. And he did it with a kind of miniature force, a pick-up force at that, of militia and partisans.

Interviewer

How well trained were these partisans?

Dr. Ira Gruber

Well, these partisans don't take orders well. If it suits them and it pleases them they'll show up and take hand. If it doesn't or if they're offended in any way and they have very delicate sensibilities, they won't show up.

So he managed to get people like Pickens and Sumter to show up often enough that they in fact overran all of the British posts in the interior and by July of 1781, they liberated the south. Greene knew what he was doing. He immediately got the civilian leaders to return to Georgia and South Carolina to reestablish civilian government so that in the event of any kind of war, the United States would have claim on those states and they wouldn't be returned to Britain.

Interviewer

So he was already beginning to affect any type of peace agreement?

Dr. Ira Gruber

Oh yes. And beyond all this, he was trying to pacify Loyalists. I mean this man was very political if "war is politics by other means." This person understood that so instinctively and so wonderfully that he took this tiny little force and he liberated this vast area.

Now, George Washington was up to something else but Greene and Washington are connected in this. Washington with his miniature force of a couple thousand effective soldiers had been up on the Hudson River watching New York and he had Rochambeau with the 4,000 Frenchmen with him. When they heard that a French fleet would come up from the West Indies, 28 ships of the line, plus another 3,000 soldiers and there was another French squadron at Newport in Rhode Island with a siege train. The question is what could, how could they work together to get something more impressive, a bigger bang out of the campaign?

So, what they decided to do, it took Washington for one, he kept wanting to attack New York and Rochambeau who had looked at Washington saying [something like], "Man, we can't do that. They've been there a long time. They're dug in. That's a real army and you guys are not attacking them." Rochambeau's idea was that Cornwallis and British forces in the Chesapeake who weren't well established there, who hadn't been there for years would be a much more likely target.

Nathaneal Greene, who was Washington's most trusted advisor, wrote to Washington, saying, "Listen, I hear that this fleet is coming from the West Indies. What are you likely to do with it? You could attack New York. You could attack Charleston, big places, or you might attack those British forces in the Chesapeake. My advice is that it'd be a lot easier and a lot more effective to attack in the Chesapeake than either New York or Charleston where the British were well, much more well-established and much better prepared to resist. "

Well, Washington resisted this. Then he did a reconnaissance in force to take a look at Manhattan and he agreed. Greene, the reconnaissance in force, Rochambeau, and then news that de Grasse (the French commander from the West Indies) had taken his whole fleet and come to the Chesapeake or was coming to the Chesapeake – they all got busy immediately in August and set out over land to from essentially the Hudson River to Philadelphia to the head of Chesapeake Bay, Head of Elk, and then on down to Williamsburg and Jamestown, especially Williamsburg where they understood the British Army was establishing itself. That post would be a place called Yorktown, York on the York River with a little complementary post across the river at Gloucester Point.

So, in August and September, Washington and the French forces made this very sustained march over land. They were held up briefly because they didn't have enough shipping on the Delaware. They were also held up at the Head of Elk because de Grasse had arrived and he'd gotten to the bay at the beginning of September but the British showed up and he had to put out to the sea, engage the British, and drive them off to allow the other squadron from Newport to join him and enter the Bay. By the time Washington arrived in the middle of September, the fleet had come back but he wasn't really confident. He got to Head of Elk earlier but he couldn't embark his own troops because he was afraid that the British might be in control of the bay.

Well, by mid September when he got to Williamsburg, it was clear that de Grasse was very successful in clearing out the British, had control of the bay, had a siege train in place, and sent transports up the bay to bring the remaining Continentals and French troops down to Jamestown, Williamsburg, and then over to Yorktown.

Interviewer

So this is very complex, the operational planning, all of the logistical coordination required in order to set the stage for this siege and with it the hope for American victory?

Dr. Ira Gruber

Yes. Without exaggeration, it is supposed to have been the most magnificent planning and operation in the age of sail. I mean it's an amazingly complex coordination of forces from West Indies with the cooperation of the Spanish or the French Allies at this point.

They agreed to this. They helped plan it. They launched it. They stole a sail. We used to say steal a march but this was actually getting a sail in advance on the British. The British did not match their redeployment from the West Indies and were never able to challenge them effectively in North America.

So, it took some cooperation from the British. They had to let the French go for the West Indies without matching their redeployment but anyway, something had happened: Greene, with this wonderfully imaginative use of irregular forces to recover territory and Washington, working with conventional French forces in a conventional siege to capture a British Army. And they knew what was at stake. Both understood that what they were doing would have an impact on any negotiations that might end the war. All these years of French forces and no result and suddenly a chance for a real result at which they seized.

Interviewer

With the American and French victory at Yorktown, then, the war did not just end.

Dr. Ira Gruber

No, no, no. Washington was very hopeful that this would have an impact in Europe but he immediately began planning for the next year, for 1782. He corresponded with the French Admiral de Grasse and he said, "Will you come back in the spring?" He sent word through the Marquis de Lafayette who was now one of his subordinates and a very trusted advisor who is going home to France for the winter and he asked Lafayette to go to the French Court and say "We're really close. More money, another loan, and a fleet again next year and we've got them.

Interviewer

So what convinced the British then to finally give up?

Dr. Ira Gruber

What convinced the British? The British had been at this war, which had become a world war and which was not going very well. They lost Burgoyne in 1777, brought in France, now they lost Cornwallis. The first thing that Washington and de Grasse did was send a frigate to Europe to let people know what they've done, that they had captured this British Army and 200 guns and 8,000 men.

This was a big victory. Well, the diplomats in Europe and the politicians got this. The first thing that happened was [that] the British House of Parliament said it was not going to go on with the American War. That brought down the North Ministry, the government that had run the war throughout. It was replaced by a ministry called under the Marquis of Rockingham and with a couple of prominent politicians, men named Shelburne and Charles James Fox. The British knew they weren't going to go on with the American War. They did not know immediately that they were going to grant American independence. It took a few months for people to digest what had happened and then they began to see that they were going to have to do this and they did it. The British became interested in American independence, not because they were Anglo-Americans and English speaking union and trading partners, which was all true, and they shared tradition, a long association but they did it because they wanted to split the Allies, the alliance. They hoped that negotiating with the Americans would fragment the European Alliance, once the Americans became beneficiaries of that.

Interviewer

So as the British target the coalition, the coalition itself is falling apart and the British are willing to trade the 13 colonies in return for the larger objective of breaking up this alliance between the Spanish and the French and other European Allies, which they perhaps regard as a great threat.

Dr. Ira Gruber

They were very keen to make short work of this war and if they were going to make concessions they were going to make them to the United States, what was now the new United States of America. It took them a period of about nine months or so beginning in about March of 1782 and ending in November to come to what we would call a preliminary peace. The Americans in the course of this ignored their instructions from Congress with a wonderful disregard for the laws of the game.

They made a peace that anybody would have thought was quite wonderful. They got not just independence for the United States but they got a territorial domain that was quite beyond anybody's fondest wishes. They matched Congress's best hopes from 1779 but Congress had been willing since 1779 to settle for less.

Interviewer

They struck gold.

Dr. Ira Gruber

They got this wonderful domain, Atlantic to the Mississippi, Florida to Canada, which is a very expansive piece of property. They got essentially the withdrawal of all British forces, an end to hostilities. They got fishing rights and navigation rights. I mean it was a terrific treaty and it included the recognition, the diplomatic recognition that goes with it.

Interviewer

So, can we examine this with the respect to some of the criteria we have come to associate with war termination? How does this peace compare with the war aims that the Americans had set out to accomplish at the beginning?

Dr. Ira Gruber

The war aims that the Americans had when the war began were national domain, independence, a loose confederation, republican governments, no standing army, no taxes and the Americans actually finished realizing their war aims almost immediately after the war was over. They did it by dismissing the army, paying the officers but, hey, less than the officers wanted to be paid. Paying the officers essentially five years of full pay instead of half pay for a lifetime, which the officers had hoped they might get. The rank and file got nothing and went home sort of muttering.

Congress was imagining that it was going to run the nation's future national security based on militia volunteers.

Interviewer

So if you had to say that there was any effect on American military doctrine or a lesson that we could take away from the American victory and the ensuing peace treaty, what would you say that would be?

Dr. Ira Gruber

Well, it was that the American people are not fools and they tried to create a small kind of pickup force after the war of essentially volunteers, a little token force, and it took very little time to figure out that that wasn't adequate for the defense and the frontiers to control the population, to enforce the law and as soon as they figured that out there were bids such as Daniel Shay's rebellion in Western Massachusetts which persuaded people that the militia won't enforce the law, the states won't contribute to a national force to enforce the law, and so you needed something more. Let's say it took them a decade to essentially identify the problems with what they'd achieved and to get a new constitution and a new mandate for the central government of the United States. That government could tax and raise armed forces. It could conduct foreign policy. It could print money and you know it could behave like an independent government. The best part of the Constitution is the states couldn't do that any more. They couldn't have armed forces…They couldn't conduct foreign policy. They couldn't interfere, in effect, with the Confederation.

Interviewer

So peace was kind of like eating a large meal. It took a while to digest.

Dr. Ira Gruber

I'll say! The new Constitution, of course, has the beauty of creating power and not sacrificing liberty. So, the country emerged from this remarkable campaign of 1781 with a nation that immediately realized war aims but actually realized them in the longer term and the Washington administration did that beautifully so that he is a central character in both stories.

Session 1

The Battles of Plattsburgh and Ending the War of 1812

by

Dr. Wayne Lee

In the summer of 1814, the American war with Britain began to take an ugly turn for the United States. Britain was ending its war with Napoleon and the war-weary nation sought a quick, if also honorable and decisive, end to the war with America. To that end the ministry dispatched veteran regiments from France and the Mediterranean to North America. Defending the Canadian provinces had always been the priority, and so it remained, but now the balance of forces had shifted and the British could take the offensive. In doing so they hoped to gain and hold the territorial chips necessary to dominate the looming peace talks. The British planned a series of attacks all along the eastern seaboard and in the Gulf of Mexico but all were fundamentally diversions designed to open the way for the main army based in Montreal. General George Prevost, Governor and Commander of British forces in Canada, chose to follow Lake Champlain deep into New York with the hope to threaten New York City and thereby force territorial concessions from the Americans. On 1 September 1814, as many as 12,000 British troops crossed the border south of Montreal and marched along Lake Champlain shadowed by a newly built frigate, the *Confiance,* and her sister vessels, designed and built with the intent to immediately establish naval dominance on the lake. Waiting for them at Plattsburgh was a scratch force of 1,700 regular troops, 700 New York militiamen, and 2,500 militiamen (technically volunteers) from Vermont commanded by Brigadier General Alexander Macomb and a small and hurriedly expanded squadron of ships under the command of Commodore Thomas Macdonough. Macdonough flew his flag on the *Saratoga*. It would need to live up to the promise of that name.

Background

The United States Congress declared war in June of 1812 from a strange confusion of motives. In hindsight, it makes sense to blame the outbreak of war on two separate arenas of Anglo-American friction. British maritime policy regarding neutral trade and forcibly stopping American vessels and impressing crewmen from them, clearly infringed on American sovereignty while at the same time, the western frontier remained a turbulent zone of competition between American settlers and the Indians. Americans blamed the British for stirring up the Indians, most recently the Shawnees, defeated at Tippecanoe in November of 1811. As a minimum, the British could be blamed for giving the Indians hope for support in their efforts to hem in the westward expansion of the United States. If it is too much to blame the war on western land hunger and greed, it is not too much to blame it partly on the western states' collective sense of insecurity.

Fundamentally, the only way for the United States to exert pressure on Britain was to attack her Canadian provinces. Originally a diplomatic strategy sought to use attacks on Canada to force British concessions. As the war dragged on, many people in the United States began to see the war as one for territory or at least for the freedom to expand westward. For Britain, preserving Canada remained central but with the defeat of Napoleon looming in 1814, they were able to commit resources on a new scale. Both sides escalated their hopes for the meaning and outcome of the war. Later in 1814, as the Americans began to fear the ending of the Napoleonic War and as the British faced domestic war weariness after two decades of struggle, both sides returned to their opening vision of war as negotiation, something John Lynn has termed for an earlier era "war as process," in which military operations sought not true state territorial conquest so much as slices of the other's territory, most often to be used as bargaining chips in a nearly constant ongoing process of diplomacy.

Early American offensives in the far western theater around Detroit and the Niagara peninsula were generally defeated, until Captain Oliver Hazard Perry cleared the British fleet from Lake Erie in September 1813. That victory solidified the American position in the West but did not prove capable of sustaining a major territorial offensive within Canada (although the killing of the Indian leader Tecumseh during the 1813 campaign here undermined any further role for the Indians in British military campaigns). In a separate campaign against the Creeks, General Andrew Jackson defeated one of two rival factions there and then forced the Creek nation to cede 23 million acres of Alabama and Georgia to the United States. In the Niagara peninsula in the summer of 1814, the US Army troops performed much better but were unable to convert limited battlefield success into territorial control and, in fact, were forced back into Fort Erie and there they endured a long siege into the fall. Meanwhile, British naval power, now undistracted by Napoleon, began to exercise a crushing blockade. American export trade dropped from $130 million in 1807 to $25 million in 1813 and then $7 million in 1814.

Indeed, it was the surrender of Napoleon on 13 April 1814 that seemed set to change the character of the war from one characterized by failed American offensives, stalemate in the North, Indian wars in the South, and a strangling blockade, into a war of decisive and destructive British offensives. A whole new array of options emerged that combined Britain's until-now slumbering naval superiority with veteran regiments from the European theater. This new accession of military power led to the most spectacular moments of the war; the burning of Washington and the American defense of Baltimore at Fort McHenry. Ironically, as spectacular as they were, they were but diversions within the overall British plan for the summer of 1814.

British Operations: Summer 1814

In June 1814, Lord Bathurst of the Ministry of War wrote to Prevost to outline the summer's campaign plan. He promised Prevost some 3,000 men immediately with 10,000 more to arrive in waves. He was to use those forces to commence offensive operations although he was not to risk the loss of his force. His primary mission remained protecting the security of Canada but such security demanded clearing the American threats on Lakes Erie, Ontario, and Champlain. Prevost could dispose the forces as he chose but Bathurst expected him to go on the attack and to support such an attack in the interior. He assured him that, "It is also in contemplation . . . to make a more serious attack on some part of the Coast of the United States. . . . These operations will not fail to effect a powerful diversion in your favor."

This scheme made Prevost's troops and ships gathering in Quebec and Montreal into the British main effort. First, they would establish superiority on Lakes Champlain and Ontario and then they could roll down into Lake Erie and reestablish control stage by stage as far as Detroit. British forces to the west, whether around Fort Niagara or as far away as Mackinac in northern Michigan, would have to hold the line until Prevost could reinforce them which is something they did successfully. Meanwhile as Prevost gathered his forces together and constructed his fleet on Lake Champlain, the "diversions" began. Between July and 1 September, British forces captured much of eastern Maine and asserted their sovereignty there and forced the locals to swear allegiance to the British Government. The more (in) famous diversion came in the form of British raids along the Chesapeake to include burning Washington, DC and attempting to repeat the same at Baltimore. The latter raid failed after the garrison at Fort McHenry successfully resisted a two-day bombardment on 13-14 September.

In one sense, these diversions as well as other distractions, accomplished their mission. Prevost's force gathering in Montreal in late August faced almost token levels of American forces along Lake Champlain. Prevost's existing forces on the Niagara peninsula had bent but not broken and even now (from 1 August to 21 September) they were laying siege to the Americans at Fort Erie. His reinforcements were streaming in and he successfully deceived the American high command into thinking he intended to attack into Lake Ontario and especially toward the American naval yard at Sackett's Harbor. The American commander at Plattsburgh, Major General George Izard, doubted those intentions but his superiors ordered him to march most of his army west, leaving behind the token force under Brigadier General Alexander Macomb (described earlier). Finally, Prevost had pushed through the rapid building of a full sized frigate on Lake Champlain, the *Confiance* (31 long guns and six carronades, the latter being short range large caliber guns that proved extremely useful in the narrow waters of the lakes). Prevost was confident that it immediately would establish British naval supremacy on the lake and with it a truly decisive territorial bargaining chip.

He should have been right but a divided command, rushed construction, a lack of transports, and an inspired American naval defense set the stage for ending the war. The British would be advancing into Clinton County in New York, a region scantily populated at best, home only to about seven people per square mile. In contrast, Ulster County, Ireland at that time had about 368 people per square mile. This level of population produced neither the subsistence nor the roads adequate to the movement of a major force. Prevost's army required waterborne logistics and close cooperation with his naval forces. Unfortunately, Prevost and the regional naval commander, Commodore James Lucas Yeo, did not get along and their commands were literally divided. Yeo answered to the Admiralty in London, not to Prevost, and the Admiralty tasked him to "cooperate with" Prevost. They agreed on the necessity of a frigate to command the lake but at several other points, especially the last minute change in command of the Lake Champlain fleet from Captain Peter Fisher to Captain George Downie, their inclinations clashed. Fisher had supervised the building of the *Confiance* and then Yeo appointed Downie to command that ship and the lake fleet within mere days prior to its launching. Worse, the *Confiance* was green in timber and crew. Her new captain barely had time to practice his gun crews (many pressed from the infantry) before he and his fleet were tasked to cover Prevost's march into New York. Lacking transports, the British infantry trudged south along the poor roads that paralleled the lake. One British officer reported during their march that the roads were; "worse than you can imagine and many of our wagons are broken down...the road through the woods at Beatville [Beekmantown] is impassable, therefore our only dependence is upon water communication." This conjoined land and water movement in a narrow corridor followed an entirely predictable path, a path for which the Americans could plan.

On the American side, Major General Izard had long suspected a summer offensive of some kind and he assumed that Plattsburgh would be the first stop in a British advance. Most of the town lay north of the Saranac River gorge and could not be defended but the river itself presented a fine line of defense and Plattsburgh Bay was a complex and shoal-filled harbor from which an American naval force could bombard a marching British column while sheltered from the lakes' weather. Izard dug in south of the river. Even better, the reports of the construction of the *Confiance* led the Secretary of the Navy to speed carpenters and a shipbuilder to Vermont and within a remarkably short span, they built the sloop *Saratoga* (eight long guns and 18 carronades), the *Ticonderoga* (12 long guns and five carronades), the *Eagle* (eight long guns and 12 carronades), and rehabilitated 10 gunboats (oared ships with one gun each). Like the British, these ships plus the extant *Preble* (seven long guns), had inexperienced crews but their commander, Commodore Macdonough had had more time to train them and to consider his defensive position. Izard and Macdonough jointly formed their plans for the defense of the town and were entirely in agreement on the necessary steps.

Unfortunately the War Department swallowed Prevost's feint and ordered Izard with most of his force to march west. Izard resisted and delayed but in the end he departed Plattsburgh, leaving Macomb with 1,700 assorted regulars and orders to raise the militia. Macomb raised 700 New York men and at the last minute 2,500 Vermont men crossed the lake, technically not "militia" (since they had crossed state lines), but volunteers in federal service.

The *Confiance* slipped off on 25 August and on 1 September, Prevost marched across the border into New York. He hoped to win the population to him and he carefully ordered that there be no plundering and that all provisions be paid for. Such care flew in the face of reports arriving that week about the burning of Washington. Prevost quickly pushed through the one effort to slow his march north of Plattsburgh, moved into the town, and began seeking a way across the river, while the two sides commenced bombarding each other.

Macomb lacked the forces to defend the town north of the river but feeling the "eyes of America" upon him, he also felt he could not retreat further south. The river had only two bridges and Macomb could cooperate more easily with his own naval forces while beside the bay. Meanwhile Macdonough moved his fleet into an anchorage designed to cover the American position at Plattsburgh, while also forcing the longer-gunned British fleet to enter the bay almost already in range of his shorter guns and having to approach him head on which was the worst possible position for a ship in the age of sail.

From Prevost's perspective, all the American eggs were now in one basket. He had the main American force in front of him and an inferior American fleet locked up in the bay. To his surprise, Downie initially objected (on 8 September) that the *Confiance* was not yet ready, claiming even that the American fleet was "considerably superior in force." Nevertheless, within two days, Downie reassured himself and coordinated a plan with Prevost to simultaneously attack the American land and lake positions with the navy's guns to signal the start of the mutual attack. Prevost planned to hold the Americans' attention in central Plattsburgh while a flanking column marched three miles upstream to a more lightly guarded ford. Meanwhile, Downie was to sail in and dominate the American fleet with his longer ranged broadside.

Instead, the British fleet rounded the Cumberland Head to enter the bay with their bows facing the Americans' broadsides and as they came around the head, their wind died and they slowly drifted toward the American line, absorbing the blows first of the few American long guns and then of their carronades, all while without being able to answer effectively in return. As the distance closed, the British ships finally turned and a brutal broadside to broadside combat ensued. The Americans fought from an anchored line, blocking the bay, and Downie had sailed in to concentrate the fire of *Confiance* and two other smaller ships first on the *Eagle* and then the *Saratoga*. Within the first 15 minutes of fighting, an American shot dismounted a British cannon which flew into Downie's chest and killed him. Damaged but continuing to fight, the *Confiance's* heavier broadsides poured into the *Saratoga* and nearly evened the game by taking out virtually all of the guns on one side. Macdonough then used his pre-set kedge anchors to spin his ship around in place and bring his other broadside to bear. The *Confiance* attempted the same maneuver but lacking Macdonough's careful pre-battle preparations, she became fouled and struck her colors at 10:30 a.m. The smaller British ships either grounded or surrendered, while the gunboats fled.

Without a covering fleet, the future of the British land advance was probably doomed but matters were made worse by a failure to properly coordinate the timing of the two attacks. Downie commenced the fleet attack between 7:30 and 8:30 in the morning but Prevost's flanking column was under orders not to attack before 10:00. By that time, the British fleet was on the verge of defeat and as Prevost realized that his fleet was fleeing or captured, he recalled his successfully advancing flank attack. Prevost almost immediately began a wholesale retreat, covered by a heavy rain (Macomb lacked the forces to pursue at any rate). Prevost had been steadily stockpiling stores, especially artillery ammunition, and now he lacked the transport to bring them back to Canada. One artillery officer complained that; "several wagons & carts from being overloaded [in order to remove as much as possible] and the extreme badness of the roads [being] broke [*sic*] down, leaving [*sic*] no alternative but to destroy them and their contents." As for the retreat itself, Prevost later explained to Bathurst; "Your Lordship must have been aware…that no Offensive Operations could be carried out within the enemy's territory for the destruction of his naval establishments without naval support…The disastrous and unlooked for result of the naval contest…rendered perseverance in the attack of the enemy's position highly imprudent as well as hazardous." Prevost also blamed the poor state of the roads and the growing threat of a militia "raising en masse around me, desertion increasing & the Supply of Provisions Scanty." Without "the advantage of water conveyance" both problems were insoluble.

The Battles of Plattsburgh, on land and lake, generated relatively few casualties and represented only one campaign among many that summer and fall of 1814. Furthermore, the British had one more major campaign already under way against Mobile and New Orleans. Plattsburgh nevertheless was the key to ending the war. In the competition for territorial bargaining chips the British accession of forces that summer seemed to have given them the advantage. In August, as the British summer offensives were getting under way, the British commissioners offered terms about which the American peace commissioner Henry Clay could only say; "The prospect of peace has vanished...It would be offering an unpardonable insult to our Government to ask of them any instructions [regarding those terms]." Plattsburgh made the difference, although other American defensive efforts contributed - especially the defense of Baltimore. The British had not exactly put all their effort into one roll of the dice at Plattsburgh but it had been their main effort and it had been the one *designed* to acquire that territorial bargaining chip needed to tilt the peace talks to their advantage. Henry Goulburn, one of the British peace commissioners, agreed; "If we had either burnt Baltimore or held Plattsburgh, I believe we could have had peace on our terms." Recognizing the failure of their main effort, the negotiations began to make real progress. The two nations' representatives signed the treaty of Ghent on 24 December 1814. The Battle of New Orleans occurred in January of 1815 but before the news of the treaty arrived in North America and it had no effect on its terms.

Recommended Reading

Black, Jeremy, "The War of 1812 in the Age of Napoleon," Norman: University of Oklahoma Press, 2009. This is a recent narrative of the war that places it fully within the international context.

Everest, Allan, "The War of 1812 in the Champlain Valley," Syracuse, N.Y.: Syracuse University Press, 1981. This is the best available study of the war within this region and includes a well-researched and scholarly narrative of the Plattsburgh campaign.

Fitz-Enz, David G., "The Final Invasion: Plattsburgh, the War of 1812's Most Decisive Battle," New York: Cooper Square Press, 2001. This is a solid if somewhat idiosyncratic campaign study of Plattsburgh that includes some heretofore lost documentation.

Hickey, Donald R., "The War of 1812: A Forgotten Conflict," Urbana and Chicago: University of Illinois Press, 1989. This is perhaps the standard modern scholarly narrative of the war, one which helped launch a number of more detailed studies in the 1990s.

Mahon, John K., "The War of 1812," Gainesville: University Press of Florida, 1972; reprint, New York: Da Capo Press. This is a classic detailed narrative that retains value especially for the diplomatic and naval fronts but weak on the Canadian perspective.

Quimby, Robert S., "The U. S. Army in the War of 1812: An Operational and Command Study," East Lansing: Michigan State University Press, 1997. This is an enormous two volume study of Army operations; excellent for detail but limited by its titular focus on the US Army.

Session 1
Interview
Dr. Wayne Lee

Interviewer

What can you say is unique about the treaty and the conditions that lead to the end of the War of 1812?

Dr. Wayne Lee

Well, I'm not sure that the treaty is unique so much as the experience the United States has in combining military operations history with diplomatic negotiations to end the war is relatively rare in American history. It's not rare in European history.

In fact, one of the things that I try to suggest is that it's the only cabinet war that America fights. The cabinet war is an expression from the 18th century, the idea that you're fighting for dynastic purposes or limited territorial gains at the expense of another state and that you fight operations that are designed to achieve certain sort of what appear to be territorial bargaining chips that you can trade, a gain here for a loss there. You're literally conducting military operations at the same time you're conducting diplomatic negotiations to see how you can influence the table with the battlefield.

In some ways, this is almost the only war that the United States does that and where literally the peace negotiations begin in August of 1814 and in the middle of the campaign season. They go on all the way through the fall and into December.

So the whole time that negotiations are going on, battles are taking place, campaigns are being initiated, launched, and included in the reports of those campaigns that are arriving at the peace table, which is actually in Belgium. So there is a translator communications problem.

There are delays. So the negotiators are in the middle of processing the arrival of what might be inaccurate reports. They want to get the final and full report, make sure, "Did we win? Did we lose?" None of these campaigns tend to be extremely decisive. They're constantly in that game of assessing "What have we gained? What have we lost, and how can we use that? We go back to the negotiating table tomorrow."

That's relatively a unique thing in the American experience.

Interviewer

So battlefield successes directly translate into diplomatic power.

Dr. Wayne Lee

They should, except, that in the War of 1812, you don't get a lot of really obvious battlefield successes. There are battlefield successes. They don't tend to create momentum. There's no trajectory that follows on from them.

In 1814, one of the key facts is that you get British successes and American successes and the trick is going to be balancing them. "What do we consider to be the most important and therefore what do we give up here because of what they gained there?"

They do tend to balance out. So in many ways, the treaty is a draw, but the one thing that the Americans didn't think they could live with in the treaty is probably granted to them by the British because of what happens at Plattsburgh.

Interviewer

Explain.

Dr. Wayne Lee

Well, in August, when they first convened peace negotiators, one of the main sticking points that the Americans resisted was the idea of an independent Native American state on the western frontier. That was a major plank for the British treaty negotiators. They were insisting on it in August of 1814. That was the one thing that the American negotiators just would not tolerate.

The British wanted it because they thought it would create a buffer state between British interests and American interests. The Americans didn't want it because they saw it as hampering their ability to expand westward.

Over the course of the next couple of months, you had campaigns launching in Maryland, around Washington, and in the Gulf of Mexico. Then also the most important effort from the British point of view was the one that was launched from Montreal down towards Plattsburgh.

From the British perspective, that was their most important campaign. That's where they put the most troops, the most resources, and that's there they expected to get their biggest result. When that was defeated, when it was stopped at Plattsburgh, both in a sea battle and then in company with a land battle, when that was stopped, the British looked at the situation and said; "We can't get any more out of these campaigns." Because all of the other campaigns, the launch, the raids on Washington, the raid on Baltimore, the intended raids for the Gulf coast, those were all intended as diversions for the campaign that ended at Plattsburgh.

The British government and the negotiators knew that. When their main effort was defeated, they had to start making compromises in the peace treaty.

Interviewer

Now, overarching the War of 1812, of course, are events in Europe. The British had been fighting against Napoleon. By 1814, as you've written, the British public seemed to be rather war weary. You think perhaps this failure, the British forces at Plattsburgh, this is sort of the diplomatic final straw that compels the British and the Americans to the peace table?

Dr. Wayne Lee

Well, no, because they aren't at the peace table in August. Plattsburgh's fought on 11 September. Actually, it makes it easier to remember that date. The peace negotiations started on 8 August. The issue is the campaign season and what you think is going to happen because the campaign season is essentially the summer and fall. So the key is the timing. You're exactly right as to what happened in Europe. In the spring of 1814, Napoleon abdicates. As soon as that happens, you've got two things. You've got a war weary British population desperate to end this other sideshow war in America.

They want to do it on their own terms. The government, in particular, wants to do it on its own terms. So they've got, they know they have a limited amount of time where they have all of these resources that are now freed up from fighting Napoleon that they can throw into the American war maybe for one last campaign season before the public is going to give up on this and they're just not going to let them keep fighting it.

Essentially, it's a race against time for the British. They're going to launch this. They're going to take all of these resources freed up from Europe, throw them in North America, and try to achieve some decisive result in various places. Again, it ends up being the Plattsburgh campaign is where they choose to be the most important of those campaigns.

If they don't, then, politically, they're going to be in trouble. They're going to have to end the war. The one thing that they do achieve in those other campaigns is they actually do reconquer most of Maine. That was one of the British war aims from the outset was to gain an overland connection between New Brunswick and the Montreal region.

They do, in fact, capture Maine and the citizens, the American citizens of Maine, take an oath of loyalty to the king. That's considered re-conquer. So that's the one big territorial bargaining chip that the British have by the late fall of 1814 but that wasn't seen by the Americans as quite as important as the defense at Plattsburgh.

One of the British negotiators says; "If we had captured and burned Baltimore or if we had won at Plattsburgh, then we would have gotten the treaty we really wanted to get." So they're fairly explicit about these being the most important issues.

Interviewer

With that in mind for historians and students of war, military history oftentimes has emphasized the battles, but how do you feel about the importance of studying the conclusions of these wars? What kind of lessons can we take away from the example from the War of 1812 on how the war is concluded and how war itself evolves?

Dr. Wayne Lee

There are different kinds of conclusions. There are historical conclusions and policy kinds of conclusions. I think, for the War of 1812, in particular, one of the things to take away from it as an historian or somebody who is interested in the past, is to try to get American events into a broader context. It's often studied as an American war. In fact, it's really not. It's European. It's embedded in the European conflict.

In fact, literally one of the things that's happening in December is they're getting right to the end of the treaty negotiations is the British are in the middle of negotiating the treaty of that the Congress of Vienna is trying to close out the Napoleonic War. This is all a surprise. It's not about North America. It's about "how do we rebuild Europe?"

They're actually afraid that the Russians are going to try to occupy Poland. So Britain and France and Austria conclude the treaty to attack Russia in December of 1814 if Russia invades Poland. That's in the context of trying to end 25 years of warfare against Napoleon and trying to end the sideshow of war against America. So they're desperate to end that war.

So for us to understand why the British end their war with the Americans in December of 1814, we have to understand what the British are thinking about the Russians in December of 1814. That's not the way that most Americans learn the story. You've got to put this whole thing into a European or even in a global context. I think that's true of almost all American history but it's particularly true when you talk about our wars. They're not fought in isolation of the rest of the world's events.

In terms of sort of broader lessons about war termination or historical processes, again, I think the War of 1812 is a little bit unique for American experience in terms of this ongoing diplomatic process.

On the other hand, one of the things that I think is true of all wars is that actions within war are acts of communication. Everything that you do in a war is designed to convince your opponent to do something or to respond to you in a certain way. What you have to figure out is what messages is that person going to be willing listen to, what kinds of signals do you think of a battle as a signal. If you win it, you get a particular kind of signal. If you lose it, it's a different signal.

Think of a raid as a signal. If I raid Washington and burn it, I'm sending you a very specific set of messages about what I want out of this war, especially if I don't occupy it. If I get back on my ship and I go back out to sea, then I'm saying something specific to you and you're going to have to respond to that also. So I think you can see the dynamics, especially in the last month of 1814 where there's military operations and diplomatic negotiations are occurring simultaneously, although at this translating time lag where you can try to understand how people were interpreting and understanding signals that are embedded in war.

I think that's still true. We're still sending signals when we do things in war but we need to figure out how the enemy is interpreting our signals.

Interviewer

With the War of 1812, the Americans and the British, although we had a kindred background, it didn't necessarily mean that we understood each other's intents.

The Burning of York, for example, followed by the counter burning of Washington. You're absolutely right when you say that we send messages, we send signals, on the basis of the way that we conduct our wars. Perhaps that was the British way of saying; "You escalate further, and we'll continue to escalate." From accounts, it seemed like the British response was rather restrained.

Dr. Wayne Lee

I think there were restraints. In fact, one of the things that I spent a lot of time talking about is when this retaliation happens and when doesn't it happen. In fact, the Americans and the British during the American Revolution were pretty good at threatening retaliation all the time. They're constantly threatening each other with retaliation but it's usually; "I only retaliate only if you do that." Fairly rare for someone to actually do something that the other considered a major violation. So it didn't cycle out of control.

In the War of 1812, it almost started to cycle out of the control at the burning of York and the burning of Washington but they more or less, as you say, partly because of that similar cultural background, were able to understand that signal, that the burning of Washington was interpreted as a signal and response to the burning of York.

As much as we might have rhetorically said, "we can't believe you did this, you evil British people," we nevertheless fundamentally understood what that meant and what that process was about. So I think that that helped keep that war from getting worse than it was.

Interviewer

Going to war, it seems is evidentially easier than trying to stop war once it's begun. Looking forward to the future of the 21st century war, do you think there are some lessons that we can take from the peace treaties that concluded the War of 1812?

Dr. Wayne Lee

The lessons are not obvious but there are a few things. Again, because this is such an odd little war but there are a few things. One of them is that a great deal of British power, especially in the interior of the North American continent, came from their alliance with the Native Americans.

So here you have a state that's allied with the tribal people operating on a vast continental scale. Not talking about campaigns in New York or the campaigns in the Gulf coast but you're talking about Indiana territories, the Illinois territories, the Michigan territories, just a vast continental scale. So the tribal peoples are actually really good at moving around on that continental scale and presenting themselves as threats on a strategic and political level.

One of the things the United States is able to do is disrupt those alliances partly through military defeats of the native peoples and partly through understanding the fractures within tribal societies that you can take advantage of the fractures inside a tribal confederation and pull apart individual pieces.

When you do that, in fact, a lot of Indian peoples signed treaties with the United States in 1813, two years really before the end of the war because they've been defeated here or pulled away there or weakened enough in this other place. None of these were pretty operations. None of them were things that we should necessarily be proud of.

In terms of understanding how tribal societies function in trying to get at tribal societies' relationships with an allied state, I think there are things we can learn about the ways that looks and how does a state make indigenous people, especially tribally organized indigenous people, into an ally and one of the weaknesses in that relationship.

Interviewer

The fact that the end of this war is so tied up with negotiation – that gives you a rare insight, don't you think, into how countries viewed the acceptable conditions for victory?

Dr. Wayne Lee

Yes, well, one of the beauties of doing this period, in talking about any sort of cabinet war is that we have all the records of the treaty negotiators. You get their correspondence back to their home governments. Then you get their journals. We actually literally have the diaries of Henry Clay. He was one of the American treaty negotiators.

So we can see how they're trying to balance all of these different factors. They are complicated. They change. Again, they're ongoing with ongoing operations. It's not like you get the occupation of Germany, and this didn't happen, but I'm making this up. You don't get the occupation of Germany and then you say; "All right, so what are we going to do now?" You've got an ongoing process of fighting with an ongoing process of negotiation and also changing demands. One of the demands that are changing that is particular to the American experience is the fact that it's a democratic republic.

So what is in the newspapers? How loud are the voices in the street and how will those voices affect who gets elected next? So how do I now not just balance military operations with my sense of the other side's diplomatic willingness to negotiate but how do I balance with what the electorate is going to do to me in the next election?

Session 1
Dubious Means and Unworthy Ends:
Colonel William Worth's Campaign to End the Second Seminole War

by

Dr. John Hall

On 31 May 1841, Colonel William Jenkins Worth became the seventh overall commander of a seemingly interminable war against the Seminole Indians of Florida. Beginning with the spectacular "Dade Massacre" that initiated the conflict in December of 1835, little had gone right for the previous commanders, three of whom had requested relief from command. Among these was Brigadier General Walker Keith Armistead, who left Worth with a demoralized force that had suffered as much from Florida's climate and demagogic politicians as from an elusive enemy. To compound matters, a disconsolate electorate and a common cold virus combined to thrust strategic direction of the conflict upon the third president of the United States in as many months. His secretary of war, mindful of the electorate but hoping to turn around the moribund war, issued Worth the seemingly contradictory guidance to wage a vigorous offensive war while at once slashing its costs. The colonel did not disappoint on either count, mounting two major offensives even as he reduced forces in theater by half and operating costs by a quarter. More significantly, he provided his president a framework for ending a war that, for nearly seven years, had consumed the army and drained the treasury. On the basis of these accomplishments, on 10 May 1842, President John Tyler reported to Congress the effective termination of the Second Seminole War.

Since the beginning of the war, the primary war aim of the United States was as clear as it was contentious and, as events would prove, unachievable. Pursuant to the Indian Removal Act of 1830 and a pair of contested implementation treaties, every Indian in Florida was to immigrate to a reservation in Arkansas. Most of the 5,000 Seminoles, however, were indisposed to leaving. In 1835, the United States resorted to force and war resulted. Within two and a half years, the war settled into a low-intensity guerrilla conflict in which the Indians generally (and very successfully) avoided contact with the troops, instead raiding settlements and waylaying travelers. Since then, the United States had tried all manner of offensive and defensive operations: deceit and bribery to induce the remaining Seminoles to emigrate. Nothing worked, and when John Tyler assumed the presidency in April of 1841, the prospects of ending the expensive and unpopular war seemed as remote as ever. By then, no more than 1,500 Seminoles remained, but they were the most implacable and experienced and they had mastered the art of avoiding discovery.

Worth proved no more capable of finding them than his predecessors, but he succeeded where they had failed because he and the administration he served grasped the nature of the conflict. Whereas Winfield Scott sought decisive battle with Seminole warriors and Zachary Taylor attempted to physically control all of Florida's 47,000 square miles, Worth eventually realized that the Seminoles' center of gravity was the will of their noncombatants. Although this was not evident in his inaugural guidance to "Find the enemy, capture, or exterminate," Worth had commanded a regiment in Florida since the previous autumn and he appreciated the unlikelihood of doing any such thing.[1]

If he could not find the enemy, however, he could discover their strongholds; if he had little hope of eroding the Seminoles' combat power in battle, he could dash their hopes of a better tomorrow by destroying their homes and provender. Thus demonstrating that they had no refuge, he would extend to the Seminoles an olive branch, often via the hand of unwilling Indian intermediaries and always with ensnaring strings attached.

Worth's method was not entirely novel. For nearly three centuries, Europeans had targeted settlements and food sources as the most effective (if not ethical) means of fighting Native Americans, but Florida's physical geography and climate offered the Seminoles advantages that other Indians lacked. Consisting of vast swamplands and impenetrable hammocks, Florida's terrain was as forbidding to American troops as it was protective of the Indians. Similarly, Florida's tropical climate accounted for more than three quarters of the Army's 1,466 fatalities yet helped sustain Seminole life. Not only could Seminoles raise crops year round, but the deadly summer heat deterred the Americans from attacking during the most productive part of the growing season. While the crops then raised were important to Seminole subsistence, the respite from incessant war was *crucial* to preserving Seminole morale. Worth meant to deny them this psychological sanctuary and he began preparations for the war's first large-scale summer offensive the moment he assumed command.

The location of this campaign was nearly as important as the timing. Although some of the most dangerous Seminole bands resided in the Everglades of southern Florida, no one else did, as this region was devoid of white settlements. Consequently, Worth was more concerned with those bands hiding among the hammocks of central and northern Florida. On 25 June 1841, columns of the 2d, 6th, and 8th Infantry Regiments (each comprising 200 infantrymen and mounted detachments) sallied out of their several posts and marched for the Withlacoochee River. The army conducted some of its earliest offensives in this region but had since modified its tactics substantially. According to Worth's aide, operations assumed "a partisan character" as 20-man detachments peeled off from the main columns and conducted "scouts" in their assigned zones.[2] Simultaneously, riverine forces of 60 to 70 men descended the Withlacoochee and ascended the Ocklawaha River to the southeast. For 25 arduous days, Worth drove the Seminoles from their sanctuaries. Despite capturing only five Indians, Worth's soldiers destroyed 32 fields, some as large as 20 acres, and burned 180 huts. Although the operation took a dreadful toll on their health, most of them recovered. Seminole morale did not.

Less than a week into the offensive, Seminole leaders gathered to address the impending crisis. Already their followers had suffered terribly and Worth's offensive threatened to shatter their collective will to resist. Unbowed but alarmed, the chiefs vowed to execute any Indian who communicated with the Americans about the possibility of surrender. Their desperate policy was less effective than Worth's response. Intending to exploit the conditions his offensive had created, Worth sent friendly Indian envoys among the Seminoles with assurances of a better life (and cash) in Arkansas. Similar efforts in the past had foundered because the Seminoles, envoys and militants alike, knew that the "better life" was a lie, but the summer offensive convinced many Seminoles that anything was preferable to continued resistance and they braved the threat of death to enter negotiations with the Americans. Once they did so, Worth left nothing to chance.

Four years earlier, Major General Thomas S. Jesup had seized the Seminole war leader Osceola under a white flag of truce. Vilified by the press, Jesup retorted that such measures were not only expedient but justified. As the Indians had so frequently entered diplomatic discussion in bad faith, he and many others believed, officers were not bound to honor conventions their enemies refused to respect. Other officers found the practice distasteful but none could dispute its effectiveness, least of all William Worth. Thanks to his summer offensive, many Seminoles were genuinely eager to emigrate but others were undecided. If Worth suspected prevarication, he decided for them; seizing as many chiefs, diplomats, and followers as dared to enter his snares. By mid-October, Worth had shipped 207 Seminoles westward and refined his formula for ending the war using the stick to make Indians willing to negotiate and a loaded carrot to ensure their removal, voluntary or otherwise.

As this methodology began to pay dividends in central Florida, Worth turned his attention to the Everglades. In mid-August, he established a forward operating base 80 miles south of Tampa Bay and subsequently pushed reconnaissance forces and a chain of supply depots into the southern peninsula, most of which remained as an uncharted wilderness. These preliminary operations proved the most productive of the entire operation, as one of the scouting forces surprised a Seminole camp in early November and ultimately secured 63 prisoners. Nothing else would come easy in the Everglades.

The actual offensive began in late November, when elements of the 2d Infantry Regiment attacked southward along Florida's east coast and into a blocking position east of Lake Okeechobee. Simultaneously, 150 soldiers of the 3d Artillery and a similar number of Sailors and Marines under Navy Lieutenant John McLaughlin, moved into staging areas on the eastern margin of the Everglades. In the west, 13 companies drawn from the 2d Dragoons and 4th, 6th, and 8th Infantry did the same. As December dawned, 1,100 troops from all three services plodded or paddled into the Everglades and two months of the hardest service they would every know. With uneven assistance from Seminole guides, 20-man detachments branched out on scouts lasting as long as a week. When they had the good fortune to encounter moist land (for there was none that was truly dry) sawgrass palmettos slashed open their legs, creating wounds that did not heal under water. They had little to show for their troubles. On 20 December, elements of the main column crept toward an enemy village only to have a disoriented flanker fire his musket in distress. Thus alerted, the Seminoles covered the evacuation of their village masterfully, killing two Americans without loss to themselves. As in the north, the Americans contented themselves with the destruction of huts and fields but the only morale that seemed to sag was their own. Starved for intelligence, they were "wandering in the dark" in an alien landscape.[3]

However, it did not matter and Worth knew it perhaps before the operation was even underway. Prior to launching the attack, he intimated to one regimental commander that there were more sensible ways to wage this war than by beating the bush in search of meaningless engagements. On 9 December 1842, he delegated command of the Everglades offensive to the same subordinate and returned north to oversee the strong arm diplomacy effort that promised far greater returns for a fraction of the effort. Yet neither was this program free of disappointment. Worth had been lured north, in part, by word that militants had assassinated two of his Indian envoys. The situation had improved by the time Worth established his headquarters in Tampa on 16 December but soon afterward Halleck Tustenuggee's band attacked an unsuspecting settlement in northeastern Florida and threw most of the territory into a panic. Worth, however, stayed his course, even when he learned that one of his "converted" militant-chiefs-turned-envoys had been working against him for nearly two months. Worth did not set aside the stick entirely, but he used it selectively and energetically against those bands unwilling to enter negotiations.

By the end of January, however, Worth conceded the futility of further offensive operations in the Everglades. His frustrated officers agreed. "The idea of catching Indians," one company commander confided to a friend, "was looked upon as perfectly ridiculous."[4] Accordingly, Worth withdrew all but four companies from the Everglades, leaving future operations there to Lieutenant McLaughlin and the Navy. Among the forces he redeployed were nine companies of the 3d Artillery, which had served in Florida since the very early days of the war. Small detachments of Marines assumed the 3d garrison duties but nothing replaced its combat power. After a valedictory sweep of the region east of the St. John's River, the soldiers of the 3d Artillery were to board ships for duty elsewhere.

Far from sad to see them go, Worth looked forward to their departure as a benchmark of progress. Upon assuming direction of the war, he commanded eight of the army's 14 regiments with a ninth inbound in time for the winter campaign season. Once his peace initiative began to show signs of progress, however, Worth recommended cancelling scheduled deployments and sending other units out of theater early. He did so partly in obedience to the wishes of the administration but primarily out of conviction that these forces were not needed. Indeed, his recommended force levels were routinely too low for the comfort of the administration, which saddled Worth with more combat power than he wanted. By mid-February, he retained half of the combat companies in the Army, not nearly enough to secure Florida's 47,000 square miles but far too many for the mission as Worth conceived it.

On the basis of his operations to that point, Worth concluded that removal of the remaining Seminoles could be achieved "by pacific and persuasive measures, or not at all." He also realized that such persuasion entailed compromise, something he, as the operational commander, could not authorize. Accordingly, on 14 February 1842, he wrote to the War Department recommending a strategic reappraisal. Estimating that only 301 Seminoles remained in Florida, Worth argued that "Every exertion of force...places the object in view, his total expulsion, more remote."[5] To see them eventually removed, the United States would have to first let them stay, and Worth requested permission to conduct future negotiations accordingly.

To weigh such a momentous proposal, Secretary of War John Spencer convened a council of the Army's senior leaders. Worried that anything less than victory would tarnish the Army's reputation, all but one officer advised against the recommendation. The lone dissenting vote came from Major General Jesup, who had employed similar methods, reached the same conclusion, and offered a nearly identical recommendation four years earlier. The secretary of war at the time had dismissed Jesup's proposal out of hand but Spencer was more receptive. Reluctant to overrule his generals, he made no immediate judgment on Worth's proposal, instead waiting for the right opportunity to take it to the president. That opportunity came in late April of 1842 as the traditional campaigning season drew to a close and Worth's fight-to-negotiate methodology yielded (Miccosukee leader) Halleck Tustenuggee and 114 of his followers. Within two weeks, John Tyler promulgated Worth's proposal as administration policy and gave the theater commander authority to declare the termination of hostilities when he saw fit. After a summer spent in peaceful negotiations, Worth did so on 14 August 1842.

By the time Worth concluded his negotiations and seizures, he had shipped over 900 Seminoles to Arkansas. If the 600 who remained were more numerous than he realized, they were not inclined to jeopardize their hard won but fragile hold on a Florida homeland. This concession by the United States was an essential component of Worth's success. Although he directed the war with as much vigor, prudence, and ruthlessness as any commander could, he could not claim full credit for ending this regrettable war. This required more than the balancing of operational ways and means. It demanded an honest reassessment of the ends to which they were applied. Worth had the good fortune to serve an administration willing to provide this reassessment and sagacious enough to realize that enough was enough.

Endnotes

1. John T. Sprague, "The Origin, Progress, and Conclusion of the Florida War," (1848; repr., Tampa: University of Tampa Press, 2000), 274.

2. John T. Sprague, "The Origin, Progress, and Conclusion of the Florida War."

3. John T. McLaughlin to Worth, 26 December 1841, quoted in John T. Sprague, "The Origin, Progress, and Conclusion of the Florida War," 380.

4. McCall to "My Dear E," 27 February 1842, George A. McCall, "Letters from the Frontiers: Written during a Period of Thirty Years' Service in the Army of the United States," (Philadelphia: J. B. Lippincott & Co., 1868), 396.

5. Worth to Winfield Scott, 14 February 1842, H. Doc. 262, 27th Cong., 2nd sess., Serial 405, 11.

Session 1

Interview

Dr. John Hall

Interviewer

Why did you choose to focus on the second Seminole war rather than all three Seminole wars together?

Dr. John Hall

One of the issues that's come out in our discussions about Indian wars is it's often times difficult to distinguish where one war begins and another begins. I think that with the Seminoles, obviously, as an enemy of the United States, there were three peaks in the early 19th century, through the mid-19th century.

The First Seminole War is somewhat distinct from the second and third but the second was the most significant of these. Depending upon how you date the start and end of the conflict, it lasted approximately seven years and involved the vast majority of an army of first 12 and then 14 regiments. They had to expand the army to fight this war.

At its peak, the largest operation conducted in the winter of 1837 and 1838 included some 9,000 troops: volunteer forces, the Marines, the US Navy, the US Army. So this is a unique Indian war in the American experience in terms of its size and in terms of its duration.

Now, the obvious thing about the end of this conflict is that it's not really the end because there is a Third Seminole War.

Interviewer

You've written a lot about Colonel William J. Worth, the war's final commander. Why?

Dr. John Hall

Well, he's not generally celebrated for his accomplishments in bringing this war to a close and there are several reasons why I think this is the case.

First of all, he didn't win the war. Contrary to what a lot of people want to believe, the United States was not undefeated in its wars, by any stretch of the imagination. This is a conflict that's rather unique in this regard in that it's a conflict that, even after the third Seminole War, you cannot make a claim that the United States won the war.

Another reason why Worth is not celebrated is because he used techniques and methods that were deemed unethical or objectionable by many of his contemporaries, including brother officers and certainly elements of the press.

Like one of his predecessors, Thomas J. Jesup, he entered negotiations with Seminole chiefs and laid traps for them. The moment he thought negotiations weren't going the way that he wanted them to go, he triggered the trap and captured the chiefs and as many of their followers as he possibly could. So there's another reason why he's not really celebrated, but

I think the most obvious one is it doesn't really end the war and why would you celebrate unethical conduct that's not victory and doesn't produce an enduring peace?

Interviewer

Okay, but why did he fail?

Dr. John Hall

The reason he's not able to produce an enduring peace and none of these commanders are, is that no operational commander has the wherewithal. He has the capability of reducing the drivers of conflict in these kinds of wars, which, in the case of the Second Seminole War, and most other Indian wars, I would say they're incompatible visions of the land and the Indians' place upon it…

One of the ironies of this history, I think, is that while Worth's not remembered for this conflict, he is remembered for his contributions in the war against Mexico, which was neither the most just nor moral war the United States has ever fought but it fits familiar patterns of what wars are supposed to look like against the conventional enemy. It provided the commanders and the nation with a sense of conventional military victory and glory that resonated with them. The Seminole War did not provide that to them.

Worth, like Jesup before him, is one of these people who use exceptional measures to capture Indian leaders. You can make an argument, undeniably, that conduct was unethical in accordance with notions of military honor that prevailed at that time and since then. But in a roundabout way, you can also make an argument that there is something morally just in the way that Worth pursued war termination in that anything that sped the conclusion of dishonorable war and preserved lives, anything that moved the United States to the point where they could terminate hostilities and preserve life, in a broader sense, actually served the collective good of both of these combatant groups.

Interviewer

Was this a popular war with the American people?

Dr. John Hall

No. Never. It was very divisive from the beginning because it was framed around the morally contentious issue of Indian resettlement.

Interviewer

Well, unlike the Cherokee, for example, the Seminole resisted removal and resisted movement to Indian Territory and fought the United States. Now, you've brought up a number of very important points.

Victory, under dishonorable circumstances, is not palatable to the American public. In addition to that, it's not acceptable for the military as an institution or the American people in general. When you consider the ultimate conclusion of those wars, do you think that perhaps the American people, and the American government, understood that their "victory," if we could call it a "victory," against the Seminoles, was incomplete?

Dr. John Hall

They certainly understood it was incomplete. I think you could generalize. You could talk about the nation at large and, by the early 1840s most Americans have ceased paying attention to the Seminole War. They call it the "Florida War." Outside of that region, other more pressing matters have entered public consciousness – the debate over the chartering of a national bank and debate over territorial expansion…

In the case of the Second Seminole War, it is largely a nuisance to most people. They just want it over and done with. The only people that are really committed to the absolute rule of the Seminoles for Florida are people who had an ideological hand in promoting the policy of removal in the first place and are touting the necessity of this war and those Floridians who think that it is inconceivable to have a Seminole state within their territory. So it's a rather polarizing sort of debate.

What ultimately enables William J. Worth to end this war are his methods, which are very effective. They're very ruthless but, in large measure, they're the same methods that Thomas Jesup, the fourth overall commander, had employed several years earlier and achieved similar results, demonstrating marked progress over that time.

The reason that Worth is able to end the war while Jesup had not been able to is because he works for an administration that's actually willing to say, "Enough is enough."

The first six commanders all worked for administrations that for ideological, political, and personal reasons could not bring themselves to modify United States policy. So the operational commander is to exhaust all of the means and ways at their disposal, trying to find the right combination to bring this war to a close. The missing ingredient was the ability to tweak the war aim so that you actually could come up with a strategic solution that made sense and served American interests. So Worth does everything an operational commander could possibly do so that there's nothing wanting in Worth's conduct from the perspective of the War Department. If there's anything wanting, it would be more ethical conduct towards the Indians that he misled.

He would not have been the last commander were it not for that change in strategic direction that was able to say; "This really is enough and it's time to end the war."

Interviewer

So at least in the case of the United States, it's the political which guides the military by providing the goals, by providing the desired end state, and conditions for peace.

Dr. John Hall

Absolutely.

Interviewer

With that in mind, then, why is it important to study how these wars ended? What could current military practitioners take from the Seminole Indian wars, especially the Second Seminole Indian War, in terms of professional education on war termination?

Dr. John Hall

Well, it's a very thorny subject because obviously we want and need complete subordination of our military to civilian control...I guess the right questions to ask of this situation, or any other situation are: What really are US interests? What are the vital interests that have to be served and what are these lesser things that might masquerade as interests but really are elements of pride, maybe even vanity?

One of the great tragedies of this conflict is it goes on all of this time in the name of national honor, not because it's really vital to national interest that every last Seminole Indian be out of Florida but because it would be looked upon as a stain on national honor to let a miserable band of, the officers at the time might have said, 4,000 half-naked savages defeat this US Army.

The US Army has something of an inferiority complex at this time. There's a siege mentality. It does not have a very well established place in American society. This is at the time at which the height of Congressional calls to eliminate West Point as an anti-republican institution. The frontiersmen really believe coming out of the War of 1812 that that conflict and Andrew Jackson's astonishing but meaningless success at the Battle of New Orleans demonstrated the superiority of the militia or the indispensability of the militia.

So the Army, too, is part of this. The operational commanders and the people who are stuck in Florida figure it out very early. This is the kind of conflict that is not going to be solved by military force ultimately. There are limits to force and excessive force, the last four commanders all concluded; "We've crossed the point of diminishing returns where every further exertion of force is making the object in view more and more unobtainable and we need to take a different line. The only way to do that is to permit, whether temporarily or permanently, some Seminoles to remain here."

The great irony in the broader view is this war is waged in pursuit or supposed defense of national honor. Yet in historical retrospect, the war itself, the waging of the war, is the stain upon national honor. It's not that they gave up. What was dishonorable was that they waged a war that most of the officers corps recognized was unjust for as long as they waged it all in the service of not national honor but really the pride and principle of particular parties and particular interests for the United States.

Interviewer

So how does this relate to officers today?

Dr. John Hall

I do think officers need to have a conception of what they're doing that transcends... the immediacy of the tactical situation.

Interviewer

Do you see any parallels between the Second Seminole War and what's going on now in Afghanistan?

Dr. John Hall

Well, I do see some parallels because, inevitably, both conflicts are going to end by proclamation rather than by decision. This is something that people have said routinely about the current conflicts. There will be no Battleship Missouri ceremony. That is an anomaly.

The question, the million dollar question, is how much is enough? When can you tie it off and say, "This is really good enough?" The question, of course, that's always associated with that is will we have peace with honor. If we leave now and things go badly, will we have defended the honor of our nation?

So I guess to that extent, that's one of the things I'm talking about with the Second Seminole War. If you are thinking about prolonging a conflict simply out of a concern for national honor, in historical terms, you are probably working against national honor.

Interviewer

Is this one of the difficulties of guerilla warfare? For the conventional force, you have a number of different objectives? For the guerilla force or the insurgent, victory may be symbolized or signified by simply surviving.

Dr. John Hall

That's certainly the case in the Second Seminole War, that the Seminole population. They very much celebrate their perseverance.

Interviewer

So it's possible for a war to end and both sides to claim victory without either side having fully achieved it?

Dr. John Hall

That's the way these kinds of conflicts usually end is not with a clean termination, but a messy one, just until the next violence emerges.

Interviewer

Do you see this, perhaps, as one of the trends for the 21st century?

Dr. John Hall

Well, one of the things that I think some of the people who write army doctrine and have been paying some attention to recently, that makes a lot of sense, is the importance of establishing the conditions for a self-stabilizing, long-term peace and that when engaged in stability support operations, that you're not trying to achieve victory. You are trying to achieve a set of conditions that at some point you can withdraw the elements of United States power and leave things on a self-sustaining course...

Certainly, the military of today understands fully the limits of armed force. I think that the claim that, when you have a hammer, everything looks like a nail, that that probably was an act of criticism of the US military in the early phases of these conflicts but here today in 2010, I really don't think that that's an act of criticism whatsoever.

The people who are familiar with these current conflicts claim most frequently that this sort of problem is not going to be solved with a military solution.

Session 1

Questions and Answers

Colonel Matthew Moten

We've got six propositions about war termination. We have a war in which we had war aims and we achieved them and found out that they were the wrong ones. We had a war for bargaining chips and finally, we had a reckless waste of blood and treasure, an interminable elective war. There is a member of the fourth estate here, who asked me the other day, what it is that the US Army could learn from studying 200 year old campaigns. I'm certain that none of the things that I just said have ever happened again. With that, I'll open it up for questions.

Question

I had talked with Wayne about this a few months ago. One of the goals that Madison has in the War of 1812, based on his political philosophy, is to keep the government from growing during the war because he sees that as a result of war, the government has to grow in power. Arguably, he was very susceptible to this. I'd like to ask the panel. These are kind of three different wars in different eras. We are always talking about how World War II and other wars where you have a massive stance against the government bureaucracy. How, in your cases, did you see that it is happening or not happening? How does the US Government grow in power and sculpt these wars, or is the United States hurt by them?

Colonel Matthew Moten

Let me just summarize Colin's question for the purposes of our taping. His point was that President Madison tried to make sure that the US Government did not grow during the War of 1812 and how prevalent has it been, in each of these wars, that the government, the bureaucracy or army might have grown as a result of the military operations.

Dr. Ira Gruber

I probably ought to start because I'm at the beginning. We worked really hard as a people, to keep the government from gaining any power. I mean the whole idea of rebelling against Britain was to release the American people from an alien, distant, ungovernable administration and they had no idea that they were going to create a strong central government and they certainly did not. They couldn't agree on the most basic stuff and of course it was not, the Articles of Confederation could not be modified in any realistic sense because it took unanimity and Rhode Island was sure to stop them, whatever they wanted to do. Rhode Island, you guys ought to know that South Carolinians summered in Rhode Island which will connect the Revolution to the Civil War. That's a very important historical connection.

I think that the whole problem with the Revolutionary War, was that you didn't want the national government to have any power and the government was of course broke almost immediately, in default, printing worthless currency. The inflation tables are staggering. The Continental Army went from reasonably effective and robust at the outset, to pitiful by the end and wholly dependent on the militia and the militia of course, were doing just whatever they wanted to do.

71

Question

It just seems that this particular period of history seems so different from what's going to come later.

Dr. Ira Gruber

I would certainly say the Revolutionary War is really different because you almost never have ideologues in charge and Madison of course, is leftover from the Revolution, doing exactly what you'd expect he would do, I think.

Dr. Wayne Lee

Yeah, I think I remember talking with you about that and Colin and I looked at Gordon Wood, who makes that argument. I think he misses the fortification program however. I mean the postwar fortification program is an expansion of the bureaucracy and certainly it involves expenditure. I mean obviously, it's sort of, in hindsight, kind of a big waste of money but that certainly was a major change that occurred after the war. A lot of the fortifications that were built in the United States before the war, were built at state expense, at least partly at state expense and after the war, they're being built at federal expense, and so that's a change.

On the other hand, I wish Andy Bacevich was here. In his new book "Washington Rules," when you think about his argument about the establishment of an unquestioning set of assumptions about the American policy in use of force and maintaining an establishment, you don't get that in this period. So partly, I don't think you get that because of New Orleans. I think New Orleans does have that impact. It's already a compromise when Calhoun tries to create an expansible army program. The expansible army program is already a compromise toward, let's rely mostly on the militia, and Congress won't even buy off on that and so I think at the same time they do the fortification program, they're also unwilling to spend in the other direction.

Dr. John Hall

The fortification building program extends throughout and there is a reinvigoration of it during the Second Seminole War. As a matter of fact, Fort Monroe is one of the forts, 1841 or thereabout, and is at the tail end. It's indicative of, if there's any governmental expansion that's somewhat related to this, although this goes over into the territorial expansion as well. The creation of the Department of the Interior in 1849, does have a relationship to the end of the Second Seminole War, with basically the enunciation by the US Army that we don't do Indians and so the creation of the Department of the Interior provides the US Army with the ability to push off onto civilian bureaucracy, that mission set that it doesn't want to do. Part one of these tragic ironies are those of you that are more familiar with later Indian wars, are where by the 1860s and the 1870s, the US Army is bemoaning the lack of unity of command over these damn civilian bureaucrats and they're trying to pull control of Indian affairs back underneath the war department because they have no control over the Interior Department agents. So there's the expansion.

Question

Since it's our goal here to find threads that we can use to kind of stitch all this together, I noticed that two of you talked about national honor, or the credibility of the US Military rising in importance as the conflict itself seems to go less and less well. I guess I ask you does the rise of that as a war aim reflect indicatively of other problems in the campaign, with establishing achievable war aims across the history of these campaigns. We see the rise of national honor as a war aim; does it tell us something about the war?

Dr. Wayne Lee

National honor doesn't necessarily rise as a war aim in so much as it becomes the only one left to achieve, that can be achieved in 1812 because the war starts in many ways because of national honor; you know the idea of them taking seamen off of ships. So honor is crucial to the beginning of the war but by 1814, the Americans are starting to realize that the only thing they're going to get out of this hopefully is honor, and so that they're still fighting in the sense that they need to achieve something in order to get out with honor. Although again, as I said, the whole issue in August, Clay, the American Treaty Commissioner, in August, says, this clause about the Indian state is so unacceptable so we cannot take it because it will stain national honor. That's the way he defines it as the problem. He doesn't say because we won't be able to expand to the Pacific, he says because it will stain our national honor and so that's what the next three, four more months of fighting is essentially enough to create the conditions that okay, now we can do it.

Dr. John Hall

The Second Seminole War is similar in some regards, except that the tactical and operational army considered the war itself inherently, if not dishonorable which many of them regarded the conflict itself, as dishonorable, at least there was no glory to be had in it. Don Stivers has not done a print of the Second Seminole War for a reason. No one wants to celebrate that in their office. It was more at a political level, than that element of the Army that was most intimately involved at the top level. This sort of struggle is still ongoing about the role of the professional Army vis-à-vis the militia in national defense policy. That battle is still going on at this time and they don't want to give any satisfaction to the militia advocates because those frontier Indian fighters are convinced they know how to fight Indians better than the US Army. By the end of this war, the US Army is just kind of willing to swallow its pride and let the frontiersmen have it because they don't want duty that stains their honor, even when they're effective.

Dr. Wayne Lee

I should say, just as a quick follow up, national honor gets defined in a republic, even at the beginning of the 19th century, it's partly defined by; "Am I pissing off enough people who are going to vote or not vote for me in the next election." So what does the public think about what we're doing? Does the public think that our honor has been violated and will that have political consequences for me?

Question

This question is directed to Roger. Which federal theorists, if any, did you find useful in the drafting of your essay, in what ways?

Dr. Roger Spiller

Which theorist did I find most useful in drafting?

Colonel Matthew Moten

Political theorists, right?

Dr. Roger Spiller

Did you pick any theorists?

Question

Besides me you mean?

Dr. Roger Spiller

Clausewitz, without question, is always depicted as a cold blooded apostle of battle above all of us but I found him, in certain passages, especially in books one and two, to have quite a supple mind on this question of the duration of success in battle. I understand from readings that he himself rarely used the term seek victory. He used something else. He had kind of a very practical idea of what battle could accomplish. He used to say the results are never final and he thought that of war in general too. Those are a couple of instances in which I was a bit surprised at how muted he was compared to his reputation in a great deal of literature. He certainly can't control his image and we attach an image to this fellow for our own purposes as much as anything but if you go back through, especially the first two books were very powerful. There was no one quite equal in influence in my work, with the possible exception of Mao Zedong and when I say Mao Zedong, I suppose I mean part Mao Zedong and part his chief theoretician, who really only joined him in 1938. This was a fellow by the name of Chen Boda, who has not been written about in the west very much at all. Jonathan Spence, in his latest book, a brief biography of Mao which I would recommend to everyone by the way, has a splendid piece of work. It has some very interesting things to say about the influence of this Moscow-trained theoretician on Maoist theory. It won't hurt your head and it's not very long. It's only a couple of pages but it's really quite compelling.

At the same time John Spence's book came out, this huge doorstop of a thing came out, that really put Mao in the dark. It was a work of accusation and I think rather agenda driven. That's not Spence's line at all. He has a much more balanced view, much more nuanced, and I think much more historiographically up to date view of Maoist thought than anyone recently. It's not a work of theory as such but Roger Ames' translation of the Silver Sparrow Mountain excavations done in China, in the 1970s and 1980s which he translated in English. Roger is the head of the East-West Center, I think, in Hawaii, still, and quite a practiced historian of ancient China. He did about a 100 page introduction to his edition on *Sun-Tzu* which I found extremely helpful in considering eastern war from the theoretical viewpoint. So those especially were important to me.

Question

Thank you. It's a question as a group but as open as well. I was really interested by this division between war aims and peace needs. Given the fundamental nature to American independence, why does the United States manage to become the beneficiary of peace, whereas France, Spain, really do suffer for their involvement?

Dr. Ira Gruber

There wasn't time of course, to deal with that but the United States instructed its representatives, who turned out to be very talented people: Franklin, Jay and John Adams, to essentially follow the lead of their allies but use their own judgment and gave them instructions on such questions as the national domain which they then allowed them to modify and improve modifications. The other powers that were involved in the negotiations, had such separate interests, that the British were able to begin the negotiation with the United States and exploit that negotiation and the United States representatives quickly understood that the Spanish and the French were not to be trusted and shouldn't be followed. So, they ignored their instructions from Congress. The British were eager to end the war. They had a big war on their hands and they'd been fighting it for seven years by the time the negotiations were going on and they would have been delighted to get out of that war with the terms of 1763, that is the world as it had been and so they undertook to negotiate with the Americans and try to get a deal to break them away from the other allies.

Franklin was shrewd. He notified the French that he was negotiating separately but that he wouldn't do anything that didn't link his peace with theirs. He really did surprise them in the end and he got wonderful terms for the United States because the British were eager. Of course, Parliament had said it was finished with the American war, that's a help. The King held out against independence. He didn't want to grant it, Shelburne was uncertain. The English interest was to get out of the war and to divide the allies and so they made wonderful terms. The allies and our diplomats were smart enough to take advantage of that and exploit the differences. They got a surprise of course because the British negotiated treaties with Spain that trumped our treaty and we thought we had a treaty on the Mississippi that would have had the Mississippi open. Of course this treaty between England and Spain gave Florida to Spain, with an indefinite frontier and the Mississippi to us and of course the final treaty had suspension clauses in it. If we didn't pay up debts owed to British merchants, if we didn't see some restitution for loyalist property seized, they then had some pretext for not abiding by the treaty and they didn't.

So the negotiations are extremely complicated and it's really difficult to explain them succinctly and clearly but other peoples' interests aligned in a way that was favorable to the United States so that our campaign was made extremely productive. That is the campaign that ended the war and Franklin was nothing if not shrewd. He said to the French after he had surprised them with these remarkable terms for the United States, "Now we don't want the Brits to think they've divided us, so how about another loan?" and the French gave him another loan. That is shrewd.

Question

This is a question for Dr. Hall and then reactions from everyone. Talk about how new administrations can redefine strategic aims of the war. Can you talk about contemporary reactions to the redefinition of strategic aims?

Dr. John Hall

The contemporary reaction to that was local in nature. The rest of the nation was sick and tired of the Second Seminole War. It had already drifted off of newspaper pages. Most Americans weren't paying attention. They call it the Florida war, by its final phases, even though Worth has 5,000 regulars and eight of the US Army's 14 regiments in this operation. Most of the nation is transfixed by the promise and problems associated with territorial expansions which is of course what everybody remembers Tyler for; not for ending the Second Seminole War.

Floridians are, for the most part, livid with the settlement. It's muted somewhat because it's a territory at this point which means that the administration has the ability to appoint the territorial governor, who, of course, is from the same party as the administration. So the Whig party, in its newspapers, people think that partisan press is a phenomenon of the late 20th and early 21st century. The newspapers are purely partisan in nature and the Whig press in Florida does a good job of drumming up support for Worth's program of shifting the negotiated settlements. In terms of congressional debate, it's really only southerners and Floridians in particular, that are upset about the negotiated compromise. Did I answer the question?

Colonel Matthew Moten

I think we have time for one more short question and answer.

Question

I have a question. This relates to several points. First, Dr. Spiller's point that original methods were constantly revised and then Professor Lee and Professor Hall brought up two points which I thought were interesting which is this idea of honor and how important it is. It makes me wonder, if you enter a conflict on the one hand, with a set of ideas about how you're going to proceed, how it's going to end, what you're going to accomplish. On the other end of the scale, you also have a very wide range of possibilities of how you can achieve this in reality, some of which don't bear relation to these ideals that you start off with. So the question is for all of you. Does the appointed conversions that occur in these conflicts, where ideals and a wide range of pragmatic possibilities come together, create a final solution and terminate the conflict?

Dr. Roger Spiller

This was by an acceptable degree of honor.

Question

What is the acceptable degree of honor?

Dr. Roger Spiller

Well, both sides have to define it, and then define it in relation to one another, not in relation to an abstract which is what you only do at the beginning. You can go on and on about national honor but giving it a substance. After the General asked his question about the point at which national honor appears in a conflict, I started cycling through the various wars, trying to think of exactly when the rhetoric about national honor became more publicly prominent. That is to say that when the rhetoric tended to take over reality, the most notorious example being the Vietnam War of course, and the peace with honor movement under President Nixon. I'm sure, if we think about it a little bit more, we can find other points. It would be interesting to chart, exactly when the rhetoric of national honor begins to swell up. I have a feeling, and it's just that it's a warning sign. When you can't say anything more specific or concrete, when you cannot point to concrete results that satisfy the constituency for whom you were fighting presumably, then you begin to engage in all these kinds of vapid and rhetorical predictions about what you're going to do. I call that a hypothesis, something to be looked at. It's a very interesting question.

Dr. John Hall

In the Second Seminole War, the point of which you speak, for the operational commanders, they have reached that essentially. Each of them reaches it in their own course. I'll give them the benefit of the doubt and say they come in and try to do everything to the best of their ability but all in their own course, everyone from Jesup forward. Jesup reaches this realization, or at least he articulates it to the administration, as early as 1838. They think that they've crossed that point, where national honor needs to be reconciled to fit within the realm of the possible. It's complicated and particular in that conflict because the foe that they are fighting is regarded as so contemptible by so many people. Jesup has 9,000 troops from all three services. He has 4,500 state and territorial militia troops against an Indian band that at that point, probably numbers around 3,800 or so and only two fifths or one third of those are men capable of bearing arms. I hate to resort to presentism but it evokes recently a Lindsey Graham question, how many tanks do they have? How many airplanes do they have? It doesn't matter, they can't do anything but it makes people that are remote from the conflict, reluctant to concede, that when you have such an explicit overmatch, that that is beyond the realm of the possible.

Colonel Matthew Moten

So we talked about the hope that we would tease out new information, new concepts in this conference. It just occurs to me, as we think about this, that if you're unambiguously winning, you don't spend a great of time talking about your national honor.

Dr. Roger Spiller

The victorious have no need for introspection.

Colonel Matthew Moten

Right, that's all the time we have for this panel, before we start encroaching on the time of the next one which is an impolite thing to do.

Session 2

The 300 Year War

by

Dr. Peter Maslowski

The only way Captain Walter Clifford avoided the stench was to put his nose inches from the sweet flowing water.

Two hundred and sixty three bodies from General George A. Custer's command, baking in Montana's late June sun, provided the stench. The Little Bighorn River provided the relief.

For the third time in the last four months, Indians had defeated the US Army and no amount of obfuscation and self serving denials could conceal that fact as they had done after the first two defeats.

War between the United States and the Sioux (in alliance with two weaker tribes, Northern Cheyennes, and Northern Arapahos) came near the end of The 300 Year War. Following the establishment of their first settlements, whites waged more or less continuous warfare against Native Americans from the early 1600s to the late 1800s in order to acquire their land. Now, in the winter of 1875/1876, Ulysses S. Grant's administration provoked a conflict so that the United States could seize the Black Hills which belonged to the Sioux by every legal and moral obligation. Such considerations never deterred Euro-Americans in their insatiable quest for Indian land and getting the Black Hills seemed especially urgent. An economic depression hit the country in 1873 followed by the discovery of gold in the Black Hills the next year. Officials believed newly mined gold would stimulate the economy by alleviating the monetary shortage. In addition, the Sioux threatened vital trans-continental routes and roamed over millions of acres of rich prairie land which whites thought they wasted because they did not farm.

By the mid-19th century, white Americans almost universally agreed that all Indians must be shunted onto marginal plots (reservations) where they could be saved from extinction and become whites in everything but skin color by imbibing "civilization:" education, Christianity, and sedentary farming. But dominating Indian lands was always the primary war aim; "Civilization" came in a distant second.

Shunting aside the Sioux was not easy. They were more numerous and more powerful than other tribes in part because their nomadic lifestyle protected them from the worst effects of European diseases of smallpox, cholera, and so on, which reduced more sedentary tribes by 50 to 90 percent. In 1832, the US government inoculated some Sioux bands against smallpox which mitigated that scourge's impact.

The war began with a preemptive attack before the Indians even knew that war was contemplated much less at their tepee-flap entrance. The military high command ordered two converging columns to descend on Sioux winter camps, which was when and where Indians were most vulnerable. In summer, the nomads dispersed in small mobile hunting and war parties but in winter they huddled together in larger encampments. If the Army surprised a winter camp, the snow and cold, grass-fed ponies' weakened condition, and presence of women and children all made resistance difficult. Even if the Indians escaped, soldiers burned their lodges, food supplies, clothing, and bedding, leaving them susceptible to starvation and the elements.

However, wintertime campaigning was difficult for the Army and, paralyzed by foul weather, General Alfred H. Terry's column never left Fort Lincoln. The other column, under Lieutenant Colonel George Crook's overall direction, marched northward from Fort Fetterman in treacherous conditions. A vicious north wind pummeled men and horses, snow piled up, and on three nights, the mercury congealed in the thermometer. Crook placed the 3d Cavalry's Colonel Joseph J. Reynolds in formal command of the expedition but since Crook went along as an "observer" he was the actual commander.

On March 16, scouts discovered a village along the Powder River. Leading a 375-man strike force, Reynolds attacked the next morning, drove the defenders onto nearby bluffs, seized the pony herd, and began destroying the village. Native Americans counterattacked, sending the troops in undignified retreat and recapturing most of their ponies. Defeated by approximately 200 warriors, many fighting nearly naked in sub-zero weather, Reynolds rejoined Crook and the entire command returned to Fort Fetterman. Crook made the expedition seem successful by implying that Reynolds attacked 210 lodges, double the real number on the Powder River, and made him look better by blaming Reynolds for the fiasco.

The failed winter expeditions mutated into a summertime campaign of three converging columns. Crook moved northward from Fort Fetterman with more than 1,000 troops and 262 Crow and Shoshone allies. Departing from Forts Shaw and Ellis, Colonel John Gibbon led 450 soldiers and 25 (later reduced to 19) Crow auxiliaries eastward. Marching westward from Fort Lincoln was General Alfred Terry with 925 soldiers including General George Custer's 7th Cavalry and 37 Arikara scouts. Terry also eventually borrowed six Crows from Gibbon. Each column was strong enough to fight up to 800 warriors, more than anyone expected to encounter since everyone knew that Indians dispersed in the summer and that the grass and food supply in an area could not sustain a large population.

The Army's high command believed it confronted the usual problems in Indian warfare. First, it had to find the hostiles who were scattered in small bands over a vast region. To overcome this difficulty the Army relied on Indian allies who could follow trails that officers could not even see and locate a village without alerting the occupants. Second, the Army had to make the Indians stand and fight because they normally fled when bluecoats approached. The idea behind converging columns was to prevent their escape by compressing them into an ever-smaller area. Eventually they either had to give battle or surrender. Although converging columns reduced the Indians' ability to escape, the widely separated units were vulnerable to defeat in detail.

Unknown to the Army, its assumptions about the enemy's behavior were wrong. The unprovoked Powder River attack enraged the Sioux, Cheyenne, and Arapahos, who united in a powerful coalition to fight a defensive war to protect their homeland. As Indians concentrated in unprecedented numbers, including perhaps 3,000 warriors, they had no intention of fleeing.

Crook discovered the Indians' fighting temper first. On 17 June, as his command rested along Rosebud Creek, the Sioux and Cheyenne attacked. After being saved from immediate disaster by the desperate fighting of his Shoshone and Crow auxiliaries, who bought time for the troops to get organized, Crook engaged in incessant combat for six hours along a disjointed battle line extending for three miles. Although outnumbering his adversaries (1,300 to fewer than 1,000), he never gained the initiative. Because the Indians eventually withdrew and left the battlefield in Crook's possession, he proclaimed victory but his subsequent actions proved otherwise. Instead of pursuing the hostiles, he retreated to a camp on Goose Creek and spent the next several months refusing to move until he received reinforcements. In a stunning command failure, Crook failed to warn the other columns about the Indians' unusual strength and determination.

A week after repulsing one converging column, the Indians shattered another. Terry, Gibbon, and Custer met on 21 June to coordinate their searches. No one worried about defeating the Indians, only on preventing their escape. Crow scouts had seen smoke toward the Little Bighorn, which meant the Sioux could be on the Rosebud, Tullock's Fork, or the Tongue but were most likely on the Little Bighorn. Terry planned accordingly, directing Custer to ascend the Rosebud to its source, searching Tullock's Fork on the way, then cross to the Little Bighorn and drive downriver, preventing the hostiles from escaping to the south. Ideally, Custer would not attack any Indian village until 26 June, when Gibbon's command, accompanied by the remainder of Terry's column, would arrive at the Little Bighorn's mouth to block the Indians' escape northward. However, because no one knew when or where a village might be located, Terry gave his subordinate wide latitude, writing that Custer should conform to his orders "unless you shall see sufficient reasons for departing from them." Starkly put, Custer's strike force was to attack a village at the first opportune moment without feeling bound by Terry's directive.

On 24 June, Custer followed an Indian trail westward from the Rosebud, planning to stop in the morning darkness of 25 June, resting his men all day while searching for the village's exact location, and then attacking early on the 26th, the day Gibbon and Terry reached the Little Bighorn. On the morning of the 25th, however, he received reports that Indians had seen the 7th Cavalry. As an experienced Indian fighter, Custer knew the opportunity to strike a hostile village was so fleeting he had to attack now before it fled. To increase the chances of trapping the foe he deployed his regiment in detachments, sending one to the south, another into the village, and a third under his personal command to encircle the village from the north. If the converging columns invited defeat in detail at the strategic level, Custer's dispersion risked tactical defeat in detail, especially since he had no knowledge of the village's strength and, most importantly, his assumptions were wrong. The village was larger than anyone anticipated and instead of fleeing the Indians fought.

Out of the 647 men in Custer's command, 256 were killed on 25 June including all 210 in Custer's detachment and seven more the next day before the Indians broke camp that evening. The rotting bodies assailed Captain Clifford's nostrils when he arrived on the slaughter field with Gibbon and Terry on June 27th.

Victories at the Rosebud and the Little Bighorn yielded the Sioux no long term benefits. For those few days, the Indians were united in unprecedented strength, confident and superbly led but in accordance with their nomadic lifestyle, they were unable to sustain a cohesive effort. Separate bands drifted apart to find fresh grass and hunt bison in preparation for the coming winter. Meanwhile news of the Little Bighorn motivated the Army to seek retribution, which came not in spectacular battlefield victories, but through relentless pursuit, a grinding persistence that depleted the Indians' strength and morale until even reservation life seemed preferable to being hunted and watching elders, women, and children suffer.

Retributive efforts by Crook and Terry were slow to get underway as they idled away six or seven weeks in their respective base camps, awaiting powerful reinforcements before venturing forth to risk another confrontation. After they finally moved out, their columns wasted the late summer in futile wanderings since they lacked much intelligence about the enemy's strength and location and what little information they gleaned was consistently misinterpreted. Only by blind luck did Crook have an encounter with the Sioux. Because of poor logistics planning, Crook's command was nearing starvation when a detachment that was pushing ahead to get supplies discovered a small village at Slim Buttes. The soldiers attacked at dawn on 9 September but most of the Indians escaped and began fighting back. Crook soon arrived with the rest of the command just in time to fend off a counterattack by 200 warriors, many of whom had rushed to the scene from another village. Although outnumbered ten to one, they forced Crook onto the defensive and kept him there until his column made a fighting retreat. The general proclaimed Slim Buttes a victory but the success was unheroic and miniscule. With good reason, an authority on the Sioux War labeled the Crook-Terry expeditions "a farce."[1]

The succeeding campaigns were no farce. During the fall and winter of 1876 to 1877, troops campaigned unremittingly, even in the coldest temperatures and the deepest snow, hunting Native Americans as if they were big game animals. When soldiers found a winter encampment such as at the Dull Knife Battle in November and the Battle of Wolf Mountain in January, Indians suffered mightily as their possessions went up in flames. They lost pony herds and irreplaceable warriors were killed or wounded. The Battle of Muddy Creek in early May was little more than a pathetic denouement to the Great Sioux War. By then, virtually all Indians had moved onto reservations. "I am tired of being always on the watch for troops," lamented Red Horse. "My desire is to get my family where they can sleep without being continually in the expectation of an attack."[2] Only on reservations could Indians sleep soundly.

The United States had humbled the Sioux, its most powerful Native American adversary.

The Sioux War of 1876 to 1877 was not The 300 Year War's final campaign but it was the terminal campaign in that it more directly affected the peace "settlement" than did the few subsequent expeditions. Campaigns in the Rocky Mountains against Utes, Sheepeaters, and Nez Perces and in the desert Southwest against Apaches, occurred between 1877 and 1886. Although dramatic, they transpired in areas that were less important to the national interest than the Great Plains and the hostile bands were less powerful. When the Nez

82

Perces capitulated they had fewer than 100 warriors led by Geronimo. The last Apaches off the reservation (fewer than 50 men, women, and children) surrendered in 1886.

The war's ending seemed definitive. Whites owned virtually all the land that once belonged to Native Americans, who were now confined to reservations, but in fact, it portended a messy future because the question of the Indians' status in American society remained unresolved. They did not become an extinct species as so many predicted nor did they become "civilized." Whites tried to destroy tribal culture on the assumption that as Natives lost their "Indian-ness" they would dissolve as identifiable groups and merge into the broader society as individuals. Convinced they knew what was best for Indians, paternalistic do-gooders tried to force them to farm rather than hunt, eat beef instead of buffalo, abandon their religious practices, learn English, and send their children to boarding schools to learn Euro-American values.

In the face of this concerted effort to compel Indians to live a life they did not want, Native Americans struggled not just to live but to live <u>as Indians</u>. Despite defeat, demoralization, and hardship, for more than a century, they have displayed endurance and resilience, converting reservations from jail-like enclaves into micro-homelands where Native children learned the old ways of. Communal lifestyles and tribal affiliations survived. Indian religions and languages endure and efforts to live meaningful lives on their own terms succeeded.

"But we will never be white men," Olney Runs After affirmed. "We can talk and work and go to school like the white people but we're still Indians."[3]

In addition to the sources listed in the endnotes, see Francis Paul Prucha, "The Great Father: The United States Government and the American Indians," (2 volumes, University of Nebraska Press, 1984); Colin G. Calloway; "First Peoples: A Documentary Survey of American Indian History," (Bedford/St. Martin's, 2004 second edition); Jeffrey Ostler, "The Plains Sioux and US Colonialism from Lewis and Clark to Wounded Knee," (Cambridge University Press, 2004); John S. Gray, "Custer's Last Campaign: Mitch Boyer and the Little Bighorn Reconstructed," (University of Nebraska Press, 1993 paperback); Robert M. Utley, "Frontier Regulars: The United States Army and the Indian, 1866-1891," (Macmillan Publishing, 1973); Jerome A. Greene, ed., "Lakota and Cheyenne: Indian Views of the Great Sioux War, 1876-1877," (University of Oklahoma Press, 1994).

Endnotes

1. John S. Gray, "Centennial Campaign: The Sioux War of 1876," (n.p.: The Old Army Press, 1976) p. 211.

2. Robert M. Utley, "The Lance and the Shield: The Life and Times of Sitting Bull," (Henry Holt and Company, 1993) p. 174.

3. Peter Iverson, "We Are Still Here": American Indians in the 20th Century," (Wheeling IL: Harlan Davidson, 1998) p. 19.

Session 2

Interview

Dr. Peter Maslowski

Interviewer

We're here today with Dr. Peter Maslowski. You have written a provocative piece entitled "The Three Hundred Year War."

Dr. Peter Maslowski

Yes.

Interviewer

The war against the Native Americans [was] a 300 year war. It's, for those individuals who believe a long war is, for example, Afghanistan, 300 years is incredible.

Dr. Peter Maslowski

Yes, well I took the view that historians look at the Indian Wars as just discreet, individual elements of the Seminole war, First, Second, Third Seminole wars, and the Sioux war and the war against the Apaches. I took a different view of it and looked at the whole continuum from the early 1600s through the late 1890s as one single, long war with many campaigns in it, but a single long war with the purpose for the whites to acquire dominion over the Indians so that they could acquire the Indians' territory and the bounty and resources that came with that territory. The first conflict occurred the first day that permanent English settlers arrived in the new world, which was in April of 1607. So the conflict began that day and it lasted, well all the way to the late 1800s.

Interviewer

Do you think even from the beginning that the ultimate objective of the American colonists, whether they're from England or from the Netherlands or in some cases the French, for example, do you think their ultimate objective regarding their wars with the Native Americans ever changed? Do you think it went from, for example, territorial dominance to genocidal extermination? Or do you think that was the objective from the beginning?

Dr. Peter Maslowski

There were always some whites who advocated genocide, even as the war came to an end in the late 19th century, particularly out on the frontier. There were those who advocated genocide, but I think certainly by the mid 1800s, even before that, most would settle for far less than genocide. They just wanted the Indians out of the way and the first idea was to put them in a so-called permanent Indian territory, in which case the Louisiana Purchase was a godsend because it then meant that you could remove the Indians from the fertile farmlands of the east and get them out of the way somewhere in the west. Of course, the idea of a permanent Indian territory somewhere in the Louisiana Territory, Louisiana

Purchase, breaks down with the events of the 1840s: the Mexican War, the Oregon Cession, and the discovery of gold in California. So the idea of letting the Indians have a permanent Indian territory is superseded by the idea of moving them on to little, isolated, marginal plots of land that we call reservations. So there was always that exterminationist element, but I think it was pretty quickly superseded, and the exterminationist element might have been more widespread in the early 1600s than at any time after that because in the early 1600s it was a matter of absolute survival.

Interviewer

Exactly, when we look at earlier wars against Native Americans, especially those in New England, King Phillip's War for example, that seems to be a very strong case as to why war aims might be the complete destruction of an enemy. As the United States moves west and more and more territory was incorporated into the Republic, do you think perhaps the objective of, instead of exterminating another group, . . . placing them on a reservation became more palatable to the American public?

Dr. Peter Maslowski

Oh sure, yes, and there is always a split between those who are on what we call the frontier, who are in direct contact with the Native Americans or directly threatened by them, and the east.

Interviewer

So proximity to the Native Americans –

Dr. Peter Maslowski

The proximity, oftentimes I think, hardened attitudes and made them more likely to embrace an exterminationist policy and that's why so many of the frontier battles actually end up being massacres, and oftentimes, of friendly Indians because they didn't care if they were friendly or hostile, they just wanted the Indians to be dead. I think that that's a minority sentiment within the nation as a whole by, I don't know and I'd hate to put a date on it, but certainly by the mid-1800s and probably earlier than that.

Interviewer

It's interesting to note that removal, especially the removal of the . . . Cherokee, . . . was accomplished as a military operation. It wasn't voluntary, it was a military operation. It was a forced removal. It's not a war, but it's very much a military operation. When you look at the Trail of Tears and the removal of the Cherokee from the east to Indian Territory, how do you think that affected the military's doctrine? Do you think that had any doctrinal affect at all given the congressional emphasis on Indian removal later on as well?

Dr. Peter Maslowski

No, I don't think it had much influence on doctrine. It was just a distasteful duty. I don't think that the United States Army embraced that duty and if you look only at the Cherokees, of course you're misunderstanding removal, because it's all of the so-called "five civilized tribes": the Choctaws, the Chickasaws, the Seminoles, and the Cherokees. I'm missing one. I'm sorry I can't remember what the fifth one is right now. There is also removal of the Indians in the northwest. It leads, for example, to the Blackhawk war in the 1830s. So there is removal. The Cherokees might be the most famous or infamous, but they're not the only ones. It's a national policy that takes place in the southwest, southeast, and in the old northwest. I don't know that it has any affect on United States Army doctrine. I don't even know that you'd use the word doctrine in association with it.

Interviewer

[How about] policies, perhaps?

Dr. Peter Maslowski

In the 1800s, no.

Interviewer

The United States military fights a number of wars against Native Americans.

Dr. Peter Maslowski

I call them campaigns.

Interviewer

Campaigns.

Dr. Peter Maslowski

In one long war, but –

Interviewer

One long war with no—

Dr. Peter Maslowski

I accept your terminology for purposes of the question.

Interviewer

Yes, sir. It fights a number of campaigns against Native Americans. It utilizes a number of different methods against the Native Americans but when it comes down to it, do you think perhaps that one of the primary points of contention is the definition of victory? What do the Native Americans regard to be victory or an acceptable outcome versus what the United States regards to be victory with conditions for victory?

Dr. Peter Maslowski

Well, I think if you'd ask any Native American group it would have been to be left on what they considered their homelands, most of which were conquered from other Indian tribes. For example, the Sioux had this homeland that embraced the Black Hills and eastern Montana and eastern Wyoming, but they had conquered that from the Crows. If they had had their choice, they would be left alone, not bothered by the whites on their homeland and that would be true whether it was the Cherokees or the Seminoles or the Sioux or the Comanches down in the southwest. That would have been their definition of victory.

Interviewer

Do you think that that forms the way they react when they sign treaties with the United

States and then those treaties are then broken?

Dr. Peter Maslowski

Well, treaties are very complicated instruments in part because Indian tribes were so badly divided and factionalized. Usually there was no one main Indian chief although the whites in treaty negotiations would designate an Indian leader or two as the chief who can sign for the tribe. Well in fact, a Teton Sioux could not sign for a Yankton Sioux or a Brule Sioux couldn't even sign for another member of the Tetons. You know a different band of the Tetons. So to take those treaties seriously in the first place, I think, is a mistake. They're almost always fraught with fraud on the part of the whites, and oftentimes knowingly, and they're often signed by compulsion. You have additional difficulties in that being their languages are oral, ours are written. To Indians, many of the ceremonies that went on before a treaty was signed, the giving of presents and the kind words that were spoken back and forth were the key, whereas for the whites, those were all just preliminary to getting words down on paper. Oftentimes the Indians did not understand what they had signed away. Even those who had been compelled to sign didn't understand, in part because sometimes the translators were not particularly competent but oftentimes because the whites purposefully did not tell them what they had signed away.

Interviewer

You had to have someone, as a representative, to make the document legal.

Dr. Peter Maslowski

That's the white viewpoint of it, yes. Indians were far more individualistic than Americans who pride themselves on being individualistic and, even if a chief signed willingly, he had no power to compel the members of his tribe to follow that treaty. In particular, it was extraordinarily difficult in many of the Indian societies where warfare was the one true path to honor, prestige, status and wealth. It was particularly difficult for an older chief who had seen his days at war, to sign a treaty that said we're not going to fight war any more. So oftentimes you had the situation where some chiefs would sign and the whites said that obligated the whole tribe, but the whole tribe did not agree with that. Then you had chiefs who have signed and there was no way that they could compel the young warriors to obey by a treaty that decreed that they stay off the warpath. Now whites would always interpret that as the savages being duplicitous and, in essence, would use that as a justification to go ahead and seize more of their land. There may be an exception to this but I'm tempted to say that 100 percent of the treaties that were signed were facades, just strategies.

Interviewer

It's almost as if they're a series of armistices. Rather than the peace treaty, it's an armistice that neither side really fully understands the other, so from the very start it's a temporary cease fire, perhaps.

Dr. Peter Maslowski

That might be looked at. I mean that's a reasonable way of looking at it. Oftentimes the Indians were just sort of overwhelmed by the might of the wave of white settlement that came. They just basically had no choice ultimately [but] to go onto the reservation. The whole series of temporary cease fires might be one way of looking at it. I personally have never thought of it in that way, but it's a pretty interesting insight. The cease fires always—yeah, probably shouldn't use such a strong word, I'll say invariably, which leaves a little weasel room in there—worked to the benefit of the whites. The delay, since these are usually done on the cutting edge of the American empire, the cutting edge of the empires that moved westward, always worked to the advantage of whites because more whites were coming—a tidal wave of whites.

Interviewer

It wasn't just military operations either. It was an economic and environmental war against the Native Americans. Could you say that those were forces that were very actively in play, whether it is disease or the slaughter of the buffalo?

Dr. Peter Maslowski

Well, the disease was certainly crucial. In many cases it just devastated tribes long before they saw a white man. The Pequot war which is one of the first of the wars in the mid-1630s was a really brutal, nasty affair. The Pequots, even two or three years before, had probably numbered 12,000 or 13,000, but because of the devastation of disease when the war began they're probably down to certainly no more than 4,000, probably closer to 3,000. So the whites are almost invariably fighting Indian tribes that have already been demoralized in part by these losses, which are much weakened because many of the ones that have lost are warriors and leaders. So the whites are constantly going against tribes that are already in a weakened state and a disorganized state and a demoralized state. Now the Indians do quickly get caught up in the market economy and they rapidly want access to white goods like firearms, for example, and brass to make arrow points. They have to get a constant resupply of ammunition. Alcohol plays an important part in the sort of the demoralization of the Indians and the Indians get caught up in that. The decline of the buffalo begins long before the whites begin the systematic slaughter. It's sort of a commonly held belief that it's the whites who went out and slaughtered the buffalo. But that was the way that Indians got these goods and they were a matter of survival. If one tribe acquired firearms and horses—you were at a tremendous disadvantage if you were still foot bound and using war clubs. So there was an incentive then for these other tribes to kill buffalo because it was one of the things that they could trade, the hides for the items that they needed in this sort of arms race that developed. So, the decline in the buffalo herds really begins in the 1830s, and then the whites do sort of adopt it as a systematic policy [and] as a way to bring civilization. I assume you know that I don't need to put that in quotes. I mean that in a way that they, the whites meant it, to bring civilization and what better is the way to tame the West. You kill both the buffalo and therefore the Indians will no longer roam the plains and they can be more easily shunted aside onto the reservation. Some of the treaties, I'm going on too long here, but some of the treaties were very clever in that they said the Indians maintained these lands as long as they can hunt buffalo. So, you see, if you hunt the buffalo, if you kill all the buffalo, the Indians could no longer hunt them, so it then gives the justification to go in and move them onto the reservation.

Interviewer

Well, in your chapter you talk about a group loosely termed the Snakes. If you could again, the geographical area in which these Native American groups are based, what part of the United States is this?

Dr. Peter Maslowski

The sort of great interior basin of Idaho, Oregon, Washington, out in that area where the Snakes included a couple of different groups: the Paiutes, the Shoshone and the Bannocks. I believe I'm calling on a lot of memory here and we collectively called them Snakes. That was the most deadly Indian war in the West in that it killed far more people, Indians and whites combined than say, the Sioux war, including Custer. It was about two to one. The Snake War it is called.

Interviewer

So the fighting between the United States and this group known as the Snakes, the fighting that occurred there was amongst them, this was the final campaign of the 300 Year War?

Dr. Peter Maslowski

No, no, it marks the beginning of the end of the war. It's fought from 1860, really hard to tell exactly the date you want to use to start this war but it's basically 1864 to 1868 and it marks the beginning of the final campaign. That final campaign I look at is beginning in about 1865 and lasting until about 1880. So the final campaign is 15 years long and it involves not only operations against the Snakes but operations against the Sioux, operations against the Comanche, operations against the Utes and the Sheep Eaters and the Bannocks and the Apaches and there are others that I am forgetting.

Interviewer

There are many different groups and they're all grouped together as Indians?

Dr. Peter Maslowski

Yes.

Interviewer

[The war is] against this cultural sociological monolith known as –

Dr. Peter Maslowski

Racial

Interviewer

Racial monolith known as –

Dr. Peter Maslowski

No, we don't want to forget that word.

Interviewer

The Indians –

Dr. Peter Maslowski

Yes.

Interviewer

So how then did the United States define victory in the end? How was victory defined?

Dr. Peter Maslowski

First of all, let me be sure to emphasize that it's only the whites who looked at them as Indians. The Indians looked at themselves like Europeans look at themselves.

Interviewer

Sure.

Dr. Peter Maslowski

You're not necessarily a European, you're a German, or you're an Italian, or you're a Spaniard, or you're a Brit, or something. So, in almost all of the Indian languages, they referred to themselves as the people, not a people, but "the People." It's the whites who impose this racial category on them. They had no great collective sense of racial identity. There were some Pan Indians who tried to develop that sense of Pan-Indianism in a racial identity that's distinct from the whites, but it had limited success. Now I went off on that tangent and I forget what the thrust of your question was, for which I apologize.

Interviewer

Well, that actually answers the question fairly nicely. I would ask then, given that the way that the United States Army fought this 300 year long war against Native Americans –

Dr. Peter Maslowski

But it's not – I'm sorry to interrupt you, but it's not just the United States Army –

Interviewer

The United States, period?

Dr. Peter Maslowski

The Army is a specific institution and a lot of this is carried on by sort of ad hoc forces. A lot of it is carried on by state raised volunteer forces and not by the Army.

Interviewer

Not by a regular army.

Dr. Peter Maslowski

Not by the regular army. Some of it is. I don't mean to say that all of it was done without a regular army, but there are a lot of just citizen groups. Sand Creek, for example, is done by Colorado volunteers.

Interviewer

This is an excellent point. Oftentimes, regular army expeditions or campaigns were accompanied by militia or volunteers or civilians or armed groups or vigilante groups.

Dr. Peter Maslowski

Ad hoc groups.

Interviewer

Sure.

Dr. Peter Maslowski

"Ad hoc vigilante groups" is probably a good phrase for it, yes.

Interviewer

If we could pull some meaning out of this doctrinally for the United States Army itself, the Regulars, what do you think the United States Army, the Regular Army learned from this 300 year long war?

Dr. Peter Maslowski

I don't think the regular army was interested in learning much from it. There is no romance in this. There is no glory. There is not a great deal of heroism. It's nasty, grinding, persistent, ugly, difficult, torturous campaigns in which you spend a lot of time searching for the enemy and very little time ever fighting the enemy. You primarily wage war against Indian villages and resources. When you've captured an Indian village the Indians usually had scattered so you burned the village and burned their possessions and if you captured their pony herd, you slaughtered the ponies to deprive them of mobility. You waged war against their crops and their fishing weirs. There wasn't much to appeal to a regular army in this. As far as I know, the United States Army at the end of this war, like I say, beginning in the late 1880s and the early 1890s didn't look back and say well; "We're lucky to find another one of those wars again." The Indians were no longer a threat, so there was really no reason for them to necessarily think that they'd ever fight Indians again. The Indians were penned up on their reservations.

Interviewer

I was just going to ask, do you think it was kind of sort of like the United States Army took a big sigh of relief that this long, grinding, tortuous, unpopular series of campaigns was over?

Dr. Peter Maslowski

I think they were very happy to be done with it. I think almost all Army officers and just anybody in the Army was pretty happy to have this over with, particularly the leadership of the US Army. It could now get on with what it perceived as the real army purpose which was to prepare for a major war. The US Army is an institution. It always considered the Indians as a nuisance, not a long-term, serious threat to the existence of the United States. It wasn't a matter of survival for the US Army as an institution. It was a nuisance and they were happy to have the nuisance over with and now they could turn to real war, manning the fortifications that were recommended by the Endicott Board. That's one of the first things they did, was to consolidate all of those scattered posts throughout the West into fewer and fewer posts so that they could begin to conduct practice for regular war in larger units and formal tactics and so on. So I think they were very happy to have this over with, and they could get focused on what they thought was real war.

Interviewer

So the end of the war is not, as some individuals have described it, a battleship Missouri-style surrender, but rather a final and complete exhaustion of the Native American forces?

Dr. Peter Maslowski

I think that what happened in, I'll use the Sioux war as an example, which involved Custer's last stand. I think by the spring of 1877 the Indians were so depleted and so demoralized that the interests of the whites and the Native Americans, say the Sioux in this case, had converged, and the Sioux decided that they would rather live than die. Consequently they accepted the reservation as preferable to being hunted like wild beasts, as preferable to watching women and children and old folks suffer. They wanted a place where they could sleep soundly at night without having to go to bed thinking, well, is an army going to attack in the morning? The only place they could do that anymore was on the reservation. At the same time I think that converged with white interests, particularly those who were not of the exterminationist bent. They were, by that time, the vast majority who were happy to stop killing Indians and just wanted them warehoused somewhere out of the way. I think that's probably an accurate phrase, just warehouse them out in some isolated, marginal piece of land. So the two interests had converged. The Indians had decided they preferred to live and the whites who were happy to have them out of the way where they no longer presented any threat to any white interest and allowed the whites to dominate the vast amount of arable land and the vast amount of resources in the continental United States.

Interviewer

Thank you very much, sir.

Session 2
Final Campaign of the Mexican-American War:
Winfield Scott's Capture of Mexico City and Difficulties with Guerrillas

by

Dr. Joseph "Chip" Dawson

Introduction

Fighting against Mexico for more than a year, forces of the United States needed to conduct multiple campaigns to terminate the war. One required conventional operations against the Mexican Army, leading to the capture of Mexico City, that nation's capital. The other involved months of unanticipated guerrilla warfare.

Festering disagreements pushed America and Mexico to war in May of 1846. Mexicans expected their army to defend their nation and regain the disputed province of Texas. To take parts of northern Mexico, American President James K. Polk ordered US Army units and new volunteer regiments to conduct several attacks. By December of 1846 Americans had seized New Mexico and California. To Polk's surprise and despite the outcome of those campaigns, Mexico's leaders vowed to fight on.

Consequently, Polk designed another campaign intended to end the war on favorable terms to the United States. Although the war's previous American campaigns had been risky due to long marches and logistics problems, the capstone campaign was the riskiest of all. Assembling an invasion force of around 14,000 men of regulars, volunteers, and forces of the Marines, Polk ordered Major General Winfield Scott, Commanding General of the Army, to capture Veracruz which was Mexico's primary port on the Gulf of Mexico. If capturing Veracruz did not bring negotiations, Polk authorized Scott to march inland until negotiations concluded, even if that meant taking Mexico City, 250 miles from Veracruz. Scott landed on 9 March 1847 and captured Veracruz on 29 March. No negotiations resulted and on 8 April, Scott began his campaign into the Mexican heartland.

To increase his chances for success, Scott limited alienating Mexican civilians. He depended on civilians for supplies and paid for food and animals. At the same time Scott set up military courts to put American Troops on trial if they were charged with crimes against Mexicans. Scott's plan was surprisingly effective and many Mexicans cooperated with the invading army.

Depending on aggressive American units and officers, Scott developed a winning formula in several battles. Staff engineers, including Lieutenants P. G. T. Beauregard and George McClellan, evaluated the Mexican defensive positions. Scott designed his operations to outflank the defenses and turn the Mexicans out of their entrenchments. A major battle at Cerro Gordo resulted in high casualties among the Mexicans and modest American losses and in part due to disease, Scott's forces steadily lost strength. Yielding the city of Puebla, Mexico's leader, General Antonio López de Santa Anna, retreated with his army to the capital.

Final Campaign

Mexicans expected Scott to take a direct route into Mexico City from the east and Santa Anna had devised his strongest defenses there. Hindered by marshy terrain and lakes outside of the city, the Americans again conducted careful reconnaissance. Over 30,000 Mexican Troops defended the capital but Scott's staff probed the defenses for vulnerabilities.

Avoiding the eastern fortifications, Scott began testing the substantial southern defenses on 18 August, leading to several battles. At Churubusco, Mexican units, including the "San Patricio Battalion" composed of American deserters, offered exceptional resistance. Scott's military engineers, especially Captain Robert E. Lee, found trails to move troops through a lava bed ("el Pedrégal"), rough terrain that Mexicans had decided an army could not cross. Taking advantage of miscommunication between Santa Anna and his subordinate commanders near San Gerónimo, Americans escaped a cul-de-sac and continued attacking. More combat at San Angel and Contreras (Padierna) pushed the Mexicans back. Losses of nearly 1,000 American casualties in these engagements drained manpower from Scott's Army and convinced him to try diplomacy.

On 24 August, a ceasefire allowed the two armies to stand down during negotiations. Two weeks later, the Mexicans had not agreed to terms with the US State Department's Special Envoy, Nicolas Trist, whom Polk assigned to negotiate a treaty. Therefore, more battles resulted to decide the fate of Mexico City, either producing an American retreat or Mexican capitulation.

Santa Anna was unable to equally protect all avenues into the capital and some of his forts on the west were undermanned. One of the key elements of the Mexican defenses was Molino del Rey ("the King's Mill"). Some reports indicated it was the site where the Mexicans manufactured cannons. Spearheading the American assault on 8 September, troops from the division of Brigadier General William J. Worth carried the position only after multiple attacks resulted in heavy casualties on both sides. The Molino contained no cannon making equipment.

After viewing the western defenses, some of Scott's staff and top subordinates advocated pushing ahead from the south. Others, notably Lieutenant Beauregard, pointed to potential advantages in the west. Scott settled the matter by stating; "Gentlemen, we will attack by the western gates!"

Scott's decision meant that his troops were going to assault Chapultepec, the castle-like buildings of the Mexican Military College, where a few young cadets still manned the walls alongside other infantrymen. Chapultepec appeared so strong that the Americans should have bypassed it. Well sited cannon emplacements looked across supporting fields of fire but Santa Anna was unable to allocate enough troops to completely fill all of Chapultepec's defenses. The castle also assumed a potential psychological significance for both sides. By holding it, the Mexican defenders might inspire their comrades elsewhere but the fall of the castle could undercut Mexican morale and lift American *esprit de corps*. On 12 September, Scott ordered all kinds of units: regulars, US Marines, and volunteers, to join in the assault. American artillery batteries directed a sustained barrage prior to the infantry battle lines closing on the objective. Two hours later the flag of the United States flew atop Chapultepec but hundreds more Americans had been killed and wounded.

Naturally, America's capture of Chapultepec dismayed some Mexican troops but others were determined to stand fast at the Belén Gate and the San Cosme Gate, the main western "garitas" into the capital. Demonstrating one of the many examples of rivalry and ill will between America's volunteers and regulars, Volunteer Brigadier General John A. Quitman decided he must strike at the Belén Gate before Scott forestalled the attack and picked a regular outfit to win the honor. Quitman's infantry division also opened its assault before Scott learned if capturing Chapultepec would deliver Santa Anna to the peace table. While Quitman's volunteers leveled their bayonets at Belén, General Worth prepared his division to attack San Cosme. The generals gave directions but in many instances determined leadership of American junior officers (for example, Captain Ulysses S. Grant and Lieutenant Daniel H. Hill) inspired enlisted men to follow through with Scott's plans.

By nightfall of 13 September, the Americans had broken through the gates and entered Mexico City. Scott demanded the capital's surrender. Santa Anna's defenses and his troops had not held the Americans at bay or turned them back. Deciding to retreat, he opened the capital to the invaders instead of ordering his troops to resist street by street. Such urban warfare would have been likely to produce considerable destruction and civilian casualties. The next day, Scott and his staff, along with several regiments, flooded into city. Their arrival culminated an extraordinary campaign.

Terminating the War and Dealing with Guerrillas

Sometimes appearances are deceiving. Most Americans believed that capturing Mexico City would end the war. Frustrating the Americans and causing more United States and Mexican casualties, the Mexicans shifted to guerrilla warfare. This shift sent American conventional units and officers into action against Mexican irregulars. As guerrilla activities extended over a wide area, General Scott and his subordinates needed to administer an extensive military government. Mexican officials granted commissions to guerrillas who challenged America's military occupation.

Scott's military government focused on Mexico City but reached 250 miles back to Veracruz, along the National Road, the vital communications link to the coast. United States troops acted as police in the capital and other cities, conducted mounted patrols, and guarded wagon trains. Obtaining reinforcements from the United States, the American Army (regulars and volunteers) became the arbiters for operating businesses, conducting local elections, and protecting churches. Scott designated one of his volunteer generals, John Quitman, to become military governor in the capital. US Army courts adjudicated the cases of American military personnel charged with serious crimes. These steps contributed to American dominance over major cities and kept open major roads between them. The occupiers needed to remain in place until a treaty concluded the war. At the same time, American forces also occupied the provinces of New Mexico and California, as well as locations below the Rio Grande. Soon enough, President Polk recognized that the regulars and volunteers forming his army were not numerous enough to occupy or annex "All Mexico" as some Americans advocated.

From September of 1847 to February of 1848, nationalistic Mexican guerrillas threatened America's occupying army. Guerrillas particularly preyed on poorly protected supply trains or weak patrols. In response, Americans placed heavy guards on convoys and strengthened units riding on roadways. Creating more trouble, bandits, without commissions and under no official command, accosted merchants and troops. Enduring harassment and suffering casualties, the Americans kept major roads open and never surrendered one of their depots.

During January and February of 1848, American and Mexican negotiators held diplomatic discussions and drafted a treaty. State Department Representative Nicholas Trist gained all of President Polk's war aims: Mexico recognized Texas as an American State and gave up the provinces of California and New Mexico while America paid an indemnity to the Mexican government. After both governments ratified the Treaty of Guadalupe Hidalgo in March, diplomats announced that they had arranged for Mexico City to return to local control in the summer and that the American Army was planning to evacuate. By August America's remaining units left Mexico.

Results of the War

At the operational and tactical levels, a number of important points became evident by the summer of 1848. For example, multiple American field forces completed extensive overland marches before going into battle against the Mexicans. Instead of sustaining logistical connections with the United States, Americans bought food and other necessities from Mexicans. In the future, the forces of the United States could not rely on obtaining supplies in enemy countries.

Regarding generalship, America's senior Regular Army commanders Zachary Taylor, Winfield Scott, and Stephen Kearny, achieved a creditable record. Americans effusively praised all three but Scott's leadership and management can be rated as superior to the others. Taylor seemed more intuitive and less attentive to details of operating an army. Nevertheless, in his first engagements, Taylor led mostly regular regiments against some of Mexico's best regular units. In urban combat at Monterrey and at the Battle of Buena Vista, Taylor manipulated an unwieldy combination of volunteers and regulars to win hard-fought victories, the second against Santa Anna himself. Kearny led an expedition consisting mostly of volunteers to control the province of New Mexico and then marched to California. There he balanced the interests of regulars, volunteers, and the Navy, fought the Mexicans, and emerged victorious. Scott was fortunate to conduct an unopposed amphibious landing near Veracruz and his use of turning movements on the 250 mile march from the Gulf to the edge of Mexico City could have resulted in a treaty. Instead, he maneuvered his army to seize the capital. Scott also had to work effectively with the US Navy, something that Taylor did not face. His campaign in Mexico's heartland deservedly became the object of study by military students and officers.

Wartime behavior and accomplishments of the Army's junior officers gained the respect and admiration of Americans. Captains and lieutenants of regulars, especially engineers, artillery, and infantry, all demonstrated their capabilities. Many of those officers were graduates of the Military Academy at West Point and their conduct boosted the Academy's reputation.

On the other hand, the actions of America's volunteer officers and troops of other ranks created controversies. President Polk seized the wartime opportunity to appoint only men from his Democrat Party to become volunteer generals. Some of them were effective but most of them lacked military experience and their performance on campaign varied from poor to mediocre. Volunteer officers frequently engaged in disputes with regular army officers over military matters large and small. If they decided that haughty regulars failed to give them recognition or accolades, volunteer officers were particularly insulted and responded antagonistically. The regulars denigrated the volunteers, castigating them for their lack of discipline in camp, on road marches, and on the battlefield. By harming Mexico's unprotected civilians and damaging their property, volunteers aggravated relations with the Mexican populace.

Perhaps the most unappreciated aspects of the United States-Mexican War were the necessity of establishing American military governments and engaging in widespread actions against guerrillas. Annexing California and New Mexico into the United States required the army to administer those territories. California was under army supervision from its capture until statehood in 1850. Most Americans discounted occupying Mexico's heartland. The Army's occupation of Mexico City, Veracruz, and other cities–necessary until diplomats negotiated a treaty–appeared to be a temporary distraction, not an example of probable postwar duties in the future. Clearly, the Americans' outlook and training focused on conventional war or battle with the enemy's uniformed army. Americans usually separated combat against irregulars and Native American tribes from war against European-style opponents, often labeling combat against guerrillas as less than honorable and something to be avoided if at all possible. Reaching those conclusions, Americans put aside the relevance of guerrilla warfare and military government.

Even after they believed that they had been victorious and brought the Mexican War to a decisive conclusion, the United States met unexpected challenges. On an ad hoc basis, Americans created military governments in New Mexico, California, and Central Mexico. Likewise, they engaged in combat against Mexican guerrillas without formal doctrine. Writing such doctrine would not become routine until the 20th century but the termination of the United States-Mexican War shows that America became involved with intricate matters of civil-military relations early in its national history.

Recommended Reading

Addressing the causes is David M. Pletcher, "The Diplomacy of Annexation: Texas, Oregon, and the Mexican War," (Columbia: University of Missouri Press, 1973). Excellent evaluations of the conventional war, military government, and the guerrilla phase are in Timothy D. Johnson, *A* "*Gallant Little Army: The Mexico City Campaign*," (Lawrence: University Press of Kansas, 2007). An important study of the guerrillas is Irving W. Levinson, "Wars within War: Mexican Guerrillas, Domestic Elites, and the United States of America, 1846-1848," (Fort Worth, Tex.: Texas Christian University Press, 2005), while William A. DePalo, Jr., "The Mexican National Army," (College Station: Texas A&M University Press, 1997) analyzes the conventional army. Mexican veterans' views are in Ramón Alcaraz, "The Other Side, or Notes for the History of the War," (1850; reprinted,

New York: Burt Franklin, 1970). A substantive overview is K. Jack Bauer, "The Mexican War, 1846-1848," (1974; reprinted, Lincoln: University of Nebraska Press, 1992). Scott's personal account is "Memoirs of Lieut. General Scott," (New York: Sheldon & Co., 1864). Paul Foos, "A Short, Offhand Killing Affair: Troops and Social Conflict during the Mexican-American War," (Chapel Hill: University of North Carolina Press, 2002) stigmatizes faults of America's volunteers. Additional analysis of volunteers and regulars is Richard B. Winders, "Mr. Polk's Army: The American Military Experience in the Mexican War," (College Station: Texas A&M University Press, 1997). Examples of accounts by United States officers are T. Harry Williams, ed., "With Beauregard in Mexico," (Baton Rouge: Louisiana State University Press, 1956), and Thomas W. Cutrer, ed., "The Mexican War Diary and Correspondence of George B. McClellan," (Baton Rouge: Louisiana State University Press, 2009).

Session 2

Interview

Dr. Joseph "Chip" Dawson

Interviewer

We're here today with Dr. Joseph Dawson who is speaking about the Mexican-American War. One of the goals of the TRADOC Conference is to determine how wars end and to look at all the different factors that play into the diplomatic and military functions of a peace treaty or armistice. When considering the peace treaty that concluded the Mexican-American War, what would you say is the most important factor, or factors, to consider?

Dr. Joseph Dawson

Well, [key to] the overwhelming United States military victory was that the capture of Mexico City played an extremely important part. It was very convincing to many in Mexico that there was no longer a purpose in continuing a conventional military resistance. So that led to the decision on the part of a number of former members of the Cabinet, the Congress, that the Americans would be susceptible to a guerrilla campaign. That began just a matter of days after the United States forces occupied Mexico City. Plus, the forces were very weak, 6,700 capable men. Others were sick or wounded, or whatever the case might be, not really available for service. The Mexicans, while they were dealing with the problems of their outright military defeat, thought that the Americans could be vulnerable. Winfield Scott had already put in requests for additional troops. Reinforcements were soon on their way, but whether or not the Americans could be pushed out or persuaded out, whether or not there was any chance on the part of the Mexicans to reassert any control in central Mexico, if it wasn't going to be by conventional means, they were going to try guerrilla means. It became clear that General Scott, for the Americans, had organized a military government, had begun a systematic set of responses to the guerrillas. Really, within a month or so, most of the Mexicans realized that the guerrilla war option was not going to be a deciding factor. It could be a penalizing factor. The Americans were going to be penalized and suffer for it, but Scott made it plain he was going to maintain the occupation until the negotiations were complete.

Interviewer

So, therefore, war, especially in conventional war, although it may be brought to a successful conclusion against a conventional foe, that's no guarantee that the peace treaties will necessarily be observed by combatants.

Dr. Joseph Dawson

That's right. So for some weeks after Scott's successful campaign, really no Mexican authorities wanted to step forward to assume the responsibility for the negotiations. It wasn't until some weeks later that it was evident that the Americans, by all appearances, were willing to stay as a supervising, really comprehensive occupying power, comprehensive to deal with virtually every aspect of Mexican life. That convinced some of the Mexicans to conclude: we've got to begin some negotiations, at least discussions, in a preliminary fashion, what terms can we have, what's it going to take for the United States forces to leave.

Interviewer

That's an excellent point. How do you conclude a peace when the opposing government, the United States' foe, no longer exists?

Dr. Joseph Dawson

Well, there were several leaders in the Mexican Congress who were prominent enough, including one who had been chief justice of the Mexican Supreme Court. Within a few weeks time, enough of his own backers realized that he was probably the single most prominent authority figure in the old government. Once it was evident they weren't going to have General Antonio Lopez de Santa Anna return, yet again, having been previously president more than once, the Mexicans had to have someone step in and provide representation for the country.

Interviewer

The Mexicans, having realized that at that point, recognized that a guerrilla war wouldn't necessarily meet their national objectives.

Dr. Joseph Dawson

Right.

Interviewer

Would you say that the Americans' objectives going into the war and then their goals during the peace process, would you say that they had changed between the start and the conclusion of the war?

Dr. Joseph Dawson

The only changes came in the amount of military force that the United States would apply. So the goals were to secure Texas as a state in the union, which had already gone through a sequence of steps to make it official, the annexation process. Part of the reason for the war getting underway is that Mexico refused to recognize that annexation and still claimed Texas as a part of Mexico. So that the next obvious goal that President Polk had enunciated was to initiate a purchase arrangement with Mexico for California and probably New Mexico. The Mexican leadership really united otherwise fractured Mexican politicians who could agree on the idea that Mexico would not make a sale of that kind. The difficulty was that many new Mexican officials then also realized that their army was thin, widely spread, probably not as capable as it should have been. But all of that needed to look back a couple of years, improved recruiting, improved training, so that if there was a war with the United States, the army would be improved. Supposedly, it enlisted 30,000 men. The United States had about 8,000. So on the official count, Mexico should have been in much better shape than it was. That didn't turn out to be the case once the war was underway. Obviously, Mexico was seriously deficient in the amount of forces allocated to Santa Fe, New Mexico, and to California.

Interviewer

So the conditions, then, for peace in the United States was for the US to secure Texas as well as potentially purchase additional territory. Whereas, for the Mexicans, victory, or at least a peace that would be acceptable, meant the least amount of loss of territory and state power as possible.

Dr. Joseph Dawson

Yes, so from Mexico's point of view, that's a very good question. From their point of view, this uniting of political factions was in agreement that a defense of the nation was the goal. The aim was not to lose any territory, any of the northern provinces. Then the more difficult matter of trying to regain control of Texas, which practically had been independent for almost 10 years. So, the Mexicans were providing themselves a number of really significant challenges: regaining control of Texas, defending New Mexico with the nucleus being Santa Fe as the capital of the province, and defending California. It just proved to be impossible for them to do with the military force they had on hand. So from President Polk's point of view, he expected to apply a modest amount of military force, keep the prospect of some sort of a purchase involved in opening negotiations and bring the war to an end as soon as possible. So that by a partial application of force, Mexico would realize it could not maintain a Long-term war and Mexico would concede. It would give up the land that President Polk announced that the United States wanted to possess.

Interviewer

So a very important question at the end of the Mexican-American War, why didn't the United States just simply annex all of Mexico?

Dr. Joseph Dawson

There was a very strong movement to do so. It was a difficult pursuit for the US population and US politicians, whether national politicians and Congress in Washington, DC, or state politicians. This was based partly on the notion that sooner or later the United States would control all of North America including British Canada. So, now, it seemed 1847, 1848, to them, it seemed to be the perfect time. For a while, probably not much more than three or four months, President Polk tinkered with this notion. Very soon, he was forced to the realization that the United States just did not have enough military forces on hand. He called on several of the states to bring volunteers forward, but not enough soldiers materialized to occupy all of northern Mexico, maintain control in California, maintain control in New Mexico, and to occupy central Mexico, much less to go much south of Mexico City. In other words, the military forces just weren't there to gain dominance over the entire Mexican nation.

Interviewer

So rather than keep the entire pie, the Americans kept to their original objectives. Either way, it was a victory because of the territorial concessions of the Mexicans.

Dr. Joseph Dawson

That's right.

Interviewer

Why would a student of history, a student of military history especially, or a soldier, be interested in the conclusion of the Mexican-American War? What about the conclusion of the war is especially applicable in this period of time, in 2010?

Dr. Joseph Dawson

[There are] a couple of different ways to approach that. First, the longstanding expectation is that the United States Army will be a conventional, effective force first. As it turned out, that's what General Scott deployed to Mexico and that's what produced the apparent end result of the war. In other words, the United States didn't divide, having some units conventional and some units under territorial control or Indian fighters, or whatever. All the conventional—even the volunteers were supposedly, presumably, trained in some way to stand with the regulars in a conventional format. So there are any numbers of potential applications in the 21st century for conventional warfare. The difference comes, I think, in the war with Mexico, that many of the American officers saw conventional war as their purpose. They didn't like guerrilla warfare. It wasn't appealing. And dealing with any sort of unofficial, irregular, unconventional, guerrilla fighters, also, was unappealing and, many of American officers decided, a dishonorable way to fight. So, it was not something that they would acknowledge that whether a seven- or eight-month guerrilla campaign in Mexico was something that was tiresome and troublesome, distressing, quite challenging. Some units were nearly cut off. Even in the city of Pueblo, they were surrounded and reinforcements had no access for days. These were all unconventional guerrilla fighters. So that even with these kinds of examples, by the time the war was over, American officers from the senior levels all the way through to the captains and lieutenants, they didn't want any further part of that in the future. It demonstrates to students of history and officers today that conditions can change. They can change unexpectedly. They can shift even away from what had been the apparent direction of the conflict and, within a very short time, produces a different kind of circumstance, a different kind of challenge for them.

Interviewer

The war you start might not necessarily be the war you finish.

Dr. Joseph Dawson

That's right.

Interviewer

Excellent point, one more question, then, relating to doctrine. How do you think that the Mexican-American War affected American war fighting doctrine, especially post-Mexican-American War? Many of the individuals who reached prominent positions in the Civil War received their first experience in the Mexican-American War. How do you think that their experience affected American military doctrine?

Dr. Joseph Dawson

Well, the approach, especially of how officers expect to lead soldiers in tactical combat conditions, the basic level of war, to be participants in a larger operational effort, this conventional outlook permeated the army. None of that was expected to change. Most soldiers didn't want it to change. So the experiences they had, either on the conventional battlefield or on patrol, guarding convoys, protecting a city that was under occupation, none of those things brought the individuals themselves or the War Department back in Washington to come to the realization that perhaps some units could be designated as territorial patrol or guerrilla fighters. This has been, I think, something that wasn't going to detain or bother or cause any doubt to most American officers. There were always a few who saw unconventional or irregular war as somehow a break with tradition, a break of a pattern, and they wanted to be different. That's a tiny minority. Otherwise, the bulk of the army is going to remain focused on conventional fighting. So if there's a difference or an outlook in expectation that also may have a potential connection with early 21st century, it was the shift in weaponry for officers who were veterans of the war with Mexico and became, in some way, once again, assigned to combat in the Civil War because the weapons in Mexico became outdated by the new weapons, shoulder weapons for soldiers to carry, which had a long potential killing range, extended two or three hundred yards, depending on the skill and capability of the soldiers' had in them. Some officers found their experience in the Mexican War to be seriously in doubt, because they could go within less than 100 yards of the Mexican infantry and expect probably not to have any serious casualties. So, in the Civil War, they found that they could come under fire two or three hundred yards away instead of 50 or 60 yards away. But that's more at the tactical level rather than a War Department doctrinal decision.

Interviewer

Do you think it would be fair to say that although the United States military has extensive experience fighting conventional wars that, often times, after peace has been obtained through treaty or by defeat of the enemy's conventional forces, that it is logical to expect some form of dimension of civil protest or resistance, whether it's groups not recognizing the peace treaty or continuing the fight through guerrilla warfare?

Dr. Joseph Dawson

Much of that may depend with using the war with Mexico as an example. Of the attachment of individual groups and distance from the national capital, or in some other way, distance from influence, national influence, in California in particular, there were a number of California separatists who were almost glad the United States arrived because that would put those separatists out from under Mexico City at least. So, instead of protesting against the US occupation of Mexico, some of them were actually in favor of trying a drastic departure, to be sure, but it was going to be a departure from previous neglect, inadequate funding, and sometimes thoughtless administrators sent from Mexico City to supervise California. So the closer to Mexico City, the closer the supervision was and the more likely opposition was going to be. That's why the guerrilla fighting was most intense between the Gulf of Mexico, the city of Veracruz and the National Road to Mexico City. That's where the strongest opposition was, either violent opposition or, in some cases, simply trying to not sell food or horses or some other kinds of supplies that the United States forces needed simply by withholding that potential supply to the invader. A Mexican could, in a sense, show their opposition to the American occupation of the nation.

Interviewer

Well, thank you very much.

Dr. Joseph Dawson

You're welcome.

Session 2

Termination of the Civil War

by

Dr. Joseph T. Glatthaar

Lieutenant General Ulysses S. Grant had been waiting a long time to launch a critical turning movement. Since mid-June 1864, his Army of the Potomac and Army of the James had besieged the Confederate forces outside Petersburg and Richmond, Virginia. With each passing month, Grant had extended his lines to the northeast and west, attempting to sever rail connections and choke off supplies to the Confederates. By late March 1865, after the arrival of Major General Philip Sheridan and his massive cavalry command, Grant was now ready to swing well to the west and compel Confederate troops to abandon the cities or suffer capture.

Once warfare had settled into a siege below Petersburg, Confederate General Robert E. Lee knew he was in trouble. In the face of overwhelming Union manpower and resources, it was simply a matter of time before the Army of Northern Virginia would have to abandon both Petersburg and the capital city and industrial center, Richmond, unless Lee could somehow break the siege. He tried detaching a corps under Lieutenant General Jubal Early and sending it north. For a time, Early raised a panic by routing various Union commands and actually approaching to the outskirts of the Union capital, Washington, DC. Eventually though, Sheridan's cavalry and supporting infantry crushed Early's forces at the battles of Winchester and Cedar Creek, dashing Lee's best hope of lifting the siege. After mid-October, Lee could only try to prevent Union efforts at cutting the railroads into Petersburg and Richmond and seek a mistake that would allow him to deliver a powerful blow against Grant's columns.

Throughout the siege, Lee employed his own cavalry skillfully, using their mobility to block Federal efforts to extend their lines and interrupt rail lines until Confederate infantry could arrive to bolster the defense. Yet, with every Union effort, Grant lengthened his own lines as well as Lee's, slowing down the arrival of supplies and compelling Lee to stretch his defenses thinner and to live on less and less. That winter, troops in Lee's army seldom ate more than 900 calories per day, a diet so inadequate that Troops lacked proper vitamins and minerals to digest the meager rations they consumed. As hopelessness set in, desertions soared to an average of 100 men per day. By February 1865, conditions had declined so badly that Lee warned Confederate President Jefferson Davis that he might not be able to hold on much longer. Through deserters and prisoners, Grant was fully aware of Lee's predicament.

For his grand turning movement, Grant invited President Abraham Lincoln to visit the Army around Petersburg. No one had borne such a unique and heavy burden as the President of the United States. Hundreds of thousands of dead Troops and hundreds of thousands more wounded had weighed heavily on Lincoln. After four years of stress and frustration, the end was near and Grant wanted Lincoln there to enjoy the moment.

On 25 March, hours after Lincoln arrived at City Point, Lee attacked Union troops east of Petersburg at Fort Stedman. The Confederate commander hoped the blow would force the Federals to pull back, enabling his army to steal a march westward. The only Confederate chance in the East rested in the hope that his Army of Northern Virginia could escape, march south, and merge with General Joseph E. Johnston's small army in North Carolina.

For this critical task, Lee assigned his aggressive Corps Commander, Lieutenant General John B. Gordon. Gordon planned carefully. He chose the area around the Union's Fort Stedman, along the eastern part of the line as his target. Gordon directed small parties to penetrate Union defenses, silencing Yankee pickets and opening small gaps in the obstructions. Additional troops would cut larger openings in the Union works through which his troops would attack. All this would occur in the dark so that by dawn when the bulk of the Federal army awoke, Confederates had already breached the line. Lee authorized an attacking force of well over 11,000 troops, with an additional 8,000 in reserve. Lee also prepared a cavalry division to exploit the breakthrough.

Initial reports of the predawn attack were favorable but by sunrise, Gordon's assault had failed. Stout resistance, interlocking fields of fire, and the general strength and depth of Union lines proved too difficult for Confederate troops to overcome. The plan failed, costing Lee some 2,700 men while inflicting 1,000 casualties.

The huge Confederate buildup along the eastern part of the line meant that the Confederate west flank had been weakened and Grant intended to exploit the opportunity. Two Union corps overran enemy picket lines, giving them valuable terrain from which to assault Confederate lines. Four days later, Union forces launched a powerful turning movement around Lee's right flank, threatening the Southside Railroad. Lee responded by detaching infantry and cavalry under Major General George Pickett and Major General Fitz Lee. As Sheridan's horsemen passed through Dinwiddie Court House, they encountered sharp resistance. Superior Confederate strength compelled Sheridan to fall back into a defensive position.

That night, Grant ordered the Union Fifth Corps under Major General Gouverneur K. Warren, the nearest infantry command at six miles away, to march to Sheridan's support. Warren and his corps had a reputation for slowness and Grant authorized Sheridan to remove the corps commander if Sheridan felt it was necessary. The cumbersome Union command structure, with Warren reporting to Major General George G. Meade and Sheridan communicating directly with Grant, delayed the coordination and muddy roads and swollen streams impeded progress of reinforcements. Still, Warren's movements lacked the urgency that a campaign to turn Confederates out of Petersburg and Richmond and capture or crush Lee's entire army warranted. Sheridan hoped for a dawn attack, yet two divisions of the 5th Corps had just begun to march at that time. Early on 1 April, Pickett detected the movement and withdrew to Five Forks, a valued crossroad, and fortified a position near White Oak Road, the east-west thoroughfare. The next morning Sheridan located the Confederate lines and formulated a simple plan. His cavalry would fix the enemy while Warren's men would strike and turn the Confederate eastern flank. By the time Union infantry columns were finally ready to attack after 4 p.m., Pickett had assumed no major fighting would take place and was far to the rear, enjoying baked shad with Fitz Lee and Brigadier General Thomas Rosser. He had left no one in charge. Hearing distant gunfire, he responded only slowly. Warren's men bulled their way into Pickett's rear, and without someone to direct the fight, Confederates failed to coordinate effectively and suffered a disastrous rout. The Army of Northern Virginia lost more than 3,000 casualties, most of them as prisoners. Lee rushed reinforcements out to protect the remnants of Pickett's columns and began planning his army's retreat. A few days later, he ordered Pickett relieved from the Army of Northern Virginia.

The Union victor too lost his job that day. Sheridan felt Warren had not pushed his men hard enough and removed him from command. No longer would officers like Grant and Sheridan tolerate delays and excuses. They demanded aggressiveness.[1]

The next day at 4 a.m., Grant followed up the success at Five Forks with an assault all along the line. From the picket areas Federals had seized a week earlier, Union forces crashed through the Rebel works. Confederate 3d Corps commander Lieutenant General Ambrose Powell Hill tried to rally his men, when a bullet struck him down. A mile and a half to the northeast at Fort Gregg, Confederates fought desperately against white and black troops. When they exhausted their ammunition, troops employed rocks, clubs, and bayonets to keep back the blue tide. Nothing worked. Lee tried to inspire and direct his men in the early afternoon and in the course of the fight, he exposed himself to a "most terrific fire from the enemy light batteries." Somehow, he escaped uninjured but his personal intervention accomplished nothing. Federals had crushed his line and secured control of the Southside Railroad. Late that night, Lee ordered the Confederate defenders to abandon Richmond and Petersburg.[2]

Amid the glow of burning tobacco warehouses and the periodic explosion of ignited ammunition and arms that the Confederacy could not carry, Lee's men abandoned the two cities along four different routes. Some troops had to cross to the north side of the Appomattox River to make their escape while others were already on the north side. Lee hoped to consolidate his forces around Amelia Court House, which would require his entire army to cross to the south side of the Appomattox River. From there they would attempt to join Johnson's army in North Carolina.

Grant directed Sheridan to take charge of pursuit leading cavalry and several infantry corps. He instructed Sheridan to advance along the south side of the Appomattox. Lee's men would have to cross over to them to escape and they could prevent the crossing. Lee, moreover, had a 12 hour jump on the Federals. After all the recent rain, Sheridan's men would make better time moving along roads that Lee's men had not churned into mud baths.

Most troops in the Army of Northern Virginia knew the end was fast approaching. For some days, they had expended excessive amounts of ammunition in battle rather than risk their own lives. No one wanted to be killed or wounded in the closing moments of a war. Somehow, against all hope, a few clung to some miracle that Lee or God would save them and the Confederacy. "I must not despair," a Louisiana private scribbled in his diary. "Lee will bring order out of chaos and with the help of our Heavenly Father, all will be well."[3]

Although Lee may have wanted to abandon Richmond and Petersburg sooner, he could not do so. His animals were too weak and too few in number to chance a retreat. This time, he had no choice and the reduced numbers and strength of his animals, on top of the poor conditions of the roads, slowed the advance painfully and made each day's march more difficult.[4]

His beloved Troops fared disastrously on the retreat. Perhaps 60,000 left on the retreat but that was a ghost number. Prolonged inadequate diet had resulted in a breakdown of muscle mass, preventing thousands from keeping up over the next few days. Unlike previous campaigns where Troops purposely straggled, many just could not keep up on this march. In a telling assessment, Dr. J.W. Powell, Medical Director for the 3d Corps, reported two months earlier; "While there was not found much absolute sickness existing, there were many weak and feeble men, who cannot be relied upon to undergo any great physical exertions." Thousands dropped out of the retreat, some falling into Yankee hands and others working their way toward home.[5]

At Amelia Court House, close to 50 miles from Richmond and Petersburg, Lee's hungry army arrived on the morning of 4 April. Several weeks earlier, Lee had pre-positioned ammunition and, he thought, food and fodder there. Upon their arrival, everyone was dismayed to discover nothing to eat. Lee's troops had to spend the day hunting up food and forage with limited success. Meanwhile, Lieutenant General Richard S. Ewell, the commander of the Department of Richmond, had picked up a division of Lee's men and moved with his own troops from Richmond toward Amelia Court House. When he reached the Appomattox River, no pontoon bridge awaited him, and his command had to trudge southward and plank the Richmond & Danville Railroad Bridge to cross. His supply wagons, however, took what he thought would be a safer route, only to fall into the hands of Union troops. Another Confederate division would go without food that day.[6]

This delay to forage gave Sheridan a chance to strike part of Lee's Army at Saylor's Creek on 6 April. Union troops occupied Jetersville, which blocked Lee's route to Burkeville. Instead, Lee swung around toward Farmville, where supplies in Burkeville could reach his dwindling army by rail and he could then head south to link with Johnston's command in North Carolina. Harassment from Union cavalry slowed Lieutenant General Richard H. Anderson's columns along with Ewell's troops and Gordon's Corps and they lost contact with Lieutenant General James Longstreet's 1st Corps ahead of them. Ewell directed the supply train along a safer route to the north and Gordon, with his command, followed it. Farther south, Anderson and Ewell took defensive positions but a combination of Sheridan's cavalry and Major General Horatio Wright's 6th Corps enveloped both Confederate flanks and utterly crushed them. Ewell stayed behind trying to rally his whipped men and fell into Union hands. Some 6,000 Troops in Lee's army were casualties. The Union 2d Corps under Major General Andrew A. Humphreys then caught up to Gordon and struck with superior numbers. Gordon fought them off until early evening when Federals delivered a crushing blow and "drove him from the field in much confusion." Gordon lost hundreds of wagons and 2,000 men in this fight.[7]

The Saylor's Creek disaster marked the beginning of the very end for Lee's Army.

Not only did it lose 8,000 men and large numbers of guns and wagons, but the battle was emblematic of the collapse of the Army's fighting prowess. Exhausted physically and emotionally, the men of the Army of Northern Virginia could no longer resist the vicious strikes of the Union Army. Union cavalry would attack, forcing Confederate infantrymen to halt and fight them off. Meanwhile, gaps developed in the retreating columns and the delays enabled Union infantry and artillery to arrive and join the battle. Against overwhelming Federal strength, Confederates could not resist. On the night of 6 April, Lee told Pendleton, "It was all over—Ewell's Corps captured, Anderson dispersed, Gordon's the only organized body of troops in the whole left wing." Only Longstreet's Corps remained intact. Sheridan too sensed the Confederates' enervated condition and closed for the kill. That night, he telegraphed Grant about his victory, concluding with the assessment, "If the thing is pressed I think Lee will surrender." The next day Lincoln scanned Sheridan's victory telegram and injected pithily to Grant, "Let the thing be pressed."[8]

Once again, Lee's Army continued its march at night, stumbling into Farmville that morning. There, officials issued rations but before everyone could receive food, Lee had to withdraw the trains, fearing the Union would attack once more. Lee resumed the retreat westward. By nightfall on 8 April, the lead elements filtered into Appomattox Court House. Yet straggling persisted. The Army of Northern Virginia was dissolving.[9]

On 7 April, Grant made an overture to Lee for the surrender of the Army of Northern Virginia, suggesting that "The last week must convince you of the hopelessness of further resistance." Lee thought it was premature but asked what terms Grant would offer. The Union Army commander replied the next day that all he insisted upon was, "that the men and officers surrendered shall be disqualified for taking up arms again against the Government of the United States until properly exchanged." He offered to meet Lee personally or to designate representatives to draft terms at any location Lee suggested. On the evening of the 8th, Lee refused the offer, stating, "To be frank, I do not think the emergency has arisen to call for the surrender of this Army." He still had some minute hope of escape. Lee did offer to negotiate on behalf of all Confederate Armies, a proposal Grant quickly rebuffed. Lincoln had conveyed to Grant the authorization to negotiate only the surrender of the army in his front.[10]

Lee still had one final chance. He laid his correspondence before his corps commanders with Fitz Lee present. Yankee cavalrymen had blocked their passage westward and the group decided that Fitz Lee's men, supported by Gordon's troops, would spearhead an attack to rock back the Union horsemen enough for the army to slip through the pursuit. If Federal infantry had arrived, they were to notify Lee, who would then agree to terms. The original intention was to strike at 1 a.m. but the muffled sound of troops shuffling into place convinced the commander to delay the movement until first light so that Fitz Lee and Gordon could see what kind of opposition confronted them. At first, the attack drove back enemy cavalry but then resistance stiffened. White and black Union infantrymen, who had marched 25 of the last 28 hours, arrived the next morning just in time to block Lee's attempt to break through the Federal cavalrymen. The Confederate escape route was sealed.

Lee requested Grant meet him to accept the surrender of the Confederate Army on the terms the Union Commander had offered. It took some time to arrange a temporary truce and to contact Grant. Lee, resplendent in his best uniform, along with his aide Charles Marshall and Grant's aide Orville Babcock, settled on the McLean House, owned by the same family who lived amid the battleground at First Manassas, for the drafting of terms. Grant arrived an hour later in a dirty uniform with only the insignia of a lieutenant general on his shoulders. After some slightly awkward conversation, Lee drew them to the business at hand.

As guidance for the actual surrender proposal, Grant relied on earlier instructions and conversations that he, Major General William T. Sherman, Admiral David Dixon Porter, and President Lincoln held in late March. Lincoln was uneasy that Lee might escape and the thought of any more major battles pained him. If Lee and Johnston's armies surrendered, however, Lincoln believed the other Confederates would lay down their arms. Grant walked away with the sense that Lincoln though that surrender terms should be magnanimous.

The Grant document paroled the men of the Army of Northern Virginia as long as they agreed not to take up arms against the United States unless properly exchanged. According to the terms; "Officers and men will be allowed to return to their home, not to be disturbed by United States authority so long as they observe their paroles and the laws in force where they may reside." They would surrender weapons, although officers could keep their side arms, and those who owned horses could take them home. Lee signed an acceptance statement. While staff copied the agreement, Lee commented that his men and their Yankee prisoners needed food. Grant directed Sheridan to provide it.[11]

Terms were promptly conveyed to the Secretary of War and the President. Neither voiced objection to Grant's agreement. Not long after the surrender, some northerners demanded that the Union prosecute Lee as a traitor. Grant reacted by throwing his enormous prestige behind the surrender agreement. As long as Lee abided by terms of the parole and obeyed the laws where he lived, he would not be disturbed, and the deal could not be abrogated.

As Lee returned to his camp, Rebel troops rushed to him. He confirmed what all had suspected—the army had capitulated. When he reached camp, Lee gravitated toward an apple tree where he remained all afternoon. Brigadier General Edward Porter Alexander meanwhile, formed his artillerists along the road where Lee would have to pass to reach his headquarters, hoping to pay a silent tribute. As Lee rode along the peaceful gauntlet, discipline failed them one last time. Men broke ranks and rushed to their commander.[12]

The next day, Lee and Marshall wrote General Orders, No. 9, Lee's farewell to the Army, in his ambulance. "After concluding, the tears ran down the old hero's cheeks," Staff Officer Giles B. Cooke recorded, "and he gave way for the first time that I ever knew him to do so since my connection with him."

Before the fighting in late March, Lee commanded approximately 67,000 men according to his estimate. Only 7,892 infantrymen and a couple of thousand artillery and cavalry kept up with the army. Over the next few days as Yankees paroled them, large numbers poured into Appomattox to surrender. By April 12, 26,018 had consented to a parole.[13]

Lee considered launching a guerrilla resistance and then rejected the option. "A partisan war may be continued and hostilities protracted," he advised the president 11 days after his surrender, "causing individual suffering and the devastation of the country but I see no prospect by that means of achieving a separate independence." Of course, Lee reassured Davis respectfully that the decision was the president's. "To save useless effusion of blood, I would recommend measures be taken for suspension of hostilities and the restoration of peace."[14]

Word of the army's surrender struck Confederate supporters like a thunderbolt. So many thought that Lee's Army was invincible and that somehow, the general and his men would extricate themselves from the disastrous loss of Richmond. The army had come to symbolize a dream and both now vanished. "How can I write it?" Catherine Edmondston of North Carolina expressed her feelings, "How find words to tell what has befallen us? Gen[eral] Lee has surrendered, surrendered the remnant of his noble army to an overwhelming horde of mercenary Yankee knaves & foreigners." She simply could not believe that "The Lee, Lee upon whom hung the hopes of the whole country, should be a prisoner seems too dreadful to be realized!" When Sarah Dawson learned the news, she wrote, "Everyone cried but I would not," trusting that God would save them "even though all should apparently be lost." Once Johnston learned of Lee's surrender, he and Sherman negotiated terms. After the Federal Government rejected the first set of terms, Johnston accepted the same agreement that Grant had extended to Lee. Within weeks, all other Confederate field forces surrendered.[15]

The Civil War, by far the bloodiest in United States history, had come to an end.

Endnotes

1. Report of Major General Gouverneur Warren, 21 Feb. 1865[6]. REPORT of Sheridan, 16 May 1865. Lee to Breckinridge, 1, 2, and 2 Apr. 1865. OR 46 (1): 796-800, 1101-105, and 1263-265; Thomas Rosser, extract for Philadelphia *Weekly Times*, 5 Apr. 1884. John Bolling Folder, CWTIC, USAMHI; Thomas T. Munford to Captain, 2 Aug. 1870. W.H. Taylor to General, 19 Feb. 1903. Fitzhugh Lee Papers, UVA; Fitz Lee to Taylor, 9 Jan. 1903. Taylor to Lee, 15 Jan. 1904. Walter H. Taylor Papers, NPL; John C. Evans to Annie, 30 Apr. 1865. John Craig Evans Papers, AHS; William Marvel, "Lee's Last Retreat: The Flight To Appomattox," 214-17. There is no contemporary written evidence of Pickett's dismissal, but there are pieces of inferential evidence, which Marvel develops well. For an overview of the Army of Northern Virginia and its final days, see Joseph T. Glatthaar, "General Lee's Army: From Victory To Collapse."
2. REPORT of Grant, 22 July 1864. Lee to Breckinridge, 2 and 2 Apr. 1865. REPORT of Lee, 12 Apr. 1865. OR 46 (1): 54-5 and 1264-265; A. Howard to Lane, 3 June 1867. Geo. H. Snow to Lane, 13 May 1867. James H. Lane Papers, Auburn U.; Giles Buckner Cooke diary, 2 Apr. 1865. Giles Buckner Cooke Papers, VHS.
3. Briscoe G. Baldwin to General [Gorgas], 31 Mar. [1865]. Briscoe Baldwin Papers, VHS; REPORT of Lt. Col. Briscoe Baldwin, 14 Apr. 1865. Box 3, Lee Headquarters Papers, VHS; Eugene F. Levy diary, 3 Apr. 1865. Marcus, ed., "Memoirs of American Jews", III, 312; Taylor, "Some Experiences of a Confederate Assistant Surgeon," 112-13; Edward C. Anderson to wife, 19 Nov. 1864. Joseph F. Waring Papers, GHS.
4. Peter Wellington Alexander, "The State of the Confederate Cause," 17 May 1865. Columbia U.; Lee to Breckinridge, 22 Feb. 1865. OR 46 (2): 1247; REPORT of Lee, 12 Apr. 1865. OR 46 (1):1265-266.
5. REPORT of Lee, 12 Apr. 1865. OR 46 (1):1265-266; J.W. Powell, Medical Director of A.P.

Hill's Corps, [Feb. 1865], addendum to IR of 3rd Corps by Maj. R.J. Wingate, Jan. 1865. IR, R15, F286. RG 109, NA. Thanks to Dr. Boyd Switzer, Professor of Nutrition at UNC Medical School, who assisted me here. Lee's men consumed about 35 to 40 grams of protein per day and needed 55 to 70 grams. Based on a adult male, average size 5 feet, 8 inches tall, 150 lbs., he received 62.5% of calories, 6% of Vitamin A, 15% of Vitamin E, 3% of Vitamin K, 9.9% of calcium, 8.8% of Iodine, 41% of Potassium, 32.5% of Folate, along with all sorts of B-Vitamin shortages. Conversation wit Dr. Boyd Switzer, Dec. 12, 2006, and printout. See Glatthaar, "General Lee's Army," 461.

6. Captain B.H. Smith, Jr. to Lt. Col. Latrobe, 13 Mar. 1865. Ser. a, Box 3, Lee Headquarters Papers, VHS; Pfanz, "Richard S. Ewell", 428-35; Marvel, "Lee's Last Retreat," Appendix B, 207-13, challenges Lee's statement in his REPORT. It seems extremely unlikely that Lee would order ammunition stockpiled for the army at Amelia Court House and not food and forage.

7. Gordon to Lee; 6 Apr. 1865. Ser. a, Box 1, Lee Headquarters Papers, VHS; REPORT of Lee, 12 Apr. 1865. OR 46(1): 1265-266; Pfanz, Ewell, 436-39.

8. W.G. M[cCabe] to Miss Mary, 7 Apr. 1865. Early Family Papers, VHS; Maj. Campbell Brown diary, 26 Jan. 1866. George Washington Campbell Papers, LC; Taylor, "Some Experiences of a Confederate Assistant Surgeon," 111-13; Sheridan to Grant, 6 Apr. 1865. OR I, 46 (3): 610. Lincoln to Grant, 7 Apr. 1865. Roy P. Basler, ed., "Collected Works of Abraham Lincoln," VIII (New Brunswick: Rutgers University Press, 1953-55), 392.

9. REPORT of Lee, 12 Apr. 1865. OR 46 (1): 1266; GO, No. ___. HQ, 1st Army Corps. 8 Apr. 1865. Osmun Latrobe Papers, MDHS; Gallagher, ed., "Fighting", 527.

10 . Grant to Lee, 7 Apr. 1865. Lee to Grant, 7 Apr. 1865. Grant to Lee, 8 Apr. 1865. Lee to Grant, 8 Apr. 1865. Grant to Lee, 9 Apr. 1865. OR 46 (1): 56-7.

11 . REPORT of Grant, 22 July 1865. Grant to Lee, 9 Apr. 1865. Lee to Grant, 9 Apr. 1865. OR 46 (1): 57-8; Marshall, "Lee's Aide-De-Camp", 268-74.

12 . E.P. Alexander to Longstreet, 26 Oct. 1892. James Longstreet Papers, NCDAH; Goree to Alexander, 6 Dec. [1877]. Goree, ed., 301-03.

13. Lee to Davis, 20 Apr. 1865. Lee Letterbook No. 3, Robert E. Lee Papers, LC.

14. Lee to Davis, 20 Apr. 1865. Lee Letterbook No. 3, Robert E. Lee Papers, LC; Gallagher, ed., "Fighting," 532-33.

15. Catherine Edmondston diary, 16 Apr. 1865. Crabtree and Patton, eds., "Journal of a Secesh Lady," 694-95; Eliza Andrews diary, 18 Apr. 1865. Eliza Frances Andrews, "War-Time Journal of a Georgia Girl," 151-52; Sarah Morgan Dawson diary, 19 Apr. 1865. Sarah Morgan Dawson, "A Confederate Girl's Diary," 435.

Session 2

Interview

Dr. Joseph Glatthaar

Interviewer

We're here today with Dr. Joseph Glatthaar. The theme of this TRADOC conference is the resolution of combat, the termination of warfare and negotiation of peace or a truce. Your particular piece was about the Civil War. You're an expert on the Civil War, widely known for a number of pieces you've written. In fact, one of them has to do with African-American soldiers during the Civil War. Could you, just for the record, tell us the name of this work?

Dr. Joseph Glatthaar

"Forged in Battle."

Interviewer

It's almost as if the United States fought two wars, the war before the Emancipation Proclamation and the war after the Emancipation Proclamation. President Lincoln issues this emancipation granting freedom to the slaves in the Confederate States. It doesn't grant it to those in the bordering states that are still slaveholding Union states. Was this a huge risk for them?

Dr. Joseph Glatthaar

Oh, without a doubt. I think Lincoln felt restricted by his constitutional obligations, that is, he could declare it for the states that were not occupied, that were still in a status of rebellion but he felt that he had no authority to declare it for individuals who occupied states.

Interviewer

Didn't this change the goals?

Dr. Joseph Glatthaar

Absolutely, it went from a war that was to reestablish the Union as it was intended in 1860 to a war to reestablish the Union and abolish slavery which, incidentally, negated the original proposition, that is, you couldn't have a war, or you couldn't reestablish the Union as it was in 1860 and free the slaves. So it completely transformed the original war goal.

Interviewer

Why, then, would he issue this emancipation in 1862? Why not begin another war?

Dr. Joseph Glatthaar

I think Lincoln had hopes that the Union would be able to win the war expeditiously. By the summer of 1862, the war hadn't progressed very well for the Union. The Union was having difficulty raising additional manpower and Lincoln came to the conclusion that the amount of bloodshed had reached a point where the nation couldn't be restored as it once had been. If the nation was to move beyond this, they had to abolish the institution of slavery. If he did so in areas that were in rebellion that would really start the process of the destruction of slavery throughout the nation.

Interviewer

Other historians have advanced the argument that, by emancipating the slaves, President Lincoln not only changed the goals for the Union forces but he also was able to achieve a diplomatic isolation of the South. The war, because it went beyond Union and also now included emancipation, suddenly, it was the idea of the British and the French aligning with the Confederacy meant that they were aligning themselves with the slave power. How much influence do you think that decision had on the outcome of the Civil War?

Dr. Joseph Glatthaar

Well, I'm not so sure it had a huge impact because I'm not convinced that Britain and France were going to come into the war anyway. I think the British or the French would have had great difficulty really affecting the war from a military standpoint. Keep in mind that the British and French practically starved their troops to death in the Crimea some eight years earlier.

The British had commitments all round the world. I'm not confident that they would have had that much an impact, nor am I confident that you would have been able to get the British government to go in because, even if Lincoln didn't emancipate the slaves, it was clear that the Confederacy had seceded to protect the institution of slavery.

There were strong business ties between the Union and Great Britain. So, for a variety of reasons, I'm not so sure how significant it would be but, unquestionably, by declaring the Emancipation Proclamation, the Union had the moral high ground and that eliminated any possibility.

Interviewer

To reiterate, issuing the proclamation in the middle of the war, the Union was not winning the war at that point. It was a risky gamble.

Dr. Joseph Glatthaar

Yeah. That's why they delayed the issue. It's because it would have looked like a desperate effort on the part of a losing power. If they waited until after the Antietam victory, then they could declare the Emancipation Proclamation from a position of greater strength.

Interviewer

Even then, it wasn't a popular measure.

Dr. Joseph Glatthaar

No. There was a lot of divisions. For those who opposed slavery, it helped them reconcile two very different issues. That is, they knew that the war was about secession and some say seceded for slavery. They had moral difficulties accepting slavery. So it eased their moral qualms by putting the nation on the road to the elimination of slavery. So I think, in that regard, it was a really good feature.

Interviewer

Well, let's look at the Confederate's surrender at Appomattox. General Lee had a number of options available. Why do you think he chose not to conduct a guerilla warfare campaign?

Dr. Joseph Glatthaar

I think Lee, . . . said to Edward Porter Alexander, and then later communicated to Jefferson Davis, about the guerrilla option. Lee thought that the South had already suffered terribly during the course of the war and that a guerrilla operation would only enhance the suffering, that the army would suffer and the civilian population would [too]. It wouldn't be just from Union personnel. The guerrillas themselves would be plundering farms and things and making hardships even worse in the South. He felt like the guerrilla war wouldn't win an independent Confederacy and so, therefore, it didn't make much sense. He also thought about the spring. If the army surrendered at that point and soldiers went home, they'd be able to get crops in the ground and it would avoid massive starvation come wintertime. So what he really wanted to do is look after those who have survived the war, make sure they got home, took care of their loved ones, feed their families, things of that nature.

Interviewer

Do you think he was also considering the lawlessness and certain parts of the Confederacy, especially states like Arkansas, for example, where armed bands seemed to control large sections of territory because of a lack of essential state government?

Dr. Joseph Glatthaar

Yeah, I'm not so sure he would have known that much about what was going on in Arkansas but he didn't have to look that far. All he had to do was look at Virginia and North Carolina. The mountain areas were pretty lawless. You had bands of deserters. He had to detach troops to go after them on a number of occasions. So he was fairly well aware what was taking place in those mountain regions. Of course, Sherman had rode through Georgia, had rode through South Carolina, and was halfway through North Carolina. He knew that the letters from home were prompting soldiers to desert. That was affecting his army too. So he had a good sense of the chaos on the Confederate home front.

Interviewer

Right, it's been written by some authors as well that, at this point, the Confederate military is racked by disease and malnutrition as well as having all these concerns on the home front. As the Union negotiated surrender in Virginia, there were still viable Confederate armies in other parts of the South. You wrote about Grant exerting pressure on his subordinates to take a less harsh instrument of surrender. Can you delve a little bit more into that?

Dr. Joseph Glatthaar

Sure. I think what was taking place here was that Lincoln and Grant and others knew that Lee's army was the symbol of the survivability of the Confederacy. As long as Lee's army survived, there was a chance the Confederacy could win. So it was imperative that they defeat Lee's army, capture it and destroy it. So Grant was able to box it in, but Grant also offered very magnanimous terms. [In] part of that he got guidance from Lincoln. Lincoln had been involved with Grant on a few other episodes where some Confederates wanted to surrender and Grant was in an awkward position and Lincoln took the matter into his own hands so that Grant was removed. Then Grant had received instructions from Lincoln that he was to only negotiate for the surrender of the army in his front or on minor and fairly unimportant military matters, say, an exchange of doctors or [if] something were captured or something like that or passing bodies between the two lines. In this case, what Grant did was he wrote the surrender agreement and stated that the Confederates would not be bothered by the Federal government as long as they abided by the paroles and obeyed the laws where they resided it. So that, in effect, was a pardon. After the war, as you probably know, there was a movement to prosecute Lee for war crimes and Grant put his reputation on the line, which was, of course, staggering that he had signed an agreement with Lee. Lee was bound by the surrender agreement. He had not violated the local laws. He had not violated his parole. He had to be left alone. He could not be prosecuted. Ultimately, Grant, with his enormous prestige, was able to compel the Union government to drop those issues.

Interviewer

Jefferson Davis is another individual. There were quite a number of cries for his execution too.

Dr. Joseph Glatthaar

Yes, there were. Of course, he was in prison for a while but it would have been difficult. He would have been tried in Virginia. It might have been difficult to get him convicted. Passions dissipated after a while. Eventually, the Union government felt like they might not have a good case and it was probably best to just let him go.

Interviewer

Unconditional surrender, it seems to be a term that comes out of this era, out of the Civil War, unconditional surrender. What exactly does that mean?

Dr. Joseph Glatthaar

Well, Grant, of course, wrote that in his terms for the surrender of the Confederate forces at Fort Donelson that he demanded their immediate and unconditional surrender, which meant that they would be prisoners of war. It didn't mean that they would be executed or anything of the sort. Of course, they were sent to prison or war camps and then ultimately exchanged. I think that's simply what they were intended.

Interviewer

It seems, though, that the precedent was set for unconditional surrender and that influenced American surrender instruments after this period of time.

Dr. Joseph Glatthaar

Unquestionably it did. The terms under which Joseph E. Johnson surrendered and other Confederate armies, technically weren't unconditional surrender. They were paroled and they couldn't – they had to obey their paroles — unless exchanged. That was unlikely with the Confederacy imminent collapse by that point. Then, of course, they would not be prosecuted unless they violated the laws, the local laws.

Interviewer

Sure, if you could say there was a particular effect on the American way of war that came out of the Civil War at the end of the conflict, what would you say the end of the Civil War had as far as an influence on the American way of war?

Dr. Joseph Glatthaar

I'm very uncomfortable with the concept of an American way of war, because I think the United States adapts its approach to war based on the circumstances, the enemy, the weapon systems that are at disposal, and so on. I think what emerged in this, of course, was the dramatic and overwhelming use of strength, economic strength, manpower strength, and excellent leadership. Those three things played huge roles in the defeat of the Confederacy. Remember that the Union did embark on the raiding strategy, which had critical economic components. There was a psychological element to it. Marching an army right through someone's home state brings huge psychological burdens to the soldiers. You join the army in the Confederate case to protect your loved ones. If an army marches through your home county, how well have you done your job?

Interviewer

Right, there's no confidence. You've proven that you're impotent in face of the enemy.

Dr. Joseph Glatthaar

That's exactly right.

Interviewer

If you had to say there was a particular impact on how wars are fought in the 21st century, what would you say is the impact the American Civil War?

Dr. Joseph Glatthaar

Well, I think you'd probably see elements of it in World War I and World War II, in the sense that the United States mobilizes hugely from an industrial standpoint, commits enormous amounts of economic resources, and raises really large military forces that are exceedingly well supplied by world standards. By World War II, these forces are the most mechanized in the world. Our allies are mechanized because we're able to provide them with the mechanization. So, I think the lesson there is to draw on the great strengths but there's also a really important lesson and it's ultimately forgotten by the time we got to Vietnam. That was that you need to convey to the American people in a very clear fashion what it is they're fighting for. I think Lincoln was exceedingly clear about that and, as a result, the Union was willing to sustain 362,000 deaths and continue fighting, which is a pretty extraordinary achievement when you consider the population was only 21 million people. So, Lincoln really convinced the northern public that the price was worth it and that the sacrifices were worth it. I think, in World War II, it was pretty clear what we were fighting for and that the sacrifices were imperative. I think, as we got on, perhaps less so in Korea and certainly much less so by Vietnam that the American public wasn't convinced that this was a situation of vital national security and, of course, Vietnam is much more complicated as Gian will tell you.

Interviewer

Well, thank you very much.

Session 2
Questions and Answers

Colonel Gian Gentile

Can we have a round of applause for all of these very excellent papers and presentations? So I'll open it up in a minute to the questions. These were three excellent presentations and I've just got two pages full of notes and a number of things that I saw that seemed to be somewhat common at least as far as themes of all three. I've already mentioned a couple of these. An army fights and transitions to an army that has to occupy, how armies learn after war. Then just to build on a couple of the things that Pete said that I thought were really interesting in his presentation is this key essential most important point about how an army, how a state translates tactical success into strategic success which I think at least has been a key element in the thinking about my own work on Vietnam. The last thing that I think is also certainly common to all three presentations and how Pete ended his talk which is about the ending of wars and that when wars end they tend to be messy and not clean and are often unclear which makes me think again about Chip's talk on the Mexican War and when folks thought the war was over and then a guerilla war popped up and then the ending of the Civil War with the messy problems created by reconstruction.

So with that and my comments as the moderator, I'd like to open it up for questions. Please, if you don't mind, in order for us to capture the important questions that you have if you could move over to the microphone which is to my right to most of your left right up there and give your question to the microphone so that we can record it. Thank you and then once you get done with your question, the microphone is portable and so we can move it around.

Question

Hi. The question I had was regarding the first two papers. We've talked about the lessons that the United States Military tries to learn. After the Civil War they're confronted with the second situation where they've had to run a military administration. Regarding the first paper they were not mature enough to accept this lesson but after the Civil War you have many officers who had served in that conflict being presented again with the situation of a military administration and reconstruction. Why did they not choose to learn those lessons especially since they were ready to change tactical and operational doctrine from learned lessons? Why are they not aware of that issue of postwar settlement that they've been called upon not only to do once, but now twice?

Dr. Joseph Glatthaar

Personally, I think that most of the senior officers who had influential or important assignments in New Mexico, California, and the central part of Mexico were not on active duty in 1867 after the Military Reconstruction Acts were passed. Many of the junior officers I would assert were just not paying attention and certainly didn't see this assignment in any sort of military administration, military government in 1847-48 as something that was going to be a long term matter for them to deal with.

Dr. Joseph Dawson

I think there are several factors that you need to keep in mind. One is that the officer corps generally was conservative. It was much more likely to be democratic than it was likely to be republican and so in the policies that they were implementing, there were largely radical Republican policies and people didn't necessarily agree with those policies. Furthermore you're implementing reconstruction on Americans. It's a very different situation and so you know these are your former countrymen and so it's a very delicate area. Furthermore, most of the US Army officers thought that African Americans were inferior beings so why don't they just shut up and listen to the white people? They know what they're doing and that's the quickest way to recover but of course the white people had no interest in recognizing or honoring the civil liberties of African Americans. It's a complicated situation.

Dr. Peter Maslowski

The question wasn't directed at me but hell I'm a historian and I love to talk.

Colonel Gian Gentile

Go Pete.

Dr. Peter Maslowski

One of the interesting things and John Hall alluded to this in the morning, is that the Indian administration, I mean that runs the reservations? Well the United States Army fortunately is left out of that because reservations are in the hands of the Interior Department. There are disputes and it would make a paper in itself between the US Army the War Department and the Interior Department, particularly the Bureau of Indian Affairs, as to who has control over the Indians and I think the US Army was lucky that there was a Bureau of Indian Affairs to run things on the reservation so that the US Army didn't get stuck with that duty, that occupation duty as it might be called.

Dr. Joseph Glatthaar

One other quick response is that a couple of the officers who were given considerable responsibility by General Scott or by the War Department were volunteer officers and not regular officers in 1847-1848 and so they weren't a part of the institutional memory.

Question

This is more of an observation but I thought maybe it went to General Dempsey's point earlier about thinking about the title of the conference and maybe one way to think about it is more in terms of political consolidation and the US Army's role in that because a theme that has come up now with six talks and I imagine this afternoon as well, is that that's really what we're talking about and linking it and thinking about it in the framework of war termination. This sort of puts this in the literature that actually is not that relevant, the old literature to what you're talking about. So that was my main point but essentially all of you are talking about the US Army's role in shaping the politics on the ground if these conflicts come to a close both at the strategic level from what general officers had to do like General Scott but also at the lower levels of troops on the ground.

Colonel Gian Gentile

Go ahead Will.

Question

I have a thought on the changing of prerequisites for recognizing war aims and this comes out of Dr. Dawson's point that Scott gets to Mexico City, takes it, and then is surprised when everything doesn't fall apart. This does tie into two sort of general academic constructs of warfare during this period. In the 18th century, the whole idea is that your focus is on taking enemy capital which is the store house of the political will to resist and at some time in the 19th century, you see a transition to where suddenly the capital is no longer the store house of political will or the repository of resistance but your army becomes the repository of political will and thus you have to take out this army, not necessarily destroy it but break its ability and willingness to resist before you can begin talking about achieving other war aims. Because you represent such different varieties of conflict, the questions for you three: are there specific points that you see in the record where United States authority has recognized that (A) the enemy's military force is the repository of the political will to resist and continue the fight and (B) when you see this transition, must we take this source of resistance out before we can really begin to address anything else?

Dr. Joseph Dawson

Very good question and I think there are a number of different features. I'll just touch on a couple of them in regard to Mexico. While I'm not thoroughly familiar with each and every thought that General Santa Anna had, I think he was beginning to realize the war just was completely going against Mexico. As Scott's Army made progress about halfway, I think he was seriously considering what sort of negotiations might benefit Mexico and the Mexican Congress forbade him to go into negotiations that would resolve the war. So once it was confirmed that the Mexican Army was so defeated in detail as you indicate, then the Mexican Government, which only recently had told the general not to negotiate, fell apart and so Scott and the State Department Representative Nicholas Trist (who was with him) had difficulty finding anyone who could be thought of as an official representative of a government that had collapsed. So it was both a political collapse and a military collapse.

Dr. Joseph Glatthaar

I think it's pretty clear that the Confederate Army is the manifestation of political will and I think President Abraham Lincoln recognizes that very fact. What Lincoln ultimately does of course, is to force Grant into the Overland campaign in 1864 which is not the kind of campaign Grant wants to choose. Grant has alternatives and Lincoln doesn't understand the alternatives but he's very frustrated with subordinate commanders who won't target the enemy army and won't sustain the overwhelming Union force and so he forces that campaign on Grant. Of course General Lee's Army is the most successful institution in the entire Confederacy so it becomes the embodiment of the Confederate cause just like Washington's Army was the embodiment of the American Revolutionary cause and so the defeat of Lee's Army is much more significant than merely the defeat of an army. If the army in Tennessee got defeated at Nashville, I mean shattered remnants survived but the army never really survived in total, that didn't bring the war to an end. Until you defeated Lee's Army, the war was going to go on. So I think that's my answer to your question.

Dr. Peter Maslowski

In the Indian Wars and I think John Hall made this point earlier too, the US Army's problem with the Seminole campaigns and with every other campaign was (A) to find the Indians and then (B) once you found them, make them stand and fight. The fact of the matter is that the Indians would rarely stand and fight. So consequently whites thought that they were cowardly that they were unmanly, that they waged this skulking way of war and they hid in the swamps and the forests like wild beasts and so on. Consequently white military forces rarely waged warfare against warriors. They waged war against Indian resources. When they captured pony herds out on the Great Plains, they slaughtered them by the hundreds because the ponies were so essential to the plains way of warfare. They waged war against women and children. It's no accident that many of the events that you've heard of between whites and Indians are sometimes called battles but more often they're called massacres because that's who you could get your hands on, the women and the children beginning with the attack on the Mystic Fort in the Pequot War in the 1630s and bring it right on up through Bear Creek in -- I may have my dates off so don't hold me to this but I think Bear Creek was 1863, Sand Creek was 1864, the Marias was the early 1870s, Wounded Knee. While these are considered battles they're really in a sense massacre. Most of the people who are killed are women and children because that's who you could make war upon. You could just wage war against the Indian resources.

John didn't have time to get into it but I know in his paper he talks about crop destruction. You go in and you destroy the Seminoles crops. You can't fight the Seminole Indians because they won't stand up and fight, so what you do is you wage war against the foundations of Indian society.

Dr. Joseph Glatthaar

Of course you also launch winter campaigns because the Indian ponies can't feed on the grass because blankets of snow cover it so that the ponies become weak. That means there's no mobility for the Indians and you can actually get at them.

Dr. Peter Maslowski

Well, and the Indians, the warriors you can force to stand and fight because the women and the children are there.

Dr. Joseph Glatthaar

That's right.

Dr. Peter Maslowski

Indian winter campaigns were damn hard on the US Army. They were out there campaigning when the temperature was so low that the mercury congealed in their thermometers and stuff. It was just really brutal and lots of men died of course and suffered loss of limbs and digits and so on from frostbite. These were brutal campaigning conditions.

Question

I wanted to offer a comment on learning. We've talked here about learning and since this is a Training and Doctrine Command conference, one thing you should know about army learning in the 19th century is that it tends to be very, let's say rigid and mechanistic. Colonel Moten's written about this in his book. Andy suggested in writing for TRADOC that the Army does learn things through kind of common sense and verbal discussion passing things on, but if you look at their doctrinal publications as it were, they're either logistics or ordnance kind of supply manuals. With these, you know you can write everything out and a lot of it can be qualified and you have forms and you say this is the form you use. Or it's tactical and their tactics are very mechanistic. Their tactics, especially earlier, are more linear, it is the more mechanistic. So a lot of the learning that we're talking about here and that we're looking for here is a political learning that's much more complex and much less linear and much less mechanistic than what they normally do in terms of doctrine. They really do not have anything at a kind of strategic political level of doctrine and as we've pointed out in so many cases. When you're dealing with American citizens, it's kind of hard to set up a doctrine to figure out how you're going to govern American citizens. So military government, I don't think it's necessarily that they disdain it although there are certainly issues with that, but it's that they don't think intellectually. They don't think in a way that helps them structure those questions and those answers.

Colonel Gian Gentile

Anyone want to take a question of political strategic learning by an army?

Dr. Joseph Dawson

Right. I think Sam makes a very good point particularly for following the Mexican War into Mexico territory where volunteer soldiers really led the supervision and in central Mexico although it would seem the opposite because Winfield Scott's in charge for such a long time and then he's replaced by another senior regular officer. Both of those were considered so short term, I think to be of less consequence. In California it was the opposite, where regular officers are in charge and they're in charge from 1847 until California becomes a state in 1850. Regular officers participate in writing the state constitution.

Colonel Gian Gentile

Kearny has a lot of experience doing not exactly military government but military diplomacy on the frontier. So here was the guy, they don't have the doctrine, they don't have a conceptualization of it, but they do have some experience that they can bring to these situations.

Dr. Joseph Dawson

There were enough examples from 1847 to 1848 that the Army could have gave them closer attention than that.

Dr. Joseph Glatthaar

I think we need to keep in mind something. There's a triangle. Organization, doctrine, and technology are three that have to work together and the problem you have in this time period is that you certainly have an organization but because you don't have the technology you don't have great flexibility in doctrine. I think it's only when you develop more effective means of firepower and most importantly communication, so you have command and control, that it gives you much greater flexibility in the development of your doctrine.

The second thing I want to point out is remember too that when you were in the old frontier army you had to solve all sorts of problems because you were the Federal Government's representative on the frontier. There were all sorts of instances where soldiers, as certainly Sam recalls and Mac Coffman knows, where officers were prosecuted in civilian courts for enforcing federal laws and they had to pony up large amounts of money for lawyers to defend themselves. Usually they got reimbursed by the Federal Government several years later but that was one of the big problems and so they were setting policies that had a huge impact on civilians. So in that regard, quite a number of the US Army Officers had that experience but those would be at the highest levels and of course the young guys who would be implementing most of these decisions would be captains and they would be probably 22 to 26 year olds because they have been in the US Army for four years and they are not going to have had that sort of experience. So for them, it's all brand new learning.

Dr. Peter Maslowski

I think in order to be an effective Indian fighter, you almost had to learn personally. There was no doctrine, there was no agreed upon way to do this, and they did come to some sort of common understanding that good Indian fighters learn. For example, converging columns. You rarely just send out one column to try to track down the Indians because they'd always escape. So for example in the Custer campaign, there were three converging columns and that is designed (A) to have a better chance to find the Indians and then (B) to force them to stand and fight but you also had to learn sort of at a personal level that you just couldn't campaign effectively if you didn't have Indian allies.

There aren't any wars where it's whites against Indians. All the wars are whites and some Indians against other Indians and oftentimes, for example, during the colonial period and Ira might have mentioned it or maybe Wayne did, it's Indians and whites against Indians and whites. You had to have Indian allies and some were more comfortable with Indian allies than others. You had to learn to love to campaign in really atrocious conditions because once you got on the trail of the Indian band you just had to stay on it in all sorts of weather and some officers are more comfortable in those conditions than others. It was a very personal experience and you could count the number of really good Indian fighters probably on the fingers of one hand. These guys really learned and became sort of famous as Indian fighters.

Colonel Gian Gentile

You mentioned in your talk about the continuity of the war aim for the American Army and the expansion out west which was essentially conquering and taking land. That is a rather total war aim. So if you have a total war aim like that, does it eliminate the need for strategy because what you were just describing, there were really the tactics and operations of all this and with that kind of total war aim, does it eliminate Indian strategy?

Dr. Peter Maslowski

Well they certainly did have tactics but whether or not they had a strategy as to how to do this, I don't think it would be strategy in the common understood sense today but it was sort of an agreed upon concept among those who were the best at how you had to go about doing this. The most important strategic concept in the post Civil War Indian Wars was this idea of converging columns and winter campaigning because that's, as Joe pointed out, when the Indians were most vulnerable. The use of Indian allies and the waging of war against resources, those were sort of agreed upon understandings. I don't know, maybe together they would collectively comprise a strategy. I don't think it was ever written down anywhere.

Dr. Joseph Glatthaar

You probably read and many of you may have Don Connelly's book on John M. Schofield and the politics of generalship, which is a really interesting study because Schofield does occupation duty in Missouri and then later on because of his experiences in politics and his Democrat party affiliation, he gets chosen to be the acting Secretary of War when Edwin M. Stanton was removed. Then, of course, later on in his career, Schofield comes back in as Commanding General and works in conjunction with the Secretary of War to insure a clear and clean flow of command authority from the President through the Secretary of War to the Commanding General. Then the Commanding General would then have an ability to project his influence over the bureaus and bureau chiefs as well as the line and that was kind of a precursor to the creation of the general staff and the chief of staff.

Question (Thomas Spoehr)

Major Tom Spoehr. So a quick question for Dr. Dawson. It gets at this issue of measures the US Army implements to end the war and to target the will of the people. In Mexico, Winfield Scott, around December of 1847 in addition to attacking the guerillas aggressively, implemented some measures in Mexico City. They expanded the occupation, put a heavy tax on the Mexicans, and also brought in significantly more troops and got up to about 24,000 eventually. I guess my question for you is did that matter? How significant were these measures that the US Army implemented to ending the war and if they didn't, what did the US Army do to affect an end to that conflict and get the Mexicans to agree to these terms?

Dr. Joseph Dawson

Yes. Scott established this military administration and worked closely with the church. In fact you make an extremely important point and I appreciate you doing so that Scott realized at the beginning of his supervision of the capital that less than 10,000 soldiers were just not going to do it in a city of that size and so he began receiving troops that were already in the pipeline to come to him as reinforcement should the campaign have continued. He put them to good use in operating as patrols on the national road as well as in Mexico City itself and so that presence especially from the end of the fighting in mid September for about 70 or 80 days until some sort of representation came together that Nicholas Trist could deal with in negotiations, was absolutely crucial to have the American Military presence there over several weeks. This continuing military government that Scott instituted all that played an important part.

Dr. Conrad Crane

Something struck me. I know it's going to come out in one of our panels. Also in the panel this morning, there's another theme that has been evident to me in these presentations and it deals with learning but also the role of historians learning. I guess the way I'd sum it up is the accepted narrative about how the war was ended had a significant impact on military institutions' defense policies. So it's not just that the war ends but it's how people perceive war ends. For instance, the Mexican War is a good example. The part about Scott and the guerilla war gets lost. That doesn't come out in the narrative. The narrative is very much about the conventional fight. Reconstruction gets left out. The point is about the conventional fight. We'll get into our stuff this afternoon and we'll talk about the way that the endings get interpreted and influence defense policies. I guess the question is in the examples you were talking about. I know in the Indian Wars it comes out as well. What is the battle over the narrative? What is the battle over the institutional narrative to shape how the institution is going to be influenced by those wars?

Colonel Gian Gentile

Let's start with Pete if you don't mind.

Dr. Peter Maslowski

You're going to start with me instead of Chip? The US Army was in one sense left in the lurch when the Indian Wars came to an end because the primary reason for having an army had been as a frontier constabulary. The phrase that was always used all the time was to police the Indian frontier. Once that was gone, there was this search for a mission. Although I see Brian Linn just shaking his head no. He doesn't agree with that. There was certainly thought given to other purposes for the US Army but that was its primary use out on the Indian frontier. When those Indian Wars ended, I think Brian tell me if I'm wrong, but did they not speak about going into Indian country in the Philippines?

Dr. Brian Linn

The people that were doing that weren't veterans of the Indian Wars.

Dr. Peter Maslowski

Yes but there was no institutional memory of them.

Dr. Brian Linn

My point is the most successful thinking when all this stuff is going on is the Endicott Board. The US Army has got other things to worry about including the mission that it really has as the defense of the United States.

Dr. Peter Maslowski

Yeah but the Endicott Board comes at the tail end of the Indian Wars.

Brian Linn

Right but the big success is how to get back to national defense, fighting the big war. All this stuff that you're doing is fleeting.

Peter Maslowski

They're happy to have it in the rear view mirror. Well I guess they didn't have rear view mirrors in the 19th century, but they were happy to have it gone. One of the first things they did was to consolidate their posts. The fewer posts they had, the bigger units they could have to begin to train for conventional warfare.

Dr. Brian Linn

My point was that when you said the primary justification was the frontier and I would say that in many cases the US Army didn't define it that way. All the graduates of this great institution, the best of them went into the Corps of Engineers and went on to coastal fortifications. So in the self definition, they viewed themselves in an issue of national defense. I don't think they thought of the frontier.

Dr. Peter Maslowski

The Corps of Engineers also engaged in internal improvements. For example, an exploration of the West, all of which had to do with conquering the continental domain.

H. R. McMaster

I have a couple of comments. One I'm pulling out of Conrad's point. I remember this comment. Battles as they're written about are apt to be two different things and, of course, people who have written reports of battles understand this and, of course, historians understand it. I mean it's absolutely right. Who really has read that much in books on the Mexican War about the guerilla war? Who has really read much about Scott's administrative things afterward? I mean that's not his legend you know and is not thought about. The question I wanted to raise and I thought about that in the earlier panel, as I sat there it's so obvious that actually I dealt with it in my paper without really putting a name to it or spelling it out. It's the impact of the popular will, pro and con, where it waxes and wanes during a war, the impact on the political leadership and the military leadership which might be very different?

Colonel Gian Gentile

We'll make this the last question and we'll start with Chip.

Dr. Joseph Dawson

Well, I think they both are related just as Mac pointed out and I think it is this emphasis on the successful victorious national narrative that was much more of a positive outcome to your question Conrad, than trying to deal with a very unpleasant, as I said from the officers' point of view, dishonorable way to fight that this was nothing close to what the American Officers were prepared to do or wanted to do and certainly wanted it reduced or cut off as quickly as they could. So the contrast was this dynamic sweep from Texas to California, this consistent string of victories even though a couple of them were very narrow victories. Scott's always sort of counting noses, how many soldiers do I have left today to continue this campaign and then in winning so that this all totaled up to be the kind of outcome that Americans wanted to remember not the contest against guerrillas not the matter of months or even two years of administration in California.

Dr. Joseph Glatthaar

It seems to me based on my experiences and then thinking of Gian's paper on Vietnam and the American Civil War and some other events, that the public will pull the political will. In the Confederacy's case, the Confederate people had just had it. The soldiery had just had it. Confederate President Jefferson Davis would have loved to have fought for five more years. He just couldn't get the soldiers to continue fighting. He couldn't get the southern people to continue fighting. If you look at Gian's paper, Tet is the classic example. It's a huge battle and clear American military victory tactically but it just highlighted in the minds of the American people the lies that had been told by the political leadership about how the war was progressing and all of a sudden the public will just collapsed on us.

Colonel Gian Gentile

Pete, since you had the longest war you'll have the final word on narrative and political will in war.

Dr. Peter Maslowski

The 300 Year War against the Indians fits very nicely into the great national narrative of western expansion which is the triumph of civilization under God's divine providence. They just sort of fit together.

Question

Gentlemen?

Colonel Gian Gentile

Yes, sir.

General Martin Dempsey

This is not going to be a question, but I can't stay for this afternoon so I wanted to pose another challenge, like you need another challenge, but I'll do this up here so I can be recorded. You know that what we're going to try to do with this body of essays from these contributors is find these threads of commonality about how conflicts typically end and then I'm also going to take it and take some of the work and merge it into the Leader Development Strategy. How do we develop young men and women to be older young men and women who are giving the strategic advice to national command authorities? It occurs to me that one of the themes that have come out in both panels and I suspect that will come out this afternoon again, is that the war aims and the peace aims for that matter, tend to change over time. You don't finish conflict the way you start it because it just has a dynamic, it's human and so it changes. The challenge I think for readers because someone asked me, I forget who at one of the breaks, if the war aims are changing, how does the senior military leader who is giving this advice share it? Do the war aims share in a transparent way or could you find yourself perpetuating the conflict as it's been given to you. Have the war aims changed either transparently either deliberately or in some cases, they change of their own weight and if so our responsibility as mentor besides giving advice is then to propagate the campaign and report on its progress. Do we have the initiatives? The word initiative came up twice this morning in the panel. How do you answer that question? Does history instruct us on how we answer that question to our national command authorities?

Now I've also read, as you know, I'm looking for ways that this work will kind of balance other works in my life, in "Supreme Command," Eliot Cohen suggest that this is a gross oversimplification but I can get away with it because I'm an English major. He suggests that war is too important to be left to generals and that therefore and because war is a political animal more so than a social animal, that the senior political leaders oftentimes have to grab (to use a tanker's analogy) TC override. I wonder again, just how much of that is because the war aims have changed, the senior military advisors and leaders haven't been part of the change, they've been left behind and if that's the case then they're measuring something that isn't consistent with the outcome that the political leaders want to achieve at that time. So there's a gap which becomes a credibility gap for the military leader and is there something that the history of these 12 or 13 different campaigns can tell us about how a military leader can become someone attuned to that dynamic and give the kind of advice without crossing that fine line in our profession from transition and from giving advice to being an advocate of a particular outcome.

Stated one other way, because this is very complex stuff, I think that what is emerging and one of the themes that I'm walking away from is fairly or unfairly, rightly or wrongly, that the military leader and the national command authority political leaders need to co-create in some way the context which produces the outcomes we see as opposed to them being imposed by one group or another and really, sometimes run afoul, or sometimes we lose our way, as if one group or the other in isolation makes those changes because then we find ourselves pulling apart. I'm just curious if that is a lesson that could be drawn out of this and in so doing, help me understand how to build future leaders.

Colonel Gian Gentile

I know could comment on that question and those important points but since we are out of time, I will use my prerogative. Joe's writing something. Actually, I was going to talk about Vietnam and just to comment on what you say. Actually, I think sometimes war aims often do change but sometimes they don't and maybe it's important for the state that's fighting an enemy, who doesn't have changing war aims, to assess those and what that means for (at least in the case of Vietnam) our own. The last point that you made sir is this question of military leaders along with political leaders and the co-creation of an outcome. I'm sure Joe could have a lot of interesting things to say about President Lincoln and his generals in the Civil War but I will touch on that in my talk on Vietnam this afternoon. At least in my reading of the final years of the war, between General Abrams and President Nixon, there is not a co-creation. In fact, the two actually become separated in terms of how they see using military force to go about ending the war.

So with that, I would like to conclude this excellent second morning panel and thank all of the presenters for their talks and for the excellent questions as well.

Session 3

Philippine War

by

Dr. Brian Linn

The Samar campaign is widely seen as the *nadir*[1] of American counterinsurgency in the Philippine War. The surrender of General Claro Gueverra and the last 90 members of the nationalist forces on 27 April, 1902, took place amidst a desolated, disease-wracked, and starving island. For almost a year, American soldiers aided by sailors and marines, had conducted a brutal campaign to forcibly separate the population from the guerrillas. Joint Army-Navy operations had destroyed houses, livestock, boats, crops, and even fishing weirs[2], forcibly relocated tens of thousands of Samarenos into concentration camps, and had killed hundreds of suspected combatants. With heavy handed irony, critics have contrasted President William McKinley's 1898 directive that "The mission [of the] United States is one of benevolent assimilation, substituting the mild sway of justice and right for arbitrary rule," with Brigadier General Jacob H. Smith's command: "I want no prisoners. I wish you to kill and burn. The more you kill and burn, the better you will please me." That the officer who received Smith's orders, Lieutenant Colonel Littleton W. T. Waller of the United States Marine Corps did kill, burn, and summarily execute prisoners, only compounds Samar's bad reputation. Just as My Lai and Abu Ghraib have become iconic, if mistaken, measures of US troop conduct in more recent pacification campaigns, so Samar serves as the archetypical example of the Philippine War.

The origins of American military involvement in the Philippines are one of the greatest controversies in American historiography. The cascading consequences of apparently random decisions and events ranging from an obscure plan drawn up by a handful of Navy officers to President William McKinley's intuitive and opportunistic strategy, defies lineal analysis. Surely there must be more rational or more sinister explanations: an imperialist conspiracy, Anglo-Saxon racism, Manifest Destiny, declining or expanding markets, the need for naval bases, irresponsible media moguls, the insidious influence of Theodore Roosevelt. That the Filipino side is equally confusing only compounds the problem. After the defeat of an 1896 revolt in the Tagalog tribal region surrounding Manila, its exiled leader, Emilio Aguinaldo, returned in an American ship to declare an independent Philippine nation with himself as dictator. Simultaneously, anti-Spanish revolts broke out throughout the archipelago, driving out the Spanish and established governments. Many of new polities refused to acknowledge Aguinaldo's authority and the recently proclaimed republic on Negros Island requested United States protection. All of these new polities, and especially Aguinaldo's government, were composed of wealthy landowners, businessmen, and political chiefs; the peasantry that made up the vast majority of the Filipino populace was excluded. No wonder historians cannot determine if the ensuing conflict was a Tagalog rebellion, a conglomeration of tribal and regional uprisings, a nationalist revolution, a revolt of the masses, a Filipino-American war, or (as the United States officially termed it) an "insurrection." What is clear is that Commodore George Dewey's 1 May 1898 defeat of the Spanish flotilla at Manila Bay opened a host of possibilities for McKinley and his military advisors. Based in part on Dewey's misleading reports, McKinley decided to send 11,000 troop expedition to assist him. Reflecting abysmal ignorance or unbridled confidence, McKinley declared the expedition's dual objectives were to complete the "reduction" of Spanish authority and provide peace and order to the archipelago's inhabitants. In so doing, McKinley assumed Dewey's victory had effectively transferred the governance of the Philippines to the United States, a claim he would insist on in subsequent peace negotiations.

On the evening of 4 February 1899, fighting broke out between the 21,000-man American force inside Manila and Aguinaldo's besieging army. The ensuing three-week Battle of Manila was a decisive American victory, destroying many of Aguinaldo's best units and much of his military supplies, and securing Manila as a logistic and administrative center. For the rest of the year, the United States Army drove Aguinaldo's increasingly fragmented forces north until they dispersed in November. As he began his flight into the mountains of northern Luzon, Aguinaldo declared that henceforth resistance would be continued by guerrilla war. His instructions had far less impact on the conduct of the war than McKinley's insistence the Army should lay the foundations for colonial government, a mandate that required soldiers to conquer and rule the Philippines. What had been a relatively conventional war fought almost entirely in central Luzon became an archipelago-wide struggle between small garrisons and local revolutionaries for control of individual towns, provinces, and islands. Both sides integrated political and military responsibilities. An officer was often simultaneously his town's mayor, chief engineer, sanitation inspector, school superintendence, and tax collector. His guerrilla opponents were usually locally raised militia who lived either in the garrison town or its outlying barrios. They gathered periodically to harass the troops, collect supplies and taxes, and intimidate collaborators. As American post commanders came to understand the nature of the resistance in their specific areas, they developed intelligence contacts, established effective and loyal government agencies (particularly police and militia), and through a mixture of coercion and benevolence, secured popular compliance. By July of 1901, organized armed resistance was over and a civil government under William Howard Taft had assumed control in all but a few provinces.

One of the exceptions was Samar, a 5,200 square mile island in the Visayas islands whose 195,000 inhabitants, with the exception of a few wealthy merchants and landowners, eked out a precarious living growing rice and hemp and fishing the island's treacherous coastal waters and rivers. Dominated by jagged [and] jungle covered mountains that restricted its population to coastal or river villages, Samar's terrain, climate, foliage, and diseases posed daunting obstacles to both Americans and the indigenous resistance movement under the loose control of Vicente Lukban. The first expedition in January 1900 captured the two northern ports of Calbayog and Catbalogan, but was unable to advance into the interior. After a bloody skirmish at Catubig in April, the high command reduced Samar's garrison to a battalion and to the two ports. Lukban and other political military *jefes* (bosses) had over a year to organize military units, build supply caches, and mobilize popular support. Although Lukban's proclamations convinced Americans (then and now) [that] he was the supreme warlord of Samar, most guerrillas were locally raised and led, and some, such as the devotees of the Dios Dios cult, pursued their own interests and waged private wars.

In May of 1901, the collapse of resistance in most of the archipelago and the declaration of civil government in the neighboring island of Leyte made heretofore neglected Samar a new priority for the senior commander in the Visayas, Brigadier General Robert P. Hughes. Hughes' pessimistic appraisal was that after a year and a half, soldiers "know nothing beyond gun shot range of their stations, except what is learned through uncertain sources." He brought in the 1st and 9th Infantry Regiments and some squadrons of the 10th Cavalry and began sending troops into previously unoccupied areas along the coast and river valleys. Recognizing the futility of chasing guerrillas through Samar's mountains, rivers, and cane fields, Hughes targeted their food supplies and access to hemp [which was] their main source of funds. Army patrols began what soldiers referred to as "burning;" destroying crops, livestock, shelters, fishing boats, and anything else deemed of military utility. Hughes encouraged his troops to herd civilians found in the interior into garrisoned towns, frequently devastated in previous fighting. Samar's guerrillas reacted with ambushes and their own burning campaign. The result was an ecological and demographical catastrophe with thousands of malnourished and diseased noncombatants overwhelming the efforts of bewildered, frustrated, and often outraged post commanders. Hughes' propensity for large region-clearing punitive operations led him to neglect local security and strip the town garrisons. On 28 September, guerrillas under Major Eugenio Daza and the townspeople of Balangiga attacked Company C of the 9th Infantry, killing 48 officers and men.

The "Balangiga Massacre" both panicked and enraged Division of the Philippines commander Major General Adna R. Chaffee. General Smith later claimed Chaffee told him to make the interior of Samar a "howling wasteland," a phrase he subsequently repeated to Waller. By the end of the year, infantry strength in Smith's 6th Separate Brigade on Samar had grown to 11 infantry battalions, including Waller's Marines, and eight companies of Filipino Scouts. Off the coast, a flotilla of Navy gunboats provided transport for military expeditions and fire support for isolated garrisons. Hughes and Smith and their naval counterparts, quickly lost the ability to command and control these forces. Smith provided almost no guidance to his staff, left his headquarters (and his communications) for days on end while he wandered around the countryside, and issued fiery statements to his post commanders that essentially ordered them to pursue a war without mercy. Navy officers expanded Smith's 27 October directive that "all natives found passing between [Samar and Leyte] or afloat on either shore will be fired upon and killed" to cover all of Samar's waters. Smith pursued similarly draconian policies on shore, telling one officer; "I want this war carried on with more severity. In fact, it is more killing that I want." When another officer asked for assistance in feeding the refugees, Smith told him, "Let them die, the sooner they are all dead the sooner we will have peace." He ordered his officers to target rich and influential civilians, including priests, and to assume that all civic officials were actively assisting the guerrillas. Under his directives, Samarenos were arrested and imprisoned, forced to guide patrols or serve as translators, and otherwise persecuted. Smith dispatched officers, especially Major Edwin F. Glenn (his brigade provost), to arrest and interrogate suspected insurgent sympathizers. He continued Hughes' policies of sending both large cordon-and-sweep operations and small patrols into the countryside to destroy guerrillas and their supplies. One such expedition, under Waller, was a disaster. He disregarded advice, told no one of his location, abandoned his command, and then failed to report them as lost, thus indirectly causing the deaths of 11 United States Marines from exposure. Even worse, he summarily executed 11 Filipino porters on grounds of treachery, when all evidence indicates that without their assistance even more of the US Marines would have died.

By the end of 1901, there were disturbing indications the campaign on Samar was spinning into violent chaos. American patrols, having burned out most accessible areas, now had to march for days to get to "hostile" territory. A number of reports claimed large numbers of insurgents killed but captured virtually no prisoners or weapons, indications of both inflated estimates and indiscriminate shooting. Most of Lukban's guerrillas had dispersed and hidden their weapons, and the guerrilla chief's escort had shrunk to a handful of guards. To many officers, Smith's harsh policies were counterproductive, actually impeding peace and stability. Post commanders demanded the means to feed the thousands of starving refugees and issued passes to fishermen and merchants to bring in food. Smith's interdiction of trade and his insolence and contempt for civilian rule, along with Glenn's kidnapping and torture raids enraged both Leyte's governor and the Philippines' civil government. Even more alarming, rumors of Waller's executions spread by boasting United States Marine officers, soon found their way into press. Chaffee, belatedly trying to exercise control and mitigate growing pressure from Taft and Washington, visited Samar in late January and was appalled. He cancelled or moderated many of Smith's harshest directives, restricted Glenn's activities, stopped indiscriminate destruction, and told officers that they were no longer to regard all Filipinos as enemies. Shortly afterwards, Smith was relieved of command. He was subsequently court martialed and retired from duty.

In February, a patrol of Visayan Scouts captured Lukban. His successor, Claro Guevarra, surrendered to Smith's successor on 27 April. Samar was transferred officially to civil government on 16 June, and on 4 July 1902, President Theodore Roosevelt formally declared the insurrection in the Philippines over. With villages, brigand gangs, and machete wielding cultists all quick to use violence, Samar was far from pacified. Army forces returned to the island in 1904 and stayed for almost three years to assist the civil government in suppressing the Pulahan Revolt. To this day the island is the scene of fighting between government forces, communist guerrillas, religious sects, private armies, and brigands.

The immediate effect of the termination of the Philippine War on the military was to relieve it of an unpopular and unsustainable obligation. The demands of overseas service had justified the reform agenda of Secretary of War Elihu Root in 1900 but they also inhibited change. The constant shuttling of officers and units back and forth from the Philippines resulted in organizational and personnel turbulence, delaying the establishment of schools, training facilities, and troop concentration in the United States. Moreover, by the end of the war, the United States Army was running out of men. Chaffee had to discharge 4,500 soldiers from the Philippines in March of 1902 alone. In order to improve the continental forces, the overseas garrisons were stripped to dangerous levels. American troop strength in the Philippines declined from 68,000 in 1901 to 13,000 in 1904. Although troops, particularly the 5,000-man Filipino Scout force, were occasionally called in to suppress civil disturbances, their primary mission was defensive. By 1913, the United States Army had concentrated all but a few of its troops to guard Manila and the vast fortification system guarding its harbor. Concurrently, the United States Army created a permanent colonial army, rationalizing the overseas deployment schedule at the cost of acknowledging the Philippine garrison was incapable of defending the archipelago. For most of the next three decades, until Douglas MacArthur's grandiose revisions, the garrison's wartime mission was limited to protecting Manila Bay until relieved by the Navy.

The conquest of the Philippines, and the concurrent acquisition of Guam and Hawaii, appeared to provide the United States with a far superior strategic situation in the Pacific and the Far East. It was soon clear to most civilian and military leaders that while Hawaii was essential to North American defense, the Philippines were, in Roosevelt's words, America's Achilles heel. Some, such as Leonard Wood and MacArthur, argued that with more troops and a strong naval base, the Philippines would serve as a springboard to Asia, securing intangible benefits to American political, economic, and moral influence throughout the Far East. Others argued the Philippines were not only indefensible but their very weakness, when coupled with American pretensions to dominate Asian trade, was likely to provoke war with Japan. For decades, in both Washington and Manila, military policy was paralyzed by this debate between imperialists and continentalists. By the time it was resolved, in the continentalists' favor, it was too late. The results were graphically and tragically displayed in both Hawaii and the Philippines in December of 1941.

Recommended Reading

Andrew J. Birtle, "US Army Counterinsurgency and Contingency Operations Doctrine, 1860-1941," (Washington: Center of Military History, 1998)

John M. Gates, "Schoolbooks and Krags: The United States Army in the Philippines, 1898-1902," (Westport, Conn.: Greenwood Press, 1973)

Brian McAllister Linn, "The US Army and Counterinsurgency in the Philippine War, 1899-1902," (Chapel Hill: University of North Carolina Press, 1989

Brian McAllister Linn, "Guardians of Empire: The US Army in the Pacific, 1902-1940," (Chapel Hill: University of North Carolina Press, 1997)

Brian McAllister Linn, "The Philippine War, 1899-1902," (University Press of Kansas, 2000)

William T. Sexton, "Soldiers in the Sun: An Adventure in Imperialism," (Harrisburg, PA: Military Service Publishing Co., 1939);

John R. M. Taylor, "The Philippine Insurrection Against the United States, 1898-1903: A Compilation of Documents and Introduction," 5 vols., (1906: Reprint, 1971, Pasay City, P.I.: Eugenio Lopez Foundation)

Richard E. Welch, "Response to Imperialism: The United States and the Philippine-American War, 1899-1902," (Chapel Hill: University of North Carolina Press, 1979)

Endnotes

1. Lowest point of greatest adversity/despair
2. Traps/enclosures in a stream to catch fish

Session 3

Interview

Dr. Brian Linn

Dr. Brian Linn

My name is Brian McAllister Linn and I'm a professor of history at Texas A&M University.

Interviewer

So, let's go right to the work of the conference and then we'll backtrack from there to some of your early academic history and some of the things that you've produced. Tell me what the subject was that you tackled in the essay for the TRADOC conference on war termination.

Dr. Brian Linn

I dealt specifically with what happened after the end of what's now called the Philippine-American War and used to be the Philippine Insurrection and I call the Philippine War. So I sort of studied the last campaigns that occurred in 1901-1902 and then carried it out to sort of see what the problems they had with ending the war after it had been officially declared over, some of the impact that it had had on the United States Army, and then the long-term strategic results of occupying an overseas empire.

Interviewer

I guess what you just described as the war that has three completely different names says something about war termination in itself, doesn't it?

Dr. Brian Linn

Right, exactly. We were never sure what the war was and in fact, there was a legal problem because we officially didn't take possession of the Philippines. The treaty wasn't signed with Spain until about two months after the war had begun. . . .

Interviewer

Go on for a moment, before we get specific about the Philippine war, to some of the themes that Roger Spiller outlined in what, I guess, was in some respects the kind of broad introductory essay about war termination and its historical importance, if you could.

Dr. Brian Linn

Well, I should point out there was enormous discussion at the meeting we had in January about how to define war termination and what this project would actually be. Everyone that deals with it has to deal with a variety of things. You obviously have to talk a little bit about how the war began. Then you have to sort of talk about how it ended. Now do you want to spend a lot of time focusing on how the war ended, or do you want to breeze through that and talk about the short-term consequences and the long-term consequences? I think, and to the credit of the people that organized it, we didn't get a checklist. We weren't sort of given a master outline that we had to follow, and I think Roger's problem, then, was to try and impose coherence on a group of essays in which people were focusing on very different things. I've read five of them and there are similar themes in them, so I would guess that Roger's great contribution is to put the sort of coherence on there that the individual essays might not necessarily have, and I think he's probably the one you should interview on how he fit that together.

Interviewer

Allowing that freedom was necessary, because each war dictated its own special understanding of a way that a war ends and it also is dictated from the perspective from which you're viewing it. I mean, if you go out 20 years later you might see that the significance of an earlier battle was more important than whatever was the last campaign.

Dr. Brian Linn

Right.

Interviewer

In your case in the Philippine War, really it's very hard to mark what the end was because the insurgency overlaps and tangles itself with the war itself and then beginnings and endings are really hard to tease out. Is that right?

Dr. Brian Linn

Well, sort of. Two points. One of them is the first book that we were following, "America's First Battles," had in it a study in unpreparedness. There was a unifying theme, but that was in part driven by TRADOC's desire to show the consequences in unpreparedness. Right now, we're in a situation in the current operating environment where those lessons aren't nearly as clear and it's not nearly as vital for people to know: the consequences of not winning the first battle.

Interviewer

Given what General Dempsey just outlined and what Professor Spiller mentioned, you could say it's a study in uncertainty.

Dr. Brian Linn

Right, but it's a lot easier to prepare for unpreparedness than it is to prepare for uncertainty, almost by definition. In my particular case, the war essentially ended because Teddy Roosevelt declared it was over and he picked 4 July, but the initial commander in military operations, who was General Elwell Otis, wrote, I think, in March of 1900, "The war is over and all that's left is a big job of policing." This has been said, by the way, about Afghanistan; that we have essentially won that war twice. We just haven't recognized that we won it and pulled out. That we won it allegedly when the Taliban were driven out, and we could have declared victory and come home; and we won it in 2004 when the first election occurred, and we could have declared victory and come home. Neither choice or decision was made to do that, and now we're in a situation where it looks like it may well be completely unraveling and we will simply sort of have to pack our bags and leave, because Karzai and no one wants us anymore; and it's simply, we can't afford economically or in terms of our world position to continue to fight it. So war is difficult. You have to know when to say it's over.

Interviewer

I would like to come to the parallels between the Philippine situation and Iraq and Afghanistan both, but just before we get to that, I do want you to describe to me the story of the Philippine War, but historically, there's also an argument that the First World War's end doesn't happen until the Cold War ends, right?

Dr. Brian Linn

There are also issues of definition. If you see the war in the Philippines as essentially a military struggle over who was going to impose government on the villages and the provinces, that war, in fact, you could argue is over a year before it's declared over because the United States essentially controls so much of the Philippines that there's almost no possibility that the nationalist resistance is going to be able to do that, and it's essentially mopping up operations. By June of 1901, if not earlier, that's certainly the case. So in a way, Roosevelt's taking a year after the war to declare what everyone knows, and that sort of leads to what, some would argue, those wars aren't really over until the Moro wars end in 1913 or the Japanese invasion or, now look, you've got violence in almost every area that the Americans had problems with after. You've got problems in Southeast Luzon, we've got Samar, Mindanao. Where were the problems after the end of the Philippine War? It's the same areas.

Interviewer

Or you could argue, I guess, the war could have been "over" with independence in 1934. Again, it depends on where you want to define it and how you want to define it, but where you want to choose to stop.

Dr. Brian Linn

Right, if you want to talk about the war being over when there's no more sort of endemic armed resistance against the government of the Philippines, that war is still very much going on and we now supposedly have special forces troops operating in areas that Pershing was operating in, helping the Philippine Army.

Interviewer

Tell me the story of the Philippine War. You're speaking to an undergraduate, let's say. You're just telling them what the war was from the period of McKinley, Roosevelt to the whole story.

Dr. Brian Linn

Well, there are problems that you could probably do it in one sentence and you could do it in a paragraph and you could do it in a 400-page book, but anything in between is very difficult.

Interviewer

Let's try the paragraph.

Dr. Brian Linn

Okay. The war is a completely unplanned war in the sense that we're at war with Spain to liberate Cuba, a very limited war. I mean, this is a limited war objective. We're not talking about invading Spain and, in fact, the initial plan was simply to blockade, which would have achieved most of these objectives. But the first military action of that war is a strike by the Navy's Asiatic squadron on the Spanish squadron in Manila Bay.

Interviewer

Why are we interested in this in the beginning?

Dr. Brian Linn

Now this is very complicated, and I think it's got some relevance for today. It was a militarily sound action without people really thinking, "Okay, once we do this what are we supposed to do with it?" Well, the fact that we can do it doesn't necessarily mean you should do it, and so Dewey sails out and he wins this tremendous and completely unexpected victory and you have to remember, except for the wars on the western frontier, which weren't wars, this is the first war since the Civil War.

Interviewer

What year are we now?

Dr. Brian Linn

This is Dewey's victory in 1898.

Interviewer

Describe Dewey for a second.

Dr. Brian Linn

Well, Dewey is a Civil War veteran, a Vermonter who's out in the Far East. He's actually in Hong Kong with the Asiatic squadron, which is largely to protect United States trade in the Far East, mainly China trade. He's got a very small squadron out there, but relative to the Spanish, it's quite possible. He does a very brave thing. He steams through the defenses, which for all he knew he was going into what they called torpedoes; we would call mines, and coast artillery. In fact, the Spanish hadn't put those out because they had all decayed. So he steams through. Once he does that, the Battle of Manila Bay is essentially pretty much a massacre. Well, news of Dewey's victory comes back.

Interviewer

Go back a minute. Why did Dewey engage there? What were the terms of engagement, to put it that way, for Dewey and what political motivation inspired it?

Dr. Brian Linn

Well, I'm not sure he's certain. The idea is that you're at war with this country as a target of opportunity. There's no smoking gun in the sense of there's no document from McKinley saying if we destroy the Spanish fleet in the Philippines, we can trade the Philippines for Cuba, or we need foreign trade, or we need to capture the Philippines so we'll have a base in the Far East. These are all ideas that are brooded about, and the new left has made much of this, but McKinley himself as a strategic leader kept everything to himself. And he had the wonderful ability of talking to people and looking at them very sincerely and speaking in platitudes and at the end, they were absolutely sure they agreed with him, but they couldn't really remember much of what he said. He didn't like to write anything down, and he liked to talk to people and he listened, but he kept his own counsel; and so despite enormous amounts of effort by scholars, we really don't know what's in his mind. He rarely committed himself and if you read his speeches, he would try out different ideas, depending on the audience and sometimes he would say one thing and sometimes he would say something else and he would sort of get the temper of the American public from that.

Interviewer

Where is the great biography of McKinley? Where is that?

Dr. Brian Linn

I don't think there is one. I mean he's too complicated and people have tried.

Interviewer

He's sort of opaque in that way.

Dr. Brian Linn

He's very opaque and he's very frustrating because he doesn't give. I mean I used to teach McKinley to military officers as a case study in the Powell Doctrine because he violates every tenet of the Powell Doctrine, and yet, I would argue he is the most successful wartime commander in chief we've ever had.

Interviewer

So walk me through both those points real quickly.

Dr. Brian Linn

Okay. He does not provide clear guidance. He doesn't have an end state. He doesn't go in with overwhelming force. If you go through, I guess he secures popular consent but not really because he doesn't really allow the Congress much knowledge on the Philippines until he's already done it. I mean he doesn't do anything. He doesn't provide the American public with what we're supposed to be doing there. He keeps everything quiet. He never commits himself. The best McKinley story I can tell you is Wesley Merritt, who McKinley has appointed to be the commander of this mission to the Philippines comes down and spends several hours with McKinley, talking about what McKinley wants, goes back and there's a telegram in the War Department reports from Merritt, sort of saying, "I don't know if you want me to occupy Manila or the entire Philippine archipelago." Now think, a man who can sit down with his commander for three or four hours and talk to him, have this discussion and at the end of it he still doesn't know.

Interviewer

He does not know?

Dr. Brian Linn

McKinley doesn't tell him. There's no letter back saying, "Oh, just Manila" and these military officers get very angry at McKinley and they say, "Oh, why is he doing this? He's being a politician. He's being wishy-washy." I say no. He's being strategic. He's one of the most brilliant strategists in the world or in American history because what does he have to gain by committing himself? That's a question that needs strategic analysis. What does he have to gain by committing himself? The Powell Doctrine assumes you will always gain by committing yourself, but the one case study where Powell claims it worked, in fact we lost enormous amount by committing ourselves. We should not have said we're not going to Baghdad in retrospect. That was a very silly decision. It was a very silly decision on a strategic level and on numerous occasions, his ability as a strategist was shown to be mediocre at best. McKinley doesn't commit and at any time, as a result, up until he sort of tells the delegation in Paris that we want the Philippines, which is quite late (after the war is over), he could pull out. If the situation doesn't work, if he gets a defeat, he has not risked his personal prestige. He has not risked the nation's prestige. He can withdraw. So he sends people out and sees what's going on. He's a Clausewitzian—war has its own dynamic. Things will turn up. The Powell Doctrine assumes that no good opportunities will arise, that you know this all when you go in, and that's why you have an end state. McKinley always assumed that war could go one way or the other and it might throw up disasters, but it might also throw up opportunities.

Interviewer

It also strikes me that by keeping his cards close to his chest, he reminds me a little bit of Eisenhower in the 1950s. Will he do the worst thing possible? Will he do the best thing possible? You don't know and that uncertainty, when presented by a strong executive figure, can be a powerful deterrent to a war itself.

Dr. Brian Linn

Yes, and he was a very capable and very strong executive and you think about it, the war really starts in late April. It's over by 13 August 1898. With May, June, and July, it's barely a four-month war and in that, he gets the Philippines, he frees Cuba, he gets Hawaii and Guam, and he creates this empire at minimal cost to the nation. It's really hard to beat that. I mean, compare that to the Gulf Wars – not nearly as successful an operation. So you have to throw this back at military officers when they're dealing with McKinley, to explain why he's successful. If he's completely inept, why is he so successful? The fact is that he's a strategist in my mind in the sense of recognizing war is chaotic and let's seize opportunities, and for him, that's a very good way to be.

Interviewer

So go back to the story of the war.

Dr. Brian Linn

Okay. So you have a commander in chief who's like that to begin with and as a result, the war, especially the Philippines dimension of it, is completely unexpected because McKinley is into opportunity, he does provide very specific guidance but it's not the guidance his commanders in the field want. He provides guidance about civil government, about how to treat the Filipinos, about what your mission is. From the beginning, McKinley sees this as an opportunity. He sees the army's mission not just an opportunity but as one essentially of governance. Whether that's going to be permanent governance or not, he doesn't commit to anything.

Interviewer

Is this going on the white man's burden notion then?

Dr. Brian Linn

Well, again, with McKinley it's very tough to find out because he rarely commits himself.

Interviewer

That's a big discussion there. I mean that's part of the conversation at the moment.

Dr. Brian Linn

Actually, the poem "White Man's Burden" is written by Rudyard Kipling at this time. I mean it is [written] to the United States upon the occupation of the Philippines. I mean, that poem is directly written by a British Imperialist to the Americans on what they need to do. So the term wasn't used before then, because it didn't exist, but it becomes very popular. Now currently, there's an enormous amount of focus in America on race and the question is whether race is a factor or is it the driving factor? I just haven't seen enough in the documentary evidence to see it as a driving factor and again, I can tell you what Henry Cabot Lodge thought about it, and Alfred Thurman thought about it and perhaps what Teddy Roosevelt thought about it. The fact that these people are there and even if you can prove they're talking to McKinley doesn't prove that that's United States policy, and this is a problem that the new left and the race-oriented or gender-oriented explanation (that this is a test of American manhood) always has. At a certain level, you have to show cause and effect and there's no cause and effect. There's a good article in the "American Historical Review" a long time ago that said this was the worst chapter in any American history textbook, and it's about this period. It's inherently true in the Philippine War. People from the beginning cast the war in ideological terms. I mean, from the beginning it was cast as either imperialism (America's destiny) or anti-imperialism, this is the final breaking of the Republic. The ideal of Jefferson that ideological debate actually supplanted any narrative history of the war is what Mark Twain and George Frisbie Hoar and the anti-imperialists are talking about. No one really cared about the events, except as they fit into this ideological interpretation. The imperialists spent a great deal of time proving the Filipinos were unfit for government and were committing atrocities and this proved their unfitness for government. The first task of the newly formed Intelligence Bureau is to gather Philippine documents to show that the Filipinos caused the war and that Aguinaldo caused the war and that they couldn't be trusted. So that's going on with the government side and on the anti-imperialist side, the same thing is going on. They take sections from soldiers' letters, some of which were later shown to be bogus, to prove the Americans are conducting operations in a genocidal manner and, I hate to say this, but many of my colleagues in academics 106 years later are still at that level. They haven't advanced the dialogue very much at all. They're perhaps doing more research, but their interpretations were formed by Mark Twain 106 years ago and they haven't really moved beyond that.

Interviewer

What is your interpretation?

Dr. Brian Linn

I really wasn't interested in either one of those. I mean, I really wasn't, and I think that was my saving grace. What I was interested in when I started looking at it, was that no one had ever written a book about how this war was actually fought on either side. There was just a lot of mythology, but no one had really sort of gone down and tried to retrace how the war was actually fought. Well, for a military historian that's rare. I mean, you can go to this library here and you can find 30 books on how Shiloh alone was fought or the second day of Gettysburg was fought. To come across an American war where there's actually no narrative of how the war was fought was amazing for me, and it happened to be that I was interested not in big unit operations, I was interested in counterinsurgency. This is an ideal war. So you've got a war that no one knows how it was fought and a counterinsurgency struggle, and so for me the real interest was not the big picture, which I don't think I'm qualified to determine and I don't think anyone else is either to be quite blunt. I mean, I don't buy the big picture interpretations of this war for a number of reasons. The main one is people haven't done the research. Now, so when I started getting interested in that, I went in saying, "Well, all I had read by people like Stuart Miller and Howard Zinn was this was a race war. Americans went in and murdered indiscriminately and shot down Filipinos in droves." What your textbook tells you, but it was because of race and so I said, "Well where did this happen?" I sort of started with these big picture ideas. Was it because American society was racist? Well, for a military historian, that's hard to prove if you're in the archives. So I thought maybe it was because as Stuart Miller claimed, they recruited all these people from the West who already had this Indian War background and they just went out there and fought them like Indians. Well, that really quickly proved to be completely fabricated. I mean, he confused two different organizations. It was completely silly. He had the guys that fought the conventional war who tended to be predominantly western but that wasn't who fought the counterinsurgency campaign. Those guys were from all over the country. So he just didn't understand that there had been a state volunteer and a United States volunteer and they're two different organizations.

Interviewer

Give me a side note here with when the conventional war begins and ends in that time period now and the insurgency/counterinsurgency continue and for how long?

Dr. Brian Linn

Well, there are two phases. Fighting breaks out in Manila. I mean, the first Battle of Manila is 13 August 1898. The Americans come in and sort of strike a deal which some of the army guys don't know and capture Manila. Emilio Aguinaldo, who claims that he represents an independent Philippine Republic, has already claimed independence on the

146

outside and doesn't get in there, but tries to get in and the Americans hold him back. So from August to February, you have this escalating tension. Aguinaldo is hoping that first the Americans won't take the Philippines and then when it's clear that McKinley has demanded that, the Senate won't vote for that, that they will reject the treaty and there's a lot of indication it's a close vote. It was won by about two or three votes in the end.

Interviewer

An anti-imperialist argument almost prevailing is what you're saying?

Dr. Brian Linn

Yes. The Army has got very few people, 11,000 or 13,000, I'm not sure, in Manila and many of those are physically broken down from disease and it can't get anyone from Cuba because those people are really hammered from yellow fever. So it's just been devastated by 1898 and it needs to build troops up. In fact, they're waiting for about 6,000 or 7,000 new troops to come in so they can send these people in who are mostly National Guardsmen who signed up to fight the Spanish. Well, that war is over and they're being stop-lossed. They're being held. I mean this is one of the first cases of stop-loss. These guys all had signed up for the duration of the war. Once that treaty is signed, the war is over and they want to go home. Well, as these two sides both don't want war and McKinley keeps saying, "Look, time is on our side. Time is on our side." Commanders say, "When can we fight?" "Don't." He keeps telling, "Time is on our side." Aguinaldo's government will fracture, which McKinley didn't have intelligence on but his gut was very good on this. Aguinaldo's government is entirely drawn from the landholding elite. Many islands aren't even represented. The delegate from Cebu was a Tagalog from Manila. Aguinaldo's attempts to impose control, even on the island of Luzon, aren't working. In many cases, like on the island of Panay where he sends an armed group, they immediately start not fighting but disputing with the local insurgents who want a Federal Republic of Panay. These people aren't fighting for a Philippines like Aguinaldo wants, a strong centralized government run by the Tagalogs. These people are Cebuano or Ilocano or Luzani. They want something like Brazil, a series of federated states, and so there's this contested period in which I think McKinley is sort of aware of and unfortunately in Manila, tensions are rising. There have been a number of alarms and on the night of 4 February, a patrol from the Nebraska regiment stumbles into a Filipino scouting party and fire is exchanged. Well, fire had been exchanged for months. I mean, this is pretty common but in this particular instance, things escalate beyond the ability of both sides to stop them. Aguinaldo is out of town. Firing escalates. The next day, the Americans go on the offensive and there's this very, very bitter battle for about two weeks; the Battle of Manila in which the Americans drive back Aguinaldo's forces and capture much of the equipment that he had captured from the Spanish and that's crucial. Mauser rifles, for example, you can't manufacture that ammunition and so they captured that. Artillery—they destroy many of the Spanish-trained units and if you've ever seen Manila, Manila itself runs like this. There's the ocean from Manila Bay but on this side, there's something called Laguna de Bay. With this big lagoon and Manila is actually on this sort of narrow land, well the Americans drive through. So between the ocean and the bay, the Americans establish this quadrant and that splits Aguinaldo's army into two. His base of strength is in the south, the Tagalog provinces of Cavite and Batangas and Tayabas and Laguna but he and his army are in central Luzon and the Americans then sort of build a defensive ring in the south and then go on the offensive in the north and the campaign from February to November is very similar.

Interviewer

In normal war theory creating a-two front war for yourself is dangerous. Is this what they had effectively done?

Dr. Brian Linn

Yeah, I mean he had circled Manila, which is good, but the problem with encircling it, if your back is to water, is once they break out, you're forced. Now then the Americans have interior lines. They can build a defense and shift troops back and forth. What they do in practice is periodically they go and knock back the southern tip. Then they focus on going after Aguinaldo and trying to destroy him. Now the Philippines is an agrarian society and most of the crop is essentially rice. To the south it's hemp, which leads to a real problem of supplying our armies. There's a reason why the Europeans developed modern war right about the time they started producing an agricultural surplus. You can't wage war in a society like the Philippines with basically subsistence. So the only way that you can subsist an army is along this railroad line that runs into central Luzon. So both Aguinaldo and the Americans are sort of tethered to this line and so what happens is Aguinaldo's army will be first at Malolos and then a series of positions along the railroad line where he's trying to supply himself, retrain his army and the Americans will drive up the railroad. One unit will sort of attack him and hold him. Another unit will march through the countryside and try and come in the rear and cut the railroad line and the problem is there are no maps, so they go off Spanish maps showing a road and it's a trail. You can move about four miles a day. So with the first day, you march past your logistic line. Second day, your troops start drinking the local water. Third and fourth day, you start having dysentery, malaria, fever. The units just collapse and then you have to sort of rebuild them and then a month later you can go on another. It's not that Aguinaldo is going to always sort of slip away. Just a day too short or a couple of hours too short, they get to the railroad blind and it's evacuated. So you have a series of very interesting encircling campaigns but by summer, the army that went to the Philippines is broken.

Interviewer

Where is command and control for the United States under this circumstance?

Dr. Brian Linn

Well, you have General Elwell Otis who is the commanding general in the Philippines and later the military governor, and he always wears two hats and he always focuses on that. When I talk about the Philippines, then I get these guys, "Well, these guys were just a bunch of old Indian War officers, they aren't professionals like we are." I said Elwell Otis had a law degree from Harvard, and by the way, while he was fighting a war, he wrote the civil code for the Philippines. Now, you find me a four-star general in the US Army that can do that. They can't. I said a three-star or two-star or probably even a one-star. You've got more generals than any organization, I think, except maybe the People's Liberation Army.

Interviewer

It's probably still the civil code.

Dr. Brian Linn

Yeah and yet, here's this old guy who could do more than you could and he's fighting a war at the same time and he's doing a good job of fighting that war and because of that, there's more legitimacy for him to tell his officers, "You will also do this." So as they're fighting their way up there, they're also beginning to establish civil governments behind them because McKinley's mission to the army is that the army's job is what he calls "benevolent assimilation," or to show the Filipinos this is the army's mission and by your actions that the United States will provide good government.

Interviewer

Then depart this nation, right?

Dr. Brian Linn

It's not even there. Sometimes there will be a colonial government coming in, but that's again not declared and there's a sort of tension that goes on with these commanding generals asking for instructions in when we can fight and McKinley saying, "Your job isn't to fight. Your job is to govern." Otis takes this very seriously. So as the Americans are moving up, they're beginning to establish civil government, but by summer, his army is just collapsing, and so he needs time to get those volunteers back to the United States and bring in a new army that's only been created, I guess, since about April. Now some of these are regular units who have been rebuilt since Cuba and they're raw recruits. I mean 80 percent to 90 percent had just joined up. So the old army is already dead by 1899 and then 35,000 of them are the special United States volunteers who are raised entirely for service in the Philippines and have a limited term enlistment and they start appearing around August. When that new Army comes, Otis launches the final offensive. Only this time, he drives up the railroad with Arthur MacArthur. Henry Lawton launches a sweeping attack and Lawton bogs down almost immediately in the mud. So he takes his cavalry corps and sends this guy called Brigadier General S.B.M. Young who's the first army chief of staff, and Young does this incredibly heroic march and at the same time, another expedition, an amphibious expedition ends at the top of Lingayen Gulf and cutting the railroad. They immediately go and around 13 November or so, I'm not sure the exact date, Aguinaldo's army is just collapsing. I mean, people are just taking their guns and walking home and Aguinaldo essentially declares, "We will now continue resistance through guerilla war," and he tries to set up regional commands. He flees and goes off into the mountains in Northern Luzon where he remains largely a figurehead until Frederick Funston captures him in I think April of 1901.

Interviewer

Eventually, he dies in captivity?

Dr. Brian Linn

No, once he's captured in this sort of great special operations mission, he comes back.

He's treated very well. He meets with General McArthur, who has replaced Otis and within about a week, issues a proclamation urging his comrades to lay down their weapons and he actually lives all the way through to the Japanese occupation. I think he dies in the 1950s. So, in the process, he writes several autobiographies that sometimes have different facts in them.

Interviewer

Well, he's commanding the insurgency after this?

Dr. Brian Linn

Well, . . . he never really commanded. He was in [command] the same way Karzai commands the Afghan government. He's a coalition leader who rules only because he can consolidate very powerful military chiefs and by November, he can no longer control. I mean, he's had to execute or murder his commanding general, a guy called Antonio Luna, because he fears he's starting a coup. His army is pretty well collapsed, but his leaders have already collapsed and they've gone back to the local provinces. Now, if you look on this war as a war between the American government and its Army and the Philippine Republic and its army, and that's how General Otis looked on it, then by December, that war is over because Aguinaldo's army has been destroyed. He sweeps down to southern Luzon and destroys General Trias' army down there and then sends out an expedition and just captures ports all the way down to Mindanao and actually into the whole lower Archipelago. That's why Otis says the war is over. There is no organized armed resistance facing us anymore, and then Otis dissolves the tactical organizations. You're no longer second brigade, first division for example, and instead he creates regional commands. He breaks up the Philippines into departments. There's the department of Northern Luzon, department of Southern Luzon, the Department of Mindanao and Hola. According to Otis's reference and the US Army's reference, these are back to the old western departments where you had like, the Department of New Mexico and then and there, there are not tactical commands but district commands. So he'll group four provinces into the first district of the Department of Northern Luzon, the second district and to Otis, the shift now is between becoming a commanding general to becoming a military governor, and that's the transition he's made in his mind. What he's doing is setting the groundwork now for that civil government. He's already written a sort of basic document for civil government. That's another funny thing is: "Well what is your document for civil government?" They give you this pile and they can give one to the marines and it's a page and a half. This is how you set up a government. That's all it is; police things and any lieutenant can do it. So he's working on that, but he also starts telling McKinley; "I want to come home now. I've done my job. I'm tired and I'm overworked and it's time for me to come home."

Interviewer

And he saw that the "end of this war" was that he had set up the Philippines for civil government.

Dr. Brian Linn

Right, and in fact, a civil government starts arriving under William Howard Taft and the Philippine commission is getting started and Arthur MacArthur takes over, the father of Douglas MacArthur.

Interviewer

Taft's role here is what?

Dr. Brian Linn

Well, Taft and the Philippine Commission is there to sort of create the conditions and what ultimately happens, it transitions to become the civil government of the Philippines. The Philippine Commission shifts from being a sort of assessment of the situation to suggesting the right form of government to that actual government.

Interviewer

Taft is a lawyer, he's coming in to establish...

Dr. Brian Linn

Right, and he's got a guy called Luke Wright who's another southern judge and so he's got a group of civilians and they're coming out to first assess and then ultimately take over, which I think was a lot smarter than what President Bush did when he sent Bremer out immediately to sort of take civil power. I mean it was really irritating to hear, "Well, we did this in the Philippines," like you told us to do in the Philippines and you say, "No, you did it exactly opposite from what McKinley wanted," but again, McKinley is a very capable and shrewd person.

Interviewer

George W. Bush's administration wasn't there? Cheney had a big interest.

Dr. Brian Linn

I know Karl Rove really had an interest. It's sort of like that great line in "A Fish Called Wanda" where the Kevin Kline, Otto, and Jamie Lee Curtis have this wonderful exchange where she says, "Otto, you big ape," and he says, "Apes don't read Nietzsche," and she says, "Yes, they do, Otto, they just don't understand him."

Interviewer

So Rove was reading McKinley without understanding, or he was probably reading into it what he wants to see.

Dr. Brian Linn

Exactly and without understanding that to run that system, you need to have Mark Hanna and you need to have William McKinley and neither Rove nor George Bush was in that league, frankly. I mean, you have one of the best wartime presidents and probably one of the worst and it's a real big difference. So a system that's personal has to have the personalities.

To get back to the war, Otis was aware of this, but he viewed this as banditry, but it really takes a long time for Manila to pick up what looks like isolated flashes and recognize there's a pattern. Many of the troops from Aguinaldo's forces in regional places like in

Panay and Samar as the Americans push out, are never defeated. The Americans land and they seize a port, but these people don't recognize they were defeated and they weren't fighting for Aguinaldo. They were fighting for local control and they had it and they've had two years to do it. The Spanish had left in 1890. Now in 1900, the Americans are showing up, landing, seizing a hemp port and saying, "You're now under the United States flag." These little flashes of guerrilla attacks, such as shooting a sentry and raids on supplies, but more importantly the difficulties the Americans are having in setting up local government and exerting control, takes a long time to recognize that what was initially a conventional war has shifted to a series of insurgencies. If you talk about a dozen little insurgencies over who is going to control villages and provinces, that is a war that the Filipinos are far better equipped to deal with than they were as a conventional war. It's hard to create an army out of nothing, but if you have a tradition of resistance at the local level, they're really well set up for that.

Interviewer

This is where the comparison to Afghanistan seems so acute, but not Iraq in the same way, right?

Dr. Brian Linn

Yeah, Iraq had tribes but yes, not. It's much better in many ways and we didn't really run into this in Afghanistan until we went into the countryside and started trying to impose order and at that point, that war suddenly shifted very dramatically because people might not care who's in Kabul but when you come into their territory, then there's resistance. Remember when there were anti-government elements for awhile? Well, I mean if these people don't recognize the construct known as Iraq or Afghanistan, how can there be anti-Afghanistan elements? I mean it's a great example of just not understanding the nature of the threat. Some people would argue that that's still very much the case in the Philippines. I mean, most of what we get from the Philippines is still dominated by people in Manila and still very strongly Tagalog. When I was there in 1996 at this conference, I met Eugene Odaza, who's a grandson of the person who led the Balangiga Massacre. He was very excited to meet me and he told me that one of the things he really liked about me was that I had restored Samar's resistance to the Samareños, that all the treatments in both the United States and the Philippines treated it as Vicente Lukban, who's one of Aguinaldo's officers and led resistance. Odaza said, "That's not true. This is our resistance. Lukban was important as a leader but it was us. We fought this war." So what I get from Filipinos is very interesting because in some cases, like people in the Manila area, they are very hostile to this because I'm essentially saying it's a local resistance. I'm challenging the idea of a unified Philippine nation, which a lot of people in Manila have bought into and it's very important that they prove that was the case in 1898, but out in Cebu or Iloilo or places like that, they have a much more positive view of this view of the war because it restores them.

Interviewer

Yeah, and it also goes to the heart of something in what General Kingston said which is that there's one layer of understanding, and then you go deeper. Then there's another layer of understanding and if you don't go deeper, you miss or you risk not knowing really what happened and whether you've achieved your objective or not.

152

Dr. Brian Linn

Right, and this is where it gets also very interesting in terms of the anti-imperialists who tend to quote MacArthur saying we're facing a united Philippine nation, but at the time he's making that statement, MacArthur is in no position to know that. He's been in Manila, and he hasn't been in the field for six months.

Interviewer

This is Arthur MacArthur?

Dr. Brian Linn

Arthur MacArthur makes that statement quite late in the war and he makes it, I think, for political reasons. He makes it because he's fighting with Taft, and Taft's challenging him. It's not a statement that people in the field would have agreed with and Arthur MacArthur doesn't have a whole lot of support out in the field. So again, when you're in Manila and you're looking at all of this, you create a one layer of understanding, which is this is a national resistance: the Filipinos are united against us. But on the local level, and I've read thousands of reports, it's much more that the resistance is local. There are certain people that are opposing this. The majority of people just want to be left alone. Or in some areas, the majority of people are hostile, but they're not hostile to us because it's a Filipino nation. They're hostile to us for local reasons. So the locals understand and every lieutenant understands the situation in this village pretty clearly. MacArthur sees this great pattern which he can then claim credit for solving and that's another thing.

Interviewer

What is Teddy Roosevelt's relationship to this story?

Dr. Brian Linn

Not really very much. I mean Roosevelt benefits in many ways from McKinley's assassination. There's a sort of protecting the McKinley's legacy and so forth but McKinley is assassinated and, really, within about a couple days later, the Balangiga Massacre occurs or what's called the Balangiga Massacre. It's a very successful locally run attack on an American garrison in Balangiga, Samar. Now at that time, everyone thought the insurgency was over. Aguinaldo had been captured and surrendered, as well as all the major leaders. There were only three areas that were recognized as still having violent resistance, the last embers, and everyone thought these were going away, and so this attack, which was the worst guerilla attack that had happened in the whole war, temporarily panics the high command in Manila who were sitting on a cauldron that's about to blow up. All of the Philippines, they're going to go back again. So they come down very hard, especially in Samar. Taft, who had a better understanding of what's going on says, "No, that is not that case, and this is an attempt for the military to take control back from us because they're talking about imposing martial law." Roosevelt, to his credit, has as his main decision to make at this point, to sign with Taft and to not put the military back in charge. Now, out of that campaign, particularly in Samar which was the last one and in Batangas Province, come allegations of atrocities, and so the second follow-through on this is a lot of accusations of Americans killing, burning, indiscriminate shooting, putting people in concentration camps, which was very emotional because we had accused the Spanish of doing that in Cuba, and so we kind of worked to free people from concentration camps and now we're doing it ourselves. So that's the second legacy and there's ultimately a Senate investigation, or Senate hearings on the conduct of American troops.

Interviewer

What's the result of that?

Dr. Brian Linn

Well, for one thing, it makes it very easy for anti-imperialists to go and cull testimony from that, right? Henry F. Graff did a book, "America Kills the Philippines" [editor's note: published as "American Imperialism and the Philippine Insurrection — 1902"]. Essentially all he did in that book was cull pretty selected testimony on American atrocities as they say, "Here's what they were doing." It taints the entire reputation of the US Army. I mean, the fact is that while there was torture and there were indiscriminate shootings and all these sorts of things that occurred before, they had not been policy. They had been sort of individual acts which have to be understood in the context of those individual acts. I mean, you have to understand why these people did this and instead, these two campaigns— particularly Samar, made it look like this was policy. It's the end of the war. They must have been doing this all the time, and it then became the task of historians like me to prove it hadn't happened rather than the case of anti-imperialists to prove it had. It's very similar to My Lai which was an isolated instance. Everyone knew it was wrong and that it was unusual, but because of My Lai, it's almost become a necessity for American soldiers to prove that they didn't do any wrongs rather than having to prove they did. A whole number of scholars are still writing books like it. I mean there's one that just came out about a year ago. These start with the assumption this was a racial, genocidal war. How do I know? Because of what happened at Samar, and I go on that assumption and it's up to someone else to prove it didn't happen that way and beyond that, it really ceased to be a matter of proof because people like Glenn May and Alfred McCoy and myself have actually gone in and traced this war at the village level all over the Philippines. The major contribution in my book was to say, "Okay, here's how the war was fought and if you want to study a counterinsurgency that's essentially a local insurgency, you study it at the local level. You get out of Manila and you get out of the headquarters and you go into the field and you know, box after box of five by eight cards are essentially saying that in this town, this was the nature of the resistance." We know this because we've captured their letters and here's what the Americans did to solve it. This was a local insurgency that the Americans solved primarily through local counterinsurgency methods and that's my thesis.

Interviewer

The lessons for counterinsurgency doctrine out of this are what?

Dr. Brian Linn

Well, there are again different levels to hit. One of them is there are a lot of techniques that I think would be pretty useful that took a long time for people to start adapting in Iraq and Afghanistan that I think if someone had bothered to show up and say, "Okay, here's enough money for three weeks to think about what the major things are." For example, green jungle. It became standard operating procedure that every patrol had to go out and map the area. Okay? That's just a sort of basic technique. They began to do surveys. They began to do identification cards and photos and dossiers and began to collect intelligence, not just at the central level but at the local level. I mean, these are really simple things, but they took a long time to develop and they developed, interestingly enough, at the captain level before they were being implemented at Baghdad, which is exactly the Philippine experience. You might save a lot of trouble by just having a sort of handbook of about five pages saying here are standard practices that we use. They learn a lot about how to patrol, how to use native spies, how to use guides, and so a lot of it is just very practical things. So on one level, the army develops a lot of really good useful techniques for operating in jungles, for amphibious attacks, for how to, and I mean this is the amazing thing, supply troops in an environment that is so hostile that people die in a couple of days. I mean, they win a lot of their campaigns against the guerillas simply because they can survive in the jungle and the guerillas can't, and the guerillas starve to death and ultimately come in and surrender. Dealing with logistics is crucial in this, which people forget because they're so used to opening their MREs. So that's one level; and the second level would probably be that at the higher levels, how to develop an intelligence network for a counterinsurgency that allows for rapid dissemination of information at the local level, but also allows the central people to develop an idea. I mean, that's MacArthur's major point. He's got a terrible intelligence service. He doesn't know what's going on most of the time. He really doesn't, if you read his telegraphs. He doesn't have a clue what's going on. He's panicking.

Interviewer

He knows he doesn't have a clue, is that right?

Dr. Brian Linn

No, he doesn't. Not Arthur MacArthur, are you kidding? As far as Arthur's concerned, he's right all the time and everyone else is wrong and they're conspiring against him, but, I mean, he's panicking when he ought to be calm, and he's calm when he ought to be panicking, and part of that is because he doesn't have an intelligence system. So that level of how do you have an intelligence system, which I think is crucial, basic processes for setting up the civil government. I mean, American officers on their own are writing to their hometowns to get book donations to bring back to the Philippines so they can set up schools, but there's a lot of just really useful stuff the Americans could have done on that level. The third level that you can get it from is the sort of how to put this into your education in terms of leadership development, just general. One thing that surprised me, for example, reading about the Moro wars, is how many people had read the Quran before they ever went or while they were in Mindanao. John J. Pershing was made an honorary chief. The amazing thing about the Moro wars is that they're fought among the Americans and individual tribes, or in a couple cases cults, but there's never a religious war. The Spanish had had a religious war there for 100 years. Americans don't and when the Americans leave, many Moro chiefs ask them to stay because they know when the Americans go, the Filipino Christians will come in and exploit them. That's exactly what the Filipino Christians did and most of that has been since the Americans left. Mindanao is quite peaceful when you consider it's an incredibly violent culture because these people have a lot of cultural sensitivity and they're not trying to convert or proselytize. They're very clear about that and the term crusader isn't there at all.

Interviewer

The Petraeus Doctrine is built somewhat on this kind of understanding.

Dr. Brian Linn

Right, and it requires an educated officer core, and these people did have a lot of time to think and read and study the Quran and contemplate what they were going to do.

Interviewer

Which would also go against the argument that this was a racial war?

Dr. Brian Linn

Yes.

Interviewer

The white man's burden was to take care of the ignorant.

Dr. Brian Linn

Right.

Interviewer

There was a respect, it sounds like, for the cultural achievements, different though they may be.

Dr. Brian Linn

Yeah, I mean they are racialist in that they're aware that the Filipinos are a different race, and the troops talked about that all the time; but my problem is that I've never been satisfactorily convinced that when people are pulling a trigger or setting fire to a village or even administering a water cure to somebody that that's geared by racial antagonism. Ninety percent of the time in any case I've ever found, there's very clear practical reasons why you were shooting at this person or setting fire to their village or torturing them, and it has nothing to do with the fact they're Filipinos. It has to do with the information you want and can get the names of someone, or just punishing someone.

Interviewer

Were the Americans different than the Spanish in this respect or in this case?

Dr. Brian Linn

Well, let's see. The Americans had a much more ambitious agenda than the Spanish. The Spanish had really only controlled Manila and then worked deals with the locals.

Interviewer

Christians…

Dr. Brian Linn

The rest of the Philippines is Catholic/Christian from before, but there was actually a schism in the church and a separate Anglican church emerged. The term Moro was a Spanish term for the moors and when the Spanish arrived there from the beginning under Legazpi it was like, "Oh, well, we know these enemies. They're the ones we fought against in the Reconquista." They'd bring that attitude immediately and the Moros bring their own attitude, which is, "Ah, yes, we know these people." So the Spanish helped make it a religious war, and I think the Philippine government until recently didn't help at all.

Interviewer

Let's bring it to the lessons that the Philippine experience provide to us in terms of looking forward.

Dr. Brian Linn

We're talking about these levels of basic counterinsurgency tactics, higher ideas on how to run a counterinsurgency campaign, the sort of Petraeus Doctrine. If you're going to be people-centric, you have to have officers sensitive to that. The lessons after that and some of the ones I'm going to talk about later, these are incredibly debilitating wars. I mean, the Philippine War only lasted about three years but it devastates the officer corps and the NCO corps; and the enlisted corps and that army has to be rebuilt, which people are very aware of now, but mainly there's a disease and so the army you go into these conflicts with isn't the army you come out with.

This leads to a second issue, which is both then and now, that the war ends at the end of the 19th century or begins at the end of the 19th century and ends at the beginning of the 20th century. I mean, the army is very aware of the new century and it's in the process of reforming itself. The Root Reforms occur as a direct result of the conflict in the Philippines and the revelations of how incompetent they were in Cuba. So as General Dempsey was talking about, this transformation issue, where are we going to go in the 21st century? That's a problem that people in the Philippines, and certainly when they come back, are addressing and the result is that the army that comes out of the Philippines is not only different in personnel, organizationally and administratively it's very different and that's another thing, how to rebuild and reform.

Interviewer

Well, I'm wondering whether these kinds of ends of wars involve the persistent insurgent element that can debilitate an army, particularly when we're fighting on two fronts.

Dr. Brian Linn

Right, and they lead to the fact that they're physically debilitating. They tend to lead to reforms, but the third issue they would raise and that General Dempsey raised today as well is: do you concentrate on the war you're fighting and think that the wars that you're going to fight are going to be like this? If we're going to face counterinsurgency warfare, then we need to structure the army in a certain way. If we're going to be occupying Afghanistan and Iraq for 10 or 15 years, we need to think about that. If, on the other hand, we're going to be fighting another peer competitor, we have to structure ourselves differently. Now at the end of the Philippine War, the United States Army has that. There are people in the United States Army saying we need to be a colonial army. We need to have civil servants, we need to train our guys and we're going to administer the empire. People like Leonard Wood and Robert Bullard are arguing that the army needs to know as much about waging peace as it needs to know about waging war. Others, such as J. Franklin Bell, are saying, "No, we need to prepare for a big war."

Interviewer

It's the same argument going on now.

Dr. Brian Linn

Exactly, and that's an argument that is won very clearly within about 10 years by the big war people and, of course, they always argue, "Well, we were right. See, look at World War I." However, everyone sort of forgets that months before Wilson declares World War I, Pershing is down in Mexico in the punitive expedition in 1916 and Bell's directives and all the stuff from the Philippines are sent down to the guys in Mexico.

Interviewer

So is the lesson an army for all things, for all possibilities and all points of view and we will be fighting big war, conventional war, and we'll be fighting insurgencies?

Dr. Brian Linn

Right, I'd say the argument you have to have is the United States Army prior to Iraq and Afghanistan was fixated on being 99 percent brilliant at conventional operations. How do we get to be 99.1 percent? You know? I wish we would have spent a lot more time saying let's be 80 percent good at conventional war and build up our capabilities in these others. That's the decision the United States really didn't make. It kept two armies for a long time, and I think it was a lot better off.

Interviewer

Well, it's the hangover from Vietnam in part. It makes us not want to fight those wars again, right? I mean that's what it is.

Dr. Brian Linn

Well, I think the army never liked to fight those wars, but officers accepted it as part of their duty. What I think was made certain by people such as General Powell is sort of a devil's bargain. We will guarantee you victory if you only fight the type of wars we want you to fight.

Interviewer

Thank you so much. This was terrific.

Session 3
The Meuse-Argonne Offensive:
The Final Battle of World War 1

by

Dr. Edward Coffman

For 47 days in the fall of 1918, Americans fought the greatest battle in their history. More than a million soldiers of whom some 120,000 were casualties defeated the Germans on this battlefield. This was neither the time nor the place for the ultimate battle that General John J. Pershing, the commander of the American Expeditionary Forces, desired. Soon after his arrival in France in the summer of 1917, he and his planners focused on what they hoped would be a war-ending campaign toward Metz in 1919.

Although the United States had declared war on 6 April 1917, it did not begin to play a significant role on the Western Front until the summer of 1918. This was because of the time taken for a massive mobilization and Pershing's determination to keep his troops as an independent force rather than replacements in allied ranks. During the first 12 months [that] the United States was in the war, 300,000 soldiers reached France. Some of the American divisions, however, did train in quiet British and French sectors while the II Corps (27th and 30th Divisions) stayed with the British and four infantry regiments remained with the French. From 1 April to 1 November 1918, about 1.7 million soldiers arrived which meant that Pershing had enough combat troops to begin carrying out his plan.

On August 10, he created the 1st Army with plans already under way to reduce the St. Mihiel salient in mid-September as the first step in the Metz campaign. Although Allied Supreme Commander Marshal Ferdinand Foch had approved this offensive, he changed his mind in late August. The commander of the British Expeditionary Force, Field Marshal Sir Douglas Haig, recommended a plan to employ the American Army as well as British and French forces in a gigantic pincer offensive in September against the huge German salient that stretched from the Meuse River almost to the North Sea. Foch then told Pershing that he wanted to modify the St. Mihiel offensive in order to make preparations for a different battle. He also recommended that a few American divisions serve with the French 2nd Army in the Meuse-Argonne sector and then have the American 1st Army with more divisions take over the sector left of the Argonne Forest.

Eventually Pershing agreed with the provisos that he would be able to carry out his original plan to close the St. Mihiel salient first and then have his field army take over the Meuse-Argonne sector. The dates set for the initiation of offensives were only two weeks apart. Fortunately, with the help of four French divisions, eight American divisions overwhelmed the Germans' weak defense and thus were able to close the St. Mihiel salient in two days, 12-13 September. During the brief interval before the second offensive began, Colonel George C. Marshall shouldered the daunting task of planning a secret movement of 400,000 troops, their equipment, and supplies to the Meuse-Argonne front.

The Meuse-Argonne would not be as easy. The front stretched 20 miles from the unfordable Meuse River to the dense Argonne Forest. Although it was a quiet sector for most of the war, the Germans had established four defensive lines together with scattered barbed wire barriers and machine gun positions throughout the area. They did not expect an attack, hence, only five under strength divisions held that sector. At full strength they would have been only half as large as the American divisions which averaged more than 25,000 officers and men.

Lack of training and combat experience was a major problem for the Americans. Of the nine divisions (4th, 28th, 33rd, 35th, 37th, 77th, 79th, 80th, and 91st) in the initial attack, only four (4th, 28th, 33d, and 77th) had combat experience. Generally, their training in the States varied as virtually all had suffered from sending replacements to fill up divisions about to sail for France and in turn being brought up to strength shortly before their crossing the Atlantic. Several divisions had not trained with their own artillery. Two days before the attack, the 77th Division received 4,000 replacements who had been in the US Army only six weeks.

The planners were aware of this problem but hoped that the great advantage in manpower would overwhelm the defense. They expected the attacking force to advance nine miles through the first two enemy defensive positions and reach the formidable main line position, the Hindenburg Line, on the first day and penetrate it the next day. Since this front was only 32 miles, the closest of any of the Allies, from the enemy main line of supply along the Western Front, the Americans assumed that the Germans would quickly move reinforcements into the sector. The planners gambled that they could seize the weakly held defensive positions before the reinforcements arrived. This optimistic assumption demanded a great deal from mostly inexperienced troops.

A heavy barrage preceded the jump off early on 26 September. Despite the fog and mist that morning, three divisions (the 4th, 80th, and 91st) covered three miles, while two divisions (the 28th and 77th) facing the Argonne only advanced a mile. Much of the terrain was unsuitable for tanks and the American tank crews had never trained with infantry. Among the casualties on the first day was Lieutenant Colonel George S. Patton, whose tank brigade supported the 35th Division. Although advance elements did penetrate the second defensive line, the key position of Montfaucon remained in German hands until the next morning.

German reinforcements began to pour into the sector even though the three Allied offensives started within the next few days. They stiffened the defense while other problems added greatly to American burdens. The lack of experience of those men and officers who had been in the Army a year or less combined with that of more senior officers new to the demands of higher command. Keeping troops and supplies moving was difficult because there were only three available roads. Rain also increased the difficulty of movement as well as the misery of the soldiers. Thus, both command and control and logistical shortcomings hampered American progress.

After the first two days, it was clear that breaching the Hindenburg Line would take much longer than the planners had anticipated. Pershing ordered continued attacks but after four days, his troops had not reached the objectives set for the first afternoon. Although three of his most veteran divisions (the 1st, 3d, and 32d) replaced the 35th, 37th, and 79th by October, advancing was still problematic.

Later, Pershing recalled that the first 11 days of October involved "the heaviest strain on the army and me." The Allies were becoming critical of the Americans' failure to advance more rapidly. The British, in particular, had made significant gains. On 1 October, Marshal Foch was so concerned that he suggested to Pershing that he give up part of his sector to a French general who would then command a significant number of the American troops. As Foch should have realized, this infuriated Pershing and the supreme commander backed down.

Three days later, Pershing made another effort to penetrate the Hindenburg Line. Eight divisions struggled forward but none succeeded in that objective. The 1st Division, however, did drive a deep wedge that made it possible for the 77th, 28th, and 82d to clear the Germans out of the Argonne a few days later. In its 12 days of heavy fighting, the 1st suffered 8,200 casualties, the most of any of the American divisions in the battle. During those early October days, two of the most famous events of the war took place in the Argonne. One was the five-day siege of the Lost Battalion of the 77th Division. On 8 October, the day after the relief of the Lost Battalion, Alvin C. York, armed with a rifle and a pistol, killed more than 20 Germans and captured another 132 as well as 35 machine guns.

Pershing ordered another general attack along his front on the 14th and gave three divisions (the 5th, 32d, and 42d) the objectives of seizing key positions in the Hindenburg Line on the 14th. The 32d and 42d were among the more experienced units in the AEF; however, the former had recently received 5,000 replacements who had only been in the service less than three months. A small patrol of the 32d Division took Cote Dame Marie while other division units captured Remagen. The 5th Division captured Cunel and two days later Douglas MacArthur's brigade of the 42d took Cote de Chatillon. The Americans had seized more than four miles of the Hindenburg Line.

After three weeks of relentless fighting, the 1st Army took the objective that the planners had thought would fall by 27 September. On 16 October, Pershing gave up its command in favor of his best corps commander who was Hunter Liggett. A few days earlier, he had divided 1st Army in two, placing another corps commander, Robert L. Bullard, in command of 2nd Army. Pershing then promoted his two best division commanders, John L. Hines of the 4th and Charles P. Summerall of the 1st to command the III Corps and the V Corps, respectively.

One reason Pershing was under so much stress is that he commanded the field army and the AEF which meant that he had to manage the operations of his troops as well as deal with the Allied political and military leaders. Although he turned over command to Liggett, he initially stayed at 1st Army headquarters and pressed for continued attacks. On the 17th, Liggett politely but firmly told his boss to go away and let him command the army.

The new commander did continue limited attacks to obtain better positions for the next offensive, but he realized that he had to give much of his army a respite to straighten out the problems that had multiplied during the past three weeks. The infantry units were under strength not only because of the large number of casualties as well as an estimated 100,000 stragglers. The transportation problem had also worsened since the heavy fighting had made the roads more difficult to traverse.

Liggett brought in a different and more sensible approach to battle than Pershing. The latter's doctrinal core belief was in "open warfare" in which infantrymen with their rifles and bayonets, would achieve the great breakthrough. Although he did eventually employ artillery in preparation fire and made some use of tanks and aircraft, he persisted in ordering mass infantry attacks. Liggett recognized the necessity for a more combined arms approach hence better coordinated use of artillery as well as of aircraft to support the infantry.

For his major attack on 1 November, Liggett arrayed three corps with seven divisions along a 16-mile front. On the left, I Corps (with the 77th, 78th, and 80th) had to deal with terrain that included two forests. In the center, V Corps (with the 2d and 89th) had the crucial mission of seizing the Barricourt Heights, the key to its unfinished defensive line, while on their right III Corps (with the 5th and 90th) was to get in position to cross the Meuse. Liggett demanded massive artillery and air support as well as extensive use of gas to support the infantry. All but a few artillery pieces and ammunition were furnished by the Allies. Summerall, commanding V Corps, was given the most support and, as an artilleryman, he knew how to make the best use of it. His corps and Hines's III Corps succeeded in their first day's mission as the massive artillery support wiped out many of the machine gun positions but I Corps struggled with defenders in the woods. Liggett was not concerned as he realized that success of the two other corps would force the Germans to evacuate that area. Besides, a heavy barrage (more than 41 tons) of gas shells had knocked out many of the Germans in the larger forest.

In addition to the support of the artillery's rolling barrages plus more use of machine guns and mortars, infantry units relied on the experience and common sense of officers and men to attack in small groups and infiltrate or outflank strong points while taking care to mop up after the initial advance. In the 2d Division, two night marches surprised the enemy and resulted in a gain of six miles. These new approaches enabled Liggett's attack to advance considerably farther in five days than the 1st Army had done in its continual attacks during the first three weeks of the offensive. In early November, the axis of the III Corps attack shifted from the north to the east where two divisions (the 5th and 90th) crossed the Meuse with the former attaining an 11-mile and the latter, a 3-mile advance.

The outnumbered, war-weary German troops were retreating not just in this sector but in the face of three other Allied offensives. The Germans and their allies were losing in all theaters while on the Western Front the German army had suffered heavy losses not only from the ongoing Allied fall offensives but also from their own offensives earlier in 1918. These severe blows and the tight naval blockade caused the morale of the starving German people to plummet. On the verge of collapse, the government was anxious to make peace. The massive American reinforcement meantime, bolstered the morale of the French and British who had also reached the limits of their manpower. On 11 November, the Germans signed an Armistice. As the last stage of the American offensive demonstrated, the combination of increasing strength and skill of the AEF was a significant war-winning asset.

Recommended Reading

In recent years, two solidly researched and well-written books on this battle have been published: Robert H. Ferrell, "America's Deadliest Battle: Meuse-Argonne, 1918," (2007) and the more detailed "To Conquer Hell: The Meuse-Argonne, 1918," (2008) by Edward G. Lengel. Also recent is the excellent analysis of the doctrinal change in tactics that had a major effect on the last three weeks of the battle: Mark E. Grotelueschen, "The AEF Way of War: The American Army and Combat in World War I," (2007). An older book still in print, Edward M. Coffman, "The War To End All Wars: The American Military Experience in World War I," (1968 reprinted in 1986 and 1998), covers the leadership in both the United States and the AEF, relations with its allies, the mobilization and training of the huge wartime US Army, and the battles those soldiers and Marines fought as well as the Navy's war.

Session 3

Interview

Dr. Edward Coffman

Interviewer

We're here with Dr. Edward Coffman. He is another historian who has written about the Meuse-Argonne Offensive as part of the TRADOC Conference on War Termination. Let's start out by asking about World War I, the Meuse-Argonne Offensive. The United States comes into the war late, 1917, but the impact of American soldiers and of American industrial and economic assistance to the French and British is noted almost immediately. So the Meuse-Argonne Offensive, why does this have such importance for students of war, for students of conflict?

Dr. Edward Coffman

Well, it's basically important because I really think there were several offensives at the same time. The British and the French had offensives and the British actually gained more ground than we did, but the major point of the American offensive and the Meuse-Argonne was [that] we put so many people in there. That is still by far the largest battle the United States was ever engaged in. We had 1.2 million people involved in that battle. In the Bulge, it was 600,000. We had 122,000 casualties. The Bulge had 60,000, I think. So it is really our greatest battle. The great impression was, although in the essay I wrote for TRADOC I talk about this, about the great change in doctrine that came about in actually the last two weeks of the war, when we really moved a lot. As far as the importance of the battle is [that] the German leaders realized with that great influx of troops, they were taking casualties. They were amazed at the guys just, you know, getting killed and all that, but at the same time, there were so many of them. The German commander of the area there said that won the war. Well, they looked and here was this enormous strength, and there's more all the time and Ludendorff had already gotten the message and quit, resigned a month or so later. So, I mean, it was the fact that we had so many people over there and they were ready to go and they were fighting hard. All of the other belligerents were scraping the bottom of the barrel and, all of a sudden, there were millions. We had two million people over there and that, in effect, was important in the battle and the Germans realized that and they actually surrendered.

Interviewer

So, that was the turning point.

Dr. Edward Coffman

That's a very critical point there. My father was a veteran of the war. He was in the Navy and he was only in toward the end of the war. By the 1950s and 1960s, they were calling it the forgotten war. . . . The largest American military cemetery in Europe, by far, is the one in the Meuse-Argonne. Do Americans go there? Very rarely. On the 75th anniversary of the Meuse-Argonne there were six tours, six American tours. The French were there and there was a contingent from the American troops. You know, they sent down a company or something and a band for the ceremony. When I visited the battle, I was really impressed that the French were there. I even had several French thank me as an American. There and at other cemeteries and battlefields but Americans, just in the past, just weren't interested.

Interviewer

Do you think perhaps the failure for understanding this battle and the American collective consciousness is perhaps due to the way that World War I concluded?

Dr. Edward Coffman

Yes, but I think there were two factors basically, two major factors. One is the Allies wanted to belittle the American effort in the war because they didn't want Wilson and the Americans to dominate the treaty, which Wilson wanted to do, and he failed. So, after that, your contribution was simply that you backed us monetarily and everything. Your military wasn't all that hot and they, you know, they didn't really do that much, but we were the ones who suffered, which they did. I mean their casualty rates, the French lost like 1.2 million people killed. We lost 50,000. The Brits lost I think 900,000 [and] you know, [that] was heavy casualties. Those were smaller countries than the United States and so, then after the war, there were fights over what we wanted to collect in war debts. They said well, you know, all you contributed essentially was money. Now, where the American people got involved is [that] they quickly became disillusioned right after the war in the treaty period. Wilson's dreams were just shattered, the idealism that he had going into a peace without victory, a world war to end all wars. This is it. On the back of the American medal, the service medal, is written; "Great War for Civilization." People very soon began to realize it didn't work out that way, and then, as time passed, it even became more so because the League of Nations was ineffectual. We never belonged. We never signed the treaty. We never belonged to the League of Nations. By the 1930s, there was this great press campaign that actually it was the "merchants of death," that the American manufacturers who had shipped war materials to the British and the French. They did it because of the money and they got us in the war in order to make sure they'd win and we'd get the money and all of that. In the 1930s, there was a strong peace movement. Ninety-five percent of Americans in a poll taken in 1935 or 1936, I think it was, said we shouldn't go to war for any reason in the future. There were 2,000 peace rallies at various places and there were later neutrality acts that we will not go to war to help anyone or anything. Even when you have a situation like the Panay that no one remembers anymore, but the Panay, an American gunboat in the Yangtze, the Americans and Brits had warships there taking people out of Nanking during the rape of Nanking.

Interviewer

This is in China?

Dr. Edward Coffman

Yes, in China. On a Sunday morning in December of 1937, Japanese planes attacked and sunk the boat and there wasn't all that much of a reaction. It excited me. I was an eight-year-old kid and a movie was made. What the Japanese didn't know is there were

20 or 30 correspondents on the boat. One guy was a cameraman. He had gotten on it to do a documentary on the thing and he's filming them. The Japanese denied it but then they had the movies, the planes coming over with "meatballs" on them and the American flags flying and they're strafing it and bombing it. So there was this great disillusionment. We'd been had.

Interviewer

Because of the way that the end of the war was negotiated –

Dr. Edward Coffman

Yes.

Interviewer

There were a number of unforeseen consequences, very significant consequences.

Dr. Edward Coffman

Yes, there were.

Interviewer

How do you think the military was impacted by the way that World War I concluded? Do you think there was any influence on American doctrine?

Dr. Edward Coffman

Well, the big influence was reduction of strength. Like there was a push to get a permanent military training program. You know, sort of a general draft and all of that [so] that every American able-bodied male would serve a year or two in the military and everything. That failed. They tried to get that, but it failed. Then they were going to have a large army and that failed. Then they were talking about an army of 500,000. Then Congress finally accepted an army and voted for an army of something like 250,000 but it never reached that strength until the mobilization of World War II. In 1938, the American Regular Army was 185,000, which would put it 18th in strength among the armies of the world.

Interviewer

Is this because the American public in general rejected the idea of military service?

Dr. Edward Coffman

Yes, and the fact that the Army was something that was just out there somewhere. I remember talking to an officer one time who had gone to the US Military Academy, and he was in the Regular Army and he went home to Columbus, Ohio, and someone asked him what are you doing? He said well, I'm in the Army. They said, what did you do that they kept you? You know, I saw only two Regular Army soldiers in the 1930s and they had brought down a scout car. I come from Kentucky. They brought down a scout car, you know, the light tank type they called it in 1937 or 1938, and they parked it at the courthouse and all the little boys and old men went down and looked at it. You didn't see the Regular Army. At that point, I didn't know anybody in the Regular Army. The Regular Army just, unless you live close to an Army post, they weren't around. At the same time, and I'll make a point of this, what saved the United States Army were the schools, because they were being trained at the schools and, of course, at the War College. Henry Gole had written a book, taught here, and retired as Colonel of Special Forces later at the War College. Henry wrote this book on war planning that went on at the War College as a student project and, of course, they had already worked out Europe first. They thought they knew [that] Japan was a threat, but they assumed [that] the major threat would be from Germany eventually. So in the 1930s they were already working the war plans, Europe first. At a time that peace movement as late as 1940 had an ad with a World War I veteran sitting in a wheelchair and he has an overseas cap on and the headline said; "Hello, sucker."

Interviewer

A particularly poignant example as a war planner is what sort of lessons could we take from the way that World War I was concluded and its aftermath? If, for example, we were to fight a war in the 21st century how do you think the results of World War I would perhaps affect our planning processes?

Dr. Edward Coffman

Well, I think the major thing that happened at the time, was in looking ahead to see what would happen in World War II, in 1943. I'm a packrat and I happen to have saved the "Time" magazine as a kid and I found it, which is even more amazing in the mess that's my filing cabinets and everything. In 1943, "Time" magazine featured John J. Pershing, who's still living and he's coming and going mentally, but he's in Walter Reed at the time. It was talking about him and then it had in there something about how he had pressed for unconditional surrender at the time. We should singly defeat the German Army because then they'd been beaten and everything or the German Army could march back. At the time, the German people, before bombing, hadn't been bombed. Their armies had fought the wars in other countries. They hadn't had any destruction or anything and then they came up with a "stab-in-the-back" idea and the Nazis, you know, really preach this: we're going to get back at them, in other words, and of course they start planning for it almost immediately. In this article, they talk about Pershing pressing this and Wilson turned him off very quickly when he started pressing for that. Wilson didn't want that. He wanted peace without victory. You know, FDR came out with unconditional surrender and persuaded Churchill to go along with it at the Casablanca Conference and that's what we had in World War II. What effect this has on a war like we're in now, I don't think is very much except be prepared for the unexpected. You know, don't assume certain things. The great message that I'm giving is, I can say the major ramification of World War I and the way the war ended was World War II. The Japanese assumed we weren't fighting, we wouldn't fight and they had a reason to believe that. They knew about our public opinion. Yamamoto and the guy, I forget his name, the guy who commanded at Iwo Jima. They knew Americans and Americans are not going to fight. Except Yamamoto warned, if we stay in here long, they might. You know, unless we can really knock them out?

Interviewer

So, perhaps one of the lessons we could take from World War I is that to have a decisive peace, one must have a decisive victory, not an enemy that is permitted to sign a peace agreement while remaining in full control of offensive capabilities, an enemy really that remains undefeated. Perhaps maybe the second lesson we could take from this is the profound effect of the presidential and public opinion and agendas on peace processes themselves. Do you think this is an accurate assessment?

Dr. Edward Coffman

Yes, because that certainly had an effect. I really wonder if Wilson's policies had gone through with the other Allies. I don't know [that] the Germans still might have their problem. They did have that great inflation and that might have happened anyway and then out of that came Hitler, you know. I had a friend who was visiting in Germany right before Hitler took over and he had talked to a lot of the wealthy German manufacturers and everything, and he asked them about the Nazis. I mean, that seemed like a far right really nutty bunch and it was, "Oh, no, you have nothing to worry about them." Within a year they were in control. So you don't know what's going to happen and in the type of war we're in now, I don't know if you heard John Hall talk about that Seminole War, that's the sort – how do you defeat these people?

Interviewer

That's true. What are the conditions?

Dr. Edward Coffman

Yeah, what are the conditions? I mean at least you had formal armies and great strength and they were fighting you, and you know you could tell you knew when you won a battle certainly. You're not always sure here. What about Afghanistan? Are Taliban still there? You better believe it. Who's the enemy? How do you know? How do you define victory?

Interviewer

Well, thank you very much.

Dr. Edward Coffman

Well, thank you.

Session 3

Waging and Ending War in Europe, 1945

by

Dr. Theodore Wilson

The final campaign to destroy Hitler's Third Reich and clear the last German forces holding out in northern Italy played out differently than had been anticipated when the United States first gave serious consideration to how to achieve victory over the Axis in 1941 if and when it entered the war in Europe. The assumptions that yielded the "Victory Plan" of the summer of 1941 and dominated Anglo-American strategic debates over the next two years presumed a war of movement and concentrated firepower or a "high tech" conflict that ensured once the Allies invaded northwest Europe, a swift conclusion to the conflict either by a German military collapse or an internal coup. Despite the addition of massive Russian military power to the Allied coalition and the successes that followed the Normandy landings in June of 1944, those assumptions proved mistaken.

In contrast to those optimistic predictions prior to D-Day and during the period of breakout and pursuit, the final months of the ground campaign in the West proved to be a slog reminiscent in painful ways of 1914-1918. American soldiers would have cause to remember such previously unknown places as Huertgen Forest, Schmidt, and Metz. Ironically, the German Ardennes counteroffensive launched on 16 December 1944 opened the gates for Allied victory.

The Battle of the Bulge affirmed how strong the links between the Allies were. Facing inexorable pressure from East and West, Hitler made a desperate gamble by ordering the concentration of 30 divisions or some 600,000 men which was the bulk of the Wehrmacht's reserves in a desperate counterattack aimed at striking through the Ardennes to retake Antwerp and crush the British 21st Army Group and the US 1st and 9th Armies. Assuming that overcast skies would neutralize Allied air superiority and lead to a stunning breakthrough, Hitler convinced himself that, as had Frederick the Great, the Anglo-American coalition would collapse in mutual recriminations. Most German commanders believed that the operation was reckless in the extreme but they kept silent.

Despite the success of an elaborate deception plan and rapid advances against a lightly defended front in the days after the Ardennes offensive was launched on 16 December 1944, Hitler's bold stroke was fated to do no more than halt for a brief time the march of Allied forces toward the Rhine. Shrugging aside irritation among senior British and American commanders following the operation named MARKET GARDEN and Field Marshal Bernard Montgomery's vocal criticism of the broad front strategy, Eisenhower placed US forces north of the German breakthrough under Montgomery's command. United States units caught in the maelstrom fought stubbornly. Aided by improving weather for Anglo-American tactical air forces and the opening of a gigantic Soviet offensive all along the central sector of the Eastern Front, the British from the north and Patton's 3d Army from the south eliminated the Ardennes salient. The butcher's bill was high: some 78,000 casualties and another 56,000 non-battle losses. The Wehrmacht lost more than 100,000

KIA and WIA, and nearly double that number missing or suffering non-battle injuries. United States forces had reclaimed all the ground lost by late January of 1945. One final German attack (Operation Nordwind) against the 7th Army manning a salient known as the Colmar Pocket which was between the Rhine and the Moder rivers north of Strasbourg on the southern flank of the Bulge, was launched on 1 January 1945. The aim was to cut behind and encircle two newly arrived American divisions and retake Strasbourg but the Germans found tough going against the inexperienced but hard-fighting Americans, deep snow, and subzero temperatures. Nordwind quickly blew itself out. Soon thereafter, a United States led attack eliminated the Colmar Pocket.

Then came the muster for the final campaign of the Allied armies to utterly destroy the Wehrmacht and compel surrender in the rubble of Berlin or some other German locale where whoever remained officially in charge was found. As of 1 February 1945, the total strength of US Army forces in the European Theater of Operations comprised 2,329,042 spread across the European continent and another 605,882 in Britain though the great majority was ASF (Army Service Forces) personnel and groups of individual replacements. United States Army ground forces totaled 1,585,242, assigned to some 60 divisions and myriad other combat and combat support units. British and Canadian combined strengths were approximately 1,090,000. In all, the Allies pushing east would soon field 85 divisions, including five to eight newly organized French divisions currently being trained and the eight French divisions currently deployed. Facing them, SHAEF (Supreme Headquarters, Allied Expeditionary Force) G-2 intelligence estimated 80 under strength divisions assuming that no large scale withdrawal from northern Italy had occurred. The Allied armies possessed a number of advantages including control of the skies, the experience gained at all levels from six months of unremitting combat, far greater stores of weapons and other materiel, and — that pearl beyond price — the challenges posed to the enemy of having to defend on two fronts.

Nonetheless, SHAEF planners viewed the task they faced as a daunting one. German defenses along the Rhine frontier were substantial. As well, the numerical superiority enjoyed by the Allies was less impressive after the operation of the invasion of Europe or OVERLORD manpower crisis was factored in. By late 1944, the US Army claimed only 89 divisions, no strategic reserve, a lack of combat replacements, and worrying concerns about growing numbers of combat exhaustion cases among units that had seen long periods of combat. A further complicating factor was the logistical bottleneck caused by inadequate port facilities.

The result was a more cautious operational strategy than desired by those demanding that Montgomery be permitted to dash for Berlin and, alternatively, complaints by Generals Bradley and Patton about favoritism to the British. General Eisenhower returned to the strategy of a broad front advance. This decision reflected a desire to avoid any further German surprises such as the Ardennes counteroffensive. It also reflected concern about Nazi fanatics holding out in a Bavarian redoubt and post surrender efforts to disrupt the Allied occupation by so called "Werewolf" terrorist bands.

Also important were the "bomb line" discussions to ensure that Allied strategic air forces flying missions in the Balkans and elsewhere in Eastern Europe not attack by inadvertence the advance columns of the Red Army. These efforts gained urgency when American P-38 Lightning aircraft in November of 1944 strafed a Soviet infantry unit, killing a lieutenant general and five other soldiers. On 6 February 1945, an agreement between the headquarters of the Soviet, British, and US Army Air Forces established a line of demarcation for air raids. A month later came a formal agreement on joint air operations to cover advancing Allied ground forces.

First to push forward were the soldiers of General Troy Middleton's VIII Corps attached to Patton's 3d Army, which smashed through the defenses of the West Wall along the Schnee Eifel, a rugged ridgeline between Belgium and Germany. Just 40 miles from the Rhine, 3d Army soldiers ran out of gasoline and ammunition.

The focus then shifted to Montgomery, who controlled 25 divisions: eight British, five Canadian, one Polish, and the 11 divisions comprising General William Simpson's 9th Army. Montgomery's plan, Operation VERITABLE, called for two converging attacks– one by British and Canadian forces southeast toward Wesel, the second by Simpson's divisions northeast toward the Rhine. A massive Royal Air Force carpet bombing mission and the most intensive artillery barrage of the British Army since 1918 kicked off the British attack.

Unfortunately, Simpson did not follow up. Blocked by discharge from the Roer River dams, his forces were unable to cross the Roer. That left Montgomery's XXX Corps vulnerable to a German counterattack. Once the flood waters subsided, Simpson's 9th Army drove into the rear of the German forces and shattered the enemy's main strength, taking more than 30,000 prisoners and inflicting substantial casualties. Only a directive from Montgomery stopped the soldiers of the 2d Armored Division from seizing a bridgehead across the Rhine south of Dusseldorf.

A central thrust, launched on 26 February, led by General Courtney Hodge's 1st Army now again attached to the 12th Army Group, pushed toward Cologne and Bonn. Once these objectives were seized, the aim was to link up with Patton's 3d Army also closing on the Rhine. Cologne fell to soldiers of General Lawton Collins' 7th Corps on 5 March. That opened the way for the 9th Armored Division to seize the railroad bridge across the Rhine on 7 March. This amazing feat made possible the establishment of a bridgehead across the Rhine. The capture of the Remagen Bridge occurred on the ninth anniversary of the Nazi occupation of the Rhineland.

To the south, an armored spearhead of Patton's 3d Army roared along the Moselle, reaching the Rhine in just three days and then turned south to link up with 7th Army units driving northward through the Saar industrial region. On 25 March, all organized German resistance west of the Rhine had ended. Hitler's "defend at all costs" policy had yielded another military disaster and the loss of more than 300,000 German soldiers. Signs of collapsing morale within the Wehrmacht and the German populace began to appear.

Exploitation of the Remagen bridgehead quickly followed. Ironically, the rapid progress of the US Army overshadowed what had been intended as the main show — a massive assault by the British 2d and 9th Armies across the Rhine north of the Ruhr. Having gathered some 25 divisions and ordered a pounding by some 3,000 artillery pieces and repeated bombing attacks, Montgomery's troops attacked the Rhine barrier on 23 March. Within a few days, all opposition by the five German divisions in the area had ended. By the end of March, seven Allied armies were east of the Rhine. It was clear to everyone except Hitler and his most fanatical supporters that Nazi Germany's situation was hopeless.

The stunning push across the Rhine affirmed the coming of age of the United States Army. From a hastily organized organization built on a foundation laid down at Fort Leavenworth and isolated posts across the nation, this army of citizen soldiers had, over the course of three years, become a formidable fighting force. Correct application of the doctrine of combined arms that had been enunciated prior to America's entry into the war took time. There were many fits and starts. In part, the Army's struggles derived from the mistaken assumptions about the nature of the conflict that it would encounter. Wrongly assuming that the warfare to be waged in Europe followed a *blitzkrieg* paradigm by emphasizing movement, rapidity of maneuver, and concentrated fires so that the rifle, as one GI observer bitterly noted, was pushed aside in favor of the typewriter and the tank. Deeply flawed personnel assignment policies made the effects of these errors of intelligence and judgment even worse. By the middle of the fall of 1944, the US Army found itself engaged in a war of attrition reminiscent of the Western Front in 1916. Combat infantrymen were carrying the brunt of the fighting and suffering the highest rate of casualties by far.

Fortunately, American battalion, regimental, and divisional commanders and the men serving under them had learned on the job. They applied existing doctrine but with flexibility as circumstances and their judgment and experience dictated. In this way, they solved many fold problems regarding the implementation of combined arms doctrine, tank-infantry coordination, the combined use of tactical air power, and artillery to support movement of infantry units, and they invented new ways of employing standard weapons and solutions to challenges such as communications difficulties, the battlefield treatment of combat exhaustion cases, and the integration of individual replacements. While German officers might scorn the quality of certain of the weapons with which the US Army was equipped, they expressed awe at the skill with which the Americans employed those weapons in coordination.

The final weeks of the battle for Germany made that fact abundantly clear with multiple Allied bridgeheads across the Rhine in Germany and no natural barriers and only outnumbered and demoralized forces to defend the homeland. General Eisenhower now controlled 90 full-strength divisions, including 25 armored and five airborne, arguably the most powerful military force ever arrayed for battle. The Allied front stretched some 450 miles from the Rhine's North Sea outlet south to the Swiss border. SHAEF's next major objective was the Ruhr, the heart of German industry. The plan was to encircle the Ruhr by an advance of the 9th Army around its northern flank and sending the 1st Army around the Ruhr industrial complex from the south. On 1 April, the two wings met at Lippstadt, trapping Field Marshal Model's Army Group B and much of Army Group H, the principal German force remaining in northern Germany. Although Hitler raved about making the Ruhr a fortress to be defended to the last man and last bullet, the surrender of its defenders (325,000 soldiers) occurred on 19 April.

Allied forces were now racing forward on all sides. The Canadian 1st Army completed the liberation of nearly all of the Netherlands. The British 2d Army had occupied Bremen and Hamburg by late April. The United States 7th Army, further to the south, took Nuremburg on 20 April and then turned south to clear Munich. Patton's 3d Army penetrated deeply into the east of Germany, reached the Czech border on 25 April, and then having been denied permission by Eisenhower to take Prague, consolidated its gains.

An enduring controversy has smoldered about Eisenhower's "go slow" policy with regard to the seizure of Berlin and other places earlier designated as within the Soviet occupation zone. Montgomery's forces were poised for a dash across the north German plain to Berlin and elements of the 9th Army had secured a bridgehead across the Elbe River only 50 miles from the outskirts of Berlin. Eisenhower, who famously said that Berlin no longer had any military significance and further that it lay within the Soviet zone of occupation, was also concerned about the persistent rumors about a "National Redoubt" supposedly constructed in Bavaria to which surviving SS forces and other Nazi fanatics would retreat to carry on the war. Although a myth, Eisenhower for a time believed that the possibility of such a bastion from which diehard Nazis could continue resistance for months or even years could not be discounted. As well, the US Army was dealing with various other demands such as the appalling discovery of the death camps, huge numbers of German prisoners of war, and an even greater influx of refugees fleeing the Soviet advance from the East, as well as the potential danger to security of so-called "Werewolf" groups.

As the end neared, interaction at the operational level became extensive. From the west, elements of British and Canadian forces under Field Marshal Bernard Montgomery as well as those of the US 1st and 3d Armies were approaching their designated "stop" lines. On the Soviet side, the drive into Germany was done by the 1st Byelorussian, 1st Ukrainian, 2d Byelorussian, and 3d and 4th Ukrainian Fronts. There occurred a series of personal meetings and radio communications between operational commanders. The coming linkup led to bilateral exchanges between Eisenhower and Montgomery with their Soviet counterpart, Marshal Georgi K. Zhukov. These communications dealt with boundaries, signals protocols, and arrangements for artillery and air attacks. Crude but functional signs and identification signals were agreed to between Soviet, American, and British forces. These ad hoc arrangements sufficed until the historic linkup of American and Soviet forces at Torgau on the Elbe River.

As Red Army soldiers moved through the rubble of Berlin, Adolf Hitler, hiding in a bunker deep below the Reich Chancellery, committed suicide on 30 April 1945. His last days were devoted to raging about all those who had betrayed him. When news arrived that Heinrich Himmler had attempted to open peace negotiations with British forces in northern Germany, Hitler drafted a political testament in which he appointed Admiral Karl Donitz as the commander in chief of the German armed forces. He then shot himself. Although earlier American plans had assumed that surrender would occur on a piecemeal basis, events proved otherwise. On 2 May, remaining German forces surrendered in northern Italy. That same day, Donitz proposed a surrender of all German forces facing the Allied armies in the west but stated that resistance against the Red Army would continue. That proposal was summarily rejected by SHAEF. Only unconditional surrender would suffice.

Germany's surrender on 7 May 1945 at Rheims was made jointly to representatives of the Allied coalition. "The mission of this Allied force was fulfilled at 0241 local time, May 7, 1945," the official communiqué over Eisenhower's signature proclaimed.

When the news spread, wild celebrations took place in all the Allied nations. Nowhere was the jubilation greater than in Britain, where, as one GI commented in a letter home, "The feeling was infectious. The strain had lifted. Years of control, black-out, bombardment, sacrifice, and hardship were over. ... I wish I had been in New York to celebrate it with you. If at last the dawn of the long night is breaking and if we could only march together and feel together as we did last night, the people of all nations should have no fear of the future." That was not to be. The euphoria of VE-Day (Victory in Europe) quickly dissipated as the challenges of managing an occupation for which the US Army was ill prepared. Dealing with the enormous economic and geopolitical challenges that confronted the United States in its relations with its wartime allies and the implementation of ill conceived and in some instances contradictory occupation policies in the weeks, months, and years after VE-Day took the United States Army into unknown territory.

Recommended Reading

Analysis of the final months of the war in Europe begins with Gerhard Weinberg's magisterial study, "A World At Arms: A Global History of World War II," (New York: Cambridge University Press, 1994). Also see the relevant volumes in the US Army Center of Military History's "The United States Army in World War II," the so-called "Green Books," especially Forrest Pogue, "The Supreme Command," (Washington, DC: G.P.O, 1978), and Charles Macdonald, "The Last Offensive," (Washington, DC: G.P.O., 1973). Recent studies include Michael Doubler, "Closing with the Enemy: "How GIs Fought the War in Europe, 1944-45," (Lawrence, KS: University Press of Kansas, 1995), Max Hastings, "Armageddon: The Battle for Germany, 1944-45," (New York: Knopf, 2994), Edward Miller, "A Dark and Bloody Ground: The Huertgen Forest and the Roer Dams, 1944-1945," (College Station, TX: Texas A&M Press, 2003), Derek Zumbro, "Battle for the Ruhr: The German Army's Final Defeat in the West," (Lawrence, KS: University Press of Kansas, 2006). Also see the rich vein of biographies of commanders such as Dwight D. Eisenhower, Bernard L. Montgomery, George Patton, and others.

Session 3

Interview

Dr. Theodore Wilson

Interviewer

We're here this morning with Dr. Theodore Wilson and the subject of our interview is the termination of war. Not just the complete stop of combat operations but the diplomatic and social events that surround the termination of hostilities. So the first question is what sort of insights do you have about the theme of war termination? What do you think you could share with individuals interested in this subject?

Dr. Theodore Wilson

Well, the first observation obviously is that this is little studied. One reason for this conference and for this project is to bring about some better understanding from a historical perspective of how wars come to an end. Termination is, for me, a somewhat fanciful notion because clearly wars end but whether they're actually terminated in a conscious, deliberate way is a debated issue. It's an absolutely crucial question. We know a lot more about how wars begin, how we get into wars, and the notion is that wars can somehow be avoided by studying the processes of how they begin. Whether that's true is another issue. We know surprisingly little, certainly from the American perspective, about how wars end and it's worthwhile. My own view as a historian is there probably is no general theory of war termination. The sort of the standard view is wars are terminated when the two sides reach some rational agreement that it is time to stop but that's not been the experience in some number of instances in our history. Wars end when one side is totally vanquished. It doesn't have, really, a voice in the matter and that really was the situation, I think, in Europe in World War II. That's been the focus of my interest over a long period of time and that's how I think it ended.

Interviewer

So on the basis of what you've said about conflict resolution, it's easier, perhaps, to start a war than it is to finish it because the termination of hostilities requires more than cessation of military action. It also requires immobilization, and in many cases a consensus of the people and even then, the peace agreement or the armistice that's arranged, may not necessarily hold.

Dr. Theodore Wilson

Yeah, that's a useful point. Peoples and nations enter into conflicts based upon some presumed set of war aims, of agreed aims, generally speaking, or response to certain situations such as Pearl Harbor, but those aims change over time. The views, the attitudes of the people, and the level of hostility can change over time. I mean, the announced aim, and probably it would have been a generally accepted aim of the United States in entering the war against Nazi Germany and the Axis in Europe in World War II, was to "destroy" Nazi tyranny. That is, to get rid of the Nazi regime and then presumably some more democratic and stable regime would come into power. Over the course of the conflict, those aims changed as the capabilities of the United States and its allies changed and as the problems that they encountered in developing their strategy to win the war changed.

Interviewer

Which brings up the point that the United States forces are engaged in counter insurgency efforts in both Iraq and Afghanistan? It is now 2010. Do you see any parallels between the American efforts in World War II as the war winds down in Europe? The war in the Pacific is still being very hotly fought. How do you think the public reacts to a war that's being fought on two fronts?

Dr. Theodore Wilson

Well, it's an interesting and important question. I think I respond to it in a couple of ways. One is to be blunt from my perspective. I was not aware of what was going on in World War II. I'm not quite that old but what we now know about public engagement in the war was much higher in World War II both for Europe and the Pacific than is the case with regard to Iraq and Afghanistan. I mean these are, sadly, from my perspective, conflicts that have still been marginalized in terms of the public's consciousness for a variety of reasons, but there are some other responses that I think are relevant. One is that as the war in Iraq wound down or our engagement has been wound down, there is a similarity between what was presumed to be happening or going to happen with regard to the end of the war in Europe and the war against Japan. The timetable that had been set up, is that the war in Europe was initially supposed to end in the late fall/early winter of 1944. It didn't happen. The war against Japan, it was presumed, was not going to end until late 1946 or early 1947. So then when the war does end in Europe in the spring of 1945, you get a massive demobilization on the one hand but then a shift of American individuals and units from the European theater operations to the Pacific in preparation for the presumed invasion of Japan. That has to some degree occurred with regard to the shift from Iraq, the re-shift I should say with the refocus on Afghanistan after Iraq, but the other point or similarity is exhaustion. This fighting on two fronts and particularly the way in which in World War II there was no mechanism for individual or unit rotation, meant that guys who had been in close heavy combat in Europe and in the Pacific were there for three years. You're having the same thing occur, from my perspective as an outsider, with regard to Afghanistan, that's beginning to occur with Iraq as these multiple deployments occur. I mean, we're on the margin. A couple of years ago I heard the Deputy Chief of Staff whom I've forgotten his name say, "The Army's broken," and I think that had the war in Europe gone on a couple of more months, someone would have said the United States Army is broken because we were exhausting our replacements. Our units were worn down. We had all kinds of ammunition to fire, but otherwise we were in a difficult situation.

Interviewer

With the public perception and the will of the people in the 21st century, do you think that, given the wars of the 20th century, we might see a difference or perhaps a change in the way wars are fought and ultimately terminated?

Dr. Theodore Wilson

Yeah, I think we have seen that change occur. It's a very complicated story and one that I as a historian am reluctant to offer any hard and fast opinions about, but in World War II which is my terrain or turf – for most of the wars of the 20th century, at least through Korea and into Vietnam, there was an enemy and that enemy had a particular place where the enemy was holed up, so to speak. So, the presumption was victory was defined as pushing the enemy out of that place and perhaps even destroying the enemy's ability to retaliate or to resist. That's not the case in the 21st century and I think that's part of what the problem is with regard to the public's difficulty. The threat is there but it seems that unless there is a shoe bomber found or unless there's somebody in Times Square who's about to set off a homemade explosive device, it really gets crowded off the front page. Whereas the march of either forward or backward, the story of what was happening in earlier wars, was given ongoing attention. We're not getting that even with regard to Afghanistan. Yes, we get sadly three more Americans killed or so forth, or now yesterday 29 or however many people killed by a car bomb in Baghdad, but that's a blip.

Interviewer

Do you think, then, that the way wars are fought and the way the termination of wars is negotiated, that increasingly the amount of information available the impact of the media is greater perhaps than earlier conflicts?

Dr. Theodore Wilson

Certainly there's more information. At some level, there's more information because of the 24/7 mechanisms that are available. Yes, we have that information. Whether it is tuned into . . . . The news channels are there but is somebody watching. I don't mean to be blunt, but is somebody watching CNN rather than America's whatever – you know "How Did I Dance" or whatever those things are that are all over the national TVs. You know, there's the other dimension too. We really have had for the last three decades a truly professional army in the sense that we have an army that is an all-volunteer force rather than an army made up of either conscripts, many of whom didn't want to be there, and saw themselves as leaving almost immediately after their term of service was up, or in previous wars, we had the hastily called up volunteers and militias and in a couple of instances, draftees. The negative side of that professionalization and the existence of the all-volunteer force is that this sense of civic obligation to defend the nation may have eroded. It's in your hands now rather than in ours. I mean, that's an arguable position.

Interviewer

Excellent point, conflict resolution at the end of World War II was fairly complex. The United States was one of a number of nations in a coalition and the war was being fought in Europe as well as in Asia. What sort of lessons do you think are still applicable from that period, how it was ended?

Dr. Theodore Wilson

Well, I guess the lessons would be the inevitable challenge to existing assumptions and the unforeseen consequences that flow from those changes. The allies assumed that, at some point as the ring closed around Germany, that the Wehrmacht would either put down its arms, and rationally that should have happened relatively soon, at least, certainly after the Battle of the Bulge, or that there would be such a coup that Hitler would be assassinated and a government would come to power with which the allies could negotiate the surrender. Whether that group was going to stay in power was another matter. It didn't happen that way. I mean, what happened was that resistance at some level continued even after Hitler's death and continued though Russian soldiers were in the rubble of Berlin.

For a period of time, the occupations of Germany and Japan have been used as sort of the gold standard for military occupations. The early days weren't nearly as positive, so to speak, as they had been portrayed in comparison with what happened in Iraq. There were the "Werewolves." There was widespread sabotage. There were attacks on allied personnel. There were punitive killings of individuals deemed to be collaborators.

Interviewer

So there are some parallels with what's going on in Iraq, for example. The Werewolves or Nazi stay-behind guerrilla elements, whereas in Iraq they had Fedayeen Saddam members who had been grouped under the general category of insurgents. So even though the conventional war has ended, it does not mean that everyone agrees.

Dr. Theodore Wilson

There was to be an official organization. There was an SS-controlled organization set up to do stay-behind activities after the occupation, the resistance activities. It didn't amount to all that much, but like the situation in Iraq, if you looked anywhere in any field in Germany in May or June of 1941, there are weapons and people could pick up those weapons, and many did pick up those weapons for their own protection, but also because they were angry still or would be angry about being occupied. So, that does continue, and at a lower level over time than was the case in Iraq. Partly because of the Soviet threat, maybe the majority of Germans came to terms with accepting the occupation of the US, British, and then the French, in preference to what was going on in the Soviet zone of occupation.

Interviewer

One final question, do you think the United States prefers unconditional surrender of its opponents because of its experiences? In World War I, for example, the German army was not decisively defeated. They didn't believe that they had been defeated on the field of battle. World War II, however, unconditional surrender was what the allies demanded. Do you think that was a result of that experience?

Dr. Theodore Wilson

Yeah, that in large part was the direct result of what had happened and of the claims of German right-wing people such as Hitler in the 1920s. That the war had not really ended and that resistance could have continued, but for the so-called "stab in the back," and so there was this determination that this time we're going to make clear to them that they have been defeated and that will necessitate a military occupation. There also, along with that, though, is that people say it goes back to the time when Roosevelt was a young man and he did a sort of a mini grand tour of Germany and was absolutely repelled, appalled by the officiousness and the Prussian character of what he saw about Germany, that he was a strong believer in punishing not just the Nazi regime, but the German people. Most Americans didn't necessarily go along with that, but that's certainly part of it.

Interviewer

Thank you very much.

Dr. Theodore Wilson

You bet.

Session 3

The Final Campaign of World War II in the Pacific

by

Dr. Gerhard L. Weinberg

Although it was designed as a preliminary to the final campaigns of the war in the Pacific – Operation Downfall, the planned invasions of the Japanese home islands and the American landing on and seizure of the island of Okinawa in the Ryukyu chain of islands southwest of Japan turned out to be the terminal struggle of the conflict. Okinawa was to be conquered in Operation Iceberg, involving a preliminary landing on a small off-shore island. There the Americans seized and destroyed several hundred special suicide boats that the Japanese had planned to utilize against any invasion force. The assault on Okinawa itself followed on 1 April 1945. It was conducted by the newly constituted 10th Army supported by massive air forces and American and British Navy task forces. Since the defending Japanese 32d Army commander had decided to concentrate on fortifying and holding the southern portion of the island as long as possible, the American landing was essentially unopposed. The airfields in the center of the island were captured quickly as the landing forces pushed from the west to the east coast, and these were relatively quickly repaired and put into use by the Americans. Marine Corps units included in 10th Army moved north and completed operations there by 20 April, having faced substantial resistance only on the Motobu Peninsula.

The major fighting occurred in the south as army divisions pushed against the entrenched Japanese beginning on 4 April. As was usual in the Pacific, General MacArthur's intelligence chief had drastically underestimated Japanese strength on the island. Furthermore, many of the Japanese were dug in deeply enough so that naval and air bombardment hardly affected them. The army units, even when reinforced by Marines who had completed clearing the northern portion of the island, could push forward only yards at a time in bitter fighting. At the same time, the Japanese tried to destroy the Allied supply operation by sending literally thousands of kamikaze planes to attack the ships off the island. Substantial losses were inflicted on the American and British ships, but even the heaviest losses of the US Navy in the war in the Pacific failed in their basic objective. The Japanese super battleship Yamato, which was also sent out to help disrupt the American naval supply and support system, was sunk along with some escorting ships by carrier-based American planes even before it reached the Okinawa area.

After considerable internal debate and an order to attack from Tokyo, the 32d Japanese Army launched a major counterattack on the night of 12-13 April. It failed with heavy losses. An American offensive on 19 April also failed but thereafter the Americans were able to push the Japanese back slowly but steadily. A renewed Japanese counterattack on 4 May, accompanied by small landings behind the American lines on both sides of the island, failed completely. The Americans thereupon took the capital of Naha, while the Japanese decided to retreat to the southwestern portion of Okinawa and fight to the death there.

The Japanese lost heavily during their retreat to the Kyan line in the southwest and

183

as a result they were unable to hold off the American offensive launched on 8 June. The American forces had been slowed down by bad weather as well as Japanese resistance but from here on, they pushed to mop up the scattering remnants of the Japanese units. The American commander, General Buckner, was killed in the final stages of fighting while the Japanese commander Ushijima committed suicide. Fighting ended on 2 July, but for the second time (after Iwo Jima) total American casualties exceeded the number of Japanese dead. A few Japanese soldiers and a substantial number of conscripted Okinawans surrendered but it was obvious that the closer the Allies came to Japan, the fiercer the fighting and the higher the casualties.

While the fighting on Okinawa raged, both the Allies and the Japanese planned for the campaigns to follow. The Americans expected to land on the southern Japanese home island of Kyushu in November (OPERATION OLYMPIC) and to seize the southern portion of it as an advanced base for the landing on the main island of Honshu (OPERATION CORONET) then planned for March of 1946. The latter operation was expected to include an American Army (the 1st) that had fought in Europe and also to include British and French units in the follow up to the initial landings. The hope was that the Soviet Union would attack Japan on the mainland of Asia as had been promised and might well follow on the reconquest of the Kurile Islands to the north of Japan with an assault landing on the northern home island of Hokkaido. It was greatly hoped that these operations would end the war in the Pacific but there was considerable concern that Japanese forces on the mainland of Southeast Asia and the islands and portions of islands they still held might well not surrender but would have to be destroyed in what were referred to as "post CORONET" operations.

In mid-June of 1945, President Harry Truman who had succeeded President Roosevelt on the latter's death, ordered that the landing on Kyushu go ahead as was being planned on the basis of recommendations from the combined chiefs of staff. Not long after, he was delighted to learn from Joseph Stalin at the Potsdam Conference that the Soviets would attack Japan three months after the end of the war in Europe as they had promised earlier. All the major Allies were beginning to redeploy soldiers and equipment from Europe to the Pacific in anticipation of what were expected to be lengthy and bloody concluding battles in which casualties between half a million and a million and a half were expected on the American side with substantial additional casualties for the other Allies.

The Japanese assumed that the Americans would invade the home islands after they had conquered Okinawa. On the basis of their prior experience with American landing operations, they further assumed correctly where and about when the Americans would assault, first Kyushu and then Honshu. They mobilized additional divisions, began to train more and more civilians to participate in the fighting, and brought some units from the mainland home to strengthen the defenses. They had also carefully hidden several thousand planes and fuel for them so that they would have a very much greater air force available for suicide attacks when the American troop ships and escorts appeared off the coast of Kyushu. Since these planes had not been sent into action when American and British warships appeared off the coast of the home islands in July of 1945, the Japanese correctly believed that the Allies would greatly underestimate the size of the air force and hence the number of kamikazes that they would face. It was the hope of the Japanese leaders that the enormous casualties that would be inflicted on the Americans would lead the latter to agree to a peace in which Japan would not be occupied and disarmed and there would be no trials of war criminals. The authorities in Tokyo assumed that the fighting during and following any American invasion or invasions would be protracted and bloody and expected that Japanese casualties would be about 20 million.

As American intercepts of Japanese messages showed the very large increase of Japanese forces on Kyushu, Army Chief of Staff General Marshall became very concerned and (for the only time in World War II) he asked General MacArthur whether he was certain that the Kyushu landing was the right operation to implement and he was told that it indeed was preferable to any alternatives. Marshall assumed that the atomic bombs that were expected to be available by the time of OLYMPIC would be utilized in its support. The Americans learned from intercepts that the efforts of the Japanese to secure some sort of peace mediation by the Soviets or their possibly switching sides were being rejected by Moscow. They also learned that the advice to surrender that the Japanese government had received from its ambassador in Moscow had been discussed and rejected unanimously. Under these circumstances; Truman, Marshall, and Secretary of War Henry Stimson, agreed that up to two of the atomic bombs becoming available would be dropped on Japan in the hope of shocking the Japanese into a new discussion of surrender with a different outcome. If that did not work out as hoped, the bombs becoming available thereafter would be held for use in support of OLYMPIC. It was also agreed and announced that if after an unconditional surrender, the Japanese people decided that they wanted an emperor, they could have one who would be under the authority of the Allied supreme commander.

Neither the call for a Japanese surrender issued by the Allies from their conference at Potsdam nor the dropping of the first atomic bomb on Hiroshima brought any major change in Tokyo, but there had been one significant change shortly before that would be important after the second bomb was dropped on Nagasaki. Emperor Hirohito had agreed with the Japanese strategy of making the cost in lives and treasure to the Americans so high that they would agree to a compromise peace. The Okinawa campaign appears to have led to a change in his thinking. The Americans were clearly not being discouraged and could be expected to continue until Japan was occupied and completely crushed, whatever the cost. Furthermore, his advisors were pointing out to him that the suffering being imposed on the Japanese people by the military losses in the fighting now compounded by the American air raids destroying one city after another might very well lead to a domestic upheaval that would end the imperial institution. It was under these circumstances that the advisors were able to have the emperor intervene when the governing council of Japan was evenly divided between the advocates of continued fighting and the advocates of surrender. While the former argued that those killed by an atomic bomb were no more dead than those killed in other air raids, the second bombing suggested to those pushing for surrender that the Americans could simply kill everyone in Japan without ever having to launch the landings that the Japanese expected to make so very costly for them. The leaders in Tokyo could also see by the Soviet declaration of war and invasion of Manchuria that there was no prospect of mediation or help from that country, quite the contrary. It was under these circumstances that the emperor intervened in the deadlock to order surrender.

In addition, War Minister Anami Korechika who was a key figure among the advocates of continued fighting, in the dilemma between his own view of the proper course for Japan and his having been present when the emperor ordered surrender, committed suicide rather than join those who tried to overthrow the government, destroy the recording of the emperor's speech, and stick with the existing policy. Under these circumstances, the coup attempt failed, and the surrender was announced. Furthermore, the surrender directive was carried to Japanese forces in the field (in some cases by members of the emperor's family) in such a way that the overwhelming majority of local commanders had their units surrender rather than continue to fight. There would be a peaceful occupation of Japan, no post-CORONET operations, and no systematic killing of Allied prisoners of war as previously ordered.

The fact that Japan, unlike Germany, surrendered before it was wholly or mostly occupied meant that there continued to be a Japanese administration under the control of the Allied supreme commander as the country was not divided into occupation zones as Germany and Austria had been. Japan was also spared the destruction that would have accompanied the planned invasions as well as the great number of military and civilian casualties that any continued fighting was certain to entail. There would be all manner of problems and conflicts in East Asia as China sunk into civil war, the European colonial powers tried to reclaim their colonies, and Korea was divided between a northern state under Soviet auspices and a southern one under American auspices but the fighting between Japan and the Allies had ended without the expected enormous casualties on both sides. The fighting on Okinawa had shown both sides what more years of conflict would be like and what the cost and the outcome was certain to be.

Recommended Reading

The best recent books on the fighting on Okinawa and the end of the war are Thomas B. Allen and Norman Polmar, "Codename Downfall: The Secret Plan to Invade Japan – and Why Truman Dropped the Bomb," (New York: Simon & Shuster, 1995); Richard B. Frank, "Downfall: The End of the Imperial Japanese Empire," (New York: Random House, 1999); Max Hastings, "Retribution: The Battle for Japan, 1944-45," (New York: Knopf, 2008); and D.M. Giangreco, "Hell to Pay: Operation Downfall and the Invasion of Japan, 1944-1947," (Annapolis: Naval Institute Press, 2009). Helpful on the Japanese side is Thomas H. Huber, "Japan's Battle of Okinawa, April-June 1945," (Fort Leavenworth KS: Combat Studies Institute, 1990). Still important: Robert J.C Butow, "Japan's Decision to Surrender," (Stanford CA: Stanford University Press, 1954).

Session 3

Interview

Dr. Gerhard Weinberg

Dr. Gerhard Weinberg

My name is Gerhard L. Weinberg. I'm a retired Professor of History, University of North Carolina at Chapel Hill, where I was a William Rand Kenan, Jr. Professor of History.

Interviewer

Great, let's begin by actually tackling the subject of this conference and then we'll go to the specifics. How would you summarize the way that wars end in human history?

Dr. Gerhard Weinberg

Well, wars end in very different ways in history. The particular portion that I was asked to deal with for this program is the Pacific part of World War II and in that particular instance, what turned out to be the final battle of that war, namely the campaign on and around Okinawa, which was not intended to be the final campaign. We had expected to invade first the southern Japanese island of Kyūshū in Operation OLYMPIC, then the main island of Honshū in Operation CORONET in 1946. There was serious concern that, even after the home islands of Japan were occupied, the millions of Japanese soldiers on the mainland of Asia and on the various islands would continue fighting and the war might go on, who knows how long. At other times, wars have ended in negotiations between the parties and at other times, wars have ended in a relatively quick defeat of one side by the other. In all cases, either the parties that are fighting have to reach some kind of accommodation or one manages to crush the other. However, there is also the possibility that happens from time to time that when one side appears to have won, guerilla warfare of one kind or another continues thereafter, and then the question of when that has ended can be very, very tricky and difficult to resolve.

Interviewer

Isn't it also true that some wars end only to encourage the beginning of another war?

Dr. Gerhard Weinberg

Well, that has certainly been the case in Europe during much of the 14th, 15th, 16th, and 17th centuries. It has also been true in Colonial wars. One fight leads to another. That was certainly true about wars with the American Indians, with the Native Americans. One conflict produced another. In other instances, a loser hopes to turn the tables and win the next time around. Those things are not, in my opinion, easily predictable, and a whole variety of contingent factors and circumstances tend to play a very significant role.

Interviewer

I'm thinking here of the First World War leading to the Second World War.

Dr. Gerhard Weinberg

I don't think it did.

Interviewer

Well, tell me that. Tell me why you disagree with that.

Dr. Gerhard Weinberg

Well, what led to the Second World War was, on the one hand, the decision of the United States not to participate in maintaining the peace settlement as the only major power to emerge stronger rather than weaker from the war. We dumped the responsibility for upholding the peace treaty on the two major countries most weakened by the war, Britain and France. That certainly made it much easier for others who wanted to start a quite different war to go ahead and do so. I know that it's become fashionable to brand the British and Neville Chamberlain for what is called the sellout at Munich, but people tend to forget that Czechoslovakia was created in the Pittsburgh Agreement and Pittsburgh, the last time I looked at an atlas, is in the United States. We created that state and then dumped the responsibility on the British and French for maintaining its independence, while simultaneously telling them by law that we would, under no circumstances, help them and even sell them weapons, if they came to the defense of that country. I think the other side of this is that the German government of the 1930s was very explicitly not interested in undoing what had happened in 1919 to Germany. Hitler always complained that these other politicians were what he called border politicians, grenze politiker, whereas he was a raumes politiker, a politician of space, that what Germany needed was not these little tidbits of land it had lost in 1919, but it needed hundreds of thousands of square kilometers of land to live on. So you had a completely different war that the Germans insisted on starting and where it was made easier for them, if you will, to start it, because the Soviets would help them to begin with and we were not prepared to help anybody.

Interviewer

So you would blame the United States as much as anyone else?

Dr. Gerhard Weinberg

Well, I would certainly put some blame on the United States. I would also put a good deal of blame on the Soviet Union, but most of the blame goes to those who actually started another war. That, it seems to me is what's critical, and I find it interesting that one of the German generals captured in Tunisia at the end of the fighting there in early May of 1943 was overheard and recorded when he was a prisoner of war in England as saying, "Oh, if we could only get another Treaty of Versailles, we'd all jump to the ceiling for joy." Well, there was no need to practice jumping, because there wasn't the slightest chance that the Germans would ever be that fortunate again, to lose only bits of territory they had stolen from others, when instead of course, they lost a great deal of territory that had been German for centuries and centuries, they had the largest expulsion of people ever in history. The whole country, not a little bit of it, was occupied and they actually, instead of paying a little in reparations and taking in more in loans than they paid, they actually paid some reparations and ironically today, 65 years after it's over, the Germans are the most pacifist people on the continent of Europe, generally speaking. I think it would be fair to say. Those Germans, Field Marshal von Leeb for example, who thought of a Third World War, don't get very much mileage from their fellow German citizens. There is no particular interest in that country that I can discern, for taking on the British, French, Russians, and Americans a third time.

Interviewer

Tell me a little bit about your own personal history. Where were you born?

Dr. Gerhard Weinberg

I was born in Hannover in Germany. After all, the kings of Hanover, on weekends, ran the British Empire for much of the 18th century; not as well as the Americans liked, which is why we're no longer under the kings. But I left Germany at the end of December 1938 and was in England in all of 1939.

Interviewer

Tell me the circumstances of your departure from Germany in 1938 and why?

Dr. Gerhard Weinberg

The family is Jewish. My parents decided that we would have to leave the country.

Interviewer

This is after Kristallnacht, right?

Dr. Gerhard Weinberg

Oh, yes, but they had decided, even before, to apply for quota numbers for the United States. I had relatives who had moved here before the First World War in one instance and in the 1920s in another. After Crystal Night, the British government, alone in the world, changed its rules and allowed people who were going someplace else to do the waiting in England as opposed to waiting in Germany. The Quakers went to what they, in England, call public schools and we'd call private boarding schools, and asked them if they would take refugee Jewish children from Germany at reduced rates. This one school in Swanage on the south coast said, "We'll take two boys" and a school not far away in Bournemouth, said, "We'd take a girl." So, my parents put the three of us on a boat on 28 December 1938 and we were then in England.

Interviewer

Your parents stayed there?

Dr. Gerhard Weinberg

They couldn't get our exit permits yet, but in the spring of 1939, they were able to leave for England, and in the summer of 1940 our quota numbers came up and we were able to come to this country in September on one of the very last passenger ships that crossed, in our case, from Glasgow to New York. The family settled in Albany, New York, not that far from here. I went to junior high school and high school there, and then, since I wanted to be a teacher, went to what was then the New York State College for Teachers at Albany. It's now SUNY State University at Albany. Interrupted for military service in the Army, in this country and then in the occupation in Japan in 1946 and then in 1947, the Army decided to get rid of its draftees for a while. It didn't start taking them again until the Korean War. Then I finished my B.A. at Albany State and did a summer semester, a couple semesters of graduate work, and then went on the G.I. Bill to the University of Chicago and took an M.A. and Ph.D. at Chicago.

Interviewer

What was your dissertation on?

Dr. Gerhard Weinberg

I wrote my dissertation on German-Soviet relations in the period of the Nazi-Soviet Pact. Out of that was eventually published as a book; "Germany and the Soviet Union, 1939-1941," which was first published, and then with a new introduction, republished some years later. Then I worked for three years on the War Documentation Project, which was an Air Force contract with Columbia University to locate and exploit captured German documents in this country, most of which were located in the old torpedo factory in Alexandria, Virginia.

Interviewer

I know that very well, yes.

Dr. Gerhard Weinberg

It's now an artist's boutique.

Interviewer

Yes.

Dr. Gerhard Weinberg

So, I worked there for three years and then went and taught as a fill-in at the University of Chicago for a year, at the University of Kentucky for a year, and was then asked to set up and direct the program for microfilming those German documents before they went back to Germany. I did that in 1956 and 1957, went back to Kentucky for two more years, and then was invited to be at the University of Michigan. So, from 1959 to 1974, I taught at the University of Michigan and in 1974, moved to the University of North Carolina at Chapel Hill.

Interviewer

I assume you left family back in Germany during the Second World War.

Dr. Gerhard Weinberg

Some.

Interviewer

Some who were lost, is that right?

Dr. Gerhard Weinberg

Some family couldn't get out or their quota numbers came up too late or what not and they were killed.

Interviewer

Let's move on to your experience in occupied Japan because that will set up the discussion we can have about the close of the Pacific War. Tell me a little bit about your experience there, your personal experience.

Dr. Gerhard Weinberg

I came to Japan in August of 1946 as a private in the 4th Replacement Depot in Zama, Japan, and for the first weeks, since they needed somebody who had some college education and I had gotten in three years at this point, I was assigned to the supply section to what was called emergency supply, which meant either going out and getting things or delivering things which were coming in regularly by train and so on. That was very interesting for me because I got to see a little of Japan in the process. I had these convoys of two, three, four, or five trucks and I would be the only American. The drivers and helpers were all Japanese, veterans of the Imperial Army who were now, as civilians, employed by the Americans.

Interviewer

Tell the story you just told a minute ago in the conference.

Dr. Gerhard Weinberg

Well, before I get to that story, I'll tell you another one, because the first day when I'm assigned, the warrant officer told me that since the trips would take the whole day, I would go to the mess hall and tell them I needed my lunch, and I would have to tell them how many trucks I had. Needless to say, I was somewhat puzzled as to the connection between my lunch needs and the number of trucks. I very quickly discovered what was going on; namely, my appetite shrank or grew, depending on the number of trucks. It was quietly assumed that at lunchtime, I would hand out to the Japanese food which they would have for their lunch and occasionally, put something in their pocket to take home. We had all been told, I learned immediately as a replacement, that the Japanese are starving. You break rules and you pay the penalty but there's one rule you don't break. You don't want to know what they'll do to you if you break it. You don't go into a Japanese restaurant, and you don't buy food. These people are starving. I never saw that rule broken. At any rate, I very quickly discovered that while no doubt the morning report from the mess hall indicated that they fed only GIs, but there were two of us GIs who suffered from this very unusual malady of expanding and contracting appetites, but among hundreds of GIs, you're going to find a few who have unusual problems.

One day, the warrant officer, who generally gave the assignment to me, said, "Private Weinberg, today you will get your assignment from the major." And the major for us in supply meant the Chief of Supply for the 4th Replacement Depot, of course, and I knew where his office was. I had never been in it before. I went there to report and the major explained that a battalion, I believe it was, was coming back and giving up a particular post that was not going to be manned hereafter. They had brought all the weapons from the post with them and I was to take a convoy of truckloads of these weapons to the ordnance depot, which was at that point in time, in Odawara, north of Tokyo. I said, "Yes, sir" and he next said, "And today you will draw an M-1 rifle." We were all unarmed at this point you understand. I said, "Yes, sir." Then he said, "But no ammunition." I was quiet for a moment, and then as a good private, I said, "Yes, sir." The upshot of this was that I was a slightly nervous GI, as the only American in this convoy. All the truck drivers were former soldiers of the Imperial Japanese Army. There were several helpers, likewise and here we are, driving through the Japanese countryside with truckloads of hardware and I have a rifle, an M-1, what we had been trained on, I mean, in basic training but with no ammunition. I was very relieved when we got to Odawara and all the rifles and bazookas and machine guns and whatever else we had had been unloaded and I was rid of them, but as I said in the session here, it is not a procedure I would recommend for any of our soldiers in Afghanistan.

Interviewer

Now you use these two stories in a way, to illustrate the cultural sensitivity that the Americans brought to the occupation. Is that right?

Dr. Gerhard Weinberg

Yes, I mean, two parts. Number one, that there was a degree of sensitivity that these are people who are in a bad way and we shouldn't do anything to make it worse and that there was no danger of incidents. I never heard of one. My brother, who is a year and a half older and the Army had sent him to Japan already in the fall of 1945, a year before I got there. All was quiet and there simply weren't incidents as there were in Germany, to some extent, in the early months of the occupation. One simply did not hear or learn and, as I said, we were normally all without arms. When, after one day, I learned that there was an Army education program school in Yokohama and we stopped a convoy there, I went and talked to the administrator about if they needed a teacher. I had had three years of teachers' college, "Oh, yes," but the major in charge said he couldn't requisition me. The major in Zama in the 4th Replacement Depot would have to release me. So, the second time I got to see the major is when I went in, saluted, and explained it to him and he released me. I spent the rest of my time in Japan from, I don't know maybe September of 1946 until February or March of 1947 teaching American history and American government to GIs who had signed up for classes there. Then, when another teacher left, I had literacy classes, literally literacy classes for American GIs for the rest of the time.

Interviewer

You began by speaking to how the end of the Pacific War and the predictions for how the Japanese would respond was clouded by the thought that the cultural attitude towards surrender in Japan would dominate and that they would fight to the end. Yet, during the occupation, there was less of an insurgent episode than there was in Germany. How do you explain that?

Dr. Gerhard Weinberg

Well, I would explain it in two ways. Three ways, excuse me. One was that the Japanese government, led by the emperor, had called for an end to hostilities. That meant there came an occupation in which the Americans did not behave the way the people had been told they might behave. Things were quiet. If anything, Americans would give candy to kids and so on. I think that that was a very, very important part. Furthermore, the country was not totally devastated by the kind of fighting over the country that took place in Europe because the Germans insisted on fighting to the very bitter end. Furthermore, from almost the beginning, there was a Japanese government and administration. It was under Americans, advised by allied supervision. This was unlike Germany where there is no government. There is military government, but there is no German government. We start with local governments and eventually provincial governments, but there's no central government even in West Germany until 1949. Whereas the Japanese government and administration, under supervision, control, purging, and what not, continues. I'm not suggesting they enjoyed having American—and in one section of the island of Honshū—British soldiers around. There were Japanese mayors and administrators and police and officials and so on, so they were, if you will, obeying their own government and their own officials who, to be sure, were getting their orders from Americans higher up. This was a country in which the occupation did not displace the local administration. The local administration was there and it must have been very obvious very quickly to the people that these strangers who were in the land didn't seem to bother them much. When I was in Yokohama, we were in Quonset huts in an area that was surrounded by barbed wire, which was the 8th Army hut area. The rule was no unauthorized persons in the 8th Army hut area. Every day, there were Japanese people hanging around in the garbage cans. Everybody understood they're completely harmless and they need whatever they're getting out. Therefore, nobody saw them. The military police would walk right by and nobody said or saw anything. One day, I was back from the school early and the word was out that General Eichelberger, the Commanding General of 8th Army, was taking the British Commonwealth Commander, on a tour of the hut area. I ran into the hut area to get my camera. Here was Major Hope, who was in charge of the hut area and who was a very tall man, towering over these two three-star generals. They're walking between these rows of Quonset huts and right next to one is a big garbage can with a Japanese hanging in it and they don't see him and if two three-star generals don't see him, he's not there. Of course, none of this is secret. All of this is, if you will, out where everybody knows and sees and understands what's going on and as opposed to some other parts of the world, what is not going on.

Interviewer

Well now, while the cities of Germany may have witnessed more destruction, the stories of the fighting in the Pacific were always stories of extreme brutality.

Dr. Gerhard Weinberg

Yes.

Interviewer

I'm curious what your take would be on the book called "War without Mercy" that addresses the idea this was some kind of race war going on. Can you speak to that a bit?

Dr. Gerhard Weinberg

Oh, yes, by John Dower. Yes, I think he's got most of it wrong. The overwhelming majority of racially Oriental people were on the American side in World War II, and most

Americans couldn't tell the difference between Chinese and Japanese. What this had to do with was not race but Japanese behavior. It is worth remembering that after the First World War and the Russo-Japanese War, the Japanese Army was held up as a model for good treatment of POWs. There is a drastic change that takes place in Japan in the 1920s and 1930s, and the Japanese behaved very differently thereafter.

Interviewer

What happened and why did that happen?

Dr. Gerhard Weinberg

Well, it is because people who shot their way into power in Japan thought that there ought to be changes and began to introduce them. The Japanese soldiers, partly because they believe in it and partly because they're under peer pressure, behaved differently toward prisoners. That hasn't a thing to do with their race, in my opinion, and the book by Gerald Linderman, "The World within War" has a chapter which very clearly shows and illustrates with examples how American GIs in December of 1941 and January and February of 1942 in the very beginning, suddenly realized that these people are behaving differently. It is a response to behavior. It is not a response to race. Now, I'm not suggesting that our deportation of Japanese-Americans from the West Coast was a wise move but what people tend to forget is that in those days we had 48 states. The February of 1942 Relocation Order applies to five states and of the five states, two altogether and three in part. I don't really believe that anybody in Washington, least of all President Roosevelt, thought that Japanese-Americans living in Spokane were racially different from those living in Seattle. What you had basically, was a reaction to our interception of lots and lots of Japanese messages that suggested there was disloyalty and the United States Army wanted to protect the West Coast. Roosevelt, the president who signed that order, was born in this state (New York) and not that far from here. He lived not that far from here and has served in the state legislature and as governor. I have never seen any evidence, and I've worked a lot in Hyde Park, that he thought Japanese-Americans living in New York were racially different from those living in California. Those living in New York stayed where they were. I lived in Albany, okay? Because I wasn't yet a citizen, I was stateless, formerly German, I was subject to the identical rules applied to Japanese-Americans living in Albany, Italians, Romanians, Hungarians, Italians, and Bulgarians and I don't think I looked any more Japanese then than I do now. The notion that this is all a matter of race is, in my opinion, a complete misreading of what happened at the time.

Interviewer

What about Dower's racial aspect working the other way, with the Americans' behavior towards the Japanese?

Dr. Gerhard Weinberg

It just doesn't seem that way to me. In the military, there were reactions to the way they fought and the way they behaved but there are these stories and pictures of Americans on Saipan, trying to keep these stupid Japanese from jumping off the cliffs into the water because they had been told, "You'd better commit suicide." As you know, the Americans tried very hard and they got interpreters to try to talk to them to keep these people from doing that.

Interviewer

Well, let's come back to Okinawa for a moment. So Okinawa was not planned as the last campaign?

Dr. Gerhard Weinberg

That's correct.

Interviewer

So you would argue, I imagine, that it is not definable as a kind of characteristic last campaign of wars; is that right?

Dr. Gerhard Weinberg

Well, in one way it is because the impact of that was enormous. That is to say, on the one hand, it encouraged the Americans also to encourage the Soviets to please keep their promise and get into the war in the Pacific as quickly as possible and not to do what the general inclination was and certainly General Marshall's inclination, which was to use any atomic bombs that became available, as they started to become available in late July or early August of 1945 in support of Operation OLYMPIC but rather to see if we could not use one, or at the most, two to shock the Japanese into thinking about their basic strategy which was to just keep on fighting until the Americans called it off. Having just been given a demonstration in Okinawa, obviously, Americans weren't any more thrilled about their heavy casualties. The heavy American Navy casualties in the Okinawa campaign are the highest of the war. Okinawa, after Iwo, is the second time the total American casualties exceed the number of Japanese killed. Nobody's enthused about this, but it clearly is not leading the Americans to call it off. On the contrary, they are very clearly determined to go on, and the Potsdam meeting is in fact held in Potsdam and the announcement to the Japanese is made from Potsdam, in part, with malice aforethought. That is to say, "Look, we made it here and if you guys got any brains, don't wait until we're issuing proclamations from Tokyo." There was, if you will, a deliberate degree of symbolism, shall we say. And of course, it comes at a time when the fighting on Okinawa is over and the Japanese are expecting an invasion. While there was then, and has been since, various discussion and speculation about American casualties in OLYMPIC and CORONET, varying essentially from half a million to a million and a half, I have found it very interesting that, as others have shown, within the Japanese government, there was no debate. That is to say, it was assumed there would be 20 million Japanese casualties and that was considered acceptable to everybody until the atomic bombs fell. Then half of them said, "Let's call it off" and half of them said, "Why?"

Interviewer

So, the bomb was really the decisive last action?

Dr. Gerhard Weinberg

I would say the second bomb.

Interviewer

Explain to me the difference between the first and the second.

Dr. Gerhard Weinberg

Well, I won't say it was just the second. What we need to keep in mind is that although we had built these things in anticipation of a German bomb, it turns out–we know this today–the Japanese scientists were further along than the German scientists and while the German scientists, when they first heard Truman's announcement after the Hiroshima, they were already interned in England, and the Brits were taping them. Their first reaction was, "This is all fakery. Since brilliant us couldn't do it, those morons on the other side certainly couldn't." Okay? Interesting enough, the Japanese scientists immediately knew what this was. They didn't, unlike the Germans, think, "We didn't build one, so they couldn't build one."

The second bomb was important in the following way: those who were in favor of continuing the war argued, not that unreasonably, that a person who's killed by an atomic bomb is not more dead than somebody who's killed in a regular air raid. As you may know, in the early March raid on Tokyo, more people were killed than in the two atomic raids put together. Okay? The people who said, "Let's call it off" used, as we had hoped they would, the second bomb as a sign. They've got lots of these. They can just keep dropping them until there's nobody left alive in Japan. They don't have to invade. In other words, the basic strategy which had been adopted in 1942 and maintained until this time – that is to say; "We will make the cost to those so-and-sos so high that they will call it quits" – could only work if you actually got to fight them. The second bomb undermined, if you will, not only the wisdom of this but the concept itself because it suggested that all the Americans had to do was produce enough of these and drop them all over Japan until there were no Japanese left and there would be no opportunity, if you want to use the term, to kill lots of American soldiers and sailors and airmen, because they didn't have to. They weren't engaged. You see because the part of all this which people today forget Is, they look at both the casualties of one bomb and the damage and forget that at the time of the latter part of the Second World War, those were not such unusual numbers, either of casualties or destruction. What was unusual was that instead of hundreds of planes dropping thousands of bombs, you had one plane dropping one bomb. The one thing the Japanese, whatever erroneous views and stupid notions they had in 1945, they knew the Americans do have a lot of airplanes and if they have a lot of airplanes, when they've built a lot of those bombs, this whole concept in other words, of raising the cost to the Americans especially the cost in lives, no longer made any sense. We know, of course, that this is all in the contemporary records. The third bomb was about to be ready and General Curtis LeMay asked whether he should drop it and, of course, he got orders, "Under no circumstances." The third and any others that were becoming available were going to be used to support OLYMPIC if the Japanese didn't surrender. Now, there were problems with that and that raised an article on this subject; namely, we were going to send our troops through this area where we had dropped the bomb. I mean, that's another story entirely. People didn't understand the whole fallout and what not and so on. You see these idiot scientists jumping around after the test in New Mexico but the point here was that, from the Japanese perspective, the second suggested, not that this was some unusual experiment.

Interviewer

As if we had an arsenal of these bombs.

Dr. Gerhard Weinberg

We either had one or obviously, could produce one. They had every evidence – all they've gotta do is look in the sky—that we had lots of airplanes, and they were within range of both land bases, I mean, in the Marianas, and on aircraft carriers. When I was teaching there in Yokohama, we had a German who was a resident of Yokohama who taught, I think, in chemistry to GIs who went to the same school and I remember talking to him and asking him when people in his neighborhood realized that the war was lost for Japan and he said it was in July of 1945, when they could actually see allied warships off the coast. I found that very interesting, from someone who lived there and talked to his neighbors.

Interviewer

Yeah, they were that close, you mean?

Dr. Gerhard Weinberg

Yeah, I mean, we did that and, we and the Brits, as you may know, in the summer of 1945, had our fleets off the coast of Honshū, while as usual, Major General Charles A. Willoughby was completely misled by the Japanese as to the numbers of planes and troops and all the rest of it. As from the Japanese perspective, I'm talking what he was saying, what his neighbors were telling him. I thought that was an interesting comment. The other interesting comment on this, I got from a former superintendent of the academy.

Interviewer

Who was that?

Dr. Gerhard Weinberg

General Goodpaster. In 1995 before the 50th anniversary of V-J Day, when President Clinton went to Hawaii, then Secretary of Defense Perry had a briefing session for the president in the Pentagon. General Harold Nelson, who had just been retired from being Chief of Military History, General Goodpaster, and I were the three briefers. I didn't realize that but it turned out that General Goodpaster had been called back from Italy in the winter of 1944-1945 and went from Lieutenant Colonel and Colonel to participate in the planning of the invasion of Japan and that's why he was one of the briefers.

There was some crisis in Bosnia and the President had to confer with the Chairman of the Joint Chiefs, so we had time to wait and chat and I chatted some. I had never met General Goodpaster. I'd met General Nelson, but I'd never met Goodpaster before. So we were talking and he made a comment to me which I found very interesting. He said he would have slept much better when he was in command at NATO—of course, the Cold War's over because we're talking 1995 now but as you know, he was over in NATO. He said he just slept much better in NATO. He'd never had either the size army or size air force that the Japanese had waiting for us in August of 1945. I thought that was a very interesting comment of the general's and when I got home, I checked on the Cold War. At no time during the Cold War did NATO have either the size army or the size air force in Western Europe to ward off a Warsaw Pact invasion. The general had it right. I found that a very interesting comment on his part.

Interviewer

So without the dropping of the bomb, and then the second bomb, there would have been an invasion of Japan. Would we have been defeated?

Dr. Gerhard Weinberg

No, we would have had very heavy casualties. The Japanese didn't have our plans but they had figured out on the basis of experience essentially, where we would land. They had a much larger air force hidden away and not sent out and reserves of gasoline fuel for them. So the number of kamikazes would have been very much higher than we expected and there were a couple of typhoons in between which would have put back our schedule. But I think that, at very great cost, we would have conquered the southern part of Kyūshū in probably November, December, or January. My guess, it would have been something like three months and not in March, as originally planned for in CORONET. Sometime in the summer of 1946, we would have landed in Tokyo Bay. As you know, one of the armies was one coming from Europe, the 1st Army, 6th Army, I guess, was going into Kyūshū. The 8th and 1st Armies would have gone into Tokyo Bay with British Corps and French Corps and the follow up and more of the divisions of what had been our 10th Army which by this time, was under General Stillwell who had taken General Buckner's place when Buckner was killed. Sometime at the end of 1946 or early 1947, Honshū would have been invaded and in the meantime, the Russians would have invaded, most likely still in late 1945 or early in 1946 and so at some point, by the end of 1946 or the middle of 1947, the home islands would have been occupied.

Interviewer

Do you think that after the second bomb, the Japanese felt that the terms of peace were certainly going to be more favorable to them if they did not keep fighting?

Dr. Gerhard Weinberg

No, what they just figured—in half of the government—was that they wanted to go on fighting. Those who wanted to stop realized that the Americans were going to continue and there wasn't any point, so why have the whole country devastated from one end to the other when at the end, you're not gonna get any better terms?

Interviewer

When they did not prevail, the half of the country that wanted to keep fighting merely accepted defeat?

Dr. Gerhard Weinberg

Once the coup attempt failed, the willingness of the emperor to proclaim defeat to his people and get acceptance enough of the military to do this caused the people to accept it, and a part of this acceptance is related to the point that this chemistry professor made. That is to say that they realized the war was being lost. What we tend to overlook is that while the Japanese never suffered the level of casualties that the Germans did, they got off easy comparatively speaking—either military or civilian—the country was in a very bad way. That is to say the destruction of Japanese shipping had stopped some of the factories who weren't getting the raw materials they needed. It stopped shipments of food. It raised all kinds of problems of hunger and depravation. What people in this country tend to forget is that while we had been at war since the end of 1941, they had been at war since the summer of 1937, so that the whole of what you might call collective strains and cumulative casualties, costs, disruptions, et cetera, of war were much heavier and while, as I said, both destruction and casualties in Japan were much less than in Germany, the war for them had been longer and the rations had gone down much earlier than they did for the Germans. Well into 1944, the Germans have the highest rations of anybody in Europe. Now, thereafter, don't get me wrong, I'm not suggesting that they don't really suffer in the winter of 1945-1946 and the winter of 1946-1947 because they do. For the Japanese, deprivation starts at home much earlier than for the Germans, and the strain of war is much longer, more than two years longer, than for the Germans, so that when people say, "It's all over," there is at least a degree of relief there, and while the Russians hold back a lot of the Japanese POWs for a while, we don't and the men come home. Those who surrender at the end don't spend that much time in POW camps and so there is a sense of relief, "Thank goodness this is all behind us now." One of the things that you may know that the American Army Air Force did in I think March and April of 1945, is to drop leaflets on Japanese cities telling them, "Get out of the city into the countryside." Well, we had then destroyed some of these cities, but hadn't destroyed others. But the upshot of this was that those in the cities that hadn't been destroyed, and the towns and villages, had no enthusiasm for having that place destroyed. I mean, one has to see this also from the perspective of people who have really been through it, who have been told that when these people come, they'll eat all the babies, and then, when these people come, they don't seem to have the slightest interest in eating any babies. I'm serious. I mean, these things obviously don't happen. Now, I mean, the other side of this is, of course, when you left the PX or went to the service club in the evening, there'd be young women outside waiting to be picked up and people like me would say, "No, thank you. No, thank you. No, thank you. No, thank you." There was a great deal of what I would call temporary prostitution, as there was in Germany, as there was elsewhere but that's fundamentally different from what the Japanese had been doing with kidnapping women and shipping them around to be sex slaves. These women wanted to be picked up, hoped to get a steady friend, and supported their families and themselves in this fashion. When they didn't need it anymore, they got off the street, and they were not being carted off to some other part of the world to service large numbers of soldiers. It was a very different kind of thing. My point here is, this is all out in the public you understand. None of this is secret or being kept from anyone. So the young women who were doing this, number one, are doing it, I don't mean by free choice. It's choice under pressure. They stop doing it when they feel like doing it. They're at home with their families, supporting those maybe younger brothers and sisters, elderly parents and what not and so on and the surrounding population doesn't talk about this much. It's not a nice subject to talk about. They're also aware of the fact that the occupation army is pouring money, cigarettes, soap bars, and chocolate in.

Interviewer

Talk to me a little bit, just as a final question, about the impact of the coming Cold War and the United States-Soviet relations at the end of the Second World War in the Pacific.

Dr. Gerhard Weinberg

In the end of the Second World War in the Pacific, it has a couple of specific things. There is the issue of what to do about Korea and the decision that the Russians will take the surrender of Japanese troops in the north and we will take them in the south and that leads to the division at the 38th parallel that somebody dreams up. The Soviets anticipated that if Japan were divided into occupation zones the way Germany had been, that they would most likely be occupying possibly the northern part of Honshū, and when they talk about this after the surrender, after they have already taken the Kuril islands and a couple of little ones off the coast that hadn't been a part of the Kirils–and that's why there's no peace between Japan and Russia yet. The American President Truman insists no Russian troops in Tokyo. This is the key issue there, so that by surrendering to the Americans and then the allies in a collective sense, the Japanese escape what happened to the Germans; that is, the country divided into zones and sectors and all the rest of it because the British occupation force is simply doing what the Americans are. So they're standing around in the western part of Honshū. It's not a zone, if you see what I mean, and they have a ceremonial presence in Tokyo, which is of no significance. So that's one area where the Cold War impacted us and the other is that there is not a coordinated handling, or agreed handling either, of the POWs. The Russians go their own way with POWs, that is, those they captured on the mainland. We go our own way. While the Russians proceed with the prosecution of those Japanese who have been involved in these horrendous biological and chemical warfare experiments, we decide, because we want to know what they've been doing, to give them all immunity, and if you ask why do we want this information, it's because we're looking toward a future where we may need that information.

Interviewer

Well, thank you very much. I appreciate your time.

Session 3
Questions and Answers

Colonel Gian Gentile

First of all, I know I'm not going to be able to really tell anything to this audience, you don't already know about, the importance of it, and especially the content of it. I'm really in awe of the historians who you assembled to help TRADOC think more clearly about the problem of war and warfare and the US Army's role in achieving outcomes in armed conflict consistent with our interests. I think you're going to help our army tremendously for a number of reasons, so I'd like to just talk with you a little bit about where TRADOC is headed in terms of our idealized vision of future armed conflict, our description of how the US Army will operate in the future, implications for our force, and how I think this project will help us think so much more clearly and comprehensively about the problem of future war.

I thought I might just begin with talking about how this effort coincides roughly, in maybe a several year period with our decision to end what we might call our holiday from history within our the US Army and our tendency in the late 1990s up until we were confronted with the realities of the wars that we're in, to really take an historical vision of future war and to emphasize change in the nature of war, without due attention to the continuities in war. I think we suffered as a result of that and I could talk a little bit about that. I think that we ended this holiday from history largely due to the difficulties that we've encountered in Iraq and Afghanistan, where we've confronted the reality of war rather than war as we would like it to be. We were defining war as we would like it to be, you could argue, in the late 1990s and really up to 2001. It's during this time, of course, that we grasped onto sort of this fantastic body of ideas called the revolution in military affairs and defense transformation, what you might call a faith-based argument, that future war relied mainly in the realm of certainty rather than uncertainty.

Then there was a series of other assumptions that flowed from that fundamental assumption. This is the belief that advances in information technologies, communications technologies, surveillance technologies, and technical intelligence collection capabilities had lifted the fog of war and would allow us to gain unprecedented awareness of every aspect of the battle area. So our future commanders, much like French commanders, thought that they could in the 1920s and 1930s, be at the handle of the fan and be able to wage methodical battle, much like some believe that the advent of the telegraph would allow a modern Alexander to command remote from the battlefield with a high degree of understanding. We bought into just the latest version of that misplaced belief that technology would allow you to achieve a high degree of certainty in future war and again, this led to a series of other assumptions that I think really led to what General Dempsey has characterized as a failure of imagination in terms of anticipating the difficulties we would encounter after the collapse of the Taliban and the Saddam regime in Afghanistan and Iraq. I think it was almost a willful sort of decision to neglect history in this period of time.

One of the fundamental assumptions or beliefs associated with the revolution of military affairs is that we could really define wars. We would like it to be well into the future. We could take a leap ahead approach to capabilities development in our Army and in the most hubristic and overconfident terms of some of the advocates of this approach, they said that if we develop these technological capabilities, we could lock out our adversaries from the market of future conflict. You remember this sort of terminology associated with this. It was very hubristic; it was full-spectrum dominance with no pure competitor until 2025. We're going to achieve dominant battle space knowledge, knowledge dominance. Everything was dominance, you know? I think there was a little part of the psychological there and maybe a Freudian problem associated with that. I think we have administered a corrective to that thinking in the form of the Army Capstone Concept and I won't go through each of the tenets of that or the draft on the operating concept. I'd ask the team here to distribute that to the participants, the Capstone Concept and the draft Operating Concept. The operating concept won't be finalized until August so if anybody has any comments, criticisms, or suggestions, we welcome those.

What we've done is we've rejected this sort of orthodoxy in defense transformation. We said war remains firmly in the realm of uncertainty because of the continuities in war and warfare, mainly the human, the psychological, and the political dimension of war which I think is something that all of the essays get at is that war is still an extension of politics. Then you can't take this sort of linear approach to either the conduct of war itself or the development of Army forces for the future because not only do we interact with adversaries in the context of the wars we're in, that makes progress in that war inherently nonlinear and impossible to predict at the outset, and that thereby puts a premium on our ability to adapt. We also interact with potential adversaries between conflicts. So if we decide well in advance that we're going to develop a certain capability that's going to be decisive in future war, we're just about guaranteeing that that capability will be largely irrelevant because of our adversaries' ability to evade, emulate, or disrupt that capability. There has been no civil war; we know that as historians, right? Submarines, sonar, bomber, radar, machine gun, and attack missile, now there was the network right? The network was going to solve the problem of future war; slice and dice future war. So now we know that's not the case obviously and so what we're taking is this grounded projection to the future.

Beginning to think about the future really requires understanding the present, and if you want to understand the present, by an examination of history. So what you're doing is immensely important for us, in laying a conceptual foundation for Army modernization. You're going to help us really develop and refine our vision of future war. That's important to us obviously, because of the specific changes we make in doctrine, organizational training, leader development and education, material solutions, and personnel changes. I saw Mike Meese in here. His team has done some great work on facilities. How we make sure that our forces prepare for the problem of future war, sort of this practical force development thing that is really important for us to understand and have an accurate projection of in the future but it also affects our institutional culture, in which General Dempsey talked about in the beginning, the professional military ethic, right? Because the kind of war you envision fighting, defines what it means to be a warrior and so if you believe that what it means to be a warrior is for you to be able to integrate just certain technological capabilities and those capabilities in and of themselves are going to deliver a high degree of certainty, they're going to enable really near perfect planning then you would emphasize a planning process in your culture. It would enable near perfect decision making in areas remote from the battlefield, you would advocate them for centralization and really strict adherence to very prescriptive orders rather than a bias in favor of execution, the planning based on mission orders and decentralization which is where we're headed, and reinforcing a long-standing idea in the US Army in the Capstone Concept. It would emphasize risk taking and a willingness to assume risk, to seize and retain the initiative and it would be a much different culture that you would try to develop with your Army or shift your culture in that direction, than that which is based on different assumptions.

I think it also will help us guard against this projection of the future and understanding really, that the wars that we're in and what we've learned from the wars that we're in, it would protect against us again, sort of artificially circumscribing our role or narrowly defining the role of US Army forces in war. I'll talk just quickly about that. I'm going to wrap this up quickly. So as Conrad said, how we interpret the wars that we're in right now, is going to be immensely important because of our understanding of our experiences in the wars in Afghanistan and Iraq, will in large measure, shape our culture and shape decisions in connection with force development. So I think this project is perfectly timed, because it will help keep us from making mistakes. It will save us from some of our most dangerous proclivities which many of us have mentioned. It's the tendency to define future war as we would like it to be, to take an engineering approach to war, to think about war in a linear fashion, to divorce war from politics and policy. I mean that oftentimes it is our comfort zone in peacetime, as we think about future war.

So what this project will do is it will help us develop I think, a more mature and accurate understanding of the experiences in Iraq and Afghanistan because it will place those experiences in a broad historical context. It will allow us to study our profession and history as we all know we should. With depth and in context and I think here are some of the specific mistakes I think it could protect from, mistakes that I think we have made, to a greater or lesser degree in the past, at the end of conflicts, largely due to a misinterpretation of the outcomes and the reasons behind the outcomes in previous conflicts. First, keep us from defining war as we would like it to be. Remember in the 1990s, war is going to be fast, efficient, rapid, and a decisive operation, right? I mean, how can you be against that? Then we ponder indecisive operations but hey that's what war is, right? You know, the requirements that we have, to be able to consolidate political gains, to be able to what we call inform the Capstone Concept, and to employ a combination of defeat and stabilizing mechanisms, and consolidating gains as we go along. We've always had to do that, right? There are those who will tell you well, that is Iraq and Afghanistan. We don't want to do wars like that anymore and they'll view that requirement for US Army forces as unique and fleeting. You don't need to know the body of work that's out there now on new wars. None of this is new, okay, none of it is new.

The second thing it will protect us from is the idea that wars can be easily categorized, and that a particular category of war is more or less likely. Again, that is due to the continuous interaction with adversaries in between conflicts, and the point that is made, I think in every one of these essays very clearly, is that conflicts evolve over time and the character of that conflict evolves over time. So, you may go into a conflict thinking you're in a particular category of war, regular, irregular. I think the utility of those terms is very limited because of the evolution of the conflict and I think these essays will show that.

The third point is that war itself will guard us against making this conclusion, that war itself, or a certain type of war is elective in nature. I think you can see this in some of the recent debates about the wars in Iraq and Afghanistan; this was a war of choice. Okay well, it was a war of choice, maybe this particular war that individuals are talking about. But are you going to say in the future, that policymakers will be completely rational and we'll go to war only based on interest, rather than fear and honor? So I think that this idea that war, or a type of war, is elective in nature, is dangerous and something that these essays will help administer a corrective to. Associated with the idea that you can categorize war and prepare for the one that's most likely, that the type of war you fight is elective, it means you can't optimize your forces for a very narrow set of contingencies. You have to have the flexibility, the depth in your organization and your institution, to be able to adapt to unforeseen circumstances and problems.

And then the last thing is that you can't seek answers to the problem of future war in disciplines that neglect the unique nature of war. There are those who say, "Well why is history relevant?" And I think the answer is because you know, as Clausewitz said and Sir Michael Howard paraphrased and all of us probably believe in this room, that wars still resemble each other more than they resemble any other human activity and this is for broad reasons. I have no requirement of this group to recap but there is a tendency to take business analogies, to take elements of social science, rational choice economics for example, operations research, systems analysis, and apply these disciplines unthinkingly, to war. Now, any discipline can provide you insight into the problem of war but there's a reason why John Keegan said in "The Face of Battle" that what battles have and I think what warfare has in common is human. You know, this has to do with the struggle, as he goes on to say, of men and women, struggling to reconcile their instinct for self preservation, with the achievement of some aim over which others are ready to kill them, so it's the psychological and moral dimension of war but this also, the human dimension also gets to the political dimension of war.

I just can't tell you how much Mike Starry, General Dempsey, and all of us appreciates what all of you are doing to help our Army think more clearly about the problem of future war by better understanding the present because you're placing the present and what we've experienced in recent years, in the context that's necessary to achieve a full and accurate understanding. So thanks very much.

Question

We've talked a lot about controlling the narrative and looking at the previous conflicts as how do institutions try to shape the narrative. The question I have concerning these, especially with the last two papers is, how has the narrative of the reconstruction of Japan and Germany controlled us in terms of thinking about future conflicts, future peace operations, and using that which I would say is a very distinct case example of these two nations, as guiding our beliefs as to how postwar or war terminations should occur.

Colonel Gian Gentile

George Herring, I'm thinking of the book "Analogies of War" but I'm going to turn it over to the panel. Go ahead. Okay, a second question, we'll take a second one from Mike. So the first question, how's the narrative of postwar occupation, reconstruction, influence us today and Mike?

Question

Actually closely related to that is, who drives the narrative? Is it the reports from the field? Is it the contemporary press? Is it historians or is it social scientists? What is it? That would give rise to where folks look at that.

Dr. Theodore Wilson

The narrative relating to Germany in particular, also Japan, that we have had driven home to us, very much like the narrative with regard to what the meaning of the Philippines conflict was, was that it was simple, it was easy, that there was not anything like what happened in Iraq, for example. That's not true. There was violence. There were the werewolves, the so-called Werewolf Organization, really they were a formal organization but also groups of frustrated youths and others, who could pick up weapons in just about any field, did undertake violent acts of sabotage. By one estimate, there was something like three to five thousand people, both allied personnel and also civilians, killed in the period, the six months or so after the surrender. Then what happens that changes that narrative, intended to cause it, from my perspective, cause it to be obliterated, that particular narrative which got a lot of attention. It was that the looming threat of the Soviet Union and the perception that we needed to give our focus to countering that threat, led to a reduction of the pressures for a full-blown recreation or reconstruction of Germany, along really tough lines, harsh lines, and the desire ultimately then, to bring Germany into the so called Atlantic Community. So that's the narrative that became dominant and to some degree, historians did participate in skipping by, as their focus was the Cold War. But I think it was mostly driven, the obliteration, so to speak, of that narrative, mostly driven by politicians and journalists.

Dr. Gerhard Weinberg

The big difference is that in Japan, there was not the kind of sporadic set of incidents and the sporadic short-term violence. Because the country surrendered, retained its local administration under American supervision and a relatively rapid release of Japanese prisoners held by us, and a substantially smaller number of Japanese because there were fewer Japanese settlers in areas from which they were expelled, as opposed to some 12 million Germans who lost their homes. So you had to be sure hunger in Japan. That was still very obvious when I got there in 1946, but there weren't violent incidents against the occupying powers, and there was a British occupation force in the western part of Honshū but there weren't incidents against the Brits in their area any more than there were in Americans in their area. But I think that a major part that is important, quite in addition to the focus on the Soviet threat, is that by and large, the Germans and the Japanese got accustomed to having been beaten and settled down into new institutions. As the Americans and Brits and French in the western zones built up new administrations from the local level to the top, slowly over the period from 1945 to 1949, there was a degree of success and similarly in the case of Japan, the transformation and changes in their constitution, land reform, enfranchisement of women, et cetera, et cetera, independent trade Unions, you had what looked like fairly successful occupations. As Americans look back on this in the more recent past, and I think that's the question that I was trying to respond to, it was with a sense, well we do know how to do this because we did it pretty successfully that last time around, with people who were not particularly promising subjects for what we hoped to do. It does seem to me that that is very important.

I would agree with what Ted has said about what the public gets to pay attention to. In that regard for the European side unquestionably, the concern over the Soviet Union, determined the development and success of the Marshall Plan. In the case of the Pacific, it's the shift to the Korean War and the utilization of Japan as our main base in a sense, for the support of our operations and the United Nations operations in Korea, that then turn the picture of the occupation into a somewhat different perspective from what may have been at the time. One comparison comes from a personal experience in the occupation of Japan. I was for a while in emergency supply for fourth replacement depot. We'd have to bring in stuff or take stuff out, depending, and one day the warrant officer said to me, "Private Weinberg, today you get your assignment from the major." Needless to say, I go in, salute the major, who informs me of the following: that the night before, an American battalion had given up an occupation post that was never going to be used again, and they had brought all their weapons with them, and I was going to take, it was either three or four truckloads of weapons, to the ordnance depot. I said, "Yes sir," and then he said, "Today, you will draw an M1 rifle," and I said, "Yes sir," because I would be the only American in this troop convoy; all the drivers, all the helpers, would be veterans of the Japanese Army, working as civilians for the Americans. His next comment was "But no ammunition." I was quiet for a few extra seconds and then I said, "Yes sir."

So there I was then, driving through the Japanese countryside, with truckloads of mortars, machine guns, a couple of anti-tank guns, several hundred rifles, bazookas and whatnot, all of the drivers, all helpers, veterans of the Japanese Army. I'm the one GI. I have a rifle with no ammunition. I do not recommend this to any of our soldiers in Iraq or Afghanistan today.

H. R. McMaster

Could I add a footnote to that? Paul Tibbets made the comment once that after he retired from the Air Force as a Brigadier General, he ran a rent-a-jet firm that they would rent their jets out to corporation people and so on and he was much involved in public affairs in Columbus, Ohio, where he was living. There was a Japanese trade delegation coming over and one of the city fathers suggested, "Why don't you help greet these people?" His response was,; "Is this really wise?" They said, "No, we want you to do it." So the delegation comes in and he goes but he sort of hangs back off to himself. Finally, these two Japanese businessmen come over to him and they say, "We want to thank you." He was a bit taken aback and he said, "Why?" He said you know, "We grew up in peasant families. We're now multimillionaires. If you hadn't dropped the bomb, we would have been still farming that three acre plot and trying to get enough to eat." That is a little twist that frequently doesn't turn up.

Colonel Gian Gentile

Brian, do you any comments on the first two questions?

Dr. Brian Linn

We sort of forget that the occupation army isn't the army that fights the war. There's this huge demobilization and so part of the occupation is contrasting these grandiose aims with reality. In fact, that army disappeared. It starts off with about eight million, and it's down to under a million in a year. There are riots in Manila and it's pretty chaotic. If you read the Eichelberger papers about what was going on in Japan by 1946, that's no longer a combat army. It's become essentially a mob, in many respects. So again, if you're at the issues of war termination, the impact on the services is huge, and I think that's often forgotten because we have this illusion that they march down 5th Avenue like the 82d Airborne does or the Grand Army of the Republic and they go back and that's the end of it. In fact, these things leave very messy endings and the US Army, in the cases I studied which is the entire 20th Century, all these costs are flat footed, expecting a residue of goodwill and sort of some time, to adjust to the victory and in fact, within a month of the victory they're told thank you and here's your hearty handshake and medals for everybody. We're gutting you back to about five percent of what you were and so part of the issue with victory is it takes five or six years to recover from that shock. You could say that it's not until 1950, just when the Korean War is beginning, that these guys are beginning to pull themselves out of World War II, and probably not until about 1958 that they've recovered from Korea.

From World War I to around 1925, they're beginning to say that okay we sort of can see where we are now, and there's an expectation, and I hate to say this but I sometimes see it in TRADOC planning, that there's going to be a breathing space to say that now we've won the war so now let's think about where we're going and unfortunately, the historical precedent isn't that. It's here's the war, thank you and now, deal with a 95 percent cut in your forces. That's why I hope you guys are thinking about that ahead of time. I know you are H. R.

H. R. McMaster

The breathing space after World War II was supposed to be occasion to buy UMT and that is Universal Military Training was to be implemented. There would be a period of training for all able-bodied American males and that there would then be this opportunity to have that ready reserve, so to speak. It didn't happen and the draft finally is reinstituted in 1947.

Colonel Gian Gentile

Yes.

H. R. McMaster

It's on a chaotic basis though. I once was one of these guys that had the opportunity to interview senior survivors of World War II. I did interview someone who was on General Christiansen's staff. He was one of the personnel planners and he said the one thing that we never got right was personnel management. He then went on to say, "This is like the late 1980s and we still haven't gotten it right."

Colonel Gian Gentile

We have time for one more question and here it is.

Question

We've gone through a lot of wars so far today and I was thinking about what Professor Weinberg just said about the differences between occupation status in Japan and what's going on in the Middle East or Afghanistan today. Nobody really talked about religious war today. I think today, with the theological nature of what's going on, I'm not sure we can pull one out of American history. We haven't actually really fought that many wars like that. Is that going to change the question you are asking to about how our enemies could be disengaged from us?

Dr. Brian Linn

Some of the Philippine rebels certainly tried to make it a religious war. The Americans were really clever and very good at dispelling this. For example, this was seen as a war by Protestant Americans against Catholic Filipinos and probably because it was a volunteer army, they got the Catholic chaplain from the California infantry and made him in charge of the schools in Manila which the church had been running up to now. In one stroke, he sort of took out almost all that resistance and then down in Mindanao, you read the diaries of Bullard and Pershing and the one thing that they were really good at is not making that a religious war. Part of it was just their personal charisma. Almost all of them read the Quran and really spent a lot of time with the religious leaders and making it clear so that when they go off to a Moro tribe, there's a consensus that these are the bad people and you're going after them as our ally, or as the enforcement agent, to take out the Moros because everyone agrees they're a problem, not the Christians.

Even the two big battles are against sects, not part of the dominant Muslim group but as sects that the other Muslims agree that the Americans should go after. It's often forgotten, the last battle, the troops that go up and the American Army has got this famous picture of the guy shooting a 45 and everyone going. Well those troops actually should be brown, because they're Filipino Muslims, going to war with other Filipino Muslims. It's that level of recognition, this isn't a religious war.

Question

Were they scouts?

Dr. Brian Linn

Yeah scouts, they're scouts, 45th Scouts I think.

Dr. Gerhard Weinberg

I think we need to keep in mind, that in the case of both Europe and the Pacific, in World War II, we were dealing with people whose ideologies and religions were so fundamentally different from ours, that the difference between us and much of the Muslim community looks like small potatoes on a comparison basis. Where I think our own government made a terrible mistake, was never to stress, in the more recent past, our effort to protect the Kosovo Muslims from Christians who were going to kill them because they were Muslims.

That is to say, several of the American interventions of the recent past— Somalia and Kosovo in particular — were for the protection of Muslims. It is, I think unfortunate, that in the more recent developments, that has been so pushed aside or talked about only in the technological, or success or failure sense, without any reference to the fact that what was actually going on was that American forces and NATO forces, were being deployed for the protection of Muslim people. Furthermore, I don't want to stress that too much but one of the reasons that the war in Europe lasted that extra year, with horrendous casualties that Professor Wilson alluded to, was the dedication of the people we were fighting, to ending the religion that both — all the religions that most Americans adhere to, and substituting for it, national socialism as the only one there was to be.

One of the more interesting studies that's been made by Germans in the postwar years is "Hitler's Cities: The Politics of Construction in the Third Reich," that in the future of Germany, there would be neither in the cities nor the villages or any settlements, any space for churches.

Dr. Theodore Wilson

Gerhard makes a very good point. It's not accidental that General Eisenhower's memoir was entitled, "Crusade in Europe." There was that sense of this being a crusade against a — I'm uncomfortable using the word religious but a fanatical sect that could only be eliminated, not dealt with, not negotiated with.

H. R. McMaster

Ted, I wanted to ask you, were most of that guerrilla warfare and those casualties in Bavaria?

Dr. Theodore Wilson

Most in Bavaria, though the British also experienced it.

H. R. McMaster

They ran into some?

Dr. Theodore Wilson

Yes.

H.R. McMaster

That's interesting. I assumed most of it was not that way.

Colonel Gian Gentile

Of course, in the role of history, this analogy came up in the early days of the insurgency in Iraq. I called Gerhard about the werewolves and did a paper on it to get the best advice to the Secretary. There's so much I think for us to take back to TRADOC, even just from this discussion today, let alone the papers. Brian's comments on the ethical, moral, psychological preparation for environments of persistent danger under conditions of tremendous uncertainty and the need to organize for human intelligence and understanding of the local situations are things we're working on right now. Mac's comments, I think are consistent with Michael Howard's long essay on the invention of peace and your observation that the termination of wars often is not really a termination but may in fact set conditions for the next unforeseen and often more destructive conflict to come. So those who think it's just going to be Afghanistan and Iraq, and then we can take that deep breath, as Brian says, and have a war treaty or a respite. I think this serves as an important correction to that.

Theodore, I think you can take an intellectual sort of strain from strategic bombing to shock and awe and elements of effects based on rapid decisive operations, the halt themes, "no" to analysis, "no" to this entire tendency to try to find simple solutions to the complex and difficult problem of war.

Gerhard, your points on the commitment to victory, I think is an important point that emerges from your work and also, I think it's important maybe, as a theme for us to maybe develop further, is how the end of the conflict — and the termination of it — shapes the basing, long-term defense commitments that influenced the geo-strategic environment in a way that we would hope obviously; stability prevents conflict and is deterrent in nature. Brian's point though however, you know that force that is positioned forward, ought to be competent as well, or maybe it won't have the deterrent effect, it won't be able to respond to crises effectively as they emerge.

On the last question, I would just say that I think an opportunity for us, something that's different, is those who use a narrow and really irreligious interpretation of Islam are in the minority in the countries in which we're engaged. Maybe you could say it's a conflict within those societies and within those regions, rather than between these societies and ours, or our forces and these people. So thanks so much for a great panel.

Session 4
Coercion through Air Pressure:
The Final American Campaign in the Korean War

by

Dr. Conrad Crane

As the conflict and truce talks in Korea continued through 1952, the stalemate on the ground and ineffectiveness of air interdiction inspired Brigadier General Jacob Smart, the Far East Air Forces (FEAF) Deputy Commander for Operations, to look for a better way to apply his resources. He directed two members of his staff: Colonel R.L. Randolph and Lieutenant Colonel B.I. Mayo, to devise better ways and means for the FEAF to put pressure on communist forces to accept an agreement favorable to American and United Nations interests. Their study was completed on 12 April 1952. Randolph and Mayo began their report with an examination of the course and results of the interdiction campaign, which had been focused on enemy railroads since August of 1951. It had not worked, despite over 15,000 rail cuts and at least partial destruction of 199 bridges. Enemy repair efforts, night movement, and MiG-15 jet fighter attacks had foiled FEAF efforts to close transportation routes. Randolph and Mayo also pointed out that the enemy's daily mortar shell requirement could be carried by only one truck or 100 coolies with A-frames and it would be virtually impossible for interdiction to stop all such traffic. In addition, FEAF losses had been heavy.

The two officers recommended instead that any air resources beyond those required to maintain air superiority be committed to cause as much selected destruction as possible in order to increase the costs of the war for the communists. Targets were prioritized based on the effect their destruction would have on the enemy, their vulnerability to available weapons, and the probable cost to FEAF of attacking them. Suggested objectives included hydroelectric plants, locomotives and vehicles, stored supplies, and even buildings in cities and villages, especially in those areas most actively supporting enemy forces.

Based on the study, Smart planned to deemphasize interdiction to concentrate on the new target systems, aiming to defeat the enemy as quickly as possible instead of wasting resources on supply routes. Smart also believed attacks should be scheduled against significant military targets whose destruction would undermine the morale of civilians engaged in active logistic support of the enemy. He knew that the selection of proper targets to influence enemy decision makers would be difficult, not only for operational reasons but because of uncertainty about just who those key decision makers were and how their minds worked.

United Nations Forces Commander and United States Far East Commander General Matthew Ridgway's initial determination to influence negotiations with air power had been tempered by his disappointment in the results of the interdiction campaign and early battles with the Joint Chiefs of Staff about bombing North Korean ports and the North Korean Capital of Pyongyang. He also appeared hesitant to risk anything that might cause the communists to break off the peace talks. They had already used air attacks on the negotiating site as an excuse to do that twice, once with apparently faked evidence and another time because of an actual UN bombing error. His successor in May of 1952, General Mark Clark, was not as skeptical about the efficacy of airpower or as reluctant to confront the Joint Chiefs of Staff, who were also increasingly frustrated by the seemingly interminable armistice discussions. Clark's previous assignment as American High Commissioner for Austria had taught him that the communists only respected force in negotiations. When FEAF Commander Lieutenant General O. P. Weyland and Smart approached their new boss about their air pressure strategy, they were pleasantly surprised to find a willing listener.

The FEAF directive outlining the policies of the new "Air Attack Program" was published in the second week of July. The first priority for the FEAF air action remained air superiority to be followed by maximum selected destruction and then direct support of ground forces. Specific targets within the second category were prioritized as:

1. Aircraft

2. Serviceable airfields

3. Electric power facilities

4. Radar equipment

5. Manufacturing facilities

6. Communication centers

7. Military headquarters

8. Rail repair facilities

9. Vehicle repair facilities

10. Locomotives

11. Supplies, ordnance, petroleum, lubricants

12. Rail cars

13. Vehicles

14. Military personnel

15. Rail bridges and tunnels

16. Marshalling yards

17. Road bridges

The new directive still required that sufficient attacks be maintained against the rail system to prevent it from being able to support extensive sustained enemy ground operations.

The first major target for the escalated air campaign would be North Korean hydroelectric plants, which had not been bombed previously because of concerns about international reaction to such attacks. On 11 June 1952, Weyland sent Clark a plan to bomb all such complexes except the largest at Suiho. In the meantime USAF Chief of Staff General Hoyt Vandenberg was shepherding removal of all restrictions on attacks against Yalu River hydroelectric installations through the JCS. Far East Command received notification of this in time to add Suiho to the target list and Clark approved the operation for 23 or 24 June, days that United States Navy carriers were available to hit eastern objectives out of the range of land based bombers.

The addition of Suiho presented a number of difficulties to FEAF planners beyond just its location on the Yalu in dangerous "MiG Alley." It was a massive structure, the fourth largest dam in the world and beyond the capabilities of FEAF to destroy. Even the smaller dams turned out to present similar difficulties. Smart reviewed techniques used by RAF "dam-busters" in World War II but discovered the USAF could not emulate them. As a result, penstocks, transformers, and power distribution facilities were targeted at Suiho and the other hydroelectric sites instead of the dams themselves. The difficulty of completely destroying those diverse objectives limited the long-term effects of the eventual attack. However, a successful strike against the Suiho complex was seen as critical to applying effective pressure on communist decision makers. While most of the other hydroelectric facilities were for home use, planners knew that much of Suiho's output went to China.

The operation began on the afternoon of 23 June. The raid on Suiho bears special mention as a model of inter-service cooperation. It began with 35 F-9F Navy Panther jets suppressing enemy defenses, followed by 35 Skyraiders with 5,000 pound bomb loads. All had been launched from Task Force 77 of the 7th Fleet which was operating for the first time with four fast carriers. Ten minutes later, 124 5th Air Force F-84s hit the target while the whole operation was protected by 84 F-86s. Within four days, 546 Navy sorties along with 730 by 5th Air Force fighter-bombers had destroyed 90 percent of North Korea's electric power potential.

The attacks had many repercussions besides a reduction in the production of Manchurian industry. The impact on North Korea was apparent to American POWs, who never got to see the end of any of the propaganda films they were exposed to that summer because the electricity always failed. The British Labor Party denounced the bombings in Parliament as a provocation that could lead to World War III and only Prime Minister Winston Churchill's announcement that he was appointing a British deputy for the UN Command in Korea mollified them. Secretary of Defense Robert Lovett publicly endorsed the addition to Clark's staff while also providing the misleading explanation to the press that the JCS had given special permission to allow the raids on the hydroelectric plants based only on military considerations. American newspapers were not fooled and speculated that the attacks which had darkened much of North Korea and a good part of Manchuria were the start of a new "get tough" policy to break the stalemate over POW treatment at the peace talks. Some Congressmen even questioned why the plants had not been bombed earlier. Both Churchill and Lovett denied that the attacks signified any change in UN policies.

The next sign of increased air pressure was an all-out assault on Pyongyang which the JCS cleared for attack in early July. Operation PRESSURE PUMP on 11 July involved 1,254 sorties from 5th Air Force, Marine, Naval, Korean, Australian, South African, and British aircraft by day and 54 B-29s at night. Psychological warfare leaflets warning civilians to leave the city were dropped before the strike as part of Psychological Operation BLAST, designed to demonstrate the omnipotence of UN airpower and to disrupt industrial activity in the city. The effort was repeated on 29 August in an operation called ALL UNITED NATIONS AIR EFFORT which involved more than 1,400 sorties and aimed to deliver additional psychological impact during the Moscow Conference between the Chinese and Russians. Smart also scheduled concurrent attacks on targets in the far northwest of the peninsula to further display the effects of UN airpower to the attendees.

Pyongyang was not the only North Korean city or town attacked during the air pressure campaign. More than 30 maximum effort joint air strikes against key industrial objectives were conducted by Navy and FEAF aircraft in the latter half of 1952. Targets included supply, power, manufacturing, mining, oil, and rail centers. On 20 July, 5th Air Force B-26s began night attacks on enemy communications centers using incendiary and demolition bombs as part of the implementation of Operations Plan 72-52, designed to destroy supply concentration points, vehicle repair areas, and military installations in towns.

Even the B-29 Superfortresses of FEAF Bomber Command joined in the attacks on communication centers. By early 1953, Bomber Command considered small cities and towns the last vulnerable link in the communist supply and distribution system. Intelligence reported them all taken over as supply and troop centers and they were too heavily defended for daylight attacks by lighter bombers. Contrail problems and bright moonlight that helped enemy night interceptors limited operations along the Yalu to one week a month. So, the medium bombers spent most of their time hitting airfields and communication targets in the rest of North Korea.

Initial optimism about the new campaign waned as peace talks dragged on through 1952 and into 1953 and the search continued for some way to apply more effective airpower to produce an acceptable armistice. Clark and his subordinates continued to grapple with how best to execute this new concept of using air forces as their sole strategic offensive by seeking new targets. The JCS supported their efforts and except for delaying an attack on a major supply complex at Yangsi because of a nearby prisoner exchange, approved all of Clark's target requests including more attacks on hydroelectric plants. However, the JCS did prohibit any public statements announcing the intent of such operations to pressure the communists into an agreement fearing that if communist prestige became threatened they would find it difficult to accept any armistice. High level statements had to treat the air attacks as routine military operations. Ironically, as the raids were directed more and more at achieving a political settlement, the less this could be admitted in public as justification for them.

Destroying the last major target system in North Korea would be hard to justify to world opinion as just another military objective. In March of 1953, the FEAF Formal Target Committee began to study the irrigation system for 422,000 acres of rice in the main agricultural complexes of South Pyongan and Hwanghae. The deployment of North Korean security units to protect key reservoirs from guerrillas during the growing season indicated the importance of those targets to the FEAF intelligence staff. They estimated that denying the enemy the rice crop from the area would cause a food shortage, tie up transportation routes with the necessity to import rice from China, and require the diversion of troops for security and repair efforts. Clark advised the JCS that in case of a prolonged recess in the peace talks, he planned to breach 20 dams to inundate the two areas and destroy an estimated one quarter million tons of rice in order to lessen the enemy's ability to live off the land and aggravate a reported Chinese rice shortage.

That was not the only proposal to escalate the air war. Weyland held back a Bomber Command attack to obliterate what was left of Pyongyang for possible later use, as another means to ratchet up pressure if necessary. He also appears to have doubted the military utility of the attack, just as he was skeptical about the desirability of the attacks on the rice irrigation system. However, his planners convinced him to authorize attacks on three dams near important railways to wash the lines away as part of the interdiction program even though among themselves, they considered that rationale as a ruse to deceive the enemy about the true objective of destroying the rice crop. The 5th Air Force fighter-bombers hit the Toksan and Chasan Dams in mid-May which was one of the most vulnerable times for newly planted rice, followed by Bomber Command night missions against Kuwonga Dam. Clark informed Washington that these few missions had been as effective as many weeks of interdiction.

The JCS quickly approved the bombing of two more dams by fighter-bombers to inundate jet airfields at Namsi and Taechon. The draft armistice agreement provided that the number of combat aircraft allowed within Korea for each side could not exceed the number in place on the effective date of the armistice and Clark worried that the Communists intended to sneak high performance aircraft into North Korea just prior to that day, possibly taking advantage of marginal weather during the rainy season. Clark knew that further dam attacks risked a negative reaction from allied forces and might affect the armistice negotiations, but he and Weyland believed the missions had to be conducted to eliminate the airfields.

Contrary to Clark's expectations, the dam attacks attracted very little notice in the world press. American newspapers were preoccupied with the exploits of the jet aces and each MiG that was downed received more coverage than any bombing raid. FEAF press releases dutifully reported attacks by F-84 fighter-bombers on the earthen dams and mentioned that the Kuwonga Dam hit by B-29s was close to key rail and road bridges. North Korea decried the raids as attacks on water reservoirs which were not military objectives but no one seemed to notice. Perhaps like the boy who cried "Wolf," the communist complaints about UN air atrocities just were not being taken seriously anymore or maybe since no mention was made about targeting rice crops, reservoirs did not seem to merit any consideration in the press as a particularly promising or questionable objective.

The last few FEAF Formal Target Committee Meetings were dominated by discussion about how best to exploit the possibilities of the dam attacks. New ideas presented, included proposals to use delayed action bombs to deter repair efforts and to drop leaflets blaming the continuing air attacks and the loss of water for irrigation, on the Chinese Communists. Weyland was adamant that the dam attacks were for interdiction purposes and vetoed a proposal by Smart for a psychological warfare campaign warning farmers and populations below all the dams in North Korea of their imminent destruction. While

Weyland and Clark justified the dam attacks as interdiction raids, neither their planners nor the Communists perceived them that way. The Toksan and Chasan attacks did flood two key rail lines and many roads but they also inundated nearby villages and rice fields. The flash flood from Toksan washed out 27 miles of river valley and both raids sent water into the streets of Pyongyang. Bomber Command delayed its attack long enough so that the North Koreans were able to develop countermeasures and by lowering the level of water in the reservoir they were able to avoid the catastrophic results of the first two raids. This tactic also worked for the last two dams. The communists put more than 4,000 laborers to work repairing the Toksan Dam and emplaced antiaircraft defenses around it. Weyland was amazed at the speed of their recovery operations. Only 13 days after the strike, they had completed a temporary dam and all rail repairs. When Clark queried him as to what targets were left to exert more pressure for an armistice, the all out blow on Pyongyang was all that came to mind. Clark had Weyland prepare a message for the JCS to get approval for the raid but it was never sent.

The resort by the UN to use such extreme measures as the dam attacks might have alarmed the enemy enough to influence their negotiating position to some degree. Though there is no evidence that warnings from the Eisenhower Administration that the United States was prepared to lift restrictions on nuclear weapons ever reached leaders in the Soviet Union or China and the president's own remarks at a 23 July 1953 National Security Council meeting imply that he did not think the communist agreement was a product of those threats. There were plenty of obvious signs that patience in the United States was wearing thin and the war might expand if it continued. Even if notice about the increased possibility of the use of American atomic bombs was never transmitted through diplomatic channels, rumors about Eisenhower's threat to escalate the war if the peace talks did not progress were rampant throughout Korea and would have been picked up by the communists from spies or POWs. There were also many other factors besides military pressure involved in the communist decision to sign the armistice. The death of Soviet Premier Joseph Stalin and continuing instability within the Kremlin combined with riots in Czechoslovakia and East Germany gave the Soviet Union plenty of incentive to disengage from Korea and shocked China as well. Late gains on the ground against Republic of Korea troops allowed the communists to save face while making concessions for the armistice. Further delays might also allow South Korea's unpredictable Syngman Rhee to further disrupt peace efforts and lead to more heavy casualties from artillery fire and bombing.

Instead of influencing armistice talks with any specific bombing operation, airpower's major contribution probably resulted from the accumulative massive punishment it delivered to Chinese armies and North Korean towns throughout the course of the war. Eighteen of 22 major cities were at least half obliterated by bombs and most villages were reduced to piles of ashes. That is what the North Koreans remember most about American airpower and their programs to develop missiles and weapons of mass destruction have been motivated to a large extent by the desire to deter any future applications of "air pressure."

Recommended Reading

The standard work on American air operations in Korea is Robert F. Futrell's "The United States Air Force in Korea, 1950-1953," (USGPO, 1983). This story has been updated with new scholarship and the best account of the "air pressure" campaign by Conrad Crane in his "American Airpower Strategy in Korea, 1950-1953," (University Press of Kansas, 2000). The best account of the war's final ground operations remains Walter G. Hermes' official Army history, "Truce Tent and Fighting Front," (USGPO, 1966). That book also describes the complex negotiations at Panmunjom, as does William Stueck's "The Korean War: An International History," (Princeton University Press, 1995), which presents a comprehensive view of the complex conclusion of the war and its international implications.

Session 4

Interview

Dr. Conrad Crane

Interviewer

Dr. Crane, the subject of [your] writings is the Korean War and the termination of hostilities from the Korean War. What do you feel are your insights about how the Korean War was terminated and how was it different from other American conflicts?

Dr. Conrad Crane

Well, there was a lot different about the Korean War from previous American conflicts. For one thing, the war is not over. We don't get a peace treaty, we get an armistice. For another thing, we're really not sure why we get the armistice. We're not quite sure why the other side eventually agrees to sign. We still don't have access enough to their archives and to their records to know what the thought process was behind it. There were a lot of assumptions made on the American side about why that armistice came about that led to significant changes in policy down the road. So, you know, perhaps the lesson here is that it's best for historians to kind of figure out pretty quickly why things happen, because policymakers are going to drive on whether the facts are out there or not. Korea has a major impact on the whole future of American security policy. It globalizes containment. It pushes us into more alliances around the world, more of a forward defense, that we get the sense that we could stop communism if we put enough military force in front of it. If we send more troops to Europe, we expand our forces. We don't really draw down after Korea massively like you do after our normal wars, because we stay armed for the Cold War. We start to rely more on nuclear weapons because the assumption that the president has is that, somehow, his nuclear threats were significant in causing the enemy to agree to the armistice. So, all the services pursue policies of expanding their nuclear capability. Again, we're still not quite sure why the other side decides to sign the peace agreement, and it's really unclear as to exactly what impact military actions of that final campaign have on that enemy decision making process.

Interviewer

Just to draw some parallels between the air campaign in Korea after 1952 and the air campaign in Kosovo. I mean, these are both campaigns that are fought from the air although there is a ground component in Korea. Do you see air power in both of these cases being used as an adjunct to diplomatic pressure, rather than simply a military solution?

Dr. Conrad Crane

Well, of course, the military and political actions are always linked, but what happens in both Korea and Kosovo is that the primary military coercive tool used to coerce your enemy to agree to your diplomatic initiatives is air power. The exercise is similar in the fact that we're not quite sure that [Slobodan] Milosevic agrees to the accords over Kosovo, either. There are a lot of studies that have been done about the air war in Kosovo which come to very different conclusions based on very similar data. So, we've got the same uncertainty there about why enemy decision makers make the decisions they make, and how much of this is a product from this particular coercion from air power. The campaigns are similar in that there is, over time, an escalation of targeting. The targets in Korea, the target set shifts from battlefield target sets to kind of normal strategic bombing target sets to hydroelectric power facilities, which are very much dual use between civilian and military agencies, then to basically destroy almost every city and town in North Korea and to destroying even their irrigation dams. So, there's a continual escalation as time goes on. There's an attempt to find something to make decision makers do something you want them to do, or to coerce them to do something you want them to do. Now, in Korea, we're really not sure if we're aiming at the Russians or the Chinese or the North Koreans. We don't know who's really making the decisions. In the case of Kosovo, we know we're trying to get Serb leaders to make that choice, but we have the same process of escalation, where on the first day of the bombing of Kosovo, the aerial raiders are forbidden from attacking barracks around Belgrade because some of the NATO allies fear there may be draftees in the barracks. As the war goes on though, it also moves to more and more dual use targets. You know, there's the attack on the TV station in Belgrade. They take out transportation networks and bridges, attacking communication networks. Eventually, the key raid that seems to have an influence takes down a power grid around Belgrade and, while it cuts down communications to the field because it knocks out the transmitters in Belgrade, it also knocks out the incubators at the hospital for instance, because that power goes as well. So, there's an escalation. There's more dual use targeting as it goes on and that's another part of these air campaigns, but again, we're still not quite sure as to what aspect of this had an impact on Milosevic. Was it the fact that as one writer feels, that these escalating air attacks convinced the people that worse action was to come? They were talking about more Tokyos or Hiroshimas. There's another theory that while the targets start to get at Milosevic's cronies and they're the ones that say, "Look, we need to end this air campaign because it's hurting me and my interests." There's an argument that there are deals struck and again, we get back to the problems of the Soviet archives as well. We're not sure what the Soviets told the North Koreans. There may have been a warning of a ground campaign to come. There may have been a ground component that disappeared, but we just don't know. There's so much about both of these campaigns in Korea and Kosovo that we just don't know enough about the enemy decision making process and yet in both cases, there are a lot of assumptions made based on our interpretation of the campaign that lead to big policy changes later.

Interviewer

To bring up a third example then, the Linebacker air campaigns in Vietnam. Do you think there was anything significantly different from what we assumed and what we now know about the Vietnamese response to these air campaigns?

Dr. Conrad Crane

You know it's interesting. If you go to Hanoi, they have a museum to the B-52 there which talks about the Linebacker II Campaign as the Dien Bien Phu of the air. This is where they defeated the Americans, shot down 15 B-52s, and the Americans left afterward. So, they portray this as a great victory. You know, our own scholars look at it and say, "Well, you know they ran out of missiles and we caused great damage and it helped achieve a victory at the peace table." There are some authors that say the major impact was on the South Vietnamese and not the North Vietnamese, that it showed the South Vietnamese we're committed to actually supporting them. There really isn't a whole lot different from the peace accords signed after the bombing and the peace accords that were proposed before the bombing. You can argue that, maybe, there's some coercion there to get the North Vietnamese to sign but really, if anybody looked at the peace accords, it was pretty inevitable that South Vietnam was going to fall before the peace accords. They're a pretty lousy deal for them, which is why the South Vietnamese were really reluctant to go along, and why we had to. Again, the Linebacker II Campaign, I think, you can see as being unique in some ways, in that it was really aimed at not only North Vietnamese, but also the South Vietnamese. That's a little bit different. Again, major conclusions are made from that campaign. The Air Force can look at the Linebacker II Campaign and say, "See we finally did bring it up to bear." You know, General Curtis LeMay said later that if we had done bombing like that any two-week period during the war, we could have ended it, that all we had to do was put that hammer down. He said the same thing about Korea. He wanted to propose at the beginning of the Korean War that we go in and destroy all North Korean cities and said the war would have been over if we had done that. So, there's certain logic of this punishing air power that can be supported either by an interpretation of what happens in Korea or Linebacker II or even Kosovo, if that's the way you want to go, and I'm sure it fuels to some extent the "shock and awe" ideas that we carried into the most recent war with Iraq.

Interviewer

Given these examples, why do you think that it's important to study how wars end?

Dr. Conrad Crane

Well, obviously the mission of any military commander, especially a higher-level commander, is you've got to think about how the war wants to end. It's the same thing with political leaders. You don't go into a war without having a sense of how you want the thing to end. Otherwise, it's kind of pointless. You've got to have some kind of objective to kind of steer where you're going. It's not war for war's sake. There are certain objectives you want to achieve. I think that what this study shows is that it's a very uncertain path to get where you want to go, and where you end up might not be actually where you thought you were going. Even when you get there, I think it's evident especially from the Korean example, that you're not quite sure how you got there. If you really look at the record, you're not quite sure where you were. You know, I got somewhere down some path, but I'm not quite sure what that is, but you've got to make some kind of conclusions based on that as best you can, and to try to give you some insights for the next time. I think one thing that strikes me from reading a lot of the other papers in this collection is how so many seeds for our future conflicts are planted by the results of the previous one. You know, that business is very rarely finished. There's always something else on the horizon that you may have not realized was there, and that's going to lead to the next conflict.

Interviewer

How do you think the fact that the Korean War was fought by two sets of adversaries composed of coalitions with the Chinese, Russians, and North Koreans on one side and the United States and the United Nations on the other, that this affected the armistice that was eventually negotiated?

Dr. Conrad Crane

Obviously, having a coalition makes negotiations more complex. One of the interesting things about Korea, if you look at the actual results, is that you have winners and losers on both sides. It's not like one coalition all wins and one coalition all loses. The biggest losers are both Koreas. Both North and South Korea are devastated, and they both see the result of the war pretty much as very unsatisfactory, because they both wanted reunification and neither of them got it and their countries are basically destroyed. So, there's great dissatisfaction in the leaders of North Korea and South Korea. On the communist side, you have to rate the Soviets as a loser because their proxy is defeated. The world sees this as a defeat for their communist movement, and it also begins to plant the seeds of the Sino-Soviet split and eventually, they're going to lose control over China. The Chinese have to be seen as a victor. The Chinese emerge on the world stage. They stand up to the United States. They have kind of asserted themselves and then begin to become much more independent of the Soviet Union. On our side, with South Korea being seen as a big loser, the United States stands up to communism. You know, it does stop the communist thrust and is seen as defending a bastion of the free world. For the United Nations, it's kind of a mixed bag. In some extent, they are successful. They do help. They do see themselves as restraining the United States from entering war, pushing the world into World War III, but at the same time, it's done in such a way that the UN is never going to do that again. They never again have a major coalition and a major war against an aggressor like that. It kind of saps the will of the UN to be able to do that again. So, it's kind of a mixed result for them.

Interviewer

And the negotiations?

Dr. Conrad Crane

Even in the negotiations, it made it very difficult for us to figure out who the heck we were negotiating with, because we didn't know who was really in charge of this North Korean-Chinese-Soviet effort. Of course, the assumptions were that the Soviets were behind the whole thing, which was an erroneous assumption at the beginning, but really shaped our strategy and what we do. There's a perception that this is a Soviet operation and that it may be the beginning of World War III. The Soviets are probing in Korea and the real target might be Europe, and we sent a lot of troops to Europe as well as to Asia. We do things. You know, we rearm Germany and we support the French in Indochina and it really expands our interests around the world as a result of trying to stop the Soviet expansion. You know, it's all based on these assumptions of what's really going on. Many assumptions were erroneous. So, the opposing coalition is much more complex than we think it is, and I think we start to realize this as time goes on. Our side: we see that the UN is going to kind of be our supporter, and yet in some cases, it becomes a drag on us. There are great fears about American expansion using nuclear weapons and when we do the first attacks on the hydroelectric dams, we think that we're trying to have an impact on leaders in Pyongyang or Beijing or Moscow. The major impact, however, is in London, where the Parliament goes ape about this expansion of the war and there's all these dire exchanges and attempts to reel back the United States. So, it makes life more complex. It does give us a lot of help on the battlefield. It does give us a lot more international sanction, but as we continue to find in other wars with coalitions, including Afghanistan today, when you bring your allies along, it does restrict your independence of action to a great extent.

Interviewer

What do you think are some of the lessons that can be learned from the termination of hostilities in Korea? Obviously, an armistice is not the same thing as a peace treaty. Even after the armistice was signed, there were major incursions by North Korean guerillas into South Korea. An example, just very recently, is of a South Korean warship being sunk by a North Korean torpedo. What are some of those lessons learned?

Dr. Conrad Crane

Well, I mean the problem with this whole phrase "lessons learned" is it implies there are lessons, which means there's something you can take from one historical situation and apply to another. This is risky and then, there's the learned part, which assumes that somehow somebody took some action based on this knowledge and actually did something positive with it. So, it's a dangerous phrase, "lessons learned." Again, a lot of the lessons we think we take out of Korea are really wrong ones, this assumption that the nuclear threat is what ended the war. The lack of appreciation for the complexity and the positions on the other side.

When we go to Vietnam, for instance, we try to build the army in Vietnam, just like the Republic of Korea Army because we think that we build up this force in Korea to stop an invasion from the north. We'll do the same thing in Vietnam. We'll set up this very conventional force to stop an invasion from North Vietnam and it ends up as the wrong tool for what's necessary over there. So, a lot of these lessons are the wrong ones. We learn a lot though about the complexity of negotiations with communists, the need to balance sticks and carrots. You have to have force. You have to maintain a threat of force, there's a possibility of force to achieve your goals. So, I think we do learn a lot about the complexities of international negotiations in the Cold War coming out of the experience in Korea.

It does reinforce the necessity for a large defense establishment, you know, which some people see as bad, but I tell you, that's one of the implications of Korea, that we can't allow ourselves to draw down the way we do after our normal wars. We've got to maintain strength. You've got to have that strength in order to make your enemy respond. So, that's kind of a long term lesson of the Cold War we will carry through.

You know, as you said and you're right, it is kind of unique in the fact we don't really end the war. There's not a peace treaty. There's an armistice. You're right. It's been very bloody since. The last statistics I saw, it's something like there have been 100 Americans killed, about 500 South Korean soldiers killed and about 1,000 North Korean killed in incursions since the armistice and, of course, the Cheonan has been the most recent. So, it's still a very dangerous part of the world and, you know, the North Koreans have said that they abrogated the armistice, and they're not even following that anymore. So, it's kind of uncertain about the long-term impacts. Even of the war, you can say that, well, it's all gone now. We're starting from scratch. Well, of course, it's not that bad, but North Korea is not as dangerous in some ways. It's not as dangerous as it was in 1950, but, of course, with this nuclear threat, it could be more dangerous. So, it's a very dangerous part of the world still.

Another impact of the way the war ended with this extensive air campaign that basically destroyed North Korea is . . . some Asian experts think that the main impetus for the North Korean nuclear program is to prevent that ever happening again. They need to be able to deter this massive exercise of Western military power that basically destroyed their country and the way to do that is with nuclear weapons. So, that's another one of these unforeseen consequences of the way we tried to end that particular conflict.

Interviewer

After the fall of the Soviet Union, the Chinese seem to have taken a much greater role with North Korea. It's 2010. The armistice is still in effect, even though, as you have pointed out, the North Koreans have said that they've abrogated it. It's still in effect. Well, why do you think the North Koreans persist, instead of signing a peace treaty? Why do you think they persist in engaging in provocative actions?

Dr. Conrad Crane

My personal view is that too much of the power of the North Korean leadership depends on maintaining this threat. The fact that they are this beleaguered state, that they are feeling that everybody's out to get them and that, I think, is the main instrument of control that the current leadership has over the North Korean people. They're defending them from all these threats. It's useful to them. I mean, it's a real dilemma for the whole international community and how do you deal with a state that has nothing to lose? I've talked with the Chinese and we always say the Chinese can influence North Koreans, and that they should do more to control some of the strange things North Koreans do, and the Chinese will say that you and we think the North Koreans are crazy. "Why do you think we can control them any better than you can control 'em?" The North Koreans have become very, very adept at manipulating people with their threats, whether it's the nuclear threats or threats of conventional action against Seoul. You know, really, that's one of the reasons that South Korea is no threat to do much against North Korea, because there's so much artillery within range of Seoul, they understand how vulnerable they would be. I saw an editorial that talked about the fact that the response of South Korea to the Cheonan sinking was a collective shrug. Kind of like, okay, they did that. There's not a whole lot we can do to change 'em. We'll just be stronger, but there's just not a lot of leverage anybody has in North Korea, including the Chinese. Again, I think that the conditions they've created that the world is against them and they need a strong defense and a collective effort is something that the leadership continues to exploit to maintain its power.

Interviewer

Well, Dr. Crane, thank you very much.

Dr. Conrad Crane

Thank you.

Session 4

Interview

Colonel Gian Gentile

Interviewer

Why don't we begin by your telling us kind of in a capsule the story of what's relevant about the end of the Vietnam War to the themes that merged in this conference?

Colonel Gian Gentile

I guess the story of the war for me as I interpret it when I wrote this essay, when I was doing the research. Once I started writing and hammering out the essay that really the story of the war for me is still grounded and made sense by George Herring's classic formulation of the war when he first wrote his book "American's Longest War." George Herring said that the war wasn't winnable based on a moral and material cost that the United States people were willing to pay. That basic interpretation of the war was on my mind when I researched and wrote the essay. That, I think, also mixes really tightly with a lot of themes that resonate powerfully today with Iraq and Afghanistan. The notion of a better war, the notion that better generals can turn a war around, the notion that has been put forward by people like [Lewis] Sorley, who argue that the Vietnam War was actually won in the south because of General Abrams. That whole theme had been built on in the 1980s based on theories that said the Vietnam War could have been won if the United States Army would have done things differently, if it adjusted its tactics and operations appropriately, all those kinds of things. Again, those things fly in the face of George Herring's formulation, which I think is still right, that the war was not winnable. Nor do I think was the war, to begin with, in our vital national interest. Then I get into the research and the writing of the final years of the war and the termination and the ending of the war. Sort of the main theme or question to me is how did the United States end a war that it had already lost and one that it started that was unwinnable? Those were my framing questions.

Interviewer

One of the points you make is that we could have continued the war as long as wanted to effectively, militarily prop up the South Vietnamese, right?

Colonel Gian Gentile

By 1971 or certainly by the first month of 1972 as the United States is getting ready to completely leave, even continuing the war politically in the United States was just not feasible. President Richard Nixon and Secretary of State Henry Kissinger never liked the idea of a time frame to leave because they felt, and they were right, it gave them a much weaker position in the negotiations.

Interviewer

It's the same theme we're facing now?

Colonel Gian Gentile

Right, and another thing I had on my mind is Iraq and Afghanistan, more so because it does look like we're leaving Iraq, who knows what we're going to do or will do in Afghanistan, but politically it wasn't feasible for Nixon to stay even if he wanted to because, by 1971, Congress was passing laws that would eventually prevent the resourcing of the war. Nixon is reelected in 1972, but it becomes significant because even though he's reelected, the number of seats in the House and the Senate for Republicans who were favorable to continuing the war was getting smaller and smaller. It was clear that politically, the Congress was going to bring about an end to the war one way or another.

Interviewer

Let's get back to your point that the war was not winnable at a price that we were willing to pay.

Colonel Gian Gentile

Right, the tragedy of ending the Vietnam War. I've thought about this a lot, and I think Roger Spiller is correct when he says that for the United States, the key critical terminal campaign was the Tet Offensive. At the Tet Offensive and after, when the war truly, for the United States, is stalemated, we can't stay there. So from there you go from mid-1968 to the end of 1972, three years and 20,000 Americans are killed, not to mention 100,000 or more Vietnamese. How do you end a war that's already lost?

Interviewer

Let's back up and tell the story a little bit of our engagement in Vietnam, get to the Tet Offensive so we can understand this complex. Let's start with the post-war period that you do in the essay, the French Indochina and Dien Bien Phu and sort of bring us in.

Colonel Gian Gentile

To understand Vietnam and America's participation in the Vietnam War, you have to start with World War II, even drawing back a little bit further. At the start of the 20th century, you really start to see the zenith—starting with the British and the Boer War in South Africa—the weakening of the major European empires. That process really comes to its completion with World War II. So much of the next 40 years is really the story of the decolonization of European empires, like French and British retracting and pulling them in and what happens during that process of decolonization. Vietnam is a part of that whole process, but that is combined and interacting with the rise of the Soviet Union, of international communism in China. You have the spread of communist states and communist revolution and that is also linked, of course, within these countries that were foreign European colonies, to desires for nationalism.

Interviewer

This, I think, is a very important point to make clear: the United States is actually an anti-colonial voice in this mix initially, except for the competing issues of the Soviet Union.

Colonel Gian Gentile

Sure, the United States is an anti-traditional European colonial voice. The United

States is very much about establishing a world order that is conducive to its security and economic and cultural interest. Some historians call that, although in different words, a form of empire. The United States is certainly not in line with supporting France and Britain in reestablishing their colonial empires, but the United States still wants to construct a world order after World War II that is conducive to its interests. The central rub or problem which brings about the Cold War is Soviet and Chinese communism, which ideologically does threaten those interests.

Interviewer

The reason I raise this is because this is a rub between the United States and France and between the United States and Britain, too, in the 1950s, that they'd be urged to pull us in as the only remaining strong power at this point. They're urged to want to have us reassert their own colonialism, the French wanted it initially. Eisenhower and the American State Department said, "We're not on the same page with you."

Colonel Gian Gentile

Yeah, they're not on the same page, but they're different chapters of the same book, if that metaphor works right. The United States did supply France close to 80 percent of its material when France was trying to reestablish itself as a colonial power in Indochina.

Interviewer

They did it for different reasons, right?

Colonel Gian Gentile

Right, the United States after World War II is not comfortable with maintaining these European colonial empires. However, that dislike flies in the face of the American main vital interest in the world, which is Europe, confronting the Soviet Union, and building a western Europe that can deal with the Soviet Union. France is a critical player in that. The United States ends up accommodating France and its desires and interests in other parts of the world to get what it needs from France and Europe, which is why it goes along with and supports France in reestablishing it as a colonial empire. Plus, for the United States, there is a cause or a rationale for doing it, and that is it is supporting France—okay, France is still a colonial Empire, we'll support them because they are fighting or dealing with a greater threat to American interest, which is the spread of communism.

Interviewer

So, set the scene then. Indochina coming apart, the French wanting to pull out, they can't sustain it economically and they probably don't have the will either. Algeria is about to explode. So you're really in this period where the French are virtually saying let's pull the plug, but they don't want to do so unless the United States sort of comes in and backs them up.

Colonel Gian Gentile

Right, the United States had been backing them up. They backed them up so well that the French really put themselves in an unattainable position at Dien Bien Phu in late 1953 and early 1954. The French hadn't given up. The French were asking the United States for more resources. In fact, the French asked the United States in carefully put ways to possibly use nuclear weapons. President Eisenhower of the United States also says no to a commitment of ground forces into Indochina. After Dien Bien Phu, the situation is such that it's in the interest of the fighting sides to come to a table to negotiate an end to the war. The Vietnamese communists or Viet Minh, think they've won, and in a lot of ways they've had.

Interviewer

Explain what Dien Bien Phu was for those who don't know.

Colonel Gian Gentile

It's an established post around an airfield in the northern part of what during the Vietnam War was North Vietnam, and what today would be Vietnam total. The French had adopted an operational method to try to inject their forces into key points in the hinterland where the Viet Minh were, so they could fight them and also establish control of major roads and things like that. Rightly or wrongly, and it ended up being wrongly, it was a flawed operational method and it ended up putting an airborne regiment on this little post that protected an airfield, but was surrounded by large mountains. The communist army, the Viet Minh under the leadership of General Nguyen Giap, very effectively surrounded the area, put artillery up on the hills, and then eventually annihilated the French at that position, which turned out to be a significant battle because it forced the French to accept that they could not defeat the Viet Minh. They also were out of money and the United States wasn't going to commit ground forced or significant amounts of airpower or nuclear weapons, which then led to the Geneva Conference where the agreement is made to separate the country in two, between the north and the south. The Vietnamese communists were not at all happy about. They wanted the French out completely, and they didn't want a South Vietnam that was going to be in alliance continuously with the French and then later the United States. The Soviet Union and China pushed North Vietnam into agreeing to a division of the country which only was supposed to be temporary and there were supposed to be national elections held in 1956 but that didn't happen.

Interviewer

We're getting ahead of ourselves with respect to Dien Bien Phu. Explain, on whom would the nuclear weapons have been used?

Colonel Gian Gentile

The French would have wanted a couple of relatively small tactical nuclear weapons to be placed on Viet Minh army units that were attacking them at Dien Bien Phu, so they would have been able to attack the Vietnamese communist military formations that were in the field attacking the French at Dien Bien Phu.

Interviewer

Was the request was actually made?

Colonel Gian Gentile

It went through the French and it ended up in the hands of Admiral Arthur Radford, who got it one way or the other to President Eisenhower. Eisenhower eventually said, "No, we're not going to do that." So, it didn't happen and for a good reason.

Interviewer

So the settlement is dividing of the country and elections supposedly for 1956, but the elections never materialized, why?

Colonel Gian Gentile

The newly formed government in South Vietnam under Ngo Dinh Diem knew that if they went ahead with elections, they would lose because of the strength of the communists, especially in the countryside. So Diem knew that he would lose, and it was after 1956 and the cancelled elections that were supposed to happen that Diem carried out a very effective campaign to destroy the remaining communists in South Vietnam. It actually produced results, and that was one of the reasons why the North Vietnamese by 1959 started to actively provide material and manpower and support to the South Vietnamese communists, because of the effectiveness of Diem's campaign against them. It then sets the stage for the increased American involvement in South Vietnam in 1958 and 1959, largely in response to Diem's campaign against the remaining South Vietnamese communists that were still in the south. That's when a large number of communists from North Vietnam begin to move into the south and when North Vietnam starts to provide materials and support to the South Vietnamese communists. That continues to build and build and build, and you start to have the formation of South Vietnamese communists who begin to be referred to as Viet Cong in 1960. They've formed military formations, infantry companies, battalions, regiments, and they are receiving supplies, guns, ammunition, and mortars from the north.

Interviewer

What is our level of participation at this point?

Colonel Gian Gentile

Well those are the early years of the significant advisory effort continuing under Kennedy. From 1960 to 1964, there's a 15,000- to 20,000-man increase on the American side and it's still largely advisory. It's when you have Special Forces there. The South Vietnamese army, called the Army of Republic of Vietnam (ARVN), is built around an American model, but they have all kinds of problems. They don't fight well, and there's rampant corruption. It's the same story that continues throughout the Vietnam War. It's not just the ARVN; it's the South Vietnamese government as well. Essentially what keeps South Vietnam's government and military intact and able to hold out ultimately is the application of American firepower, which is a theme that I develop a lot in the essay. That's critical in the beginning, and it becomes really the only thing that holds the place together in the final years of the war. So the United States between 1960 and 1964 increases its advisory role. It adds more special forces, more trainers, and more people (mostly military but some civilian who can funnel in resources and supplies to build the ARVN) to build the South Vietnamese Air Force and its small navy and to try to do economic infrastructure building. The United States has embarked on the campaign of nation building but what happens by early 1964 is that the North Vietnamese enter the war and so whenever one side acts, the other side reacts and that just keeps going on and on as a cycle. The North Vietnamese begin to infiltrate parts of their army into South Vietnam. The situation becomes critical. There are a number of significant tactical defeats of the ARVN by the South Vietnamese communists and the North Vietnamese Army. By late 1964, General Westmoreland is asking for a significant commitment of American ground forces.

Interviewer

Speak to me a little about the American command structure here. Westmoreland becomes the general officer in charge during the Kennedy years?

Colonel Gian Gentile

Right, Westmoreland goes to Vietnam in 1964 and takes over from a guy named General Harkins, and assumes command of what is called the Military Advisory Command Vietnam (MAC-V). When Westmoreland first takes over in 1964, the mission in Vietnam is still largely one of advice and support.

Interviewer

Tell me a little about who Westmoreland was?

Colonel Gian Gentile

He is highly respected, at least in 1964. You could have called him the General Petraeus of 1964. He was a fast burner. He was the Superintendent at West Point from 1962 to 1964. He graduated from West Point in 1936. He was an artilleryman. In the early years he was very involved in World War II and North Africa. He gets linked up as an artillery battery commander initially with the airborne units, and he does very well as an artillery commander in the newly formed airborne units as a part of the Normandy invasion and then becomes the Chief of Staff in an infantry division in World War II. Then after World War II, he stays an artilleryman but he had spent so much time with light infantry, especially the airborne, that in the Korean War he commands an infantry regiment in the 101st Airborne Division as an artilleryman. He does reasonably well and he continues to progress through the ranks, and I think it's in 1958 or 1959 that he takes command of the 101st, commands it, and then from there goes to West Point where he becomes superintendent, and then from there he ends up as the overall commander in Vietnam in 1964.

Interviewer

What are his strengths and weaknesses? I think you make this comparison a little bit later between Abrams and Westmoreland. They essentially fight two different wars.

Colonel Gian Gentile

No, I don't think they fight two different wars. That is the argument these days, but I don't buy that. Clearly they were very different in all ways. Westmoreland I think was very efficient, very proper, highly intelligent, a good organizer, a good manager, and a good leader. All these kinds of attributes are obvious, which is why Westmoreland, I think, moved through the ranks and ends up in command in Vietnam in 1964. I think Westmoreland ultimately fails in Vietnam not because of his military strategy or his operational method. By 1967, Westmoreland has a sense of where the war is, but continues to push his operational method and military strategy, when, I think, deep down he knows it isn't going to work. Then, he's at a point of just hoping it might. I think that's really the flaw of Westmoreland, and that's what keeps him from stepping into the ranks of the greatest is just that he is unable to do it. Ironically, if he would have done that, he probably would have been cast as the general who said this is the unwinnable war.

Interviewer

Tell me, the Gulf of Tonkin Resolution is really the starting point of much greater commitment to American forces.

Colonel Gian Gentile

Yes, I think the Gulf of Tonkin gives Johnson a mechanism to make the war seem like previous wars. Johnson always referred to Vietnam as "that bitch of a war." Classic Johnson, he was a rather vulgar, "in your face" kind of president. He did not see himself as a war president.

Interviewer

Like more into the great society.

Colonel Gian Gentile

He didn't want to fight a war, but he did want to fight a war against American poverty. He was a big daddy from Texas. He had a general concern for people and he wanted to make people's lives better. This is one of the problems for political leaders in the Cold War. In order for Johnson to get things through Congress for his great society, he has to have the political support of the right. He cannot show weakness against communism. So, he thinks he needs to do something in Vietnam. He doesn't want to be the president who loses Vietnam, like Truman lost Korea. He feels that he's got to do something. He's got his general on the ground saying we're seeing North Vietnamese regiments now, if we don't commit major American military power here, this government and this military will collapse eventually. Johnson doesn't want to be the one who has that happen to him. So, that's the situation that Johnson is in, he knows he's getting ready to make a major military commitment, beyond just advisors, to Vietnam. But this is also Johnson who came of age during the World War II era. You're going to fight a major war, but you've got to have something to make it seem to the American people like it's a war. With World War II, it was easy because you had Pearl Harbor and the Nazis. Even with Korea you still had the North Korean attack into South Korea, what do you do with Vietnam? You need something to show aggression, to provide justification. The Gulf of Tonkin gives that to Johnson.

Interviewer

What really happened in the Gulf of Tonkin? What was claimed to have happened and what really happened?

Colonel Gian Gentile

The claim by Johnson is that there was an unprovoked attack by North Vietnamese vessels against an American naval ship. There were actually two separate events that are rolled up into the same incident. The first event actually did happen. There was a North

Vietnamese vessel that fired on an American naval vessel however that American naval vessel was inside North Vietnamese waters. It wasn't a perfect unprovoked attack. We're just out there trying to do our thing. That's the first incident. The second one was because the first happened in North Vietnamese waters, you need another event to try to make it seem like something happened and that's the one that actually didn't happen. There is a report of a North Vietnamese shooting on an American naval vessel, but it doesn't happen—the story is concocted that it did, and that becomes the justification. The two events are actually rolled up into one.

Interviewer

Is this is a complete and utter lie, a fabrication in order to convince American people to go to war?

Colonel Gian Gentile

No, I think it was a careful construction of the truth. The first event did happen, the second one didn't, but they're both sort of rolled up into one so there were elements in truth in saying that there was an incident in the Gulf of Tonkin.

Interviewer

It wasn't as cynical as let's turn this into our Pearl Harbor or was it a gross overreaction on the part of the Johnson administration to what happened truly in the Gulf of Tonkin?

Colonel Gian Gentile

It was a combination of both. Johnson wants a reason. He needs a rationale for getting into the war. You take events, you construct them to cause them to look in a certain way, and then there you have it. No, it wasn't a clear cut case of outright North Vietnamese aggression. Again, I think Johnson feels like he needs to have something that looks like a North Korean invasion. It's an interesting comparison to President George W. Bush in 2003. If you're going to take the country to war, you've got to have something that looks like you were on the moral defensive as a matter of protection, that you were attacked.

Interviewer

That Bush overreacted too or he concocted that same sort of parallel or stories that we will study for generations, but he's also got a lot of legislation before Congress at this time too. As you say, he needs the support, particularly in legislation.

Colonel Gian Gentile

Right, he needs the right; not just the Republicans but you have the Democratic right in the south. Simplified, he needed the right to help get these programs through.

Interviewer

That's important though to make that distinction. Cold War Democrats were pro defense, right, and very much would have supported the war.

Colonel Gian Gentile

Absolutely, there was a consensus during the Cold War years, especially around defense issues. The problem that the Democrats have is the concern of appearance, of looking weak or appearing weak. Johnson has on his mind the loss of China and what that did to Truman. In 1949, Truman is the president. We can spend all day talking about China, but China had been in the throes of revolution from an occupation by the Japanese, and it all ended in 1949 with Mao's communists overthrowing or defeating the nationalist armies of Chiang Kai-shek, forcing them out of China. They were nationalists and Chairman Mao is very much communist. In 1949, China goes communist and the Soviet Union exploded their first atomic bomb. All these things were happening very quickly. It wouldn't have mattered if Dewey would have been elected to the presidency in 1948, China would still have been lost, it wasn't America's to own or lose.

Interviewer

This was also the time of the red scare. People had suspicions about the State Department, didn't they, with the whole idea that somehow we were being swung towards communism. The notion of that phrase, who lost China, rang for a good 15 years. What you're saying is Johnson heard this in the back of his mind as he is making the commitment to Vietnam.

Colonel Gian Gentile

You had to stand firm and all those kinds of things. . . .

Interviewer

[The Gulf of Tonkin resolution] was not a declaration of war, there was a distinction.

Colonel Gian Gentile

No, it was not. In a declaration of war, both houses would have to vote to declare war and the United States would have been in a formal state of war against North Vietnam.

Interviewer

So what is it then if it's not a state of war?

Colonel Gian Gentile

It's the Gulf of Tonkin resolution that says, "We're behind you Mr. President, do whatever you think you need to do to protect American interest and help the South Vietnamese stand up against communist aggressors" and I'm paraphrasing.

Interviewer

That is directly parallel to the fall of 2001 with the Congress granting the president the power to resist terrorist aggression.

Colonel Gian Gentile

It's similar to 1990. There were votes against whatever the resolution was before the first Gulf War.

Interviewer

Was there a tremendous debate?

Colonel Gian Gentile

There was a debate. It's almost unanimous with maybe one or two who are against it.

Interviewer

That comparison was made to the Gulf of Tonkin by saying this time we're not going to do that, we're going to have a vigorous debate in Congress.

Colonel Gian Gentile

They did, but they still didn't declare war. Declaring war has all kinds of implications.

Interviewer

So this is actually a Constitutional flaw. It's a gray area, right?

Colonel Gian Gentile

I don't know if it's a Constitutional flaw, it is how the Constitution is used now, its main point and limits of power.

Interviewer

So, Gulf of Tonkin means that we now give the president the power to send enormous numbers of troops.

Colonel Gian Gentile

Because he has to be careful, relatively speaking, yes. He doesn't want to call up the reserves, at least in a large significant way. It's a tough situation for Johnson. He's got a lot of things on his mind. He needs the support of the American people because he's going to commit a substantial amount of American conventional military power to fight the war themselves against the communists in South Vietnam. He doesn't want to ask for a declaration of war because he is worried that maybe he might not get it and the implications for that if he doesn't get it. It cuts him in so many directions. He wants to fight a war vigorously but he can only go so far. The real rub in all of this is the United States fights a limited war in South Vietnam and the Vietnamese communists are fighting an unlimited war. There are no limits for the North Vietnamese or South Vietnamese communists, no limits.

Interviewer

Tell me about the limits for the United States. You can't take the war to its natural conclusion because it would involve nuclear weapons. You don't want to excite the aggression of the Soviet Union or China.

Colonel Gian Gentile

Right, this has critical, operational and military strategic affects for how the United States fights the war in Vietnam and for good reason. It makes sense for Johnson to say to his military, "I understand you want to go into North Vietnam, but you can't. I'll let you bomb North Vietnam, but you cannot send ground forces into North Vietnam, nor can you send ground forces into Laos to try to cut their supply lines." Why? Because in late 1950 when we had American ground military power close to the border of China, China did something, and we don't want China to do something to help the North Vietnamese if the American military goes into North Vietnam. Then, that could cause the Soviet Union to come in on the side of China, which they might, which might then bring about a nuclear war, which might screw things up in Europe. The political restraints that Johnson places on American military in Vietnam have very clear and real affects on the military strategy and the operational methods.

Interviewer

It's the same with Truman and MacArthur in Korea.

Colonel Gian Gentile

It absolutely is and for good reason, sure.

Interviewer

It's this new world of unlimited war, which is post Second World War thinking, that you can't take a war to its natural conclusions because the world has become too dangerous a place.

Colonel Gian Gentile

Right, Vietnam is not worth a nuclear confrontation between the United States and the Soviet Union, nor is it worth fighting China in a major ground war because, then, where does it end? If you're fighting China and North Vietnam, tactically and operationally you have to be able to attack their supply lines in China, and if you're going to fight China in North Vietnam, you're going to need more than 500,000 troops on the ground, which is what you end up with in Vietnam. There are also domestic constraints, too. Johnson doesn't want to call up the reserves because that might require congressional support that might not be there. So, there are domestic constraints on Johnson as well.

Interviewer

There are talks in the United States after Johnson defeated Barry Goldwater in 1964, who basically was saying the hell with limited wars. It was a defeated argument since the beginning. He felt defeated to make it, but there are other people, too, in the military particularly?

Colonel Gian Gentile

Oh sure, the Air Force. In a perfect world, with any of the operational restraints and the theoretical approach that was forced on the Air Force by people like Defense Secretary Robert McNamara and others — this whole idea of increase the size of the forces on the ground, mix it up with the North Vietnamese Army, bloody their nose, we'll show them we're serious and then they'll go, "Oh, they just sent us a signal, they're serious, we better do what they want and they'll stop" — is a theory of incrementalism. In other words, war becomes almost this game of checkers or a bargaining match. We'll start off with Rolling Thunder. We'll bomb to just about . . . the 17th parallel, we'll bomb just above it. If they don't give into our demands—and our demands are essentially to stop what you're doing in South Vietnam, pull your army out, and leave the south alone. If they don't do that, we'll keep bombing them, we'll go a little bit farther, we'll increase the number of ground forces. At some point they'll get it that we're serious, we mean business, we can hurt them, and they'll stop.

Interviewer

McNamara formed this policy and thought, "What would I do if I were in Ho Chi Minh's shoes?" Rather than saying, "What would I do if I were Ho Chi Minh?" That distinction led him to make some critical strategic mistakes, because he didn't understand the dynamic present in Vietnam. Do you agree with that?

Colonel Gian Gentile

I think it was a failure to understand again that the Vietnamese communists, both north and south, were fighting a total unlimited war and they were willing to do essentially anything to win. So then strategy really demands the serious look at questions of worth and interest, which again, I think, is why the war was unwinnable. The United States wasn't willing to confront that Vietnamese communist strategy and willpower and what it would have taken to defeat it. Since it wasn't willing to do that, it ended up taking sort of a half-baked approach and method, which became essentially an unwinnable bankrupt strategy.

Interviewer

What McNamara is essentially saying is, if I keep on raising the threat, you'll back down. And what Ho Chi Minh is saying is, no matter how hard, how high you raise the threat it won't happen.

Colonel Gian Gentile

Right, and the Vietnamese documents show this, that the bombing of North Vietnam did hurt the Vietnamese.

Interviewer

It starts in what, 1968?

Colonel Gian Gentile

It starts in 1965 in Rolling Thunder. It is not a continuous bombing of major North Vietnamese cities. It starts off in the southern part of North Vietnam. Again, it's this whole idea of ratcheting up, but relatively speaking, compared to the closing months of World War II in the Pacific with the firebombing of the Japanese home islands - relatively few North Vietnamese civilians are killed during the bombing campaign. Maybe 40,000 or 50,000 deaths, which again is not that much as, say for example, World War II. The United States is not willing to do the kind of bombing that it did against the Japanese in World War II. Ho Chi Minh understands this and how far the United States is willing to go. They're also paying very close attention to American politics, and I think they start to develop the sense that if they can hold out and maintain, which is not necessarily an automatic thing for the Vietnamese communists, that they can ultimately prevail.

Interviewer

So, in 1964 with the Gulf of Tonkin, we begin ratcheting up the commitment. What's the true commitment at its peak?

Colonel Gian Gentile

It starts in early March of 1965, on top of the 15,000 or 20,000 advisors and US Air

Force personnel that are there. It starts with a US Marine regiment that is put in the Da Nang area to protect the air bases where the bombing campaign, Rolling Thunder, had just started. That really is morphed into using the follow-on American Army forces in active operations against the Vietnamese communists, both South Vietnamese and North. It reaches its peak by early 1969 of somewhere upwards of 525,000 personnel of which, maybe 380,000 are US Army, 70,000 or 80,000 are US Marines, 50,000 are US Air Force, something like that, and it expands in 1965. I think by the end of 1965, the total force is probably 80,000. By the end of 1965, you already have the Ia Drang battle with the 1st Cavalry Division. By the end of 1966, there are upwards of 250,000. By the end of 1967 now you're up to close to 450,000 to 500,000. Then you hit the Tet Offensive in 1968 and there's a little bit more after that, but it reaches its peak by early 1969.

Interviewer

So take me through Westmoreland's leadership and the strategy that is executed during those years leading right up to Tet.

Colonel Gian Gentile

Based on the political constraints that Johnson put on Westmoreland that say that you can't go into North Vietnam with ground forces or into Laos, Westmoreland adopts a strategy of attrition, which actually makes sense based on the political constraints that he was under. Now maybe a better, more visionary general would have said and figured out what George Herring figured out in 1982, that the war was not winnable. We can do this, but ultimately it's going to fail, and we need to come up with a different approach. Maybe that means telling the president, we can do this, but it's going to take a long, long time, it's not going to happen in two or three years. Westmoreland doesn't do that. Westmoreland comes up with a strategy of attrition. Since he cannot defeat or annihilate the North Vietnamese Army through a short series of decisive battles, his strategy then is to fight the North Vietnamese Army and the South Vietnamese communists . . . in order to reduce them so much that they reach a level where they can't replace the number of people and equipment that they lose in fighting against the Americans. We called it a crossover point: that the North Vietnamese and the South Vietnamese would reach a point based on fighting against the Americans that they just couldn't keep it up. It would be at that point, combined with the bombing of the north, that the North Vietnamese would say, "We've got to stop, we can't do this anymore, we quit." It didn't work.

Interviewer

Do you think he believed it or he was imagining it?

Colonel Gian Gentile

I think based on the political constraints that he was under in 1965, and understanding that he's not a visionary general that would have figured all of this out, it wasn't an unreasonable strategy to have in 1965. Again, what I said earlier, I think the tragedy and flaw of Westmoreland is that by 1967, if he didn't know it, he should have, and if he did, he should have been much more forthright than he was in explaining that this just isn't going to work. McNamara figures it out by the end of 1966.

Interviewer

Explain that to me. What is the historical record that shows us now what was going on inside the conference rooms?

Colonel Gian Gentile

This is H. R. McMaster's great book "Dereliction of Duty." He says that there was a dereliction of duty that senior generals did know, or they should have known, that this wasn't going to work the way they were carrying it out, but they just kind of all sat back and for whatever reasons, they didn't have the intellectual courage. It was for bureaucratic interests or all sorts of reasons. It was like, "Let's give this a shot and see if it will work." You're racking up hundreds of Americans dead every week, not to mention thousands and thousands of South Vietnamese.

McNamara realizes it by the end of 1966, probably maybe even a little bit sooner. He's a businessman. It really is sort of a business model in fighting this war. If we can just keep taking them down, they'll reach a point where they'll just stop, and they won't want to fight us anymore, but it doesn't work. Westmoreland is criticized by a number of analysts, academics, serving soldiers from Vietnam for not adopting the right operational method in Vietnam. The Krepinevich Argument that comes out in the 1980s, that Westmoreland should have understood the true nature of the war, that it was war for the hearts and minds for the South Vietnamese people, and to use the military to pacify and control the South Vietnamese population, but that just doesn't work. Westmoreland knows that the decisive element in the war in Vietnam is the South Vietnamese people, and their allegiance to the government, and establishing a legitimate functioning government in South Vietnam. Westmoreland gets it, the documents show that. You read the stuff that he writes, he knows that but he has a problem. If he sends out the military into the villages to pacify, to win hearts and minds, there's still, by the end of 1965 and early 1966, there's probably close to 120,000 North Vietnamese regular infantry soldiers in South Vietnam in companies and battalions and regiments and divisions. He had this dual threat. He had the conventional threat of the North Vietnamese Army and the South Vietnamese communist units, and he has also the insurgent threat, communist threat from the villages. With the cards that were handed to Westmoreland in 1965, he played them as best as he could.

Interviewer

What happens as a result of the Tet Offensive?

Colonel Gian Gentile

I think Roger [Spiller] is right, for the United States, the Tet Offensive was the campaign that essentially put the United States on a path of ending the war. It happens on January 31, 1968. Tet is referred to as the South Vietnamese Lunar New Year. I'm trying to figure out the easiest way to characterize it. Tet was a Vietnamese Communist operation, and it was a combination decision, although probably mostly put forward by the north to launch major attacks against the government in South Vietnam and its military, which was the focus. The idea was that these attacks, carried out mostly by the South Vietnamese communist military forces, the aim behind these attacks is that it would bring about a major uprising in the south. That major uprising in the south would overthrow the government there and convince the United States that they could not win the war. It was a very large scale and concentrated series of attacks by the majority of South Vietnamese communists and Viet Cong units in South Vietnam. At least the first part of the Tet Offensive in January and February of 1968 failed.

Interviewer

Was it supervised by the north or the south?

Colonel Gian Gentile

Yeah, probably planned and certainly resourced and directed by the north, but carried out by the South Vietnamese communist forces in cooperation with the north. It is the Viet Cong main force units and their militia units in the villages that are largely carrying out these attacks against the South Vietnamese government and military. It is the critical event of the war for the United States.

Interviewer

Why?

Colonel Gian Gentile

Because it is the act or it is the mechanism that brings the war for the United States to stalemate, militarily on the ground. The United States reaches a point to where, after Tet, it can't lose, because it didn't lose tactically. Tet didn't overthrow the South Vietnamese government. The ARVN did not break. Tet showed that the American military couldn't lose on the ground, but it also showed that it couldn't win. So the United States is in a stalemated situation in Vietnam, but really, the critical aspect of Tet is the effect that it has on the political and social climate in the United States, because in some ways it is, perhaps, at least in political effects, it's probably one of the most decisive battles in history. Johnson says he's not going to run for president a month later. Walter Cronkite, within weeks after Tet, goes on national TV and says that we are mired and stalemated in Vietnam or something to that affect. It has such a huge effect because just a few months before that in November of 1967, Westmoreland, who was the architect of the strategy of attrition of Vietnam, is at the Press Club in Washington, DC, where he gives the impression that there is light at the end of the tunnel. He says something like "There comes a time when the end of the war comes into view." So, Westmoreland is saying by the end of 1967 that we're winning, we're almost there, we're making progress, a couple more years and we'll be able to turn it over. I'd be interested to see what Lew Sorley has to say in his new biography that is coming out on Westmoreland. I haven't spent enough time in the Westmoreland documents to be able to answer that. I don't know. I think Westmoreland is an honorable man, he is a company man, and he is fighting the war the way his president wants him to fight the war. He's a good general, but he's not a great general. Greatness maybe would have demanded he step out of that box and not make that same speech at the National Press Club in November. That's the backdrop to Tet, and the backdrop to Tet is Westmoreland and Johnson and others saying, "It's going okay, it's going okay. Of course, there's an undercurrent of reporting and assessments of the war by people like Neil Sheehan, David

Halberstam, and others who are saying, "No, things aren't really going at all the way you are saying they are."

Interviewer

Clearly by 1971 when the Pentagon Papers are released, we know that in the Pentagon, people are saying this.

Colonel Gian Gentile

Right, sure. I mean Daniel Ellsberg starts to turn around Tet and even before. So, there is a questioning, that's what I'm saying, an undercurrent. We can look to the same kind of thing with how's the war going in Afghanistan? It's hard, but it's not hopeless, we're in it to win, we won in Iraq so we can win in Afghanistan. We've just got to figure out how to deal with this 18-month stuff, but we can make it work. There's also an undercurrent of criticism going on. Then Tet happens and it's like, what? People back in the United States are saying, "Wait a minute, we just heard three months ago that there is light at the end of the tunnel and that we were winning, and if we were winning, how could they do that? How could they put together that kind of major offensive?" This isn't really little pin pricks, this is a major operational effort that takes months and months of planning and resourcing and they carry it out. It's defeated, but it is still carried out, so it has a huge political effect in the United States.

Interviewer

This is paired with a political challenge, Eugene McCarthy's announcement for president, right? I think after Johnson pulls out, McCarthy announces he's at that point already turning against the war. So, you have political troubles at home for Johnson and then this emerges, where it suggests that there is no light at the end of the tunnel.

Colonel Gian Gentile

Johnson has his classic statement of, "If I've lost Cronkite, I've lost the war." In March of 1968, he says he's not going to run for president.

Interviewer

Explain for those young readers who don't know who Walter Cronkite was.

Colonel Gian Gentile

How would you characterize him today? You're right, the media is so different. He was it. You and I watched Cronkite when we were kids on TV. Especially the American's psyche or attitude collectively of war is still of the World War II mindset where the nation, the media, and the people are supposed to be behind it, but none of that is playing itself out the way it did in World War II. And now that we've lost Walter Cronkite, Walter Cronkite is saying there is stalemate.

Interviewer

It ended being a kind of wise and moderate kind of voice. Also of that World War II generation, it's like grandfather's loss.

Colonel Gian Gentile

Just like Johnson said, I've lost Cronkite, I've lost the war.

Interviewer

How different is it that during the Vietnam War, we are maintaining a draft versus during our present campaign as an all-volunteer army in respect to both the execution of the military strategy and the political pressure that existed during a time of draft?

Colonel Gian Gentile

You could go a lot of ways with that. There is an argument today to reinstate the draft. A good friend of mine, Lieutenant Colonel Paul Yingling, has been making that argument in a sustained way. There is something to it. There is a definite linkage during the Vietnam War between their people and their political leaders and the fighting of the war. It was a moral commitment because the American people knew that their sons, then, potentially could fight and potentially could die. There were huge discrepancies in who fought and everything else, but still it was there and the draft was there and it was a significant factor in American social and political life during the Vietnam War years. So, there was a connection between the American people and a fighting of the war, a moral connection. I think there is no moral connection between the American people today, except for the people in the military. There is no moral connection between the American people today and the fighting of the wars in Afghanistan and Iraq. That by itself is an argument to reinstate the draft. However, that runs in the face of all kinds of counterarguments. One has to do with military efficiency: is a draft army what we really need for today's and tomorrow's world? One question for today, is the reinstatement of the draft even politically feasible? I don't think it is. I think it's a pipe dream. I told Paul Yingling, I think you're wasting effort. It's not going to happen. Maybe the answer is not a draft, but an appetite suppressant by American military and political leaders on where we choose to send the military.

Interviewer

To make this comparison back to Vietnam, that was such a crushing event because you had what American people thought was going to be a fairly quick war and suddenly they're looking at sending in more.

Colonel Gian Gentile

So now you have demonstrations, which are just student demonstrations. Pete Maslowski and I talked a lot about that. A significant part of it was happening on college campuses, but there was angst throughout American society, especially after Tet, about where the war was going and how to prosecute it. It comes at a time of the Civil Rights Movement and of change in the South. They all come to a point in 1968 where you have hundreds of thousands of people demonstrating in Chicago and Washington and other places around the country.

Interviewer

So, you say that Tet was the turning point and then you have this question, as you raised it before, how do you end a war that you've already lost?

Colonel Gian Gentile

It's clear by the end of 1968, even though Vietnamization doesn't happen until Nixon takes over, that the Tet Offensive by middle to late 1968 and the dynamics of the war, especially for the United States have changed. McNamara resigns.

Interviewer

Westmoreland, is he ...

Colonel Gian Gentile

Westmoreland is replaced by General Creighton Abrams in June of 1968. Johnson is not running for reelection and you have the summer campaign for the November 1968 election which Richard Nixon, of course, wins. Nixon is sworn in January of 1969. Nixon knows that he has to get the United States out of the war.

Interviewer

He was the "anti-war candidate" in some respects in the election. He is saying I have the solution.

Colonel Gian Gentile

With Nixon, you have a secret plan to end the war. Nixon would have slugged us in the face if we said you're anti-war. He says he's not one of those hippy, dirt bag, sons of bitches. He hates war, but we've got to end this war with honor. We've got to have this whole peace with honor thing. Nixon knows that he has to end the war. Nixon, in a lot of ways, is attuned to current American culture and current American politics, and he knows that he has to end the war. He has to get the United States out of Vietnam. Actually, Nixon is fascinating with Kissinger and how he works through all of this. Probably the first six months, Nixon actually thinks he can maybe win the war. Part of his thinking is he has a secret plan to end the war. He's going to get the United States out. Vietnamization probably really hasn't crystallized in 1968 when he's running for president.

Interviewer

What was the secret plan? I thought it was Vietnamization.

Colonel Gian Gentile

It was, but deep down his secret plan was he's going to get in there and he's going to let them have it. He's not Johnson and he watched what Eisenhower did in Korea when he kind of threw the nuclear card. Nixon really does internalize this notion of the mad man theory—that he's going to create this perception of unpredictability, and he's going to combine that with aggressive use of military force. It really is air power.

Interviewer

That makes what Eisenhower did, right? Eisenhower keep everything on the table, if you read the materials, they would have gone to that final step. He wanted that to be left open.

Colonel Gian Gentile

I don't think Nixon was ever seriously thinking of the nuclear card, but certainly, the first six months, Nixon was thinking that an aggressive use of military power combined with the creation of the perception of him being unpredictable and sort of a crazy man in the office, might be enough to show the North Vietnamese that we are serious. There's a whole different team in town, and the North Vietnamese are going to get serious about negotiations, and they will negotiate an end of the war favorable for us. Early on in Nixon's presidency, there are North Vietnamese Army units leaving South Vietnam. When the final peace treaty is signed between the two, significant numbers of North Vietnamese forces are still in South Vietnam.

Interviewer

Let's go back up to Abrams. Who is Abrams, how has he arrived to replace Westmoreland, and why did Westmoreland leave?

Colonel Gian Gentile

Let's see, Westmoreland would have had four years in command, so it was about time for him to leave. Although, if the war was going well, and Tet never happened, and there was light at the end of the tunnel, one could imagine, hypothetically, where Westmoreland would have stayed easily for another year into 1969. Clearly, Tet had something to do with the removal of Westmoreland. He's brought back to be the Army Chief of Staff. People made the comparison to the recent change out between Casey and Petraeus, where Casey, some people call it a relief. It wasn't much of a relief, but Westmoreland was pulled out, probably earlier than he might have been, and it was largely because of Tet and how the war was going at that point. Abrams had been his deputy commander in Vietnam for at least a year, if not two years prior. Abrams is Westmoreland's deputy. He's a West Point graduate and I think his year group is 1939. I think he is three years behind Westmoreland. Westmoreland isn't a nationally known figure at the end of World War II, Abrams is. Abrams's 37th Tank Battalion of the 4th Armored Division of Patton's 3d Army is the spearhead that moves up and rescues the airborne units at Bastone. It was Abrams's tank unit that broke through the German lines and made the contact with the 101st Airborne Division and that becomes a huge story in the United States. Abrams is a nationally known World War II hero.

Interviewer

Was Patton his mentor in some ways?

Colonel Gian Gentile

Patton knew Abrams, and Patton reportedly thought very highly of Abrams and reportedly had said things like, there's only a few who get it like I do and Abrams is one of them. He was a first-rate, highly competent tank commander in World War II that did hard fighting through Normandy and through France and into Germany. He doesn't have combat leadership in Korea. He is a corps chief of staff in Korea. He then — I can't remember the dates — but a lot of people have played up on this, and tying some of his earlier experiences to the perceived success that some people think he had in Vietnam once he took command. He was a division commander that sent units to either Alabama or Mississippi during the whole racial problem in 1959 or 1960 and handled the situation very shrewdly with a deft and a careful application of precise military force that didn't make things worse or things like that. That's often tied to Abrams and the perception that he actually did something different and was successful in Vietnam from 1969 to 1972. He takes over in 1968.

Interviewer

Are there quite a few changes?

Colonel Gian Gentile

He changes some wording of the strategies. The mission changes for Abrams. The mission for Westmoreland is to defeat the communists in South Vietnam in order to maintain the ethnicity or something like it of the government in South Vietnam. The mission for Abrams, after he takes over, becomes essentially one driven by Vietnamization: that now the military's mission is to get the government in South Vietnam and its military into a condition to where it can take on operations on its own. The mission for Abrams changed. His focus becomes one of turning the war over to the Vietnamese, but the overall strategy and the application of American military forces, there is a shift in priority, but essentially the strategy remains the same. He still has the same problem that Westmoreland does. There are still North Vietnamese and South Vietnamese communist regular forces, and there are still communist insurgent threats to villages. It's the same problem that Westmoreland had. What Abrams does not alter is his tactical and operational methods. He still relies heavily on fire power, just like Westmoreland did. Abrams often used to joke that the B-52 was his strategic reserve.

Interviewer

What is Lewis Sorley's argument, explain that?

Colonel Gian Gentile

His argument is the same as the Iraq surge triumph method that has been built around General Petraeus. It's the same thing: the American Army was stupid, bumbling, didn't get it except for a few exceptional units. In Vietnam, the exceptional units tended to be the US Marines and their combined action programs. By and large, the American Army didn't fight the war correctly, was on the wrong track, and then Abrams comes in and takes over. Almost immediately, within hours, turns the American Army around on a dime, gets them focused in the right direction toward pacification, towards population security, does everything right, changes attitudes, gets the American Army on the right path. The Sorley thesis goes to say actually that the American Army and the South Vietnamese had won the war in the south. They had won. There's a chapter in Sorley's book, Chapter 13 entitled "Victory" that's not supported from the evidence by the Vietnamese side. It's the argument that there was a better war and General Abrams created it, he was a better general and because of those things, the war turned around. The same story is with Iraq and the surge in 2007.

Interviewer

The same argument also is that there is a hearts and mind approach.

Colonel Gian Gentile

Yeah, and it's just pure mythology. The United States military under Abrams does not change. An operational focus does shift to supporting the South Vietnamese Government in a military pacification effort, but the operations and tactical methods of the American military during Abrams' entire time there remains largely the same. There isn't a decided shift toward hearts and minds under Abrams. The American military is largely doing the same thing that they did under Westmoreland. There are some tactical and operational changes, but that's because the enemy changed what he was doing after Tet because the South Vietnamese communists had been hurt so badly that they had to pull back and away from the villages in order to recuperate. The communists change their strategy in late 1969 and decide to essentially back off a little bit and refit and reset and reestablish the Vietnamese communists. That creates an opportunity for pacification programs and processes do go forward, which Abrams and the South Vietnamese government and military do capitalize on. But there are still Vietnamese communists there, and the American military doesn't change its tactical and operational methods.

Interviewer

It's a factor of history, rather than . . . ?

Colonel Gian Gentile

Oh, absolutely. It is historians going into certain documents or evidence and only using those. I mean if you listen to or if you read the transcripts of the Abrams tapes. Abrams and his staff believed that they won the war. That's where the "better war" thesis comes from. It comes from Abrams. I think it comes from the historian Lew Sorley, for years and years, sitting with headphones on, doing a very important service for historians by painstakingly transcribing and writing down the thousands and thousands of hours of tape recorded conversations that Abrams had with his staff and commanders on a weekly basis. Sorley has provided a huge great asset for historians, but I think his argument is deeply flawed in that he gets the "better war" thesis from Abrams and from listening to those tapes. If you juxtaposed that evidence from other evidence, especially from the Vietnamese side, it becomes clear that the war was not won in the south, the south had not become pacified, that 90 percent of the hamlet villages had not become pacified as some American evaluations had said. In fact, the Viet Cong weren't dead, they were hurt but they were still active and they still maintained a moral link with the South Vietnamese people, especially in the countryside.

Interviewer

So you would say that Abrams faced the same issues?

Colonel Gian Gentile

Absolutely, change but still the same problem.

Interviewer

He acted essentially in the same way, a good general but not a great general.

Colonel Gian Gentile

Yes, a good, competent general but highly overrated. Westmoreland was a good competent general and sadly has been promoted as the single cause of failure for Vietnam, unfairly so. They were both good generals and you can find good qualities in both and qualities that probably needed improvement in them too, but neither of them were great. Certainly Abrams was not a great general. The story of Abrams being a great general is constructed. That story is more about the American Army after Vietnam than about the American Army during Vietnam.

Interviewer

There's a hangover or psychological impact of Vietnam and the wish to sort of rewrite the history in a way to say why we lost.

Colonel Gian Gentile

Absolutely.

Interviewer

They explain this as having three sorts of theses, is that right, about why we lost. One is that the politicians let us down, it was a limited war that we never got to fight, and the third was we actually had won.

Colonel Gian Gentile

Right.

Interviewer

Explain those three in more detail now. Who are the constituents who believe each of those theses?

Colonel Gian Gentile

It is a very conflicted set of explanations and interpretations for Vietnam, because it's also tied to an understanding by analysts, academic scholars, and historians as to an assessment if the war was winnable in the first place, if it was in American vital interest. It tends to work out that people who see the war as not winnable and not being an American vital interest, tend to not buy the whole notion that the war was won, in the end, by Abrams. I do think it is a narrative. It actually does begin to be constructed by the American military, even during the final years of the Vietnam War. If you read the weekly meetings by Abrams, you can see that narrative starting to be constructed. The idea that they were really making great progress in the south, things were finally starting to shape up, if we could just get those darn hippies to stop protesting and get the American people behind the war effort, if we can get these politicians on our side as we need them, we can make all of this work. Again, the "better war" thesis starts to be built by the United States military in Vietnam, mainly Abrams, and then it is really developed after the Vietnam War . . .—and again you get into the whole development of arguments by Harry Summers that the war was winnable, the American Army just focused on the wrong enemy, it should have been the North Vietnamese and not the South Vietnamese communist insurgents. Krepinevich turns that argument on its head. Both of them say that if the American Army would have done something different tactically and operationally they could have won the war, which I think, is a deeply flawed argument. The war was unwinnable, again, based on what we were willing to commit morally and in regard to material.

Interviewer

Before we turned on the camera, you and I talked about the fact that there are always potentially doctrines that work here and they kind of frame the story of the Vietnam War, we had the Containment Doctrine that then forms the need to intervene in Vietnam. Then, we have the Nixon Doctrine, which was the Vietnamization notion.

Colonel Gian Gentile

Actually, it's an acknowledgement that containment didn't work. At least American driven containment at the barrel of an American gun didn't work, so now we go to the Nixon Doctrine, which is Vietnamization large in other Asian countries. We're going to help, and it's still about containment, but you guys got to do it, and not us, because we tried and it didn't work, so now we've got to get out.

Interviewer

Now, how about the post-Vietnam Doctrine really relating to the Reagan years and Casper Weinberger and Colin Powell?

Colonel Gian Gentile

[Lieutenant Colonel] Gail Yoshitani just finished her dissertation on the Weinberger Doctrine at Duke University for Alex Roland, and it's going to be published by Texas A&M Press in a couple of months. She makes a very persuasive argument, an important argument to separate Weinberger from Powell. You noticed in my chapter I didn't say there is a big difference between what Powell said.

Interviewer

Let's first go over Weinberger.

Colonel Gian Gentile

Read Weinberger's five or six or seven tests. The reason why I close with the Weinberger Doctrine in my essay is because I think the Weinberger Doctrine is an attempt to help America deal—in terms of foreign policy and strategy—with the trauma of Vietnam. The Vietnam syndrome that comes out of Vietnam is: we tried containment at the barrel of a military gun, it didn't work. Look what happened with 57,000 Americans dead, millions of South Vietnamese dead and displaced and millions more in Cambodia as a result of the war in Vietnam. Let's just not do anything like that ever, ever, ever again.

Interviewer

So Weinberger says these are the things we need to do.

Colonel Gian Gentile

These are the tests. Actually, the tests I think are quite reasonable.

Interviewer

What are they?

Colonel Gian Gentile

I need Gail's dissertation here. I can paraphrase them: do your best to ensure that you will have a reasonable amount of American support. The amount of American military force that you commit should be commensurate or linked to the interest that's at stake. That for me, as a matter of strategy, is one of the essential tests that Weinberger put forward. This relationship between the types, the effort of military that you're going to use should be linked to the effort that you're seeking. Which I think, just as an aside, we are currently out of whack with in Afghanistan today. There should be defined clear objectives. Those are essentially three or four of his tests. I think Gail is right. Weinberger is misunderstood, it was not a framework to limit American involvement in the world, even at times with military force, it was a way to create a framework to figure out how to use [force] in a wise and appropriate way, American military force in the world to get after American interests, which is why I ended the essay on Vietnam with that.

Interviewer

What has that distinguished from the Powell Doctrine?

Colonel Gian Gentile

The Powell Doctrine was, I think, always more pernicious and harmful for proper American civil-military relations. The Powell Doctrine is a careful construction of a military voice that directs or tells our political masters how and when to use it. That's not how it works. The Powell Doctrine is a construction of a military voice saying, here's how the American military should be used. No, the way it works in our democracy is: it's the political leaders that say, this is what we want to do with you. We want you to go into Darfur to do this. It's then incumbent on the American military to say this is what it's going to take to accomplish the political objectives that you're giving us.

Interviewer

Is the Powell Doctrine an overreaction in some respects?

Colonel Gian Gentile

Yeah, and it may be an overreaction in a way that it didn't fix the problem. Then you have a military supercharged with the Powell Doctrine that's dangerously approaching militarism and saying you can't use this for that, we're only for this. No, that's not the way it works. The president says go do this, that's exactly what we'll do.

Interviewer

What is the big lesson of the end of the war in Vietnam?

Colonel Gian Gentile

Figure out when you're in a war that's not winnable based on the way that you're fighting it and end it as quickly and least costly as possible. With 20,000 American dead from 1969 to 1972, that's a substantial amount. It's the cost. Wars are fought, people die. Militaries fight wars, soldiers/service members die. It's not just that. All of that is a significant part of it, but it's all the other commitment of national blood and treasure. Also, I think with Vietnam it is also the ongoing and continuing bloodshed and destruction that occurred in the place itself. When you look at it all in hindsight, you have to ask this question of worth: was the war worth that kind of commitment and that kind of effort, which I think has very applicable insights towards Afghanistan today.

Interviewer

You can argue, I guess, and this is your point, it even perverts the understanding of how we should use force, and where in the world, and therefore, still rings into the ears of those making policy decisions now.

Colonel Gian Gentile

Absolutely.

Interviewer

That's a disturbing impact, which would multiply the cost.

Colonel Gian Gentile

It is also tied to the whole narrative that comes out of Vietnam: it was winnable, there was a better war, that bad strategy and policy could be rescued by better tactics and operations. We've embraced that so much that all we have now in Afghanistan is tactics and operations. If we have a strategy, it's bankrupt because the president's political objectives are actually quite limited but we're pursuing a maximalist approach of nation building in Afghanistan to achieve these limited political objectives.

Interviewer

This is sort of off-topic, but fascinating to hear you say. Is there some kind of dissonance, a president waging a war that he did not initially commit to, and where's the moral pinning? Is it possible to conduct a war under those circumstances?

Colonel Gian Gentile

President Eisenhower did in Korea. He didn't start the Korean War, but it came to be his when he was president.

Interviewer

But he wasn't a firm critic of it, was he?

Colonel Gian Gentile

No, and Obama wasn't a critic of Afghanistan.

Interviewer

He was a critic of Iraq.

Colonel Gian Gentile

He was a critic of Iraq. I don't know where all this leads. It was fascinating, the last couple of weeks with the relief of General McChrystal and his replacement with General Petraeus. Who knows where the president's head is at? Charlie Rose had Michael Gordon and a number of others on a couple of weeks ago, and they were all of the mind that the president now, by putting General Petraeus in there, is firmly behind the whole nation-building counterinsurgency approach in Afghanistan. The contradiction to it, though, is that he has placed an 18-month time frame on it, which I don't know, time will tell. General Petraeus, along with Secretary Gates and a number of others, as soon as the president made the 18-month statement, there were a lot of qualifications, like it's the start, it will be conditions-based. This is a real tough one because time and resources are essential elements of questions of strategy. How long do you want to commit to something like that?

Interviewer

Thank you.

Colonel Gian Gentile

Thanks.

Session 4
The Chimera of Success:
Pacification and the End of the Vietnam War

by

Colonel Gian P. Gentile

In the final years of the Vietnam War, the pacification campaigns carried out by the South Vietnamese Government with American advice and support was not predominantly a military chore. However, the military in both South Vietnam and the United States played a key role since in theory in a pacification campaign in order for the government to carry out its other programs of local governance, economic and infrastructure improvement, security had to be established through the application of military force.

Attempts at pacification in Vietnam had been an uphill battle since most estimates by 1967 placed the majority of rural hamlets and villages under South Vietnamese communist (often referred to as "Viet Cong" or VC) control. The formation of Civilian Operations and Revolutionary Support (CORDS), initially under Robert Komer and later William Colby, provided a coordinated American advisory effort to what was essentially a South Vietnamese directed but American resource-supported campaign. Military Assistance Command, Vietnam (MACV) Commander General William C. Westmoreland's strategy of attrition demanded that the main priority for the American Army was to find and fight the North Vietnamese and Viet Cong Armies in South Vietnam. Pacification of the rural countryside was a lesser but still critically important priority, wherein American military forces supported the Government of South Vietnam (GVN) and its military in the carrying out of the pacification campaigns. Through improved security, economic aid, infrastructure projects, and assistance to local governments, pacification aimed to wrest political allegiance of rural folk from the Viet Cong to the Saigon regime. Westmoreland saw both these wars as essentially one. He referred to this one-war concept by using a metaphor of a boxer whose right hand or the Vietnamese Government and military defend the population through the process of pacification while the left or the American military (and in Westmoreland's mind the less important one) is ready to strike at the North Vietnamese and Viet Cong Armies that disrupted pacification.

By the end of 1967 the war reached a deadlock where the United States had committed enough military power and resources to keep the South Vietnamese government from collapsing but could not force North Vietnamese withdrawal from the South nor could the Army of the Republic of Vietnam (ARVN) pacify major portions of the rural countryside. Perceiving the deadlocked nature of the war, the North Vietnamese and Viet Cong decided to launch a major offensive with the aim of weakening the South Vietnamese Government and bringing about a major popular uprising in the South. The Communists also hoped that the offensive would open negotiations with the United States, a halt in the bombing of the North, and perhaps even a major policy shift with the United States toward Vietnam. The initial attacks of the Tet Offensive began on 31 January 1968 by Viet Cong units and were directed at provincial and district capitals, major cities, and other key governmental facilities. Although initially caught off guard by the attacks, the Americans and South

Vietnam responded quickly and over the course of the next few weeks and months they defeated the assaulting communist forces causing heavy losses among them.

In a sense, the North Vietnamese and Viet Cong lost the Tet Offensive. A popular uprising did not come about and the horrendous losses suffered by the Viet Cong would take years from which to recover.

The reduction of the Viet Cong from the Tet Offensive created an opportunity to expand South Vietnamese Government control in the countryside and led to what became known as the Accelerated Pacification Campaign (APC).

The APC sought to fill the vacuum in numerous hamlets and villages created by the reduction of the Viet Cong as a result of the Tet Offensives. The Campaign started in November of 1968 and was completed three months later in January of 1969. It was a spasm of pacification energy aimed at establishing territorial security force presence in as many contested hamlets and villages as possible and in creating governing bodies within the villages that would help connect the rural folk to the South Vietnamese Government. In terms of an increase in territorial security force presence in the villages and in the increase of pacification programs carried out, it was a success. The system of evaluation for hamlet and village security, the Hamlet Evaluation System (HES), noted that the APC had significantly increased the number of erstwhile contested hamlets and villages to the government side. Of the 1,317 contested hamlets that the APC targeted to convert to government control, HES concluded that by the end of the APC only about 15 percent of these hamlets were left under Viet Cong control.[1]

Westmoreland's replacement, General Creighton Abrams, and his CORDS Director, William Colby, were encouraged by the apparent success of the APC and used it a to persuade South Vietnamese President Nguyen Van Thieu of the importance of continuing programs of pacification in the countryside. From 1969 through 1972 the South Vietnamese Government designed yearly pacification campaigns with American support and advice. The 1970 "Plan for Pacification and Development," for example, highlighted eight program objectives for the overall Pacification Campaign for that year: territorial security, protection of the people against acts of terrorism, self defense by the people, local administration and governance, fostering a sense of national unity within the rural population and assisting Vietnamese civilians injured as a result of the war and it included a program of information to discredit Viet Cong activities and highlight those of the government as well as an economic objective of prosperity "for all." [2]

In July of 1971 at a weekly pep talk meeting that Abrams routinely gave to his staff and commanders, he noted that the once violent Hua Nghia and Long An Provinces which were both adjacent to the western side of Saigon had become blissfully pacified. In fact, General Abrams was so sure of the success of pacification in those provinces that he would be willing to "bet a cigar or something that everybody's kind of happy out there in Long An and Hua Nghia because there isn't much going on." Although acknowledging that the Viet Cong still posed a threat, Abrams believed that the territorial forces and the government in the countryside had the "wherewithal to keep [Viet Cong] attacks and violence from happening again."

The appearance of the success of pacification programs was deceptive. To be sure many parts of the countryside had become relatively quiet and the Viet Cong had been significantly weakened by the time the United States military withdrew from Vietnam in March of 1973. A series of South Vietnamese government pacification campaigns starting with the APC in November of 1968 and continuing up to American withdrawal pinned back the ears of the Viet Cong and greatly reduced their fighting power and ability to control the population of the rural countryside. Viet Cong cadre, due to the aggressive expansion of territorial force outposts in thousands of hamlets and villages, become cut off from large segments of the rural population. Viet Cong military strength too had atrophied due to constant Army of South Vietnam (ARVN) and American military operations relying on heavy doses of firepower. They were literally pushed up against a wall in wretched sanctuaries close to the Laos and Cambodian borders and in other isolated spots in the interior.[3]

As a result, in order for the Viet Cong main force units to remain undetected, they would have to break themselves down into small units like platoon and companies since staying concentrated as battalions and regiments would make them vulnerable to American and South Vietnamese firepower. This dispersion of Viet Cong forces allowed the security component of the pacification campaign to proceed by distributing territorial force outposts throughout the countryside and further disrupting communist activities and their links to the population. A Viet Cong infantry company commander operating in the Mekong Delta in 1970 against determined American and South Vietnamese efforts to pacify the area complained of effective military operations by the American 9th Infantry Division which as he noted had "much greater firepower" than his VC forces. The company commander fretted that American tactics based on the quick application of firepower had been very "effective" against the Viet Cong forces in his area to the point where they had been put in "great danger."[4]

Even though the Viet Cong military forces and infrastructure had been seriously weakened, the Government of South Vietnam was not able to alter the allegiance of large parts of the rural population to its writ. A military adviser in Hua Nghia at the time, Major Stuart Herrington, noted that it was true that the pacification efforts were "building schools and clinics and the like but the government still was viewed with basic cynicism." According to Herrington, the reason was due to "corruption at all levels generally had the effect of angering the people." Herrington went on to observe that the only way rural folk could be reasonably assured of safety from military operations and American and South Vietnamese firepower was to move to a "district capital" or other large government controlled village. Herrington made this observation in 1971 at the purported height of the Pacification Campaign.[5]

Although there was the appearance of successful pacification through efforts such as land redistribution, the establishment of local governing cadres, and the improvement of local economies and infrastructure, such a notion was in fact a chimera. What brought about the perception that the rural countryside had become pacified was the fact that large swaths of civilian populations were made either willingly or forcibly to leave hamlets and villages that were contested between the Viet Cong and American Army and ARVN units and resettle into areas controlled by the government. A firefight here or an ambush there by a Viet Cong unit would then bring about massive amounts of American or South Vietnamese firepower, often destroying homes in hamlets and villages in the process. In order to survive, many people just left the areas where the VC were to areas closer to government facilities which would at least provide the safety from firepower delivered by airplanes or artillery.

It was not the pacification campaign itself that was proving effective but a metaphorical draining of the pond as a means to catch fish. The rural people were the water and the Viet Cong the fish. It was this very process of moving large swaths of civilians away from contested areas where fighting occurred into government controlled villages and towns combined with the spread of territorial force outposts that provided data to HES reports arguing by 1972 that 90 percent of the provinces had become "pacified." A CORDS history completed in early 1973 and looking back on almost 10 years of war noted that over "seven million Vietnamese have been forced to leave their homes due to military activities."[6] The United States Agency for International Development (USAID) concluded that in the cities of Da Nang, Qui Nohn, and Cam Ran, over 60 percent of the total population were refugees who had entered the city between 1962 and 1972.

Although the American military in Vietnam largely supported the south Vietnamese Government pacification programs through military operations, there were a few specific cases where it carried out comprehensive pacification operations on its own. The American 173d Airborne Brigade in Binh Dinh Province conducted a comprehensive pacification campaign for nearly a year between 1969 and 1970. Unlike most cases where American forces supported pacification through military operations, the 173d in Binh Dinh were building schools, constructing bridges, fixing roads, establishing local governance, and training and working alongside territorial and ARVN forces. While the 173d was deployed in Binh Dinh, impressive gains were made in pacification but the gains were paper thin and dependent upon American presence. When the 173d packed up and left very quickly in April of 1970, as HES reports showed, the province turned back to Viet Cong control.

In assessing the overall effects of pacification and its utility, if the goal of pacification was to connect the people of the rural countryside to the South Vietnamese Government, then it failed. It was not the pacification programs but the hard hand of war through firepower that made the pacification campaigns apparently seem to work, albeit temporarily, by the depopulation of the countryside.

To be sure the Viet Cong and their revolutionary movement in South Vietnam had shrunk significantly due to the effects of military operations as part of pacification. However the Viet Cong's "core was very deep" and with certain conditions in place, it could rise up again and prove to be the pivotal link between the rural population and the combined efforts of its own infrastructure and military forces with those of the North Vietnamese Army (NVA). [7] The American military and its senior leaders in Vietnam had no real clear sense of the depth of that core or its potential for quick and decisive action. Neither did Abrams and his staff truly understand and comprehend the vast amount of societal change in the rural countryside caused by the war's destructiveness.

The last American troops departed South Vietnam in March of 1973. Between 1973 and the fall of Saigon in April of 1975, the Viet Cong were still viable and active albeit reduced in the countryside, and the North Vietnamese Army in its large and threatening numbers, was still in the South. For example, in My Thuy Phuong village just south of Hue City in 1974, HES claimed that it was generally safe for the government and gave it a high rating for security. Local villagers interviewed in 1974, however, said that many of the hamlets that made up the greater village away from the main highway were Viet Cong strongholds even though HES rated them as secure.[8]

The final North Vietnamese offensive brought about the collapse of the government and military in South Vietnam with stunning speed. The link between the assaulting NVA army units and the Viet Cong main forces and militia became quite apparent. All three entities cooperated effectively to initially harass government and security forces of South Vietnam and then finally overthrow them in decisive coordinated thrusts. The offensive began in March and was over in late April of 1975.

In the end, American firepower combined with South Vietnamese programs of pacification could not break the insatiable will of the communist enemy nor could it correct the endemic problems of corruption within the government and military of the South Vietnamese. Moreover, firepower could not connect the people of South Vietnam to the government in a moral and long-lasting way. The United States could have injected firepower one more time in Vietnam in the spring of 1975, but in so doing it would have eventually destroyed the country to "save" it.

The final campaigns of the Vietnam War question the utility of military force to change an "entire society" for the better.[9] There was no "better war" that General Abrams "deserved" as New York Times correspondent Kevin Buckley suggested in 1969 about a year after Abrams had taken command.[10] In fact the notion of a "better war" is oxymoronic. Wars by their nature are destructive and commanders on the ground should appreciate the limits of what American military power can accomplish when trying to pacify a foreign land at the barrel of a gun.

Endnotes

1. "Republic of Vietnam Pacification Program," January 1970, Robert M. Montague Papers, Box 7, AHEC.

2. Central Pacification and Development Council, "Plan for Pacification and Development, 1970," Robert M. Montague Papers, Box 7, AHEC, Carlisle Barracks, PA.

3. See "Viet Cong Evaluation of the Situation in Quang Dien," [captured document from Viet Cong Political Officer], 18 October 1968, Donald A. Seibert Papers, AHEC, Carlisle Barracks, PA.

4. "Excerpts of a Diary of a VC Company Commander," Delta Military Assistance Command (9th Division), Papers of John Paul Vann, Box 1, US Army Heritage and Education Center (AHEC), Carlisle Barracks, PA.

5. Eric M. Bergerud, "The Dynamics of Defeat: The Vietnam War in Hau Ngiah Province," (Boulder: West View Press, 1991), 314-315; for very similar observations to Herrington's from a year prior see Charles Benoit RAND report, "Conversations with Rural Vietnamese," April 1970, The RAND Corporation.

6. Director CORDS, "MACORDS After Action Report," 9 March 1973, MACV Command Historian's Collection, Series II: Staff Sections: J3 CORDS, Reports, Briefings, 1967-1973, AHEC, Carlisle Barracks, PA.

7. I David W.P. Elliot, "The Vietnamese War: Revolution and Social Change in the Mekong Delta, 1930-1975," volumes 1 and 2, (New York: M.E. Sharpe, 2003), vol 2, 1211; also see Elliot's 1968 RAND study co-authored with W.A. Stewart, "Pacification and the Viet Cong System in Dinh Tuong, 1966-1967."

8. James Walker Trullinger, Jr., "Village at War: An Account of Revolution in Vietnam," (New York: Longam, 1980), 193.

9. John Nagl, review of "The Echo of Battle: The Army's Way of War", by Brian M. Linn, *RUSI Journal*, 153 (April 2008), 82-84.

10. Kevin P. Buckley, "General Abrams Deserves a Better War," 5 October 1969, *The New York Times*.

Session 4

The Cold War

by

Dr. George C. Herring

The Cold War ended not through climactic battles but rather much in the way it had been fought: through proxy wars waged by client states, fierce propaganda exchanges, bitter verbal duels, and high level diplomacy. Its ending was in some ways inadvertent with the major combatants taking steps to improve relations that neither imagined would have such monumental consequences. More than in most other wars, individuals played the truly decisive role, especially the redoubtable Soviet General Secretary Mikhail Gorbachev and the one-time hard-line anticommunist American President Ronald Reagan.

Ironically, the breakdown in the late 1970s of a short period of Soviet-American détente marked the first step in the process that brought the Cold War to an end. Moscow and Washington had initiated detente with the hope of easing Cold War tensions, curbing an enormously expensive and increasingly menacing nuclear arms race, and healing their ailing economies through trade deals.

The agreements American President Richard M. Nixon and then Soviet General Secretary Leonid Brezhnev completed at the 1972 Moscow summit immediately came under fire from both political right and left in the United States and detente never acquired a firm domestic political underpinning. Nixon's involvement in the Watergate scandal and ultimate resignation of the presidency in August of 1974 removed from office at a critical point a major architect of improved relations with the Union of Soviet Socialist Republics.

In launching detente, moreover, the two nations had operated on the basis of a fundamental misunderstanding. The United States expected the Soviet Union in return for its acceptance as a great power to forego further revolutionary agitation, especially in the Third World. The Kremlin, on the other hand, saw no conflict between detente and its dabbling in Third World revolutions. Its aggressive activities in the Horn of Africa and other regions during the 1970s further discredited detente in the United States. The two Cold War combatants never moved detente much beyond the agreements of 1972. During the rest of the decade, Cold War tensions gradually resumed.

Proxy wars in Central America and Afghanistan in the late 1970s helped spark the last phase of the Cold War. The overthrow of the brutal Nicaraguan tyrant and long-time American client Anastasio Somoza by left wing Sandinista rebels created an opportunity for America's arch enemy Cuba and its patron the USSR to exploit. The outbreak of a leftist revolution in tiny neighboring El Salvador further aroused United States concern about an area of its traditional hegemony, but it was Afghanistan more than anything else that inflamed Soviet-American tensions.

Islamic revolutions in Iran and next door in Afghanistan aroused Soviet fears of the spread of religious contagion to its own republics with sizeable Muslim populations. When a friendly Afghan government appeared threatened by rivals, alarmed Soviet officials raised the specter of American influence in a neighboring country deemed vital to their security. In December of 1979, a reluctant Politburo as a desperate defensive measure and indeed as a last resort, dispatched Red Army troops to secure its client state and suppress the expanding Islamist rebellion. As so often in the Cold War, the two sides totally misread each other's actions out of paranoia. There was little likelihood of the United States establishing a sizeable presence in Afghanistan. Americans, on the other hand, mistakenly viewed a Soviet defensive move as the first step in an ambitious effort to seize the vital and oil-rich Persian Gulf region.

The United States responded to the Soviet move into Afghanistan with everything short of a declaration of war. Traumatized by the fall of Saigon in April of 1975, ignominiously ending years of war in Vietnam and by revolutionary Iran's seizure and imprisonment of more than 50 American hostages and a humiliating failed effort to retrieve them, Americans were in an especially anxious and angry mood. President Jimmy Carter had taken office in 1977 committed to detente and even ending the Cold War but three years of frustration in negotiations with the USSR, a steadily worsening economy, and an uphill battle to get reelected left him in a pugnacious frame of mind. Under fire from both liberals and conservatives, he felt compelled to act decisively. With marked exaggeration, he branded the Soviet intervention in Afghanistan as the greatest threat to peace since World War II. In what came to be called the Carter Doctrine, he vowed that the United States would meet forcibly any Soviet threat to the Persian Gulf. He initiated the biggest defense buildup since the John F. Kennedy years and imposed on the USSR various punitive measures including a boycott of the Olympic Games to be held in Moscow in 1980. Hoping to make Afghanistan into the Kremlin's Vietnam, the Carter administration began sending clandestine aid to the Afghan rebels. By the end of the year, detente was dead.

Tensions increased dramatically under Carter's successor, President Ronald Reagan. A former movie actor, Reagan had built his political career on the foundation of spread eagle Americanism and hard-core anticommunism. During the campaign of 1980 and his first years in office, he launched full-scale rhetorical warfare against the Soviet Union, branding it (with a name taken from the recent hit film, "Star Wars") as "The Evil Empire" and accusing it of being the source of evil in the modern world. He placed a number of ardent Cold Warriors in key government positions. The Reaganites took an unyielding position on nuclear arms control negotiations and far outdid Carter in defense spending. They developed a military doctrine that called for fighting and winning a nuclear war. They sharply expanded aid to the Afghan mujahedeen, sent military assistance and advisers to the embattled Salvadorian government, and helped form a Nicaraguan counterrevolutionary group (the Contras) to overthrow the government of the Sandinistas. Reagan stunned an already edgy Moscow in the spring of 1983 by announcing his commitment to a Strategic Defense Initiative (SDI), which was a space-based missile defense system employing lasers. It was soon labeled as Star Wars. If perfected, it would render the United States invulnerable to a Soviet first strike.

Tensions increased to the level of a full-fledged crisis in 1983. While indulging in often virulent propaganda campaigns throughout the Cold War, the two sides had generally observed certain unwritten limits on the level of insult. In the eyes of the aging, Soviet leadership, Reagan had exceeded those limits and his anti-missile defense proposal was especially alarming. United States-Soviet arms control negotiations got nowhere and were eventually broken off in late 1983. The Soviet shooting down of a civilian South Korean airliner over the Sea of Japan with the loss of 269 lives, the product of nervous, inept air defenses, was branded by the United States as a deliberate and calculated act of aggression. Fears of nuclear war loomed large. In the fall of 1983, millions of Americans, Reagan included, watched a television movie called "The Day After" which was a harrowing account of the impact of a nuclear attack on the Midwest American town of Lawrence, Kansas. Unknown to these viewers, just days before, in response to a North Atlantic Treaty Organization nuclear exercise, nervous Soviet officials, fearing an attack, went on a full defense alert. Soviet-American tensions had reached their highest point since the 1962 Cuban missile crisis. In both nations there was fear of war.

Remarkably, within less than two years after the crisis of 1983, tensions had eased and major steps were being taken toward accommodation. The war scare itself contributed to the transformation that led to a new detente and in time to the end of the Cold War. The talk of war forced sober second thoughts in both countries and discussion of ways to reduce the threat of nuclear Armageddon. After a period of marked political instability in Moscow, with three, aging leaders dying in rapid succession, the onset of new youthful leadership and stability under Gorbachev enabled the government to address pressing issues. Economic distress provoked a major reconsideration of priorities leading to a de-emphasis on the Cold War and focus on domestic reform. In the United States, Reagan won an overwhelming reelection victory in 1984 thereby gaining the freedom to mount new foreign policy initiatives. He alone among American politicians had the unimpeachable anticommunist credentials to undertake radical changes of policy toward America's old adversary without fear of political retribution.

More than any other individual, Gorbachev was responsible for ending the Cold War. He turned to politics and rose steadily through the Soviet hierarchy. Unlike most of his predecessors, he had traveled widely before taking the top office, even in Western Europe where he saw first-hand the enormous disparity between the living standards there and those of his own people. Upon taking power, Gorbachev set as his main goal to saving communism by introducing basic reforms in the Soviet economic and political system which he called *perestroika* or restructuring, and *glasnost* or greater openness. To affect the reforms, he deemed it necessary to ease Cold War tensions and reduce military expenditures, particularly in the area of nuclear weapons. Learning from Western European defense intellectuals as well as scientists in his own country, he formulated new defense policies designed to cut military spending. He sought direct negotiations with the United States on nuclear arms reduction and other issues. He scrapped the traditional communist dogma of an inevitable conflict with capitalism and spoke of an "interdependent and integrated" world.

Reagan, too, was prepared for change. Some of his hard line advisors saw massive United States defense spending as a way to bankrupt the Soviet Union. The president's intention from the start had been to establish a strong basis from which to negotiate. He despised nuclear weapons and could not see how any nation could win a nuclear war.

The war scare of 1983 had a huge impact on him and from historians and his diplomatic advisers, he reached the obvious, but for United States Cold Warriors often difficult to grasp conclusion, that the Soviet people were as concerned for their security as were Americans. Eager to establish his place in history in his second term, Reagan set out to reduce the menace of nuclear war by negotiating arms reduction agreements with the USSR. A stubbornly persistent triumphalist myth holds that his fiery anticommunist rhetoric and massive defense buildup brought the Soviet Union to its knees. In fact, his anti-nuclearism and willingness to negotiate with the USSR started the two nations on the road that would end the Cold War.

Between 1985 and 1988, the two leaders, often against bitter opposition from within their own governments, took giant steps toward reducing Cold War tensions. They sparred endlessly and inconclusively over such contentious issues as the proxy wars in Central America and Afghanistan. Reagan's unflinching commitment to SDI proved the most difficult impediment to comprehensive arms control agreements. At Geneva in November of 1985, however, the two leaders began to get to know each other and to establish a sort of chemistry. During an impromptu surreal get together in Reykjavik, Iceland, in October of 1986, they came tantalizingly close to a stunning agreement that would have banned all nuclear weapons, only to be blocked by continued disagreement on Star Wars. Persuaded by his own scientists that the United States missile defense system was unworkable, Gorbachev in time stopped opposing it, permitting the two leaders to make progress on major arms negotiations. By the time he came to Washington in late 1987, the charismatic Soviet leader had become an international celebrity and his visit to the United States sparked among Americans what one writer called "Gorby fever." By this time ensnared in a domestic crisis of his own making, the result of illegal arms sales to Iran with the proceeds from which were used for illegal assistance to the Nicaraguan Contras, Reagan was desperately in need of foreign policy success to salvage his presidency. During the Washington summit, they reached agreement for substantial reductions in nuclear weapons. The next year, while strolling casually with Gorbachev in Red Square, Reagan admitted that his remarks about an "evil empire" had been about another time, another place.

In 1988, Gorbachev took further and even more dramatic initiatives to achieve his ambitious and ultimately quixotic goals. His vision was for a reformed but still communist Soviet Union, leading like-minded neighbors toward a prosperous and peaceful Europe. In early 1988, he set out to liquidate what he called the "bleeding wound" of Afghanistan by withdrawing Red Army troops. He announced a new defensive military doctrine that permitted the Warsaw Pact countries and the Soviet Union to make huge reductions in conventional forces. He made clear that the USSR would never start a war and also replaced the notorious Brezhnev Doctrine, which had ascribed for the Soviet Union the right to intervene in satellite countries, with what one Soviet official called the "Sinatra doctrine," named for American singer Frank Sinatra's popular tune "My Way," which freed the Eastern European nations to change their domestic system as they chose.

The Gorbachev reforms of 1988 made possible the *annus mirabilis* of 1989, a series of shocking and for the Soviet leader himself totally unintended consequences that led to an end to the Cold War. Taking its cue from Gorbachev's speeches and private assurances, Poland, through free elections in June, voted into power a reformist non-communist government. Revolutions followed in Hungary and Czechoslovakia, the latter so smooth that it was called the "velvet revolution." Most shockingly, in November of 1989, the Germans themselves tore down the Berlin Wall, one of the most conspicuous and despised signs of the Cold War. To the horror of many Europeans, there was talk of a reunified Germany. The United States role in these climactic events was to allow them to happen and, as Reagan's successor George H. W. Bush wisely observed, to refrain from obvious celebration. The Bush administration did, however, play a central role in bringing about a unified Germany, a feat that left many Europeans uneasy. Two years, later, in an event of anticlimax, the Soviet Union itself collapsed as a result of a bungled coup by hard-line Communists that led to Gorbachev's displacement, the separation of numerous Soviet republics, and the birth of the Russian Republic. As a result of a strange, almost surreal process, which no one foresaw, the Cold War was over. "We were suddenly in a unique position," Bush's national security adviser and alter ego Brent Scowcroft observed, "without experience, without precedent, and standing alone at the height of our power."

Recommended Reading

The standard account by a noted Kremlinologist of the breakdown of 1970s detente and the beginning and end of the last phase of the Cold War is Raymond Garthoff, "Detente and Confrontation: American-Soviet Relations from Reagan to Gorbachev," (Washington, 1994). Don Oberdorfer, "From the Cold War to a New Era: The United States and the Soviet Union, 1983-1991," (rev. ed., Baltimore, MD, 1998) is an excellent history by a noted journalist. A broad survey of the Cold War, Melvyn P. Leffler, "For the Soul of Mankind: The United States, the Soviet Union, and the Cold War," (New York, 2007) is especially good on Reagan, Gorbachev and the end of the conflict. William C. Wohlforth, ed., "Witnesses to the End of the Cold War," (Baltimore, MD, 1996) includes useful oral histories with a number of key diplomats and insightful analysis by scholars. James Mann, "The Rebellion of Ronald Reagan: A History of the End of the Cold War," (New York, 2009) skillfully analyzes Reagan's transformation from Cold War "hawk" to "dove." Anatoly S. Chernyaev, "My Years with Gorbachev," translated by Robert D. English and Elizabeth Tucker (University Park, PA, 2000) offers useful insights into the Soviet leaders motives and actions.

Session 4

Interview

Dr. George Herring

Dr. George Herring

My name is Dr. George Herring. I am retired. I was professor of history at the University of Kentucky from 1969 until I retired in 2005.

Interviewer

Are you still writing? I assume you are.

Dr. George Herring

Yes, I miss the day to day contact with people, but the freedom to do what you want to do, no committee meetings, no grading papers – it's cool.

Interviewer

So we're here to have this conference on war termination and I'm curious to know what your take would be on some of the broad definitional issues with the term "war termination" and when war is to be declared officially over. Your essay is on the Cold War. That one is not only one that may pose problems in war termination. It also forged problems with war origination, I imagine, too. When does a war begin, when does a war end?

Dr. George Herring

It's easier to pinpoint "end" there, I think, than it is the beginning. The beginning is still a matter of controversy. Did it start with the Soviet revolution in 1917? Or did it start in 1945 at the end of World War II, or February of 1946 with Churchill's Iron Curtain speech and Stalin's election speech? There are lots of different dates.

Interviewer

I mean, you really could argue, I guess, from 1917 to 1991.

Dr. George Herring

Yeah.

Interviewer

Everything else in between is somehow just a sideshow until you get to the conclusion.

Dr. George Herring

Well, my paper would argue that termination, in effect, comes at the end of 1989. I pinpoint the Malta Conference, December 1989, of George H. W. Bush and Gorbachev, where it is pretty much agreed that the Cold War is over. The fall of the Soviet Union was a very important consequence.

Interviewer

Well, speak in general, first, about the specifics of the Cold War as a story, about your notion of how wars end, given your knowledge as a historian. How do they end?

Dr. George Herring

That's a very broad and open ended question. Well, the principal ways they end are when, sort of in a classic World War I or World War II model, when one nation, or sets of nations, imposes military defeat on another nation. That's sort of the classic model, one that may be less and less likely to reoccur in the nuclear age.

Another model would be, say, the War of 1812 for the United States, or the Vietnam War model, which I've written about extensively. That is where the two sides conclude that they cannot achieve the aims they set out to achieve at a cost that's acceptable to them. So they're willing to make compromises, either because they have to, or in the case of the North Vietnamese, because they think they can eventually win by political means.

Interviewer

So that's the notion of "convergence"?

Dr. George Herring

Yeah, I think that was the word used. So those are probably the classic two models of how wars end. The Cold War is totally different, because it's not a military conflict to begin with. I mean, except by client states and proxy armies. It's different, but the classic models, I think, are the ones I've talked about.

Interviewer

The Cold War is different because of the bomb? Does the bomb define the Cold War?

Dr. George Herring

Yeah, the existence of nuclear weapons and of increasingly destructive capacity and increasingly sophisticated delivery systems means that, in the eyes of the major combatants– the United States and the Soviet Union—this war cannot be fought as a classic war.

Interviewer

Isn't there built into the notion of atomic warfare that there is no conclusion, no war termination but the ultimate termination?

Dr. George Herring

Well, I think both sides at points during the Cold War—with the United States in particular ironically I guess, at about the time the Cold War was ending—there were those who began to argue and conclude that you could fight and you could win a nuclear war. That was not the opinion of Ronald Reagan, who very much disliked nuclear weapons, who had a strong antinuclear streak in him that's not as well known as the anti-Communist streak.

Interviewer

Who was arguing that we could?

Dr. George Herring

There were people in the military and in the Defense Department. Indeed, beginning in the Carter administration there were studies done, and people were tasked to see how we can successfully fight and win a nuclear war. So it's a trend, it's the idea that gets away completely from the old notion of mutual assured destruction. In other words, we avoid war by recognition that it's so horrific that neither side could come out of it. There's a rethinking of that in the late 1970s and early 1980s.

Interviewer

Well, first tell me what inspires the rethinking at that moment, do you think?

Dr. George Herring

It's a good question, and I'm not sure that I can give you a good answer. In the eyes of many people it's the feeling that mutual assured destruction, or MAD, was too negative, that it was too crippling, and it's what becomes a neoconservative movement later on, that there are certain ideals that are more important than the possible consequences of war, that we need to be prepared to fight for these ideals.

Interviewer

So is it anti-containment?

Dr. George Herring

Yeah, exactly, anti-containment and anti-MAD (anti-mutual assured destruction), that's what you have to think of in other terms.

Interviewer

It was a combination in that, I suppose, in part given your long experience of writing about Vietnam, that Vietnam was emblematic.

Dr. George Herring

Korea and Vietnam were fought in limited ways when they should have–in the eyes of some people–been fought, particularly in Vietnam, and could have been won.

Interviewer

The late '70s were the nadir of the army in the 20th century. It was the time of the hollow force, coming out of the experience of defeat in Vietnam, with the drugs, the racism. Was there also a sense that maybe the way to wage war is not with conventional forces, that could have been inspired by the failures of Vietnam?

Dr. George Herring

No, I would say it's across the board. There's a feeling that you ought to be able to fight at all levels and you ought to be able to win at all levels up to and including nuclear weapons. So the idea of rebuilding the army was well underway, that by no means was culminating.

Interviewer

Now, you say Reagan was firmly an antinuclear voice. By name, who were those in his administration that were having this argument?

Dr. George Herring

Richard Perle would have been one of the key figures.

Interviewer

He's on the neoconservative side?

Dr. George Herring

Yeah.

Interviewer

What about Defense Secretary Casper Weinberger?

Dr. George Herring

Weinberger would have been one of the figures as well.

Interviewer

And the counter argument would be coming from Secretary of State George Shultz, I'd imagine.

Dr. George Herring

Yeah, Shultz is pushing negotiations throughout the 1980s. One of the ironic things, I think, is that the President Reagan appoints to his government a number of people who are hard-core ideologues and he appoints a number of people who are more pragmatic, beginning with Al Haig and then moving on through to George Shultz. One of the ironic things is that the timing of the Iran-Contra revelations has the effect of sort of clinching the control of policy in the hands of a pragmatist like Shultz. That has a lot of effect on Reagan's negotiations from 1987 on.

Interviewer

Because the view is that the extremists got out of hand?

Dr. George Herring

Yes, exactly.

Interviewer

And that they did that without Reagan?

Dr. George Herring

What did he know and when?

Interviewer

The question of what participation did he have in the plotting, so to speak, of that episode, has never really been answered.

Dr. George Herring

No, it hasn't been definitively answered. He knew more than he let on and in terms, at least of the support for the Contras, certainly he gave it his blessing in many different ways.

Interviewer

It strikes me that there are similarities between the Reagan Administration and the Eisenhower administration, particularly around Dien Bien Phu. There were arguments to use atomic weapons against the Chinese that Eisenhower would never seriously listen to.

Dr. George Herring

I would disagree.

Interviewer

Tell me.

Dr. George Herring

Yes, I think there's a similarity in the sense that the Eisenhower administration, in reaction against the stalemate in Korea, at least publicly insisted that nuclear weapons were fair game. Eisenhower himself once commented that it's just like a bullet. You've got it and need to be prepared to use it. This is in the early 1950s before the Soviets have developed missiles and those long-range bombers that made it more difficult. Now, here again, you run into problems. Was he bluffing? Was he a very clever poker player, nuclear poker player and bluffer? Or did he sincerely believe, or was he actually prepared to use these things? In the case of Dien Bien Phu, when the French asked for support and it involved, what they were asking for, they didn't want large scale military intervention because that would mean they would lose control of the war and that's the last thing they wanted. They didn't want the Americans to be fighting to the last French soldier in Indochina. What they were looking for was bombing of the Vietnamese positions around Dien Bien Phu and there was an understanding, I think, on the part of both countries that nuclear weapons might be used. French Premier Bidault later claimed that United States Secretary of State John Foster Dulles, in a moment when they sort of brushed against each other at a meeting in Paris had said, "You know, I've got nukes. We've got two or three. We may let you have it." Dulles denied that.

Interviewer

That's in that movie called "Hearts and Minds."

Dr. George Herring

Yeah, Bidault actually makes that claim. They've got him on film there. Now, but Eisenhower was prepared to intervene with air power, possibly with nuclear weapons, if he got the British to go along. He didn't want it to be a unilateral intervention and if the French could be persuaded to grant the non-Communist Vietnamese their independence and, of course, they were able to get neither of these things, so he was not able to get congressional assent. Without British support, French agreement, and congressional assent, then he wasn't about to go ahead.

Interviewer

Well, Eisenhower was the same in that sense?

Dr. George Herring

Yeah, he saw what the idea of American intervention would have been to help the French to win but in winning, to push them out.

Interviewer

The French didn't want to deal with that.

Dr. George Herring

That was not what they, at this stage, had envisioned.

Interviewer

Well, what I meant in making the comparison is that it does seem that contemporary historical reflections on Eisenhower himself is that he may very well have been bluffing.

Dr. George Herring

Yeah, well, there are arguments.

Interviewer

There were people right up through Vice President Nixon who advocated the use of nuclear weapons.

Dr. George Herring

Well, and Nixon differed from Eisenhower and John Foster Dulles to the extent that he publicly advocated the dispatch of army combat forces.

Interviewer

Come back to Reagan for a moment, because this is the point of the conference today, the end of the Cold War. You're really zeroing in now, sort of 1986 to 1988.

Dr. George Herring

Well, I would really zero in on the end of 1983 to the end of 1989 as the crucial period.

Interviewer

What happens in 1983 that starts this?

Dr. George Herring

There is a major war scare. It is a time that is as delicate, as volatile as any in Soviet-American relations, going back to the Cuban Missile Crisis of 1962. Reagan has come in and everything that Reagan does has been initiated by Carter. Reagan builds on it and expands it and advertises it more and so makes it more of a public sort of thing but Reagan escalates the rhetoric more.

Interviewer

This is regarding "The evil empire."

Dr. George Herring

The evil empire, focus of evil in the modern world, and statements like that are along with a huge military build-up. There is talk of nuclear war. There's an interesting conjunction of things. In the fall of 1983 there's a movie called "The Day After" which millions and millions of Americans, Reagan included, watched, and which portrayed the impact of nuclear war on Lawrence, Kansas, a little college town just west of Kansas City.

Interviewer

It was a television movie, as a matter of fact.

268

Dr. George Herring

It was a made for television movie with huge viewership. Another thing that was going on simultaneously was the shooting down of the Korean airliner. At about that same time, there was a NATO exercise, the object of which was to 1) test NATO's capabilities, and 2) to get a sense of how the Soviets would react. The Soviets read this exercise as a preliminary to nuclear war and were actually persuaded for a time that a nuclear war was possible, if not indeed likely. It went up to a high level Defense Condition. There was a story–and I think it's been pretty well confirmed–that at one point the Soviet defense system picked up incoming missiles, and as the story goes, a Red Army colonel who was observing this and in control at this time, decided that it didn't add up, that something was wrong here, and took it on his own initiative to stop the system from going forward.

Interviewer

It's amazing how there are these lone individuals in the course of history.

Dr. George Herring

I don't think it's been absolutely confirmed, but it's a story that seems to be valid. So the point is that the rhetoric was heating up on both sides, and by the end they had broken off arms control negotiations. They had been talking since Reagan came in, but they were completely broken off. First time in a long time they had been completely broken off, since the late 1960s. The threat of war is very real, and I think Reagan takes away from this the notion that there is possibility of a nuclear war, this could be a horrible thing, You can see him—actually coming out of when he saw "The Day After" and was really rather stunned by it, rather moved by it—you could see him coming away from this.

Interviewer

Of course, he's a movie man himself, right, so it would make big difference to him.

Dr. George Herring

Well, and people always said that he saw movies as sort of a form of reality and so, you see him changing in terms of his toning down his rhetoric, his willingness to reopen negotiations with the Soviets on arms reduction. It's gone beyond control to reduction by this point and the one thing that really deters him at this point is the fact that there's so much instability in Moscow. Brezhnev dies, two successors come very quickly, and it's not until Gorbachev takes power that things are stabilized, but you can see Reagan changing and once he is overwhelmingly reelected in 1984, then he has sort of a political base to work with.

Interviewer

Now, the other side, the neoconservatives are thoroughly disappointed with the second term. Isn't that right?

Dr. George Herring

They're thoroughly disappointed, yeah.

Interviewer

They feel he's been co-opted eventually by Gorbachev?

Dr. George Herring

Yes, and Shultz on this side.

Interviewer

Tell me a little bit about that.

Dr. George Herring

Well, where do you want to begin?

Interviewer

Well, so Reagan's reelected. You know, the traditional story about second terms, they always are less dynamic than first terms, but you could argue in some respects, with respect to foreign policy, the flip happened with Reagan. You had described before that there was this tension, almost a self-introduced tension on the part of Reagan to say, "Let's have some hardliners, let's have some pragmatism, let them argue it out and then I can preside over that."

Dr. George Herring

I suppose it was that well thought out, or it just happened.

Interviewer

Yes. Well, he had an instinctive approach to government, it seemed, not necessarily articulated but that was the way he managed men and women. So, what is the second term? Is it just Reagan's shift of thinking that comes from real fear that nuclear war may happen that makes the pragmatist win? What happens there?

Dr. George Herring

I think there's more to it than that. It seems obvious, but for United States policy makers during the Cold War it had not always been obvious. He developed a sense that Russians were as concerned about their security as we were. What a revelation, a startling revelation, and that made him more sensitive to their concerns and their feelings, and sort of led him to tone down the rhetoric. It leads him to look for negotiations. Once Gorbachev is in, then there is a real opportunity to do this and they move really quite rapidly, stunningly, and I guess that's the way you had to do it, if there are delays and snags over a long period of time.

Interviewer

Now, a lot of people were suspicious of Gorbachev, and Reagan wasn't.

Dr. George Herring

He came not to be, yeah.

Interviewer

They came to have a personal relationship.

Dr. George Herring

There's just this incredible personal chemistry that develops between them. It doesn't mean they don't distrust each other, and it doesn't mean one's not still a Russian and a Communist and the other is an American but they do come to, after some hard times there with that crazy weekend in Iceland.

Interviewer

Describe that a bit. It's a summit, right?

Dr. George Herring

Yeah, and all of a sudden they're talking along and there is this notion that we might be able to end all nuclear weapons. In the face of what they were talking about, first 2000, I think. And so all of a sudden the technical people are negotiating all night and they come up with these agreements. Ten there's one snag, and that was SDI, the Strategic Defense Initiative, Star Wars. Reagan wasn't able to give it up, and Gorbachev continued to insist that it had to be confined to the laboratory, and it's that one thing that prevents agreements that would have really blown people – no pun intended – away if they had actually happened. But they come back from that and then they go back to the drawing board. Over the next couple of years, they do make really significant steps forward in terms of reducing major classes of nuclear weapons. It's quite a shocking story.

Interviewer

There's the famous walk in the woods.

Dr. George Herring

That's earlier. That's Paul Nitze from 1983.

Interviewer

That was Shevardnadze too, wasn't it?

Dr. George Herring

It would've been before Shevardnadze. I don't remember the Soviet official but Nitze was, for the ardent Cold Warrior that he was, author of National Security Council 68. Nitze had developed a certain level of flexibility by that point and was interested in trying to develop a basis for negotiation, but that was scrapped. That produced nothing.

Interviewer

So you marked the end of the Cold War, you said, with the Malta Summit. Is that right?

Dr. George Herring

Yeah.

Interviewer

Tell me where that is historically in the sequence of events, including the collapse of the Berlin Wall.

Dr. George Herring

Yeah, and of course what happens is the events in Eastern Europe beginning in the fall of 1989. Gorbachev had paved the way for this earlier. He had, in effect, told the Eastern

Europeans, "If you want change, we are not going to interfere." That's what one Soviet official called a "Sinatra doctrine." Frankie's great song called "My Way," "You can do it," you can do it your way and, lo and behold, when revolution occurred—fittingly in Poland where the Cold War starts with the Soviet-American conflict over Poland through World War II and on into 1945, so fittingly in Poland—the first revolution or reform occurs and the Soviet Union, true to Gorbachev's pledge, does nothing. Then Hungary, Czechoslovakia, the Berlin Wall, the dominoes – to use our metaphor on Vietnam – fall and the Soviet Union does nothing. Bush, however, is still not convinced after all of this, which gets back to one of your earlier questions that Gorbachev's for real. Bush and his advisors are among those who thought Reagan might have been duped, that he maybe hadn't been tough enough. They came in persuaded that caution was the watchword. Let's see how these things really work out.

Interviewer

Yet ironically, if you look at that, at their pasts, Bush was much more out of the pragmatist wing.

Dr. George Herring

One would've thought, yeah.

Interviewer

Reagan was more out of the hardliner.

Dr. George Herring

Exactly.

Interviewer

Maybe that, to some degree, it was a desire to keep that coalition together politically, that Bush Sr. needed to sort of be careful about how much he took of the Gorbachev relationship.

Dr. George Herring

That could be, but it's only by December of 1989 when they meet, early in December, they meet at Malta, everything is resolved with Eastern Europe and Germany, except whether Germany will be unified and there there is real difference. The Soviets are adamantly opposed to unification, as are many of the other European nations and the United States. Bush, Baker, and the others are pretty much committed to unification, to helping West Germany pull off unification, but it's only at Malta that you've seen everything work its way out in Eastern Europe. It's only at Malta that Bush becomes convinced that Gorbachev is for real. Two or three days of talks in an incredible setting with stormy seas—Bush almost is tossed into the stormy seas one time on a launch taking him from the Soviet cruise ship in harbor out to his own ship, his base ship—but it's there that the questions in the minds of Bush and his advisors are pretty much resolved, and by the end of the conference there's a joint communiqué. This is the first time that's ever happened and they more or less declare that this thing is over. Two years later, of course, the Soviet Union falls in August of 1991, which is a consequence of the end of the Cold War. It's the final act in it, in a sense.

Interviewer

The Cold War seems unique in the study of war. Is there any comparison?

Dr. George Herring

No, and given its timeframe of almost a half century and the fact that there was never a direct clash of armies, although they prepared it. Both of them had scenarios to fight that climactic battle on the plains of Eastern Europe.

Interviewer

So what is the last campaign of the Cold War? Is there a last campaign?

Dr. George Herring

The problem with such a template is that it doesn't apply the same in all cases. My last campaigns were the proxy wars in Afghanistan and Central America, pretty much simultaneous.

Interviewer

Was this in the mid-1980s to early 1990s?

Dr. George Herring

Yeah, 1979 into the early 1980s, but also the last campaign, I think, is the rhetorical conflict. These proxy wars are the actual combat and then the rhetorical escalation that goes on from 1979 to 1983 lead up to the war scare. So it's not as neat.

Interviewer

It's interesting for a modern area, so technology driven, that it's an exchange of words and communications that ends up being a kind of last campaign.

Dr. George Herring

Yeah.

Interviewer

This again speaks to the uniqueness of the time.

Dr. George Herring

Well, the point I make is that the Cold War ended pretty much in the way it was formed, by proxy wars, propaganda, rhetoric, and diplomacy.

Interviewer

Thank you.

Terminating Operation Desert Storm

by

Dr. Andrew J. Bacevich

The senior United States field commander knew it was over before it was over. The forces under his command had accomplished what they had been sent to do. The imperative was now to wind down the war, promptly and neatly. Avoiding unnecessary bloodshed had become a priority. So too was upholding the warrior's code of honor, demonstrating that the troops under his command were not only brave but also humane. Given all that had been accomplished on the battlefield, the task of bringing Operation Desert Storm to an end did not appear to be a particularly difficult one. The heavy lifting was done.

So when General H. Norman Schwarzkopf, who commanded United States Central Command (CENTCOM) and all the coalition forces assembled to liberate Iraqi-occupied Kuwait, appeared before the press on 27 February 1991 in Riyadh, Saudi Arabia, his mood was ebullient. In assessing the situation that evening (early afternoon Washington time), Schwarzkopf turned in a boffo performance.[1]

Quickly enshrined as the "mother of all briefings," it completed the gruff general's transformation into Stormin' Norman and vaulted him, however briefly, into the uppermost ranks of global celebrity. Simply put, Schwarzkopf used the occasion to declare victory.[2]

Against tall odds, outnumbered United States forces had executed an epic feat of arms. Outgeneraled and outfought, the Iraqi army had all but ceased to exist. What Schwarzkopf described as a "classic tank battle" had left 3,700 of the enemy's 4,000 tanks hors de combat. Over the course of a mere four days, the troops under his command had "almost completely destroyed the offensive capability of the Iraqi forces in the Kuwait theater of operations." The surviving remnant, pursued on the ground and pummeled from the air, was doomed. There was no escape. "The gates are closed."[3] The road to Baghdad lay open. Yet Schwarzkopf envisioned neither the intention nor the desire to march on the Iraqi capital. Although fighting continued, he considered his task complete. "We've accomplished our mission," he concluded, "and when the decision makers come to the decision that there should be a cease fire, nobody will be happier than me."[4]

The views expressed by the field commander in Riyadh meshed with and reinforced those gaining currency back in Washington. In the desert, things had gone much better than expected. Senior United States civilian and military officials alike felt little inclination to place down further bets. It's better for the United States to stop now and cash in its winnings, which promised to be considerable. Besides, to continue clobbering an already beaten foe might give the wrong impression. Concern for appearances and reputations was eclipsing serious strategic analysis.[5]

A call to CENTCOM headquarters earlier that same day from General Colin Powell, Chairman of the Joint Chiefs of Staff and an officer of acute political sensitivity, signaled which way the winds were blowing at home. "The doves are starting to complain about all the damage you're doing," Powell told Schwarzkopf. Images of mangled Iraqi trucks and burning armored vehicles piled up on the main road leading from Kuwait City back toward

Iraq were dubbed by the press as the "Highway of Death" and causing unease. "The reports make it look like wanton killing."[6] Perhaps, Powell suggested, it was time to bring things to a halt.

Schwarzkopf's initial inclination was to continue the pursuit for another day. He wanted to "drive to the sea and totally destroy everything in our path. That's the way I wrote the plan," he told the JCS chairman, "and in one more day we'll be done."[7]

Yet when pressed by Powell, Schwarzkopf quickly gave way. A short time later in the Oval Office, the JCS chairman duly relayed Schwarzkopf's assessment to the commander in chief. "Mr. President, it's going much better than we expected. The Iraqi army is broken. All they're trying to do now is get out." "By sometime tomorrow the job will be done," he added.[8]

"If that's the case," President Bush wondered aloud, "why not end it today?" Caught off guard by the president's suggestion, Powell said he needed once more to consult the field commander. Ducking into the president's study, he placed another call to Riyadh. Schwarzkopf needed little persuading. "I don't have any problem," he replied when briefed on the president's inclination to end the fighting forthwith. "Our objective was to drive 'em out and we've done it."[9]

Schwarzkopf's views proved decisive. At 6 p.m. Washington time, after a final round of discussion with his advisers, President Bush rendered his decision. In a 9 p.m. televised address from the Oval Office, he would announce a cessation of hostilities. There was just one added wrinkle. Rather than declaring an immediate termination of combat operations, the president would designate 12:01 a.m. as the endpoint of Operation Desert Storm. White House chief of staff John Sununu had suggested that "The One Hundred Hour War" had a nice ring to it. Midnight marked exactly 100 hours since ground operations had commenced.

"Kuwait is liberated," Bush told the nation and the world that evening in his televised presentation. "Iraq's army is defeated. Our military objectives are met." The president and his administration were ready to move on. "This war is now behind us."[10]

That judgment proved premature. Even as Operation Desert Storm wound down, complications were beginning to emerge. Expectations of overwhelmingly superior United States power producing a decisive outcome soon proved to be illusory. President Bush himself was among the first to suspect that something might be amiss. "Still no feeling of euphoria," his diary entry for that night reads. "It hasn't been a clean end – there is no battleship *Missouri* surrender. This is what's missing to make this akin to World War II, to separate Kuwait from Korea and Vietnam."[11]

At the time, few Americans shared Bush's sense of unease. Most had bought into his administration's depiction of the crisis in the Persian Gulf as a morality tale, replaying the events of Europe from 1939 to 1945. That crisis had ostensibly sprung out of the blue on 1 August 1990 when the Hitler-like figure of Saddam Hussein had invaded an innocent unassuming neighbor. In defeating Saddam's legions and liberating Kuwait, United States troops (with a bit of allied assistance) had now put things right.

This reassuring narrative was deeply misleading, however. Operation Desert Storm settled nothing of importance. Instead, the One Hundred Hour War served as a precursor and catalyst for what a decade later became known as the Long War.

Why did Operation Desert Storm, briefly celebrated as an epic feat of arms, so quickly lose its luster? One answer to that question goes like this: Operation Desert Storm was a brilliantly conceived and executed military campaign, botched at the very end and thereby leaving unfortunate loose ends. The failures were military in nature, reflecting the errors and inadequacies of very senior military officers, including along with Powell and Schwarzkopf, Lieutenant General Frederick M. Franks, commander of VII United States Corps.

The charge against Franks is that he failed to accomplish his assigned mission. As conceived by planners working for Schwarzkopf, the coalition ground offensive was to consist of two essential components. First, a supporting attack from south to north toward Kuwait City would fix Iraqi forces in place. Second, a wide-flanking attack from west to east would envelop the enemy and ensure his defeat in detail. VII Corps was to execute that flanking attack. More specifically, the war plan explicitly assigned Franks the task of destroying the Iraqi Republican Guard, the best equipped, best trained, and most formidable element of Saddam Hussein's otherwise raggedy army.

The Republican Guard, although badly damaged and put to flight, evaded destruction, major elements fleeing back toward Baghdad.[12] The hit on Franks, one that Schwarzkopf in particular endorsed, was that in a situation calling for dash, the VII Corps commander had exhibited caution. Determined to minimize coalition casualties, Franks attacked methodically and deliberately, allowing his quarry to escape.[13]

In the immediate wake of Operation Desert Storm, with dissident Iraqi Shiites and Kurds (encouraged by President Bush) rising up to overthrow Saddam, the Republican Guard provided the Iraqi dictator with the wherewithal to crush internal opposition to his regime and retain his hold on power. Saddam survived, creating an abiding problem for the United States, a direct result in the eyes of some of the VII Corps having come up short.

The charge against the CENTCOM commander is broader. Simply put, over during the course of the four days during which the ground offensive unfolded, Schwarzkopf's temperament, volcanic in the best of circumstances, became a major source of dysfunction that eventually permeated the senior levels of his command. In a job that required cool, he ran piping hot, cultivating a style of leadership that emphasized bluster, intimidation, and threats of relief.

Whether due to fatigue, pressure, or sheer orneriness, Schwarzkopf erred repeatedly on issues of primary importance, a tendency that became especially evident as Operation Desert Storm wound down. Having overestimated the expected level of enemy resistance, he adjusted only belatedly to evidence that the Iraqis were far weaker than advertised.[14] Overstating the losses his forces had inflicted on the enemy, he concluded prematurely that his work was finished. By declaring publicly, with hostilities still underway, that his forces were not going to Baghdad, he made a great gift to Saddam Hussein, providing the Iraqi dictator with authoritative insight into the coalition's ultimate intentions.

The campaign's very last act served to showcase Schwarzkopf's shortcomings. Charged by the White House with negotiating a formal cease fire, the CENTCOM commander paid more attention to appearance and atmospherics than to substance, with fateful results.

As the site for this event, Schwarzkopf selected Safwan which is an obscure crossroads in southern Iraq. While President Bush was lamenting the absence of a World War II style surrender ceremony, his field commander intended to preside over a reasonable facsimile with Safwan standing in for the battleship *Missouri* and Schwarzkopf casting himself in the role of Douglas MacArthur.

After notifying Washington that he had designated Safwan as the chosen venue however, Schwarzkopf learned that the Iraqi Army still occupied the place. A garbled report had erroneously put it under the control of United States forces. This glitch proved too much for Schwarzkopf. By his own account, he now "came completely unglued," with General Franks the specific target of his wrath. "I felt as if I'd been lied to. All of my accumulated frustration and rage with VII Corps came boiling out."[15]

Moving the cease-fire talks to a different location was out of the question. Doing so might cast doubt on Schwarzkopf's omniscience and stain a campaign that all concerned were eager to portray as flawless. So for the next 24 hours nudging the Iraqis out of Safwan without instigating a major bloodletting became CENTCOM priority number one, taking precedence over all other considerations, not least of all any substantive considerations related to war termination.

Schwarzkopf himself had drafted proposed terms of reference for the talks. His own views were quite simple, "Our side had *won,* so we were in a position to dictate terms."[16] After some minor wordsmith work, Washington had approved Schwarzkopf's draft. As he headed toward Safwan on 3 March 1991, the general was in the driver's seat.

His mandate, as he himself understood, was "confined to military issues," above all securing the release of coalition soldiers taken prisoner.[17] Upon arriving for the talks, with the media assembled, a reporter shouted a question; "What exactly was going to be negotiated?" "This isn't a negotiation," came Schwarzkopf's curt reply. "I don't plan to give them anything. I'm here to tell them exactly what we expect them to do."[18]

In the event, as he sat down across from two hitherto obscure Iraqi generals, Schwarzkopf's thoughts were focused on donating the furniture to the Smithsonian Institution "in case they ever wanted to recreate the Safwan negotiation [sic] scene." He wasted little time in straying beyond his mandate and in offering his interlocutors generous concessions.[19]

However unwittingly, Schwarzkopf used Safwan as an occasion to convey to Saddam Hussein this essential message that with the status quo antebellum now restored, the United States had no interest in wresting further concessions from Iraq.

The American general assured his interlocutors that the United States and its allies viewed Iraq's boundaries as sacrosanct. United States forces were going home forthwith. "We have no intention of leaving our forces permanently in Iraqi territory once the cease-fire is signed," he announced.[20] As the talks proceeded, an atmosphere of stiff formality gave way to a spirit of mutual accommodation. The Iraqis had given Schwarzkopf what he wanted most and he returned the favor. Asked if the Iraqi Army might resume use of its helicopters after the cease fire, Schwarzkopf readily assented. "Given that the Iraqis had agreed to all of our requests, I didn't feel it was unreasonable to grant one of theirs."[21] As if to affirm that the crisis triggered by Iraq's invasion of Kuwait had reached a definitive conclusion, Schwarzkopf concluded his conversation with the Iraqi generals by exchanging salutes and comradely handshakes.

For Saddam Hussein, Schwarzkopf's magnanimity came as a welcome, if wholly unearned gift. The helicopters alone proved invaluable. At the very moment when Saddam's hold on power was most precarious here was another asset employed in his vicious campaign to suppress internal opposition. Yet even more important to the Iraqi dictator was Schwarzkopf's tacit admission that the United States had no interest in interfering in Iraq's internal affairs. Safwan assured Saddam that he need not worry about an externally mounted challenge to his continued rule.

Finally there is the charge against Powell. Here matters cross fully from the operational realm into the arena of politics. In Powell's hierarchy of aims, one priority outranked all others: as the United States military's senior serving officer, he was determined that nothing bring into disrepute the institution over which he exercised stewardship. When it came to war termination, the JCS chairman with his own agenda complementing Schwarzkopf's, served in effect as the CENTCOM commander's enabler.

When the Persian Gulf crisis erupted in August 1990, Powell had supported the deployment of United States forces to defend Saudi Arabia but evinced little enthusiasm for liberating Kuwait by force, preferring instead to rely on economic sanctions to pry Saddam Hussein out.[22] Although Powell lost that argument, he remained intent on doing everything possible to preclude United States forces from being drawn into anything remotely resembling another Vietnam.

The design of Operation Desert Storm reflected Powell's own preferences for how the United States ought to wage war. Risk avoidance was a priority. The mission, therefore, was specific, concrete, and narrowly drawn with Powell's own statement of purpose as a model of economy. "Our strategy to go after this army is very, very simple," he announced at a press conference. "First we're going to cut it off and then we're going to kill it."[23] In pursuit of that aim, the United States assembled a broad allied coalition and deployed a combat force of overwhelming strength. Deliberation rather than daring defined the spirit of the enterprise, as illustrated by the weeks of bombing that preceded the launch of the ground offensive. Once hostilities commenced, Powell worked hard to guarantee Schwarzkopf complete freedom of action, insulating him from the sort of meddling by high ranking civilian officials that had ostensibly made such a hash of Vietnam.

All of these views put Powell in Schwarzkopf's corner when it came to hastening an end to hostilities. Although aware that coalition forces had not in fact "killed" the Iraqi Army, the JCS chairman nonetheless urged a prompt and unilateral end to hostilities. "There was no need to fight a battle of annihilation," he argued.[24] Although Powell himself believed "that Saddam would likely survive the war," that was no reason to prolong the fighting.[25]

Schwarzkopf had shattered the Iraqi defenses and put Saddam's legions to flight. To give the appearance of piling on was unseemly.[26]

Largely due to Powell's efforts, generals and not politicians determined the precise terms that concluded the Persian Gulf War of 1990-1991. President Bush "had promised the American people that Desert Storm would not become a Persian Gulf Vietnam," Powell wrote in his memoirs "and he kept his promise."[27] The JCS chairman contributed mightily to ensuring that outcome. For Powell, precluding Desert Storm from becoming another Vietnam had ranked as a paramount objective. Based on that criterion, he and Schwarzkopf had collaborated to achieve a rousing success.

Setting aside his own initial misgivings, President Bush himself signed onto the proposition that something truly profound had occurred in the desert. Asked at a press conference on 1 March 1991 if Operation Desert Storm presaged a new era of United States military interventionism, the president demurred:

> I think because of what has happened, we won't have to use United States forces around the world. I think when we say something that is objectively correct, like don't take over a neighbor or you're going to bear some responsibility, people are going to listen. So, I look at the opposite. I say that what our troops have done over there will not only enhance the peace but reduce the risk that their successors have to go into battle someplace.[28]

Bush expected Desert Storm to create the foundation for "a new world order." The triumph over Saddam Hussein, enhancing the authority and influence of the United States, especially in the Muslim world, had created opportunities to take on other problems. Heading the list, the president believed, was the Arab-Israeli conflict. As a mechanism to advance the cause of global peace and harmony, the One Hundred Hour War proved a total bust. Apart from restoring Kuwaiti sovereignty, Operation Desert Storm solved remarkably little. With a defiant Saddam Hussein still hunkering down in Baghdad, the security of the Gulf itself remained uncertain. The victory achieved in the desert served as little more than a way station, paving the way for a much larger and more protracted conflict.

Recommended Reading

The most insightful and most richly documented history of Operation Desert Storm during its ground phase is Richard Swain, "Lucky War: Third Army in Desert Storm," (Fort Leavenworth, Kansas, 1994). Important journalistic accounts include Rick Atkinson, "Crusade: The Untold Story of the Persian Gulf War," (New York, 1993) and Michael R. Gordon and Bernard E. Trainor, "The Generals' War: The Inside Story of the Conflict in the Gulf," (New York, 1994).

Andrew J. Bacevich is a professor of history and international relations at Boston University. His most recent book is "Washington Rules: America's Path to Permanent War," (2010).

Dr. Bacevich did not attend the conference, but did submit this paper.

Endnotes

1. The briefing is available at http://www.youtube.com/watch?v=7BaSwaBPg6M.

2. Richard M. Swain, "Lucky War:" Third Army in Desert Storm," (Fort Leavenworth, Kansas, 1994), p. 284.

3. Michael R. Gordon and Bernard E. Trainor, "The Generals' War: The Inside Story of the Conflict in the Gulf," (New York, 1994), p. 417.

4. Rick Atkinson, "Crusade: The Untold Story of the Persian Gulf War," (New York, 1993), p. 471.

5. George Bush and Brent Scowcroft, "A World Transformed," (New York, 1998), pp. 484-485.

6. H. Norman Schwarzkopf, "It Doesn't Take a Hero," (New York, 1992), p. 468.

7. Schwarzkopf, p. 469.

8. Powell, "My American Journey," p. 521.

9. Powell, "My American Journey," p. 521.

10. George H. W. Bush, "Address on the End of the Gulf War," (February 27, 1991), http://millercenter.org/scripps/archive/speeches/detail/5530.

11. Bush and Scowcroft, "A World Transformed," pp, 486-487.

12. Gordon and Trainor, "The Generals' War," p. 429.

13. Powell, *My American Journey,* pp. 518, 523; Gordon and Trainor, *The Generals' War,* p. 419; Atkinson, *Crusade,* pp. 405-407, 426-427.

14. Gordon and Trainor, *The Generals' War,* p. 431.

15. Schwarzkopf, "It Doesn't Take a Hero," p. 475.

16. Schwarzkopf, "It Doesn't Take a Hero," p. 480.

17. Schwarzkopf, "It Doesn't Take a Hero," p. 479.

18. Schwarzkopf, "It Doesn't Take a Hero," p. 483.

19. Schwarzkopf, "It Doesn't Take a Hero," p. 483.

20. Schwarzkopf, "It Doesn't Take a Hero," p. 488.

21. Schwarzkopf, "It Doesn't Take a Hero," p. 489.

22. Bob Woodward, "The Commanders," (New York, 1991). Powell's reluctance to use force is a recurring theme of this book, which recounts the Persian Gulf crisis up to the eve of Operation Desert Storm.

23. Dan Balz and Rick Atkinson, "Powell Vows to Isolate Iraqi Army and 'Kill It'," *Washington Post* (January 24, 1991).

24. Powell, "My American Journey," p. 523.

25. Powell, "My American Journey," p. 523.

26. Atkinson, "Crusade," p. 471.

27. Powell, "My American Journey," p. 526.

28. "The President's Press Conference on the Persian Gulf Conflict," (March 1, 1991), is at http://www.presidency.ucsb.edu/ws/index.php?pid=19352.

Session 4
Questions and Answers

Colonel Matthew Moten

George has said a great deal about destroying the Reagan myth, Gian has done his best to explode the better war myth and Con has done his best to build the airpower myth. So with that, I would throw the floor open to questions. Once again, if you have a question to ask, if you'd make your way over to our lonely microphone or I will just have to talk. Let's try to do this the way General McMaster wanted to do it. Let's ask a couple of questions in a row and I'll ask our trusty participants to furiously take notes and then we'll answer.

Question

We've heard a lot lately about the idea of a war of perceptions. I was wondering if the panelists would address the issue of to what extent do the kinds of wars we've been talking about so far differ from what some people say is a new type of war today; counterinsurgency, in terms of what causes an end? Is it a perception on the part of some of the combatants or both sets of combatants, they converge on a perception that the war has to end? Is it a group of objective factors that keen analysts on each side decide okay, war's up? I missed the two panels in the morning. I know there's been some interesting comments on the end of World War II in the panel that we just heard but anything you can say on that subject, the role of perceptions.

At the beginning of your panel, Colonel Moten identified 1945 as a shift in the wars we had been fighting. I think the panel has identified a component of this shift being the United States now undertaking wars on behalf of or in protection of our proxies and allies whether it be Kosovo, Kuwait, Vietnam and I was wondering, to tie this panel back into the first one, what effect do you think this component of our new wars, if we put it that way, has had on our strategic decision making, when we are no longer fighting just for our national honor but also the honor and sometimes lives of our allies.

This question was originally just for Dr. Crane but listening to it, I think it's applicable to all three. In Dr. Crane's paper, he talked about President Eisenhower's threat to escalate the war if the peace talks did not continue or did not progress; I think is what you said. This is applicable to all three. I don't want to draw lessons of necessarily explicitly applicable but I'm curious if all three of you could talk about the threat to escalate a war, in each of your particular situations, and what led the President at that time, to make that threat.

Dr. George Herring

Do you want to deal with them individually? Eisenhower's threat is interesting because the perception is, among a lot of people in the national security establishment after that that a clear threat was made and that as a result of that clear threat, the Chinese gave in or agreed to end the war, and of course the North Koreans do the same thing. Most of the historians who have written on this, and Con may want to elaborate pro or con, conclude that the threat, if it was ever delivered, was at best vague, that it may not have gotten to the Chinese and that therefore, it's a real stretch to argue that it's the decisive thing in ending the Korean War. As Con pointed out, it's the death of Stalin. China's determination for its own reasons, that it couldn't unify Korea and therefore, somewhere, somehow, it had to get out of it but interestingly, pushing over into Gian's area, Nixon firmly believed that the threat had been delivered in 1953 and it had been the decisive factor and when he takes office in 1969, his so called "madman strategy," the idea of delivering through the Soviet Union, loud and firm threats that if something doesn't happen by 1 November, my memory says, that there could be huge, forceful consequences; the only possible conclusion you could draw with nuclear weapons and of course these threats are delivered very clearly in this case and they don't work. So in a very specific sense, I think this carries over at least through Nixon and maybe beyond that, I don't know. You may want to follow up.

Dr. Conrad Crane

I'll try to tie them together a bit. Let's start with the perceptions part. What happens in Korea is basically, and this happens in Iraq to some extent as well, is both sides get tired of fighting. People were getting worn down. There's an argument that you really can't solve any kind of simple strife until everybody is ready to accept some kind of peaceful solution. When you write about peacekeeping stuff, they always talk about sometimes you've got to let both sides fight it out for a while until they're ready to have a referee step into the middle. What happens in Korea by 1953 is that both sides are just tired of the bloodshed and there's dissent at home. People are kind of dissatisfied, it doesn't seem like they're going anywhere.

There's a couple of ways you can go on this. This goes back to the escalation question. When the 18 Rangers are killed in Mogadishu, there are two ways we could have gone with that and President Clinton decides to pull back but he could also have gone on television that night and told the American People, "You know, we just lost 18 Rangers today, I'm going to turn Mogadishu into a parking lot," and the public would have supported that. The problem is and maybe George or somebody else might comment on the way the American political system tends to work in any of these wars, is you've got kind of show some kind of progress. Americans, it's not that we're casually averse. It's just that Americans, if we're expending blood and treasure, Americans want to see some progress, so your choices become, I'm either going to ratchet things up or I'm going to pull back, the status quo won't keep. So it tends to force decision makers into the threat to escalate, it seems to me.

Now what happens in Korea even though there's no evidence the nuclear threat gets there, is there is so much other evidence that we're ready to escalate. There are F-86s going across the Yalu River every day. A lot of the Chinese believe the biological warfare accusations, that we're now doing biological warfare. There are rumors floating around and again, part of it is, it's a self-created image. Eisenhower is a general. He's portrayed in the communist press as a war-mongering general. Well he's been elected and then they tend to believe their own rhetoric; wow this guy is a general from World War II of course he's going to threaten to escalate. So there are a lot of factors that play in there. Again, escalation is a tool. The threat of escalation is something that's part of your bargaining tools that you've got when you're trying to do any kind of these negotiations. So it's not uncommon. You've got a hammer which is oftentimes what you need to get people to come over. Even in counterinsurgency which your results are coming out of, it's a combination of carrots and sticks; it's neither one nor the other.

The one thing I'll throw out on the fighting for allies comment is by the end of the Cold War, the deployment of American Military Forces during the Clinton years goes up 500 percent. Then I'll pass it on to who else wants to handle this menagerie of questions.

Dr. George Herring

You mean a number of times.

Dr. Conrad Crane

We start dealing with a lot more people, the lid is taken off. It's not numbers; it is actually the number of small scale contingencies we get involved in goes up 500 percent. We're just getting involved with more things, and that tends to strain the American Military before 9-11 because of these involvements.

When I was teaching on the faculty here in the 1990s, I had a bunch of young Majors, some of them in the audience today, who are no longer Majors, who decided they were going to take up a collection to rebuild the Soviet Empire because the war was much simpler when they were out there. Of course, now what do we have today? We have the Soviet Empire reasserting and all these other problems too.

Dr. George Herring

There are a couple of things about perceptions. I think the Cold War, and I deal with this in the paper, had no time to do it today. The Cold War is built on a lot of things. It's built on the circumstances at the end of World War II. If you blame one individual for the Cold War, blame Hitler, because it's the destruction of Europe that leaves the Soviet Union and the United States in position to be antagonistic. You can blame it on ideology but from the beginning, all the way through, perceptions and misperceptions are so important. They're very important in 1947, 1948, and 1949 when we are convinced that Stalin has aims to overrun Western Europe, and they are convinced that we are absolutely, with the Marshall Plan and other things, were beginning to try to undermine their position in Eastern Europe. The beginning of the Korean War is huge. Stalin was absolutely convinced the United States would not respond. We had done a whole lot of things that made it look that way. You can go on and on. It's a very important factor in Cold War conflicts from the beginning on through.

I haven't really thought at length, about the way these changed. One of the interesting changes that takes place in Reagan's mind, is this realization which one would think would be obvious but to Cold War era, maybe it wasn't, was that the Soviets were as concerned about their security as we were, that they were terrified of the possibility of nuclear war, as in some ways we were. Now you remember that famous speech where he talks about, I can't remember the names but John and Sally and Ivan and Anya would sit down and maybe they could solve all the world's problems because basically, we're not that different. So that's important. Gorbachev certainly brings to his task, a greater breadth of perspective and perception than his predecessors had. That's not saying a lot but he had traveled outside of the Soviet Union, he had seen Western Europe. He had seen how much better off they were, how much better they lived, and that was a real eye opener, because he had been led to believe, by propaganda, that things were different. So there are things that are operating to change perceptions. I don't know how far you can go with that.

From 1945 on, I take a little different slant on that. One of the things that blew me away in doing the big book on American foreign relations from 1776 to 2008 was how incredibly successful the United States was up to 1945. There are failures sure, but it's a record of success that is unparalleled and then you can compare that with at best, a mixed record; Korea, Vietnam, Cold War, sure but all kinds of perceived failures. The obvious thing, there are a whole lot of things dealing with the pre-1945 success, including a whole lot of luck in the 18th and 19th century. The thing after 1945 is that goals come to be attached to happenings in other countries. So the first big failure, I mean the first mammoth failure in 1949, the fall of China, was a real shock to the American psyche. The idea was who lost China? Meaning which American or group of Americans lost China, as though China had ever been. So more and more, I would argue that success and failure depends as much on conditions in individual countries, local circumstances, as it does on what we do or don't do. When our goals become so much attached to things in other countries that have their own unique histories and cultures, then we're no longer the masters of our fate, I think, in the way that we were before 1945. That's sort of a different direction.

Colonel Gian Gentile

I'll just take a quick stab, I think, and riffing off some of the things that Con and George have said. This war of perception and what comes together to bring war to an end. Roger Spiller, as I just reread his concluding essay in the volume, and he says, you know, something like most of the time wars come to an end because both sides or how ever many sides, sort of agree to bring about an end to the war and that's certainly the case for the ending of the war for the United States in Vietnam, where in late 1972, especially as I said in my talk, after the Easter Offensive, it came to be in the interests of both the North Vietnamese and the United States, to come to a negotiated settlement and to bring about an American withdrawal from Vietnam. So it is the case where two sides come together to agree to end the war. However, sometimes in war, wars end because of the application of direct military force. As I was just thinking about the question and listening to George and Con, I mean the last two years of the war in Vietnam, between the Vietnamese, actually is in some ways what Chip was talking about this morning, after the Mexican War. Little is often told about the guerrilla war that happens after the war ends. There's very little really done significantly on the last two years in 1974 and 1975. There was a lot of fighting, especially in 1975 beginning in January, and the war comes to an end in April of 1975 for the Vietnamese people, by a military offensive by the North Vietnamese combined with their South Vietnamese communist allies.

In John Lynn's chapter in "Warfare in the Western World," on the French Revolution, he's got this really striking sentence that I always like reading and reading, and he says, the Battle of Fleurus in 1794, correct me if I'm wrong, was one of the most decisive battles in world history. I think in some ways, the final offensive that the North Vietnamese conducted against South Vietnam, was also one of the most decisive battles in history, and it was produced by military force and then this is an interesting question on escalation. I wrote about the last few years in Vietnam but in order to get there, you have to think about the first years, 1965 to 1968 and this notion of escalation, first with Rolling Thunder, the idea that we'll bomb just above the 17th Parallel and if they don't do what we want, then we'll bomb to the 18th and then we'll just keep getting progressively farther and farther. We'll add sequentially and progressively, more American troops into South Vietnam. It was really based on a notion of procedure and that if you follow a certain set of procedures in war, then the enemy will act in certain predictable ways. I think the insiders, or the lesson to draw from that, is how we think about applying military force today, especially like in Afghanistan. The whole theory and practice of counterinsurgency is also based on the notion of doing a set of procedures right, and that will produce a certain effect on the enemy because our theory tells us that it should and so in that sense, I think you can draw some insights from Vietnam and the notion of escalation.

Colonel Matthew Moten

We've got time for more questions and while you're making your way to the microphone, I'd just make this point, that the verb, to escalate, implies a certain speed of action that did not exist prior to 1945, in terms of your ability to apply military power. It seems to me that you wouldn't think about that kind of speed, that kind of power, absent aircraft and add to them, the possibility of atomic or nuclear weapons. We probably would have used a different verb prior to that time, for the way one would add more military power to a conflict.

Dr. Conrad Crane

I have just one comment on Korea, the ultimate escalation. If the peace talks had broken down in the summer of 1953, the United States would go to exercise what was called Operations Plan 8-52 and it was actually talked about at national security meetings and it was on the table and it was going to be exercised if the peace talks broke down and that would involve the dropping of between 480 and 620 nuclear weapons on North Korea and China. So that would have been escalation.

Question

Matt, the answer to your question is not to escalate but to retaliate. In pre-modern to early modern context, you change the nature of the violence you're using. So you start executing prisoners, you start doing reprisals in the modern terms. So that would be your pre modern escalation.

My question is very specific for George. I'm curious. You were alluding to it I think but I'm curious and I've always been curious and you're the person to ask I guess. What role do you think the Able Archer scare had on Reagan?

Dr. George Herring

I didn't mention this. How many of you remember the television film called "The Day After?" Yeah, wow. You won't get that among students today. Lawrence, Kansas. That happened, what that showed in the fall of 1983 and Reagan saw it and was deeply moved by it. It scared a lot of people because the context is a time when the nuclear negotiations have broken down, when tensions have escalated, there's that word again, to a point as intent as any sense, October of 1962. It's in a time when the possibility of nuclear war seems to be gaining ground and it's in this condition that a Korean airliner is inadvertently shot down by Soviets, all of these things are happening and it's in this context that NATO launches an exercise called Able Archer. The purpose of this is (1) to test readiness for nuclear war, and (2) to gage the Soviet reactions. Apparently, from what we know, the Soviets took Able Archer very, very, very seriously, jacked up their defense readiness and there was a real sense, in the Soviet Union, that nuclear war was a real possibility. There's an episode that occurs while this is going on, that has not been absolutely validated. At one point, Soviet defense installations actually thought they saw missiles coming toward the Soviet Union and there was talk of the possibility of readying missiles to be fired once this was absolutely confirmed, and a Red Army Colonel, if this is all true, is one of the unspoken heroes of the Cold War intervenes and says, "Look, this doesn't make sense. I don't really believe missiles are incoming, let's stop the process right here."

So I think these things all happen about the same time. I think this is the sort of the culmination of what I call the war scare of 1983 which I think leads people on both sides, to reassess the direction they're going. Not all but some people, to reassess the direction they're going and to think about trying to calm tensions and look towards negotiations.

Question

Another question I wrote down because I thought I was going to forget for a second. What is the difference since 1945, toward the way we actually begin wars? I know this is about termination of war but in the postwar period, we actually really are more ambiguous about the way we start wars, even taking into account, the Gulf of Tonkin Resolution. We don't really declare war any more in a formal sense. I mean, there tends to be more congressional oversight these days but Congress actually tends to step back. So I wonder if the ways we're beginning wars now differently since say 1950, is in any way, changing the space in which you have to operate, the way you end wars. It just strikes me is that people are sort of buying into wars but they're actually not buying into wars at the same stage, and things are becoming I think, more ambiguous and I think much more fuzzy than they are now but things are becoming more fuzzy it seems to me, from that standpoint. Professor Herring gets to this in his book I think but it's an important question.

Dr. Conrad Crane

Again, the people at the time knew that when President Truman declares police action in Korea and takes certain actions on his own, everybody understood that something had changed and that starts it and we see of course, the changes through Tonkin and up to today. Definitely, it's a different dynamic, it's changed the rules.

Dr. George Herring

There are numerous examples, Jefferson's dispatch of ships to the Middle East and North Africa, being the first if not one of the first. There is something different. I think that the way Mac talked about this earlier this afternoon. The way that Congress had hamstrung the Executive in dealing with the situations in the mid and late 1930s, I think made it easier to argue two things. One is the speed with which things happen in the nuclear age. Coming out of World War II, of course, you remember Pearl Harbor vividly, and then they think well, look at the weapons that people will have now or will have soon, and the speed with which things can happen and this "conventional wisdom," where we don't have time for

Congress to sit around and debate, and there was sort of a consensus, at least until Gulf of Tonkin or shortly thereafter, that the Executive needed certain room to maneuver to protect the national security.

Dr. Conrad Crane

Also, I would recommend to you, Mike Ignatieff's book, "Virtual War." We've also had a different impression of what military force is, that now it's, you know in the 1990s, you have cruise missile diplomacy. It's a lot easier to fire a cruise missile into a factory than it is to go through all the trouble of sending a diplomatic note and doing the rest of that.

Colonel Gian Gentile

Just a quick point from one of the earlier panels this morning is that it was mentioned the Petraeus Doctrine and Admiral Mullen. Recently, Admiral Mullen came out with, when he gave his speech at Kansas State last month, one of the things that didn't really catch many folks' eyes but he said that now, that his experiences has taught him that military force shouldn't necessarily be seen as a last resort but now as a first resort which I think is also tied to a very different way of conceiving war and how the conditions, at least by perception, have changed which draws on the whole Rupert Smith argument that wars are fought amongst the people, and so then the way to affect a certain situation in a favorable way is to get there early and often, with the hope that military force will be able to shape things the way you want.

Question

Is there time for more questions?

Colonel Matthew Moten

Please Cliff, go ahead.

Question

As I've been listening to these three papers and reflecting back on the ones in the morning, it seems to me that it's fairly common in warfare, perhaps because of the inherent superiority of the defense, for wars to reach a position in which neither side can win an outright military victory and then at that point, it clearly is in both sides' interests, in a sort of a game theory way, to come to a resolution of some sort or another and the question is, where along that spectrum and when, are you going to come to your resolutions.

It was pointed out in the sessions this morning, rather strongly I think, that if you push somebody to the point of violating their national honor, then even if it's one of those stalemate situations where they can't win, they will keep fighting and a logical continuation of that thought would be that one of the keys to successful war termination, unless it's a war that intends to end in complete military victory, is to know where the boundaries of your enemy's national honor are and not to push them past it and so I would ask, particularly to George, do you think that one of the reasons for the successful conclusion of the Cold War was President Reagan's ability to appreciate the importance of not pushing the Soviets past what they could convincingly portray as peace with honor.

Gian, do you think that the North Vietnamese were successful in terminating their war, because they were wise enough to recognize that you had to at least give Nixon peace with honor and that maybe had they not done that, could actually still have lost the war.

Colonel Gian Gentile

I think that by and large, the record shows that the Vietnamese, both South Vietnamese, the insurgency, the communist-led insurgency in the south, and the North Vietnamese, I think through the war had a stronger strategy because they had a clear and definite war aim that really, at least within the confines of the war in Vietnam, was a total war aim. They were looking for unification of the country, whereas it becomes clear after the Tet Offensive, that America's aims in Vietnam are limited. So I guess you're used to the word honor Cliff. I would turn that into this notion of war aims and what General Dempsey was talking about this morning and that Roger also commented on and Colonel Moten has also mentioned that aims in war often change. Sometimes they don't and in the Vietnam War, at least for the Vietnamese, the North Vietnamese, and the Vietnamese communists, their war aim stayed pretty much the same throughout and so yeah, I think that's right. I mean the key element of strategy, at least on the part of the United States, is to not only understand ourselves but understand our enemy as I conclude in my essay, the potential of the enemy, and then assess and come up with an appropriate strategy that takes those things into account.

Dr. George Herring

JFK, yes, he was very sensitive in the missile crisis. Very cognizant of the pressures that Khrushchev was under and from talking with people like Llewellyn Thompson and other Soviet experts, very sensitive to Khrushchev's needs. I think there was a perception that he was in a delicate position with the hawks in his own government and if you pushed him too far, heaven knows what could happen.

As to Reagan, the answer is yes and no. In some areas, Reagan, certainly as I said earlier, he was very sensitive to the Soviets' sense of their security and recognized that, I think in ways that others hadn't before him. In a couple of areas, he was a tough negotiator. He was absolutely adamant on Star Wars. Star Wars was discussed at the famous Iceland Summit, through an incredible process and an incredible weekend, that came up with almost to the point of saying; "You know we'll eliminate all nuclear weapons in short order" the only thing standing in the way was Star Wars, the laser-based defense system. Gorbachev insisted that this be confined to the laboratory and Reagan said absolutely no He wanted to push ahead with it. It was only after Sakharov and other Soviet scientists, persuaded Gorbachev that well, maybe Star Wars wasn't really scientifically feasible, that Gorbachev finally said, "Okay, we'll forget about Star Wars."

On Afghanistan, Gorbachev begged Reagan to give him some help in getting out of Afghanistan. Almost as soon as he takes office, he knows already that it's what he calls a bleeding wound and we've got to find a way to get out without losing too much face and one way is to get the United States to make an agreement that it will stop supplying the insurgents but Reagan won't go for it. I mean in one sense, the United States may have delayed the Soviet Union getting out of Afghanistan and, of course, one of the huge unintended consequences there was the continued arming and supporting of folks who later came to be problems for us. So Reagan, there were limits, and on those two issues at least, he was absolutely not the least bit sensitive to Gorbachev's concerns.

Comments

I have a couple comments. First is reading the material around the negotiation of Panmunjom that goes on in 1951 and 1953. There's a lot of learning that goes on. We had kind of forgotten how to do that, from what we had done in World War II, where you had to beat an enemy. It's interesting, the diplomatic exchanges, where you kind of relearn the art of negotiating with a very tough opponent that was much better prepared than we were.

I'll make this point. I'll say something about political scientists. If you get into the literature on coercive diplomacy, where there's a lot of it out there and you know what effects based operations really were, coercive diplomacy without the diplomacy, if you really look at how it was designed. What it really tells you is that you're never really quite sure why the other side gives in. You can try all the theory you want, in all the history you want but in most of these cases, we really don't know why people make the decisions they do. That's why it's very dangerous to try to take a lot of lessons from a lot of these incidents.

Colonel Matthew Moten

As we have been looking at this business of war termination, as we said at the outset, there's really a dearth of literature about this, especially in history. One of the things that we have hoped to do is to fill in that gap. The only book that we've been able to come up with that looks at war termination from a historical standpoint is Fred Ikle's "Every War Must End." It's a very good little primer on war termination and I recommend it to you, but I would say that every conference must end and if you could look at all of your eyelids right now, you'd understand why I'm in a hurry to do that.

I want to thank a few people before we finish. First, it was hugely helpful to have General Dempsey and General McMaster here this morning. I wasn't kidding when I said that General Dempsey was the driving force behind this effort. He has really been stalwart in that.

I want to thank the folks who have helped put on this conference and have done all of the legwork because I've been in Chapel Hill, North Carolina, and I haven't done anything. I really appreciate the efforts of Lieutenant Colonel Greg Daddis, Major Josh Bradley, Major Andy Whitford, and Professor Antonio Thompson. Could we have a round of applause for those folks?

I have had a tremendous partner in this entire enterprise, Mr. Mike Starry from Training and Doctrine Command. He and I have got the scars to prove that we have been in the bureaucratic and legal wars to make this kind of thing happen between two headquarters and who knows what else we've probably barely escaped prison by trying to do. Mike, you have been a tremendous partner and you have shown immense patience. I know I almost worked you completely down at one point and I appreciate all that you've done. Thanks Mike. With that, I will try to find a gavel and adjourn this meeting.

Interview

Colonel Matthew Moten

Interviewer

Tell me the origins of the war termination project, how you came up with the idea, and then where it went from there.

Colonel Matthew Moten

About a year ago, General Martin Dempsey, who's the commanding general of Training and Doctrine Command (TRADOC), had an idea to edit an old book called "America's First Battles," which was written about 25 years ago. It was a collection of essays talking about the first battle of every American war.

Interviewer

It's a very important book, right?

Colonel Matthew Moten

It's used here at West Point. It's used in a number of different places.

Interviewer

Who's the editor of that book?

Colonel Matthew Moten

Two fellows by the name of Heller and Stofft, and they began with the American Revolution and went as far as Vietnam, looking at the first battles of every one of those wars. The book was meant to be an object lesson about the dangers of unpreparedness for war. They wrote it at the tactical level and talked a great deal about the problems of getting into war, the problems of mobilizing for war, and then—as often as not having a relatively untrained force—the cost in blood and treasure of that first battle.

We discussed this a bit and determined 25 years later, unpreparedness is not our problem in the American military. We are six and seven and now eight years deep into two different wars and our problem is not so much that we're not ready. We're plenty ready. We're a very combat hardened and experienced force. Our problem now is one of stamina and how do we continue to sustain the effort for two wars, one of which is now the longest war in American history. We decided rather than editing that book, we would think about putting together a conference that would look at the other end of warfare. Rather than looking at the beginning of war, we would look at the end of war and how America's wars have ended. So we decided together, in very much the way that other project did, to get some of the best historians in America to write essays in topics of their own expertise and to put these together in a package that eventually ended in this conference here at West Point.

Interviewer

What surprised you most about what came out of that work? Did you say, "Wow, I had no idea?"

Colonel Matthew Moten

Well, I guess there were two things that surprised me. One is that there was a pretty sharp breakpoint after the end of World War II, at the beginning of the Cold War, when we changed the way we thought about how wars could end and should end. Up until World War II, we and most people and nations, had thought about war as something that one enters into for a particular purpose and then you attempt to win the war. Your object is victory, however defined and paradoxically, after the bombing of Hiroshima and Nagasaki, after the unleashing of the nuclear genie, we entered into a period around the globe of relatively limited war. America, which has this exalted status as the most powerful nation on earth—shared for a long time with the Soviet Union but nonetheless, one of the most powerful nations that had ever existed—found itself in a situation where it couldn't use the immensity of that power because we didn't want war to grow, to expand to the point that it logically could with these awful weapons. So we found ourselves limiting our aims, our objectives, our methods, and we stopped talking about victory, and started talking about something different, whether that would be ending wars, the language of deterrence came into vogue. We talked about preventing wars and since then, except for the first Gulf War in Iraq, it would be hard to say that we have really ended a war with something that looked like an old fashioned victory.

Interviewer

That change strikes me as historic, not simply historic for American experience but historic for the experience of humankind, right? War has been with history since the beginning of history and has always seemed to have victory as its goal, but this is an anomaly in history of the world, isn't it?

Colonel Matthew Moten

I think it is. I would be hard pressed to think of another nation, certainly another nation as powerful as ours is today, that has chosen to limit what it can do with military power, or better stated, what it should do with military power. The other great powers of the earth from Rome to Spain to Great Britain, in the 19th century, were far less self limiting. Part of that is because of the fear that we all experienced with the advent of nuclear weapons. The possibility for human beings literally to incinerate the earth is a very important part of that change in the way we thought, but it meant that having that strength, having that capability, Americans and American leaders wanted to make sure that they never got to the point of having to use it again. I think America still bears a mark of remorse, not to say guilt, for being the only nation on earth ever to have used atomic weapons.

Interviewer

Talk to me about how you chose the historians and the breadth of work that they delivered.

Colonel Matthew Moten

Well, this was an extraordinary opportunity for me to be associated with these people. After we decided what the scope of the book was going to be, Roger Spiller and Joe

Glatthaar, and I were all in on the beginning of this book. We talked first about which essays we would like to have, which is to say which wars we would like to cover. Then we went through an all-star list of the best American military historians, the people who were most expert in those wars. We began calling them, and we had a depth chart and decided that we would try to get some of our top draft picks first and we found that when you get someone like Gerhard Weinberg to sign on to write a chapter about World War II and you get "Mac" Coffman to sign on to write a chapter about World War I, the next phone call gets a little bit easier. When I'm able to say to somebody, well, I've got Weinberg to do World War II, and I've got Coffman to do World War I and we think you're the guy to do this chapter, what you're saying to them is you're in very good company. We think that you're at the top of your field in American military history. I found that people began to say "yes" rather quickly and so we were able to assemble a very good team.

Interviewer

Well, the better historians usually will pause and say, "Do I have any particular insights into this topic before they write about something" so they can feel that they delivered original work. What were some of the insights that they did deliver to this project? You talk about what surprised you overall about it but what did you get from Gerhard Weinberg or from Roger Spiller or Brian Linn or the others?

Colonel Matthew Moten

Well, I guess although we didn't ask our authors of individual essays to generalize about the nature of how war ends, we did find that in the aggregate, we were able to reach some generalizations and probably the most important contribution that this book is going to make is a new departure in military theory. Roger Spiller has been thinking about these things for very many years. As he read the essays, he began to tease out what we call six propositions about the nature of how wars end. I'll give you one example. First, it shouldn't be surprising to anybody that the war aims that a nation has going into a war will change as the war progresses. War tends to take on a life of its own and where one intended to be at the beginning of a war is rarely, if ever, where one ends up.

Interviewer

This is a constant frustration of generals, in particular, with respect to teaching politicians about that. Isn't that right? We have historical examples of politicians who set out, perhaps a little more aggressively, toward those set of war aims thinking that they're achievable and that those in uniform are likely to say war is chaos, war is the unpredictable, we can try as much as we can to control it but expect the unfamiliar, expect to be surprised.

Colonel Matthew Moten

There's that aspect, and there's also the aspect that political leaders tend to want to be a little bit less precise about what their war aims are. I don't know that it's so much that the generals have to teach them that war is going to be unpredictable, but political leaders want their war aims to be somewhat malleable so that as the war goes on and as time goes on, they may be able to adjust what it is that they're trying to achieve.

Interviewer

Give me an example. Tell me one of the wars that you chose and how the interaction between the politicians and the generals went on this subject.

Colonel Matthew Moten

Well, in the Mexican War, for example, it was pretty clear I think that President James K. Polk went to war for reasons that were not entirely legitimate. He wanted to annex the state of Texas and that was plain, and he made that plain. What he didn't make plain to anybody except his inner circle was that he also wanted to take what are now the states of New Mexico, Arizona, and California and he kept that somewhat hidden under the table. A lot of people began to suspect it and it made it difficult for General Zachary Taylor and General Winfield Scott to conduct their campaigns in a way that was in accord with administration policy when that administration policy was not well defined, or at least not well pronounced. Everyone had their suspicions, and Winfield Scott, at least, came to grief at the end, because he was relieved after he had achieved victory in the final campaign of the Mexican War because he had run afoul of President Polk politically.

Another example that's probably a happier example, at least in terms of victory on the Americans' part is that President Lincoln went into the Civil War with the single aim of preserving the Union. He had no expressed intent to destroy the institution of slavery as he went into the war, and he maintained that war aim of preserving the Union, of reuniting the states. Even though he eventually decided that he had to add to his policy with the Emancipation Proclamation, which was the end of slavery in those parts of the Confederate States that were still in rebellion, and it was essentially the death knell of slavery if the Union should happen to succeed, as it did.

Interviewer

It was in the spirit of fighting the war that Lincoln created the Emancipation Proclamation, am I right? Otherwise, it would have had to have congressional approval and gone through the whole process.

Colonel Matthew Moten

Yeah, Lincoln, used the Emancipation Proclamation as a war measure, and he thought of it as a war measure and he greatly expanded the powers of the presidency. The debates over the limitation or the abolition of slavery had been going on since the writing of the Constitution and the legislature had never been able to come to any resolution about this, at least a resolution that both sides could accept and interpret it in the same way . . . . Now, Lincoln, as a war president used emancipation as a measure to strike at the South economically and, by extension, militarily as well without going through Congress and without asking for legislative approval of what he had decided to do, because he thought that it would help him win the war, which it did.

Interviewer

Talk to me about the termination of World War II. You spoke about the unleashing of the nuclear genie. Did President Truman know what he was doing when he made that decision? Did he have a choice really?

Colonel Matthew Moten

I'm not sure that anybody truly knew exactly what would happen when those bombs were dropped, or at least when the first bomb was dropped on Hiroshima. Understanding the enormity of that explosion, I think, was beyond most people's understanding except perhaps the scientists who had seen the test explosion in New Mexico. I think Truman knew that he had an extremely powerful weapon, a weapon that was unlike any other that had ever been used, and I think he also understood that it would have a tremendous impact on the thinking of the Japanese political and military leaders. Gerhard Weinberg's essay discusses plans for the United States mainly, but also its allies, to invade the home islands of Japan. Having looked at all of the other campaigns against the Japanese in the Pacific and looking at the advantages that the Japanese would have [had] defending their island home, the casualties on both sides were expected to be horrendous.

Interviewer

What kind of numbers are we talking about?

Colonel Matthew Moten

Oh, 750,000 to a million casualties in that single campaign alone . . . . It's interesting, looking at the choice that Gerhard Weinberg made. When I asked him to write the essay on the war in the Pacific, I had expected that he would look at the dropping of those two atomic weapons as the final campaign, but Gerhard surprised me by writing an essay about the campaign in Okinawa, which was the last land and naval campaign without atomic weapons. What the allies learned in the fighting for Okinawa helped them to understand... the costs...that were associated with the possible invasion of those home islands, and it probably helped them to make the decision to drop those bombs. They hoped to shorten the war.

Interviewer

This is part of the fun of the process of history, right, is to say, "Well, this may have happened, but it happened because this happened and that happened because this happened." You said part of the fun of this project was to look at the ramifications of those last campaigns, what and how they changed history going forward, and that each historian was given the opportunity to look as far forward as he or she may have wanted to. Give me an example of that kind of domino effect of one event leading to another to another to another on a particular war that's covered in this book.

Colonel Matthew Moten

Well, I think probably the best example would . . . the Civil War. That war ended with about as complete a victory as one could imagine. The Union Army vanquished and dispersed the Confederate Army . . . . The Union Army paraded down Pennsylvania Avenue in Washington. It was a complete victory and then the unexpected happened, the unexpected that points to the importance of what we're doing [in this project]. . . . It's not just that you need to win a war. It is how you finish this war that is important and the United States, one could argue, largely because of the assassination of President Lincoln, took its eye off the ball of the post-war occupation and reconstruction of the South that was going to have to happen. It's not so much that it neglected it, but that it went about it in a confused way. Congress and President Lincoln were not in synch with one another about how . . . reconstruction should take place. The United States Army demobilized very quickly so that they were trying to cover millions of square miles of southern territory and to enforce Federal law in states that had recently been in rebellion and they had far too few soldiers and resources to accomplish that.

Interviewer

So let's come back to that question about how wars create these domino effects that how wars end can trigger events successively through generations really.

Colonel Matthew Moten

Unexpected things happen. In the Civil War, for example, there was what looked on paper an almost complete victory, with the Union Army marching down Pennsylvania Avenue for a victory parade. The southern armies had been vanquished and the troops had been dispersed to go back to their homes. But then how you end the war and how you deal with the aftermath of the war turns out to be terribly important. After that parade, the Union Army demobilized and became a small fraction of what it had been during wartime. But still, the job of the post war occupation of the South, and reconstruction, which is to say bringing the southern states back into the fold, was not complete. The United States Army didn't have the resources or the manpower to do that job effectively. . . . Over a period of time . . . resistance to reconstruction and to the social and political change that had been intended by the Lincoln Administration [and] the 13th, 14th, and 15th amendments to the Constitution began. . . . A dozen years after victory had been declared in the Civil War, reconstruction came to an end. The old political leadership in the South returned to power. They enforced racial segregation, Jim Crow laws, and that legacy of what I would call a failed reconstruction continues with us all the way into the 1960s when, in a sense, the Civil War continues with the Civil Rights Movement and the Freedom Riders in Mississippi. One could argue that the racial reconciliation that could have begun in earnest in the aftermath of the Civil War is still playing out today. So the ramifications of not ending a war in as complete or as thorough a fashion as one might can have long lasting consequences well into the future.

Interviewer

It's interesting because when you think about it, sometimes it's the politician's error, sometimes it may be the general's error that keeps a war in a sense, simmering. Think of World War I laying the seed for World War II. Think of the first Persian Gulf War. Some argue, by not going to Bagdad, we invited a second Gulf War, the war in Iraq, more recently. Think of George W. Bush declaring the end of the war in victory, four years before the surge itself, I think it was and certainly one would argue that the insurgency was as big a challenge as the war itself, if not more of a challenge to the American Army, [after he declared] victory. Can you speak to the seesaw effects that go between the politicians and the generals?

Colonel Matthew Moten

One of the things that is a truism but we have found again by working through this project is that wars are a lot easier to get into than they are to get out of. It is important, and I think perhaps one of the object lessons of what we're doing, by trying to provide this scholarship for students of war but also for strategists (generals) and policymakers (presidents), to understand that when one embarks upon this enterprise of warfare, one needs to understand that it is not going to go where you think it is going to go. It will branch out in a number of different scenarios and one needs to think through that very carefully.

As we began the war in Iraq, it was fairly easy to see that America had the military power to invade Iraq and defeat Saddam Hussein's army and to get to the capital and take it in rather short order. In fact, we pared back the forces that we chose to send into Iraq knowing full well that we would be able to do that without much difficulty, and we did. But we did not foresee what would happen when we had achieved that part of the task. We thought of that as the task, not a part of the task, and when I say we, I'm talking about the policymakers and their advisors in the . . . Bush Administration . . . . On 1 May 2003, two months into this war, Bush stood before a banner that said "Mission Accomplished" on the deck of the USS Abraham Lincoln and expressed the thought that we had achieved what we had set out to achieve. More than seven years later, we are still in Iraq dealing with an insurgency, dealing with what had been a civil war, and we had failed to imagine what would happen when we unleashed the forces within Iraq that had been oppressed and kept down for so long by Saddam Hussein. It was a failure of imagination.

Interviewer

It seems like there's also something to be said for the fact that generals, or the army, understand war to end at a certain point and then it's the politicians' game going forward. Am I right?

Colonel Matthew Moten

I wouldn't agree with that.

Interviewer

Maintaining the peace is different than waging the war. This is what I mean to say.

Colonel Matthew Moten

It is important. I think that there is an archaic notion. Cordell Hull expressed this at the beginning of World War II as the negotiations were breaking down with the Japanese—and I won't say this exactly verbatim but he essentially said to the War Department—"I've done all I can. Negotiations have failed. It's now in your hands." It's important for policymakers, diplomats, generals, and strategists to be involved with one another in assessment and plan making, in peace time as well as in war. If there is seen to be this bright red line between policy on the one hand and strategy on the other, between war on the one hand and peace on the other, we will tend to have a fumbling of responsibility at the highest levels of government. It will cause us to have the sorts of difficulties that you mentioned earlier, for example, with the Treaty of Versailles at the end of World War I. Again, an example of an almost complete victory by the allies over the Germans and then a peace treaty that was largely divorced from clearheaded understanding of realities on the ground, but also one that, because it was draconian in the way that it treated the German people in the aftermath of that war, laid seeds of resentment and guilt that, as Marshal Foch said after the treaty was signed, all but guaranteed another world war.

Interviewer

You [referred to a] failure of imagination . . . in Iraq. . . . Imagination on the part of whom, the policymakers, strategists, politicians, the generals, the diplomats, all of the above?

Colonel Matthew Moten

The responsibility for going to war in our country rests with the political leadership. The military leadership should advise them closely and is responsible for executing policy to the best of its ability but the responsibility ultimately rests with duly elected political leadership.

There's also a tendency, not just in the war in Iraq, but in all wars, to have this expectation that we are able to see the future clearly and we have the means at our disposal to make this a short war and that is rarely, if ever, true . . . . It was clear at the outset of the Iraq War that we had the ability to make short work of the Iraqi army and the Republican Guard and Saddam Hussein's government. We did not think through, and in some cases we chose to disregard counsel that had been given to political leaders, about what would happen in the aftermath of a victory in Iraq, a victory inasmuch as we had taken Bagdad and vanquished the Iraqi army.

Interviewer

People often make comparison between the war in Iraq and the war in Vietnam . . . . The termination of the war in Vietnam had some dramatic impact upon army doctrine with respect to the willingness to get involved in a counterinsurgency. One might argue that Vietnam may have helped make us ill-prepared to bring in the notion that you said was part of the first volume or the predecessor volume of this notion of war, origins as well as war termination, ill-prepared to fight the insurgency that followed the victory or the so called victory in Iraq in 2003. Can you lay out that notion that Vietnam formed the war in Iraq, 25 to 30 years later?

Colonel Matthew Moten

I'm not sure that there's a straight line. I would say two things. One, Vietnam is a special case because it's the only war that we unambiguously lost and it's not surprising that institutions such as the United States Army and United States Marine Corps chose to turn away from the bitter lessons of Vietnam.

The other thing is that we had an immediate reason to turn away from that because we came to understand that fighting in Vietnam, in and of itself, was a distraction from our bigger strategic mission, which was an ongoing global cold war with the Soviet Union. Tying down so many resources in Vietnam distracted us and hampered us in that larger mission. In the 1970s and into the 1980s, the armed services in the United States began to focus more clearly on the global conflict, preparing for what might or might not be and fortunately this turned out not to be a hot war with the Soviet Union. But we began to put our energies, in terms of doctrine and buying weapons, in terms of training soldiers, in terms of recruiting service members, to facing that larger more important global threat. In the end, the Cold War ended and America unambiguously won it. . . . I don't think that one can say that that's a bad outcome of our choice to neglect or move away from, what we had learned about counterinsurgency in Vietnam.

Interviewer

You could argue with the last campaign of the Cold War so to speak as a war that was never but there was the build up. The American build up in response to change this doctrine more dramatically and to build up for a war with the Soviet Union.

Colonel Matthew Moten

George Herring essentially argues that in his essay. I don't want to put words in his mouth.

Interviewer

Yeah, now the book and the conference have an interesting relationship. Tell me how the conference came about.

Colonel Matthew Moten

Well, the way we made this conference work was that, having recruited the authors to write the essays, we brought them all together for a planning conference in Chapel Hill, North Carolina, in January. It was a day and a half where we were able to get everybody to appreciate the scope of what we were trying to do and clear up some misconceptions and to have everybody buy in to the purposes of the project, the scope of the project, and the importance of what we were doing. . . . . As we . . . began to talk to each other, we realized that as much as historians have looked at war, the origins of war, its purposes, its conduct, nobody—that's an exaggeration—but seldom have people looked at the end of war as a topic worth studying in and of itself. We decided that we were able to do something that was historically interesting and somewhat new, but even further, we might be able to make a contribution to military theory, and to think about this business of putting the beginning and the middle and the end of war together, thinking about war, beginning with the end in mind and to think through all of those various scenarios and consequences.

We had that conference in North Carolina, which got everybody—not thinking the same way but at least asking the same questions—and then we spent several months writing our essays. . . . Then we came back together here at West Point in June and delivered those in a conference sponsored by General Dempsey and the Training and Doctrine Command.

Interviewer

Did the experience of coming together and leaving and coming back together again, lead to any transformations from the historians themselves about what they thought about war termination given that period of study, between each other and sharing ideas?

Colonel Matthew Moten

I'm not sure that I would go that far. I would say this. Let me just talk a little bit about the process. At our planning conference, we agreed that our authors were going to tackle a common set of questions. We didn't shackle one another with a common outline but we decided that what we would look at would be, first, to talk about the origins of the particular war and then the war aims of each side, how the war began, and then because this is not a book about the wars themselves, we would quickly run through a strategic narrative of the entire war in order to get to the final campaign and look at how that final campaign played out and how the war ended. In other words, was there a complete victory, was there a peace treaty, did we have people on a rooftop in Saigon trying to get on a helicopter, how did the war end?

Then we looked at how to stop and make an assessment at the end of that war, having looked at what the war aims of each side had been, about how those war aims changed. The answer is usually yes, the war aims change, and where did [the belligerents], especially the United States, stand at the end of that war compared to where [they] had intended to be . . . at the beginning.

I asked each of the authors at that point, to look forward into subsequent history, get back to a question that you've asked earlier, and to think about the ramifications of that war and that peace on the rest of American history and particularly on how it affected the armed services.

Interviewer

When war is done well, when the mission is articulated, executed, and completed with foresight, what does it look like? What war in American history would you say was the more successful?

Colonel Matthew Moten

Well, two stand out. One is the Civil War, which I've already talked about a couple of times.

Interviewer

You made the argument that it took another 100 years.

Colonel Matthew Moten

Well, yeah, the war was done well. The victory was complete, but here is why it's important to talk about how we do the post-war operations and how to structure the peace. The better, more complete example would be World War II where the United States, under the leadership of FDR, had an opportunity to plan its entry into the war for a couple of years before the Japanese raided Pearl Harbor. We had begun to mobilize. We had thought, in a great deal of detail, what our strategy would be and when the United States found itself drawn into that war by the Japanese attack, we were ready to begin and in very short order, we declared that we were going to try to defeat Germany before Japan: the "Germany first" aspect of that strategy, and then we would turn our full attention to the Japanese. We also determined, and FDR and Churchill pronounced this, that we were going to seek nothing short of the unconditional surrender of the Axis powers. With those broad outlines and an understanding about priorities on resources, troops, and material, we then put together a global campaign that allowed us to win a war, first in

Europe and secondly in the Pacific, and then to impose treaties of peace on Germany and Japan and to occupy those nations in a way that it's hard to argue how it could have been more successful than it was.

Interviewer

Can you argue, such as you did with the Civil War, that the termination of World War II did not complete the mission, that it didn't eradicate totalitarianism from Europe? It laid the seeds for the Cold War. That territory was still under subjugation by this time by the Soviet Union in Eastern Europe. Was Yalta a failure? In other words, this here is another war that you could argue could even, for all its successes, lay the seeds for the next war.

Colonel Matthew Moten

History doesn't stop. The objectives that we tried to achieve in World War II—I would say that we did achieve them, which [were] unconditional surrender of the Germans, Italians, and the Japanese and we did it in the order that we intended to do it—that victory was complete.

In order to achieve that, we had to align ourselves with the other growing and great power on earth, which was the Soviet Union and by any stretch of the imagination, the Soviet Union shouldered a tremendous share [of the burden].

Interviewer

More than anyone else really in terms of lives lost.

Colonel Matthew Moten

Lives lost, soldiers involved, number of units. The Soviet expenditure of blood and treasure is not to be sneezed at. It was enormous.

At the end of the war, coalitions break up. You no longer have a common enemy. You don't have the purposes of the war to bring you together and it's almost inevitable that coalitions are going to go their separate ways. You mentioned totalitarianism. It wasn't our purpose in World War II to eradicate totalitarianism. It was our purpose to defeat the Axis powers that happened to be totalitarian.

Interviewer

You mentioned earlier on that Okinawa was, to Gerhard Weinberg, the final campaign of the Second World, not the dropping of the bomb on Hiroshima. This is an interesting notion because you then set the stage for the decision to drop the bomb. What other historians in the project came up with interesting surprising choices for last campaigns?

Colonel Matthew Moten

Wayne Lee [and] the War of 1812 . . . . How it ended causes one to immediately think of Andrew Jackson and the Battle of New Orleans . . . . When Wayne Lee told me that he intended not to do that, I argued with him and I said, well, you're going to miss the boat if you don't focus on New Orleans. He said, "Watch what I'm going to do." Wayne focused on the Plattsburgh campaign in Northern New York and made the argument that the Plattsburgh campaign said a lot more about where that war had gone as it evolved from 1812 to 1814 and about how the United States had developed an army that was capable of standing toe to toe with the British and in fact, when the Plattsburgh campaign was satisfactorily and successfully completed, that outcome affected peace negotiations that were already going on in Europe and the peace treaty that was settled upon reflected understandings of what had happened on the ground at Plattsburgh and in other battles in Northern New York. Of course, the Battle of New Orleans is fought after the treaty is already agreed . . . and in a sense, the battle of New Orleans was unnecessary. Wayne also made a number of arguments about what [Plattsburgh] meant for the United States in terms of its sovereignty. One could call it the continuation of the American Revolution. The British were no longer going to be an important force in North America as an adversary to the United States in that that would have happened with or without New Orleans. He made me finally agree with him that he was right to concentrate on Plattsburgh and not New Orleans. Probably the bigger outcome of New Orleans was to launch the political career of Andrew Jackson.

Interviewer

Yeah, without it, he doesn't become president, right?

Colonel Matthew Moten

Without it, he still would have been a very colorful figure but he might never have become a political figure without the fame and notoriety that that campaign brought him.

Interviewer

When did Vietnam end? What was the last campaign of Vietnam, the Tet Offensive?

Colonel Matthew Moten

Well, this is an interesting point. As Gian Gentile was writing his essay on Vietnam, we spent a lot of time talking to each other about what the final campaign was. . . . One of the issues that comes out of this that informed Roger Spiller's thinking is that the final campaign is not necessarily the terminal campaign. The final campaign of the Vietnam War, one could say, was the 1972 offensive, just before the Paris Peace Treaty in January of 1973. One could even argue that it's after the United States is already out of the war. It's the North Vietnamese offensive in 1975 that eventually reunifies South Vietnam under the Hanoi regime. But the Tet Offensive that took place in 1968, four years earlier than the United States got out, seven years earlier than the war finally ended, was the one that changed the war strategically in such a way that it was never going back. It's fascinating because in the Tet Offensive, the United States and South Vietnamese were defending against a North Vietnamese and Viet Cong offensive and, operationally and tactically, the allies won but strategically, and more importantly, politically, they lost because the American people had been led to believe that the North Vietnamese and the

Vietcong were on their last legs. "There's light at the end of the tunnel. It's only a matter of

Time," and then all of a sudden, with the Tet Offensive, they demonstrated that they had the

military capability to launch a large sustained offensive even if they couldn't win it, and the American people, who had begun to have doubts about the war before the Tet offensive, began turning against the war in large numbers after that. So politically, the war turns there and strategically, in terms of the American people's willingness to support the policy and the strategy on the ground, I think that the war could not have been won after that.

Now, I just waded into a huge historiographical thicket. There are people who would come out of the woodwork to argue with what I just said, which is one of the fun things about history.

Interviewer

Right and that goes to the heart of what would happen in Vietnam and why we lost. That's the whole debate you're referencing, which also references the notion of the terminal campaigns. What'd you compare that to a minute ago, the terminal and the –

Colonel Matthew Moten

Final campaign.

Interviewer

If fought by democracies, they are going to be different than those fought by authoritarian regimes, it would seem. The impact of the public opinion upon a war in a democracy is much more acute. The impact of the public opinion on a war that relies on the army has to be much more acute, I would think. Authoritarian armies are going to fight wars in different ways than democracies fight wars. Is that a conclusion also?

Colonel Matthew Moten

Yes, to the degree that an authoritarian regime can maintain control of its population.

Interviewer

This assumes these are wars fought by mass armies too as opposed to dedicated, fine professionals.

Colonel Matthew Moten

Right, but I would also say that to me, another interesting point is that since 1973, we've had what we have called an all volunteer military force. I prefer to call it an "all-recruited force," and one of the reasons that we have been able to sustain years' long wars—now the longest war in American history in Afghanistan, and Iraq is not far behind it—is that only one percent of the American populace is engaged in those wars in any meaningful way, which is to say that that's the percentage of the American people that have been fighting—that percentage of the people has their families worried about them back home. But if you look at where these wars register on the American consciousness, going into an election year this year—I read this morning in the paper that about seven percent of the electorate listed Afghanistan as being the most important topic on their minds, which is well behind the economy where almost 40 percent of the American people think that that's the most important thing.

So having an all-recruited army and a relatively small one in comparison with the rest of the populace and using large numbers of contractors in our current wars allows political leaders . . . to move the problems of war off the kitchen table agenda of the American people.

Interviewer

Now, that's probably good for the successful conduct of the war but it may be bad for the legitimacy and the execution of the war with respect to democratic input, right? This is a kind of balancing act here. The defining difference between Iraq and Vietnam, right, is that, more than anything else really, this war, as unpopular as the Iraq War may have been, was never as unpopular as the Vietnam War because the sons and daughters of the great middle class are not necessarily participating here in any kind of needful way..

Colonel Matthew Moten

Yeah, I think that's exactly right. There was always the possibility that one's son, and in those days, it was almost always a son, would be liable for military service and could possibly go to Vietnam. Although, there were lots of ways out of that service, one of the ramifications of the war in Vietnam was the question of who served and who didn't and how one went about avoiding that service, if one did. I don't see that as becoming a political issue in the aftermath of the wars in Iraq and Afghanistan because we recruited everybody who was going to go fight in Iraq and Afghanistan, and there is no sense of guilt or the stigma that's going to be associated with non-military service in the aftermath of these wars.

Interviewer

This is the assumption of risk when you make the decision to join, right?

Colonel Matthew Moten

Yes.

Interviewer

With respect to war termination, it has a huge impact, right, because the war in Vietnam, so depended upon what the attitude was here at home. The notion of the public input was important. It certainly can be agreed upon almost by everyone.

Colonel Matthew Moten

People were taking to the streets in the 10,000s in the late 1960s and the 1970s to protPeople were taking to the streets in their ten thousands in the late 1960s and the 1970s to protest against the Vietnam War and that sort of impetus that the antiwar demonstrators had, I think, was largely fed by the possibility that they might be liable or that their brothers or fathers, might be liable for service in Vietnam. While there is certainly an antiwar movement in the United States over these last several years, mostly directed against Iraq but now being directed more and more against Afghanistan, it's not nearly as virulent. It doesn't have nearly as many people involved in it and certainly not with the passion that had been directed against the war in Vietnam.

Interviewer

Now that the project's complete, how would you like to see this work be used and understood going forward?

Colonel Matthew Moten

I have a simple and grandiose ambition . . . and that is that some future president contemplating the awful decision to go to war will be discussing these issues with his national security team and his national security advisor will hand him a copy of [this work] as he gets on the helicopter to fly to Camp David for the weekend and say, "Mr. President, before you make this decision, you'd do well to spend a weekend with this [work]." There aren't any answers [here]. This is not a [work] of advocacy. It is not a [work] of punditry and it is certainly not antiwar, but [it] is meant to inform policymakers about the potential consequences and the unforeseen consequences of going to war. I hope that it will help them to avoid the kinds of failures of imagination that their predecessors have had.

Interviewer

Just as an addendum to what we've just discussed, I would add that it's not a grandiose thought. Leaders and policymakers, read as they are executing their policy and making their decisions. We know that President Bush and Secretary Cheney were reading John Lewis Gaddis. We know that Alistair Horne was being read. We know a whole host of other books that were on the reading list of policymakers during the war in Iraq, Eliot Cohen among them. Speak to your notion of that with respect to this war and any others.

Colonel Matthew Moten

Well, it's my understanding that President Bush was reading Eliot Cohen's "Supreme Command," which is a collection of broad vignettes about political leaders in wartime and the thrust of Cohen's argument is that political leaders need to have a hands-on approach to their direction of warfare. They need to be very forceful in the way that they deal with their military leaders and that they should not feel any compunction about interfering at whatever level they choose. I don't necessarily disagree with the conclusions that Cohen reaches about that, [and] I've got some questions about his evidence. He has picked what he considers to be four very successful military leaders and makes the argument that they should be empowered to engage at any level of warfare.

Interviewer

Who were the four that he chooses?

Colonel Matthew Moten

Lincoln, Ben Gurion, Churchill, and [Clemenceau].

Interviewer

Of course, McPherson came out with his book about Lincoln as a war strategist around the same time.

Colonel Matthew Moten

Yeah, and I think that's a very good book. The point is that I think that President Bush was reading [Cohen's] book and began to think of himself in that mold, and I think that it guided his thinking in terms of developing his war aims and the importance that he placed on being a decisive resolute leader, perhaps at the expense of being a thoughtful information-gathering one.

Interviewer

Yes, this is on the notion that a little knowledge can be a dangerous thing.

Colonel Matthew Moten

Yes.

Interviewer

In the greater breadth of kind of material that we'd hope that a chief executive or the commander in chief would undertake, would give him some humility to the approach if nothing else then.

Colonel Matthew Moten

Yeah, and if the Bush Administration had spent some more time gathering information about the possibilities that what might have happened such as with one of our authors, Conrad Crane, who was coauthor of a pamphlet done by the Strategic Studies Institute, that looked at the problems of postwar Iraq and it listed (and I may get this number wrong) 134 things that we needed to be thinking about what Iraq would look like after a successful campaign. They published that in February of 2003 and we went to war in Iraq in March. That advice, even though it was published by the United States Government, was largely disregarded and discounted.

Interviewer

Thank you very much.